The Chinese Path Toward a Leaner Government

Yining Li · Zhiqiang Cheng
Editors

The Chinese Path Toward a Leaner Government

商務印書館
SINCE 1897 The Commercial Press

Springer

Editors
Yining Li
Peking University
Beijing, China

Zhiqiang Cheng
Peking University
Beijing, China

Translated by
Zhang Ying
Beijing Foreign Studies University
Beijing, China

Beijing International Studies University
Beijing, China

ISBN 978-981-19-6717-7 ISBN 978-981-19-6718-4 (eBook)
https://doi.org/10.1007/978-981-19-6718-4

Jointly published with The Commercial Press, Ltd.
The print edition is not for sale in China (Mainland). Customers from China (Mainland) please order the print book from: The Commercial Press, Ltd.
ISBN of the Co-Publisher's edition: 978-7-100-12639-7

This book is published with financial support from the Chinese Fund for Humanities and Social Sciences.

Translation from the Chinese language edition: "中国道路与简政放权" by Yining Li and Zhiqiang Cheng,

This Springer imprint is published by the registered company Springer Nature Singapore Pte Ltd.
The registered company address is: 152 Beach Road, #21-01/04 Gateway East, Singapore 189721, Singapore

Preface

Building a leaner government (*Jian Zheng Fang Quan*, or "streamlining administration and delegating powers" in the official translated documents) is essential in China's transition from a planned economy to a market economy and in an effort to improve the country's socialist market economy.

People of our generation have all had some experiences with the planned economy. It was a time when the government managed everything from production to consumption. In other words, the government assumed the role of both the producer and distributor of goods. Little was outside the government administration. It set quotas that matched its plans and organized supplies according to the quotas. No one in China at that time had ever heard about the term *Jian Zheng Fang Quan* or streamlining administration and delegating powers. In fact, it was impossible to streamline the government then because everything was controlled by the government, every decision had to come from the higher authorities, and all kinds of stuff were placed under the quota system. When a government assigned each of its staff with a particular task to either manage or supervise economic activities, how could it be streamlined? Power devolution was even more beyond imagination. The planned economy was based on the concentration of power. If power was delegated, how could the economy and people's daily life go as the government had planned for them?

Indeed, there were times when the Chinese government was concerned about the low efficiency and poor performance of the planned economy that too much concentration of power had entailed. However, there were no better ways. China had quite a few lessons learnt in a hard way. Trials to cut government power or remove some quota all ended up in market disorder. Shifting back to old practice only stifled the economy. Such policy flip-flops occurred time after time during the period of the planned economy. It was a doomed cycle that no one was able to break.

When did the government and the people of China draw their attention to the idea of a leaner government and gradually move in this direction? In the transition from the planned economy to the socialist market economy, cutting government power became a must. This was because under the planned economy, industrial and agricultural production and distribution were carried out on a quota-based term initiated and dictated by the government. Nothing could be done without government approval, and there was no way to circumvent it. When businesses and investors were restricted by too many regulations and authorities at lower levels lacked initiatives to press ahead, market economy would be a goal too elusive to reach. For the market economy to take root, China needed a leaner government with less centralized power. This would free up the market and help businesses become real market players who operate independently in a competitive environment. Only in this way could businesses gain more vitality and the role of the market be taken into full play in regulating the economy and allocating resources. It would also enable the urban jobless to start a business of their own and join the rank of market players.

The most telling case is the adoption of the rural household contract responsibility system established in 1979. In the years of the planned economy, farmers were fixed to the land and were under heavy restrictions. Such decisions as what crops to grow, how big the growth area was, or even when to sow the seeds were made by the higher agricultural authorities and passed onto farmers through local rural officials. This was the same as how much grain should be handed over to the government as a farm tax and how much of the remaining grain can be sold and at what price. Rural residents are under a household registration system different from urban dwellers. When farmers wanted to work in cities, they had to obtain the government's prior consent. Otherwise, they would be called *Mang Liu* (meaning people who blindly flow into cities) or vagrants. The planned economy builds its success on established and compulsory plans, where hungry and poorly clad farmers had no incentive to make improvements. After the Cultural Revolution ended in 1976, farmers in some places tried the "Big Contract," or what we now refer to as the rural household contract responsibility system, which was simply unimaginable before 1976. After careful study, the CPC Central Committee praised the pilot programs and began to popularize them across the country. Only a few years later, food coupons that had been circulated across China for decades were no longer valid, farmers were allowed to work in cities, and township enterprises emerged one after another and seemed to be everywhere. As their products were not on the government's purchase list, they had to look for their own clients. An interesting phenomenon occurred in China in the 1980s. One often saw farmer-looking people on coaches and trains, dressed in suits, sometimes with ties and carrying baggage big and small. They were found to be farmers, or more specifically, managers and salesmen of township enterprises who carried product samples in the baggage and traveled across the country to look for customers. They were the ones who broke the shackles imposed on them over the years. The market created by emerging township businesses tore down the monopoly of the distribution channel by the government under the planned economy. It could be hailed as the initial achievements for administrative streamlining and power devolution. In the eyes of economists, the emergence of township enterprises and the creation of markets for their products have quietly broken the domination of the planned economy.

In the process of breaking the domination of the planned economy, the establishment of special economic zones (SEZs) was as important as the rural household contract responsibility system and township businesses. SEZs were set up in Shenzhen and Zhuhai, two towns in Guangdong Province bordering Hong Kong and Macao. Market rules were enforced there instead of the old practice. This brought fast economic growth to the SEZs with a more liberalized market, greater autonomy for businesses and massive inflows of migrants from northern provinces. This marked the beginning of a nationwide transition from the planned economy to the socialist market economy.

The release of Deng Xiaoping's statements during his trip to South China in early 1992 triggered another wave of reform and opening-up. The Chinese Communist Party set for itself a clear target at its 14th National Congress of building a socialist market economy with Chinese characteristics to replace the long-standing dominating policy of the planned economy. The reform covered many areas. One of them is administrative streamlining and power devolution.

The policy of reform and opening-up over the past two decades spanning from the 14th to the 18th National Party Congress has gradually led China onto the path of the market economy. The efforts to make the government leaner also continued during this period of time and covered the following three areas.

First, Deng's statements in 1992 encouraged many people to make investments and start businesses in Shenzhen and the wider Pearl River Delta or Shanghai and other eastern seaboard cities in Jiangsu, Zhejiang, Shandong and Fujian. They found that business traveling and home settlement there did not require as much administrative approval as before and that they could own a business as they wished in a short period of time. This was hard to imagine in the planned economy.

Second, as SEZs and coastal cities saw a surging tide of entrepreneurship and innovation after the release of Deng's remarks, labor was needed for creating new businesses, expanding existing ones and infrastructure construction. Rural laborers flocked to the south and the east for opportunities. These migrant workers did not need administrative approval to move from the countryside to the cities, as was required in the early days of reform and opening-up. Nobody could have imagined how big impact this may have on the life of the rural migrant workers.

Third, a big event that shaped the course of China's market economy in the 1990s was its bid to join the WTO. To meet the WTO criteria, China had to transform itself from a planned economy to a market economy. This included removing or reducing administrative constraints placed on the market and businesses, including domestic private companies and potential foreign investors. At that time, people in Chinese political and economic communities were all crying "the wolf is coming." They believed that once government protection of the agriculture, manufacturing, commercial and service sectors was scrapped, China would be dealt with a heavy blow. Their arguments aroused a big controversy. Ultimately, the central leadership and the State Council made the decision to accept the commitments the WTO set for China and fulfill China's obligation on inbound foreign investment and liberalization of foreign trade in a phased manner. The result is that "the wolf" did come, but instead of inflicting huge losses on China, it has helped improve the competitiveness of Chinese companies and make the path smoother for China to move from the planned to the socialist market economy. More importantly, the system of the planned economy, with fewer sectors to cover, had less say on the future of China's economic development.

The above three areas clearly show that in the period of building and improving the socialist market economy between the 1990s and the lead-up to the 18th National Party Congress, good progress was made in building a leaner government, which is necessitated by narrowing the scope of the planned economy and making the underlying structure of the socialist market economy function better.

The 18th National Party Congress brought China's reform and opening-up program into a new phase. It was reaffirmed at the congress that the market should play a decisive role in resource allocation and China must pursue law-based governance. A clear direction was set for the efforts on power decentralization.

As the process of shifting to the market economy is yet to be completed, much remains to be improved in making the system work better. The 18th Central Committee of the CPC made the decision of letting the market play a decisive role in resource allocation at its third plenum and adopted the resolution on law-based governance at its fourth plenum. More efforts are needed for enforcement. In this context, there is much to be done in cutting government power as a means to improve the socialist market economy.

First, the administrative review and approval system must match the principles in the market economy. This system is indispensable because in a market economy, lawful, well-regulated and institutional-based operations are essential for the market to remain in good order.

The microeconomic players can be divided into three groups: companies, individuals and administrative departments overseeing the market. They all have to obey laws and follow market rules, which in turn incentivizes businesses and individuals and makes them vibrant and helps administrative agencies ensure that the market is well regulated and in good order. The focus of streamlining is now law-based governance and administration, which underpins the sound development of the market economy.

Second, due to the impact of the planned economy over the years, it is likely that a few administrative review and approval policies will remain inconsistent with market rules after the reforms. It is therefore necessary to review the current policies one by one and decide which provisions are to be removed, revised or created. The government must adopt policies that motivate and energize market players (companies and individuals), remove those obsolete policies that stand in the way of the growth of the market economy and delegate power of review and approval to lower authorities. New review and approval rules should help increase the incentives and vitality of market players, companies and individuals included. Outdated policies that restrain the growth of the market economy must be abolished. A number of items subject to approval should be delegated to lower government authorities. This will increase the sense of responsibility of the agencies at the lower level and drastically improve administrative efficiency.

Third, items of administrative charge should also be checked against reality. In the past, many charges (levies and fines included) collected by administrative agencies and their affiliated bodies were connected with their economic interests. In some cases, excessive and exorbitant charges and fines that have weighed down businesses and individuals have been put into the pockets of the collectors. Making charges better regulated and rule-based will help make administrative approval more compatible with the efforts of promoting the rule of law and building a clean government.

Going forward, it is advisable to set up a system of negative lists and power and responsibility lists in line with international practice. The negative list targets market access. The power list spells out the power of the government. The responsibility list defines the responsibilities of the government and its agencies. The three lists are important elements of law-based governance.

The following are elaborations on the three lists and suggestions on ways of their enforcement that help make the government leaner.

I. The negative list on market access

The negative list on market access was first introduced to the Shanghai Pilot Free Trade Zone on a trial basis for later adoption in other cities. This means that the government lists a number of industries, sectors and businesses where investment and business operations are strictly prohibited or under restriction. All types of market players are allowed to enter on an equal basis those industries, sectors and businesses that are not on the list. It has been made clear to all market players that things on the list are redline and off-limit zones. Industries, sectors and businesses that are not on the list should give equal access to all market players without favoring one over the other.

The release of the negative list on market access is a credible means to boost the confidence of all types of market players. If it was changed to a positive list by writing down which industries, sectors and businesses are allowed in for investment and business operation, the list would go on and on and may not be exhaustive. Specifying the redline and the no-touch zone will be reassuring to the market players, as they will know the boundaries and act with more enthusiasm.

II. The government power list

A government acts according to law in a market economy. The government power list defines the power boundaries and way of enforcement of the government and its departments. This means that when the government acts, it must act within laws and regulations. Without their mandate, no action should ever be taken.

If the government goes beyond the boundaries set by laws and regulations specified in the government power list, the action it takes will be illegal and the law would require that the government make apologies to the injured party and compensation for the loss incurred and discipline the staff involved.

There is an essential difference between the market economy and the planned economy. In the market economy, the government must carry out law-based governance, and the boundary of its administrative power is clearly defined by the power list. This means that the government cannot take action unless mandated by the law. While in a planned economy, the government and its departments are not subject to the limits of laws and regulations when performing their duties. Since government acts are not confined by laws, the government will never be caught "breaking laws or regulations" for its acts.

III. The responsibility list of the government and its departments

There are both similarities and differences between the responsibility list and the power list of the government.

The similarities lie in the fact that the power list tells what the government can and cannot do. The government must pursue law-based governance and administration, and its behavior must be backed by laws and regulations. The responsibility list also requires that the government and its departments perform their functions mandated by laws and regulations instead of acting willfully.

They are different in a way that the responsibility list is more specific about legally defined responsibilities of the government. This means that the government must perform its administrative responsibilities as specified in the laws, or it will be charged with negligence of duty. The responsibility list also standardizes and clarifies the procedures of performing government functions.

At a workshop on cutting red tape, participants discussed the phenomenon that some government officials act arbitrarily while others fail to perform their duties. The former can be checked by the government power list. According to the principle that the government can only take actions mandated by the law, arbitrary acts constitute violation of laws and regulations, which will never be allowed in a law-based society. However, the government power list does not directly deal with the failure of officials to perform their duties. These officials should be taken accountable against the government responsibility list, which spells out what the government should do and how to do it. The list provides enforceable criteria for the business community and the public in their supervision of the government and its employees.

The work around the negative list of market access, the government power list and its responsibility list will be a key priority in both building a leaner government and improving the socialist market economy.

Macroeconomic control is indispensable in the socialist market economy. However, the measures should be appropriately based on China's economic reality. In this sense, it is related to streamlining administration and delegating government power.

In the years of the planned economy, although fiscal, monetary, human resource and regional development policies were employed to regulate the economy when needed, the term "macroeconomic control" that originates from the Western economic theories was hardly mentioned because it was thought that macroeconomic control was only used by Western countries as a means to stabilize the national economy.

It was not until the 1990s that the State Council of China resorted to macroeconomic control to curb the overheated economy featured by excessive investment, swelling credit and rising inflation. The problem was triggered by the reform following Deng's statements in South China, especially after the 14th National Party Congress, which set the goal of building a socialist market economy. However, the measures taken in the 1990s were more like administrative directives, which is understandable since China had just begun to transition from the planned economy to the socialist market economy.

Things are different now. The coverage of the planned economy has shrunk considerably. Private businesses account for over half of China's GDP. Private investments have entered quite a few areas previously closed to them. Therefore, macroeconomic control in today's China is characterized by the following:

I. The macroeconomic control in this context is the one under the ever-improving system of the socialist market economy. It should be law-based and shall not violate the rule of law.
II. Macroeconomic control should be used as appropriate in all market economies and suit national realities. There is no one-size-fits-all model. The government should know when to make the policy tight and when to make it moderate, when to launch and when to stop. Structural readjustment or targeted regulation also follows this methodology and should be used when necessary.
III. Macroeconomic control aims at maintaining steady economic growth. It is a means and not an end in itself. No one should take it as a "magic pill," as every macroeconomic control measure has side effects. Disproportionate measures and miscalculated intensity will only create more problems for the future.
IV. The government must refrain from taking macroeconomic control as the only way to keep the economy going. Such thinking is harmful to the market economy. If macrocontrol becomes indispensable, how can the market play a decisive role in the allocation of resources?
V Streamlining administration and delegating government power are closely related to sound macroeconomic control. They do not undercut each other's role and deal with different aspects of the issue. The former is a key measure in raising administrative efficiency and requires continuous attention from the government even if China has completed its transition to the market economy. The latter is a critical tool for the government to meet the policy goals of steady economic growth, full employment, price stability and equilibrium of international balance of payment. Mutual coordination and reinforcement between them is important in managing the "new equilibrium" the country faces.

Greater vitality of businesses and stronger initiatives of the public are the source of continuous economic growth and the lasting competitiveness of companies. In this sense, there is a huge potential in improving the market economy.

State-owned Enterprises (SOEs) in China were not real market players in the planned economy. Their ownership and investors were unclear, and they had to obey the orders from the administrative authorities without any freedom to run the business independently. In essence, SOEs were nothing but affiliates of government agencies. Therefore, the top priority for China in its "plan-to-market" transition is to reshape the basis of the microeconomy and make SOEs true market players that can operate freely and compete in the market and to ensure that their investors are responsible for any losses incurred. This was the subject dominating the debate among Chinese economists concerning corporate ownership reform since the beginning of the reform and opening-up. For a market economy to take full shape, China's SOEs must all complete the ownership reform and become true players to compete in the market as vibrant microeconomic entities.

The corporate ownership reform, which started in the 1980s and was completed in the first decade of the twenty-first century, has come a long way. Ownerships were clearly defined. A number of SOEs completed share-holding reforms to become joint-stock companies, and some were even listed in the stock market. In addition, a large number of private companies emerged. These companies generally have clear ownership structures, including some family businesses with stocks shared by family members in the form of joint-stock companies. Thus, the number of market players in China increased sharply. In the past couple of years, I have been to the city of Jiaxing, Zhejiang Province, for field studies. I have seen with my own eyes great enthusiasm among farmers after the reform of separating rural land ownership rights, contract rights and use rights. With rights and interests protected by the law, they become highly motivated to run family farms or rural cooperatives. They are pushing for the creation of the new countryside, new townships and new communities. I have also visited entrepreneurship and innovation incubators in Zhongguancun, northwest of Beijing, where many young university students, graduates, investors and researchers join each other in making business and innovation plans. In Chongqing, a large city in central China, I saw happy new owners of small and micro businesses who found it much easier to start a business than before and were entitled to more preferential treatment. Some of them were talking about the possibility of growing their ventures into medium-sized ventures in the coming years. Their potentials will be fully unleashed once they see opportunities and promising prospects.

The growth of a company hinges on its ability to seize business opportunities, tap its own potential and display dynamism. However, ultimately it is decided by the economic system of the country. There are three key questions in it. First, does a company have a solid microeconomic basis, such as clear ownership, a full-fledged corporate governance structure and a good sense of cohesion? True market players are companies that have gained growth potential and full vitality through reform. Their potential and vitality sustain the growth of China's economy and the companies' own business. Second, does macroeconomic control include appropriate steps and sound decisions, suit economic realities and mobilize all types of market entities? Third, has the entire economic system transformed from the traditional planned economy to the socialist market economy, with the market playing a decisive role in resource allocation? The questions point to the ultimate goals for China's market-oriented reform. They are not short-term targets. To meet these goals, other institutional reforms are also needed. They include the reform of the administrative review and approval system aimed at building a leaner government.

However, the experience of Chinese SOEs in transition to joint-stock or listed companies shows that no one should underestimate the rigidity of the planned economy in the "plan-to-market" reform. The planned economy is similar to a huge and tightly knit net. It will not fade away simply because the government claims that the market should play a decisive role in resource allocation. Nor will it relinquish its influence and control over businesses simply because they are now joint-stock or listed companies. It has been proven that no joint-stock companies in China, whether they are previously owned by the state or by private families, are yet joint-stock companies in the real sense. Let alone listed companies. The reason will be given in the following description of the two types of companies.

First, some words about SOE ownership reform. Some joint-stock companies that were previously SOEs complain that years after the reform, they are still dominated by the government on all things except for attracting investment. The shareholder meetings become meaningless as the state holds the dominating shares. The policy of giving companies independence in decision-making, business management and handling profits and losses thus become empty talks when you find that the government continues to treat the companies as their affiliates and decides the appointment and removal of their management teams. In this context, how can businesses be called true market players?

For some family business-turned stocking holding companies, the governance structure remains the same, and the head of the family is the boss of the company. Others see the shares spread out among the family members, with the family head serving as the board chairman. However, the business model remains the same without any reforms to support the new governance structure. It will be hard for private companies, family businesses in particular, to grow in a highly competitive market without any remodeling of the underlying governance structures.

The result of the joint-stock reform of SOEs and family businesses still falls short of the expectations for a perfect market economy. There is still a long distance to cover in this endeavor. It is fair to say that further reforms on SOEs and the transformation of private companies, family businesses included, are both necessary in improving China's market economy. Further progress in decentralizing government power is obviously important in this process.

Now, the most important thing in the government's efforts to upgrade the Chinese economy and strengthen its market competitiveness is the reform of the state capital system and the introduction of mixed ownership in SOEs, including companies wholly funded by the government and companies where the government holds dominating or majority shares. Administrative streamlining needs to match the reform in this area.

In my book *Chinese Economy in Dual Transition* published (by China Renmin University Press) in 2013, I said there are two layers in the reform of the state capital system. The first layer is the reform on the way state capital is allocated, and the second layer is the reform on the SOE management system. The two layers should not be mixed into one.

The reform of the state capital allocation system comes first. State capital undertakes more social responsibility in the market economy. Inadequate or inefficient allocation that sets more state capital idle will be the largest loss for the government. Importance should therefore be placed on higher efficiency in its allocation. This means that sound investment decisions are needed to both prevent the erosion of state capital and generate higher returns. Based on this thinking, the State-owned Assets Supervision and Administration Commission (SASAC) of the State Council has become the owner of the state capital but is only responsible for its allocation. A working structure of SASAC-state investment fund corporations-SOEs has taken shape.

At the second layer, reform of the SOEs aims to turn all companies, both those wholly funded by the government and those where the government holds dominating or majority shares, into market players that take care of their own profits and losses with sound corporate governance structure and management autonomy. They act upon the decisions of the shareholders' meeting and the board of directors in business dealings and are subject to oversight by the board of supervisors. Like other types of businesses, their social responsibility includes providing quality products and services to the market, nurturing talented people and sharing good experience and practices. Developing and expanding market share represent their biggest contribution to society.

The current reform of introducing mixed ownership to SOEs aims to make them independent market players, a goal shared by the reform of the SOE management system.

To a large extent, moving toward mixed ownership and reforming the management system of SOEs serve the same purpose. As part of the reform of the administrative system, a leaner government helps promote the reforms of both the state capital allocation system and the SOE management system.

In the reform toward mixed ownership, the corporate CPC committee must play a leading role in both the ownership transformation and business operation and participate in major decision-making of the company. It must use its special status in corporate governance to ensure preservation and increase state asset value and take part in corporate governance in more fields and at more levels as mixed ownership further develops. The following areas are especially important. First, the CPC committee must unite the thinking of the whole company on the reform. Rallying the entire company around its goals, strategies and management is its greatest responsibility. It should provide political and organizational guide to the SOE or its later form with mixed ownership to ensure full implementation of state policies in the company. This requires that corporate CPC organizations gain greater knowledge of the company, a broader vision of future development and better skills to adapt government policy to business reality. Second, the CPC committee must be a good corporate supervisor. Inadequate supervision over SOEs both from within and outside is a prevailing problem in China. Therefore, companies themselves have the obligation of supervision through internal personnel management and external oversight to make up for the institutional weakness of the corporate management system. It is indeed important for corporate CPC organizations to focus their efforts on the daily operation of the company, protect the interests of all parties and garner more drive for the company to grow faster and better. Third, the CPC committee should put the management staff under its supervision, a key role for CPC organizations in SOEs. It covers all aspects of the company's business operations. The CPC committee's decision-making power on economic incentives also helps bring corporate behaviors in line with policies from the central government. Companies are required to place corporate personnel management under CPC leadership to forestall disagreement on policies. CPC organizations at all levels of the company are entitled by law to appoint or remove members of the management team under their supervision.

The higher efficiency of state capital allocation and greater vitality and competitiveness of reformed SOEs will help the Chinese economy enjoy sustained growth. It will bring more initiatives to the individuals and the business community and more sophistication and dynamism to the market economy with Chinese characteristics. It will also foster cooperation between state capital and private funds for win–win outcomes.

There is a story in the ancient Chinese classics of *the Water Margin* about Lin Chong, a military officer who was escorted to a distant prison to serve his terms under false charges. On his way, he met a rich landlord who heard about him and wanted to give him a treat. An acquaintance of the landlord named Hong got jealous and suggested having a boxing game with him to see who had better fighting skills. Lin did not agree until he was told that Hong was not a friend of the landlord. Soon after the fight started, Lin claimed defeat on reasons that he had shackles on and there was on way to win. After the landlord had them removed, Lin defeated Hong only with a couple of punches and drove him away. Like Lin in the story, SOEs and private businesses in China are going through reforms to break the shackles on them to display their "fighting skills." This makes building a learner government a bigger imperative. It can be expected that both SOEs and private businesses will enjoy faster growth when the government cuts items for review and approval and only focuses on what truly falls within its jurisdiction.

Beijing, China Yining Li

The original version of the book was revised: Funder information text has been included on the Copyright page. The correction to the book is available at https://doi.org/10.1007/978-981-19-6718-4_28

Contents

Theory

Shifting Government Functions and Streamlining Administration—Policy Initiation, Reflection and Prospects

Zhiqiang Cheng

Policy Initiation: An Imperative to Stimulate the Market

The chapter focuses on the past and present context of the policy adopted by the State Council to streamline administration and delegate government power. It starts with a general background briefing on the period from 1978, when the reform and opening-up program started in China, to the leading-up of the 18th National Party Congress. Then, analysis is made on the factors behind the decision of the State Council to issue the policy after the 18th National Party Congress. The importance of building a leaner government has drawn more attention than ever before. Actions have been taken, and progress has been made. However, the initiative was not created by this administration. Such issues as "obstruction in the middle of policy implementation" also occurred in the trials during the 1980s. Administrative streamlining and power delegation were mentioned 134 times in documents issued by the State Council and its General Office, including 24 times in the leading-up to the 18th National Party Congress,[1] and 213 times by *the People's Daily* (official newspaper of the Chinese Government), including 56 times on the eve of the 18th National Party Congress.[2] (see Table 1).

I. Pilot reform of administrative streamlining and power delegation

The idea of a streamlining administration was raised in 1985 and 1993, well within the first two decades of the reform and opening-up (1978–1998). It was suggested in 1985 for sorting out relations between the government as an investor and SOEs to invigorate businesses, markets, research activities and the light industry and ultimately break the fetters of the planned economy for faster growth.

[1] Data source: http://www.gov.cn/.

[2] Data source: China Daily database.

Z. Cheng (✉)
Guanghua School of Management, Peking University, Beijing, China

Y. Li and Z. Cheng (eds.), *The Chinese Path Toward a Leaner Government*,
https://doi.org/10.1007/978-981-19-6718-4_1

Table 1 Number of documents on administrative streamlining and power delegation mentioned by the State Council

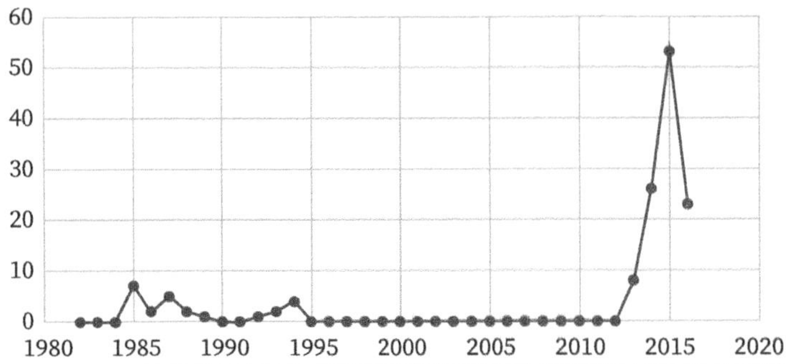

Data source China Economic Net (http://en.ce.cn/)

The State Economic Restructuring Commission issued the *Summary of the Symposium on the Urban Economic Restructuring Trial Reform* in May 1985. It said that by giving SOEs decision-making power over production plans, purchasing and product sales, the reform on streamlining administration and delegating government power would unleash the huge potential of SOEs. The People's Daily published an article stressing the importance of nurturing joint bodies of research institutes and enterprises and separating government administration from business operations. Following this guideline, local institutions with overseas business ties in Guangzhou opened a joint office in 1985, and the government of Laiwu, Shandong Province diverted a large number of officials to rural townships or service entities affiliated with the government in 1986 (which ended up in a doomed cycle for reasons to be discussed later).

Economists offered all kinds of solutions, such as improving the price regime with administrative streamlining (Guo, 1984), revitalization of traditional collectively owned enterprises (Shen, 1984), better relations between company headquarters and manufacturing plants (Yong, 1984), and removing obstacles in the middle of the reform (Huang, 1986). However, instead of stimulating growth, this round of cutting government power was followed by a GDP slowdown between 1985 and 1990 (see Table 2). The data do not mean that the efforts were made in vain since economic growth is impacted by a number of domestic and international factors. The reform in a sense has challenged or even changed the mindset of the Chinese people who had been influenced by the thinking of the planned economy and paves the way for more drastic SOE reforms.

GDP growth rate in real terms; inflation rate.

This round of reform drew full attention from the central and local governments, the academic community and the public. Efforts and reflections were made, and lessons must be gained. In a broader sense, the reform toward less government power has continued since 1978. In the transition from the economic system under which

Table 2 GDP and CPI growth rate from 1980 to 2014

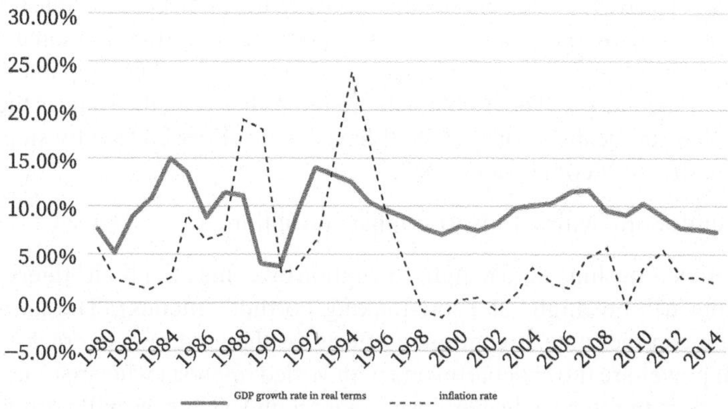

Data source China Economic Net (http://en.ce.cn/)

everything was tightly controlled to the one driven by the market, the government has been implementing various policies to loosen control and delegate power. They were accompanied by obstructions from the vested interests, as well as debates and concerns over the problems that the reform may entail. Despite the failed trial of Laiwu, which caused temporary flip-flops, SOE reforms and the WTO accession later brought the economy onto a new stable path.

II. Renewal of the policy after the 18th National Party Congress

According to the *Plan on Institutional Reform and Functional Transformation* of the State Council approved by the 12th National People's Congress, items for administrative review and approval on investment, production and business activities must be cut or passed over to government agencies at lower levels. Items for qualification and credential review and certification must be reduced. A total of 117 items of administrative approval were removed or delegated as required by the No.19 Document of the State Council in 2013. Since then, the State Council has issued 110 documents on this subject.

There are four factors behind the decision to raise the importance of cutting government power to an unprecedented level.

1. It is an important tool in advancing reforms in an all-round manner.

The 18th CPC Central Committee decided to focus the economic reform on letting the market play a decisive role in resource allocation and remove long-standing obstacles. Cutting government power includes devolving the power from the central to the local governments and from the government to the market and streamlining complicated approval procedures for higher efficiency in business operations. It is an important measure to advance the reform to greater depths, broader areas and higher levels. For example, a large number of SOEs and collectively owned companies were privatized in the 1990s, and many of the remaining ones were shifting to the joint-stock system. Going forward, the state capital monopoly in the hydropower industry will be further replaced by market competition. The power to control and manage SOEs has been steadily delegated from SASAC's local branches to the companies' management teams or the market. The problematic relations between the state as the investor and SOEs that run business on its behalf have been addressed step by step. In this way, more vitality will come back to SOEs.

2. It is mutually reinforcing with efforts to combat corruption.

The new administration is pushing hard to fight corruption by going after both "tigers" and "flies" (referring to both high- and low-ranking corrupt officials). The anti-corruption campaign can facilitate streamlining efforts, as the hard nuts to crack in cutting government power are those departments with vested interests who are reluctant to relinquish power. In return, a leaner government with less power will narrow the space for rent-seeking and sustain progress in building a cleaner government.

3. It is a perfect trigger for more market dynamism

The essence of cutting government power is to unleash the vitality of the Chinese economy. Since 2007, China has experienced a stock market crash, the global financial crisis, aging of the population and waning demographic and reform dividends. Since the 18th National Party Congress held in 2012, the anti-corruption campaign has made significant progress, and corruption dubbed the "economic lubricant" has been effectively crushed. The momentum of fighting corruption should be sustained despite weaker drive in the economy and less dynamism in the market. Cutting government power thus becomes a perfect tool to revitalize the economy and the market, while government efforts continue to combat corruption. It helps quicken the approval and launch of business projects, create development space for new business models and build synergy among the business, academic and research communities. Relations between the government and the market can thus become clearer, and the market will be under less undue government intervention. A new propeller for economic growth will be ignited.

(1) Less government power serves the growth of small and micro businesses.

Micro, small and medium-sized businesses are the main victims of a myriad of administrative approvals and controls. Innovative in business ideas but weak in economic strengths and with no means to curry favor with higher authorities, these cash-strapped businesses have to bear huge costs in the project approval and financing phase. At the same time, traditional sectors in China are in transition with less-than-expected efficiency of resource allocation. Micro, small and medium-sized businesses can attract huge amounts of idle funds, quicken the commercialization of research results and create new business models and new markets. A leaner government will help promote their growth and ultimately the growth of the economy.

(2) Less control will improve economic performance in many aspects

Streaming administration narrows government control over the market. According to Western economic classics, the government can only intervene where the market fails to play its role, and the market will reach its optimum efficiency when a few simple conditions are met (at the cost of fairness in some cases). Government control holds back economic growth and lowers all-factor productivity in a number of ways. Analyzing low economic performance caused by excessive control will help readers understand why administrative streamlining will bring high performance. The manifestation of government control and its effects are as follows.

First, state monopoly and industrial control discourage companies with lower cost, innovative technologies and high productivity from entering the market. According to economic theory, government control removes the threat from potential competitors in favor of companies in monopoly. This practice leads to lower industrial efficiency, higher profits for the monopoly and more net losses on social welfare. Less control will help the market play a better role in the economy and curb the net losses on social welfare. Mobile ride hailing apps are a good example. The traditional taxi industry is not fully market-driven, as market entry and pricing are controlled by the government, whereas the "premier cars" model on the apps makes travel more convenient and raises the utilization rate of private vehicles due to better allocation of resources. More importantly, it lets the market play a decisive role. The fares are determined by the market. It increases during peak hours and at midnight when the demand is high or the supply is low or under bad weather, such as rainstorms, when the demand–supply balance is seriously twisted. A higher price encourages supply and suppresses demand. That said, the government should also pay attention to addressing issues such as taxation for this new business model and its market regulation.

Second, government control hampers investment utilization and business operations. Market regulatory offices are immediate contacting bodies for businesses. However, their efficiency is extremely low, as applicants have to secure prior consent of at least three offices and sometimes over 10 offices within an agency for approval of any single item. Low efficiency in government approval translates into low efficiency in project commencement and business operation. As businesses and individuals obtain their impression of the government mostly from the primary-level offices they deal with, less government control will help build an image of the CPC and the government as efficient organizations.

4. This helps increase government credibility

Power is exclusive and expansive by nature. If unchecked, administrative discretion will further expand, and approval and control will be tightened in more areas for rent-seeking purposes. More power brings more responsibilities. When the government overreaches itself in exercising power, it will have to take more responsibilities than it currently fulfills and build an impression among the public that the government should take care of everything since everything is under its control. A government with too much power becomes less credible. Once anything goes wrong, the public will blame the government without rational thinking or self-reflection.

In contrast, streamlining government procedures and transferring power to the market will improve public satisfaction. Credibility is a key bedrock of the legitimacy of a ruling party. It is built up by public opinion and at the core is the level of public satisfaction.

Policy Reflection: Issues and Solutions Concerning Power Delegation, Improved Regulation and Better Services

The chapter analyzes the journey covered by the reform of cutting government power in three phases, reflects on the challenges facing the reform and provides possible solutions. The first phase was from 2013 up to the State Council reform teleconference in May 2015, when the government took the first few steps in the principle of "crossing the river by feeling the stones". The second phase was between the two reform teleconferences in 2015 and 2016 when the streamlining administration was combined with improved regulation. The third phase started in May 2016, when "better service" was added to the reform.

I. The government only cut power with low value in the initial phase and did not build enough momentum for the reform.

Between 2013 and 2014, government agencies under the State Council began removing and delegating items for administrative approval, sorting out items requiring nongovernmental review and approval, and revoking items of performance evaluation and awards and professional qualification review and accreditation. The State Council also set up a leading group on transforming government functions. For example, the State Administration of Taxation revoked or streamlined tax-related statements. The State Energy Administration moved wind and photovoltaic projects from the category of "review and approval" to that of "registration for record keeping". The Ministry of Science and Technology delegated the power of approval to set up science and technology awards.

A number of challenges surfaced during the reform. They include the following:

First, the government only cut powers of less value and kept those with big room for rent-seeking in its own hands. Many revoked items were peripheral or rarely heard of. During a meeting with non-communist party personages in July 2014, General Secretary Xi Jinping called for advancing the reform on the investment system and cutting more substantive power of the government. The general public will not be satisfied unless reform measures touch the underlying interests of the government and cut more powers of higher value.

Second, the enthusiasm gradually waned from the central to the local governments in administrative streamlining. After the reform in 2013 and 2014, the State Council abolished and devolved quite a number of items for administrative approval, but progress was slow for some provinces. Some municipal governments even failed to function after streamlining. The reform there encountered huge reluctance and was stalled. In some places, one item was divided into several subitems only to be cut later to meet the target set by the State Council. In this way, the number of items seemed to be reduced, but approval procedures remained complicated.

Third, many items require approval from more than one government agency, but these agencies failed to move in tandem in cutting power. Applicants had to go to government at a higher level to complete all required procedures because power cuts in one agency did not bring corresponding policy adjustments to other related agencies. The complexity diluted the effects of the reform.

Fourth, some government agencies at lower levels were unable to take over approval power devolved from the higher authorities. For example, when the review and approval power was passed from the municipal down to the district-level government, there were no professionally qualified staff in the district-level offices who could handle the delegated items. Ultimately, the power had to return to the municipal government.

In addressing these challenges, the State Council gradually developed a guideline of "delegating power, strengthening regulation and improving service".

II. Power delegation and tightened regulation should go hand in hand

At the Teleconference on Streamlining Administration Procedures and Cutting Red Tape held by the State Council on 12 May 2015, the idea of combining power delegation with strengthened regulation was added to the reform. Progress was reviewed on the reform. Over the previous two years, State Council agencies canceled or delegated administrative approval power for 537 items. The number of investment projects subject to central government approval was down by 76%. All overseas investment projects except for a few exceptional cases could proceed without administrative approval. For companies seeking registration, they could have their business licenses issued before obtaining administrative permits; 85% of the matters that once needed prior approval only required ex post approval; with regard to capital registration, the paid-in capital scheme was replaced with a pledged capital scheme; and annual business inspections were canceled in favor of annual information disclosure. The number of qualification accreditation and performance appraisals was cut dramatically. At the central government level, 420 administrative fees and government-managed funds were abolished or reduced, relieving businesses and individuals of their financial burden by nearly RMB100 billion every year. Some provinces moved even faster in this regard, canceling or delegating over half of the administrative approval power. Some provincial non-administrative approvals were cancelled.

The author is of the view that the aim of the State Council's decision of combining power delegation with strengthened regulation was to further streamline the government while preventing market disorder. Administrative streamlining and tightened regulation are mutually reinforcing. A leaner government will focus more on proper regulation. Only when fake products, unlawful merchants and unapproved projects are penalized can the government protect the interests of the public in a more liberalized market. The essence lies in what kind of power should be canceled, what should be further regulated, how to cut red tape and how to strengthen oversight. The author believes that there should be less direct government support to the photovoltaic industry and others to avoid overcapacity. At the same time, policy-based market access control should be relaxed. New business models should be encouraged with tailor-made implementing rules on civil and commercial law and tax codes. Taking the example of the premier car hailing market, cutting administrative approval means revoking the franchise right of the taxi companies. It is welcomed by the market. However, this sector involves the interests of vendors, drivers and passengers, and a lack of regulation will lead to a higher probability of criminal acts. At issue is what kind of mechanism (including legal provisions and industrial rules) is needed to ensure that the market operators protect the interests of both passengers and drivers and improve supervision over their behaviors. The design of the mechanism should also take in more public views instead of those of the government alone. Views of the vendors, consumers and taxi drivers should all be taken into consideration.

To make the reform successful, the academic community suggested that the government draw a power list and a responsibility list. The suggested was taken by the government. Trials have been conducted by the National Development and Reform Commission, the Ministry of Civil Affairs, the Ministry of Justice, the Ministry of Culture, the General Administration of Customs, the General Administration of Taxation and the China Securities Regulatory Commission since 28 December 2015. A negative list should also be drawn that includes production or investment items with strong negative externalities. Although the government has been exercising tight regulation over these items, a negative list is highly necessary. The three lists testify to the resolve of the government to put its power and responsibilities under an institutional and regulatory framework, since a well-established system is needed to produce a lasting effect of the reform. A spelled-out list cuts the discretion of government agencies by preventing the government, to some extent, from making arbitrary intervention in the market or seeking rent from businesses.

III. Improving government service aims to promote mass innovation and entrepreneurship and unleash market potential

The State Council held a teleconference on advancing the reform and improving public services on 9 May 2016. Compared with 2015, this conference stressed the importance of "improved service". Major achievements of the reform were summarized, including further reduction of items for administrative review and approval, integration of the business license, the organization code certificate, and the certificate of taxation registration into one document for business registration as well as one social credit code for each license. Items under central government pricing were cut by 80% to ensure better market roles. To lower the burden on companies, the government made more reductions on tax and general charges, adopted a series of taxation incentives, cancelled most of the items for intermediary services of administrative review and approval, and cancelled, suspended or reduced a large number of administrative charges and government-run funds.

Improving service is the key to a vibrant market. The initiative of mass entrepreneurship and innovation launched by the State Council aims to find new growth drivers of the Chinese economy. As cutting red tape aims to create a favorable environment for the initiative, the government needs to emphasize better service. It includes the following:

First, efforts should be made to provide an enabling environment for new entrepreneurs and, more importantly, cultivating the innovative abilities of big companies. Entrepreneurship and innovation are two key words of equal importance in this initiative. Therefore, the government must refrain from putting entrepreneurship before innovation in allocating human resources and funding. There are now a large number of industrial parks for start-ups and young entrepreneurs and incubators and joint platforms for commercializing research results. They have given a strong boost to start-ups, young entrepreneurs and the new economy. These platforms are important sources for innovation, but in reality, their innovation is low-cost based on low competitiveness and growth potential, and few research findings meet the criteria for commercialization.

For example, there are a number of university students' start-up projects in a young entrepreneurship park, such as postcards that reflect images in sunlight, university bicycle share programs, mobile phone apps, and WeChat businesses, which are popular among WeChat users. However, lack of funding and professional developers has kept the innovation at a low technology level and consequently held back the growth potential of the start-ups, let alone the prospect of becoming business giants. Even worse, in a technology incubator in Guangdong Province, a government-university joint platform on nanometers did nothing to commercialize the patented technologies transferred from the university after getting RMB70 million of grant from the provincial government for "commercializing the research results" it claimed. Too many such incubators and joint platforms originally intended for nurturing new growth drivers may eventually create bubbles and suck up funding originally reserved for traditional industries. What we need is high-tech products that are internationally competitive and world-class innovations that drive the global economy. Baidu and a few other companies that are large in size but weak in innovative capabilities are under criticism for relying solely on trade barriers and market restrictions for survival instead of creating new business models or products. In implementing the policy of "improving service", the government should give more support to R&D in incumbent companies instead of investing too much in incubators and technology commercialization joint platforms.

Second, efforts are required to tailor services to the needs of different industries.[3] The satisfaction rate varies among industrial sectors on cutting red tape. The satisfaction rate on the reform to cancel or delegate administrative approval items was 9.2% in the hospitality and catering industry, much higher than the 5.9% average. The highest dissatisfaction rate was on the reform to cut down fees and charges, which was 15.6% in the wholesale and retail sector. The lowest dissatisfaction rate was 5.0% among other industries.

[3] Data source: http://www.gov.cn.

Policy Prospects: Moving from the Old to the New Equilibrium

The following are three possible future scenarios for the reform based on historical experience.

- The government sees its functions fully transformed and its roles clearly defined. A new equilibrium is created featuring a more credible government, more vibrant businesses, greater sense of gains for the public and a booming economy.
- The cancelation of low-value administrative power brings some vitality to the economy but fails to lift it from the old equilibrium. The economy continues to run on the old track.
- The economy is plunged into a doomed cycle whereby power delegation leads to market disorder, which, in turn, leads to tighter control.

Efforts must be made to avoid the third scenario, steer away from the second one and strive for the first.

I. How to avoid the doomed cycle.

Here is the case of Laiwu, Shandong Province. In 1986, Laiwu became the first county-level municipality in China to carry out the reform on streamlining administrative power to solve the issue of fragmentation or lack of coordination between central government agencies and local authorities. Within two years, it devolved all the staff, funding and property of the municipal industrial and commercial administration, hospital, food authorities, credit cooperatives, traffic bureau and police station to townships. Despite power delegation, the municipal government continued to exercise responsibilities over township offices. Township offices had to share revenue surplus with the municipal government and could retain the balance for future use, but they would receive no subsidy from the municipal government when spending more than it collected. The reform drastically stimulated the economy at the township level with the creation of a large number of township enterprises and all sorts of streamlining efforts. It was later commended by the minister of civil affairs and the governor of Shandong Province. Its experience was replicated in other parts of the country and even appeared in *People Daily*, the official newspaper of the central government.

Around the 1990s, the new central leadership suspended the reform across China out of concern for social stability. In Laiwu, big agencies at the township level with strong revenue-generating capabilities were suddenly taken over by the provincial and municipal governments, with only government leaders' statements instead of official documents in some cases. The cash-strapped township governments were unable to hire professional staff, which seriously affected the competency of their administrative functions.

The author offers the following policy suggestions based on the experience of Laiwu and the current reality in China.

1. Higher professional competency of civil servants at the community level is much needed

In the case of Laiwu, township authorities such as the industrial and commercial administration and the traffic bureau failed to exercise the power delegated from above due to a lack of professional staff. The current reform also exposes the low level of professionalism of local government employees. The success of the reform hinges upon the professional competency of civil servants at the community level. This can be improved in three aspects.

First, efforts must be made to prevent mismatch of human resources in the context of rising size of professionals.

In the past, it was hard for government offices at the community level to have professional staff partly because they were in short supply. As the applicants with higher educational backgrounds were limited in number, community-level offices had to remove professional criteria when hiring employees. Things have changed in recent years with a growing number of universities and an abundant supply of professional graduates. Efforts should therefore be made to avoid mismatch of human resources by encouraging more students to enroll in less hot disciplines. It will help build a talent pool for the subjects concerned and prevent fluctuations in the number of professionals in specific areas that may take place years after the demand shift in the labor market. For example, life science and genetic engineering were very hot ten years ago and attracted more students than the market could manage. In recent years, the much sought-after programs of economics and finance have raised the concern that years later, there will be too many graduates flocking into sectors with limited human resource needs and too few graduates for sectors with a much bigger market demand. The publicity and educational authorities must develop a greater sense of urgency to get things under control, such as correcting the ill-informed expectation of the public on labor market demand and forestall problems that information asymmetry may entail.

Second, government offices at the community level should try their best to meet the expectations of professionals.

Generally, people with professional skills regard civil service as a good career choice, and many of them would take such jobs. However, few of them want to work at township offices. Better benefits for government employees there and more chance for them to move to urban government agencies will help meet the career expectations of the professionals.

Third, there should be fewer barriers from the heads of the community-level agencies.

The heads of these agencies have big discretion over the selection of staff, which gives them much room for rent seeking. As a result, who to hire becomes a way of maximizing their personal gains. More applicants and fiercer competition will only increase the room for rent-seeking. This explains why there are more incompetent but well-connected people than professional staff in these agencies. It is common to find a financial desk officer without any financial training background and agricultural officials who know little about farming. The practice is so widespread that it adds more difficulty to raising the professional competency of government employees in primary-level offices. The solution lies in combining an anti-corruption campaign with better institutional building. The rules must be iron-clad on the ratio of professional staff in agencies that require professional knowledge accompanied by inspections and spot checks.

2. Institutional checks must be in place to prevent arbitrary retrieval of the delegated power

In the case of Laiwu, power exercised by many township agencies was taken back by the higher authorities without an official document or proper procedures. Without an institutional check, such an act of retrieving power from the lower level offices to the higher authorities or from the market to the government can happen at any time in any place. Institutional checks must be strengthened by first adopting a power list that defines the functions of all government agencies at all levels and second setting a due procedure of retrieving the power that involves more than one stakeholder.

3. Caution is required in power delegation and service improvement

In the reform, the municipal government of Laiwu passed the approval power of many agencies to township governments without giving due consideration to the competency of the staff there. It encouraged the birth of a large number of township enterprises before clearly defining the roles of the municipal and township governments on taxation and appropriation or setting up an institutional framework of providing township government with enough funding to support their fiscal expenditure. Later, the shortage of skilled professionals and opportunities made life difficult for the township businesses and almost depleted fiscal spending of the government. It hamstrung the township governments in their role play. The lesson tells us that the government should take into consideration which power to delegate and to whom the power is delegated and which area of administration needs tightened regulation and how to do it. Sound judgment and appropriate criteria are needed before starting the reform. Institutional improvement should also be made in this regard.

II. There should be ways to break away from the inertia of sticking to the old equilibrium

The current reform must steer away the tendency of moving on the old economic track where the old norms prevail and the role of the government remains unchanged. The tendency is created by the stickiness of the old equilibrium or the reluctance of the government to relinquish its long-held power. The reluctance partly comes from the ability of the power to cash in, namely, to seek rent. Under the forceful measures of the central government to fight corruption, many officials now dare not corrupt, but there is still a long way to go in building institutional deterrence against corruption. In other words, officials dare not corrupt, but the room for rent-seeking remains big. In addition, there are many rent-seeking opportunities for petty powers, and such illegal acts are difficult to observe. The reluctance also derives from the sense of accomplishment for taking control and staying above others. These two factors have made it almost impossible for government agencies to voluntarily give up power or power expansion. The author offers the following suggestions to address this issue.

1. Breaking power inertia with sound academic reasoning

This is a plausible reform approach. For measures that remain controversial within the government but bring solid benefits to the local economy, expert teams and consultancy agencies can be commissioned to study and prove whether they are appropriate and effective. This approach will increase the confidence of the government and its leading officials in the reform measures, ensure their smooth implementation, and help break away from the old equilibrium.

2. Strengthening the sense of responsibility above everything else

Efforts to replace prior approval with interim and ex post oversight for projects have also been met with obstacles. Prior approval holds more power, as it determines whether a project can be launched or whether the plant can start production, whereas interim and ex post oversight carries more responsibilities. As few government agencies want to give up power in exchange for responsibilities, some resorted to creating sub-approval items only to be cut in the reform. The only way to follow through on the transition toward interim and ex post oversight is to strengthen the sense of responsibility as the most essential requirement for civil servants. Quantitative indicators are needed to measure the progress that projects have made after getting prior approval, and the practice of creating sub items for reduction sake must be penalized.

III. How can the new equilibrium featuring a thorough transformation of government functions be reached?

The new equilibrium in essence includes an improved sense of service on the part of the government, greater awareness of rights protection and good faith among the public and improved roles of both the government and the market. More specifically, the government function is fully transformed from controlling the market to playing a service role, with fewer rent-seeking acts and higher administrative efficiency. Big companies are more innovative and globally competitive, while SMEs and micro businesses enjoy more simplified service procedures and greater vitality.

The author has the following three points to make on the new equilibrium. First, it is an economic and political state when the reforms meet all the targets. Therefore, it requires enormous efforts to reach equilibrium. Second, it is stable, self-consistent and unlikely to be pulled back to the old one featuring unshifted government functions and an inadequate market role. Third, the old equilibrium will remain viscous and stable if reform measures are not forceful enough.

The journey toward a new equilibrium requires systematic efforts and collaboration among all parties at all levels on various key issues. The following are suggestions for future research.

1. Local governments should be encouraged to improve efficiency

Strong incentives should be given to local governments in serving the market and the public. It is important to tie public appraisal with the immediate interests of local government officials to improve their competency and market roles.

It will be good to set up a long-standing public opinion platform for collecting feedback on the reform. In this way, low administrative efficiency in some agencies will soon result in mounting public opinion pressure on government authorities at a higher level. It will help compel local authorities to address the concerns. There is no need for the government to fear these complaints, so long as they are dealt with properly. Heeding and allaying public concerns is the only way to serve public interests and improve government efficiency. The platform can be put under supervision of the disciplinary authorities at a higher level to avoid being shut down when it targets the interests of the government agencies at the corresponding level.

Another suggestion is to create a quantitative indicator system to appraise the performance of each government agency during the term of its leading officials and the efficiency of the government economic agencies. The indicators may include subjective and objective items, and the scores are publicized. The sense of service of the public servants will be strengthened through open appraisal of government service efficacy.

2. The pace of building a social credit system should be quickened

Information asymmetry is a key factor behind market dysfunction and even disorder in the previous round of administrative streamlining. Part of the reason that some agencies ask applicants to prove that their mothers are their real mothers is that there are too many fake family relationships. Some people hesitate to help out when they see an elderly individual fall to the ground for fear of running into racketeers. The lack of credibility gives rise to fakes and fraud. This may be the reason behind chaos when the market exercises oversight instead of the government. A few mercenary speculators in disrespect of rules are making money by way of cheating. They are destroying the credibility of the whole society. If no action is taken on this issue, the whole society may be dragged into a confidence crisis. In addition, that is why the government cannot and dare not transfer much of the oversight role to the market.

To facilitate a new equilibrium, it is important to reveal the credit worthiness of market players and build a social credit system that covers the aspects of culture, institutions and social entities (Zhang, 2014a). A mature credit system will further boost the reform of cutting red tape and ensure smooth running of the Chinese economy in the new equilibrium.

China has put in place an open business credit information system. More efforts are needed to improve the system and its publicity. The credit information system for individuals should be improved, and that for government agencies should be set up.

More efforts are needed in integrity education, including drawing lessons from Anron, a giant interest group that fell apart due to a lack of business integrity. As laws and ethics are closely related, building a credit system should go hand in hand with law-based governance. Dishonest behaviors must be penalized, and acts of fraud by abusing others' trust warrant heavier penalties.

3. The right sense of citizenship should be advocated, and explorations can be made on letting independent institutions act on behalf of public and business interests

Some people in China tend to criticize the government whenever they see something wrong and hold it accountable for all kinds of problems. They will blame the government for poor governance each time their own interests are affected. This is not the right sense of citizenship. It has held back the reform of building a leaner government. The government, market and citizens are intertwined in the new equilibrium, and a stronger sense of voluntary action and self-protection needs to be cultivated among the public.

More power means more responsibility. The government controls all institutions representing civil rights in China and, as a result, has to undertake all responsibilities. Probes can be made into independent development of civil rights institutions. Freedom for trade associations and workers' unions are needed so that they are able to speak for public and industrial interests and shoulder responsibilities for them. It will help the Chinese people better know their rights and responsibilities and the obligation they take to fight for their rights against rule-breaking companies or insensible behaviors, instead of putting the blame on the government on all issues and waiting for solutions and market interventions from the government.

Bibliography

Guo, G. (1984). Cutting red tape: An important way to address price distortion. *Theory and Practice on Price, 6*.

Guo, R., & Xia, L. (2014). Legal analysis on administrative streamlining–Thoughts on power list, rights list and negative list. *Journal of the School of CPC Hangzhou Municipality, 6*.

Huang, W. (1986). Removing barriers in implementing administrative streamlining and power delegation. *Business Management, 1*.

Li, K. (2015). *Teleconference address on streamlining administration procedures and cutting red tape*.

Li, K. (2016). Teleconference address on streamlining administration, strengthen regulation and improving service [OL]. www.gov.cn

Li, Y., & Chen, G. (2005). From cutting power to tightening control: The doomed cycle of administrative streamlining—Reflections on Laiwu experience. *Socialist Study, 5*.

Mao, X. (1985). How to continue the reform on cutting red tape. *Guizhou Social Sciences, 3*.

Shen, J. (1984). Reviving the old collectively owned enterprises by cutting red tape. *Economic Restructuring, 5*.

Wei, Q. (2013). Reform on administrative approval in the context of building a leaner government. *Politics and Law, 9*.

Xia, S. (1985). Necessary conditions on cutting red tape. *Social Science Front, 3.*
Yong, A., Xiao, Y., & Jian, P. (1984). Better relationship between company headquarters and plants in the reform of cutting red tape. *Economic Management, 10.*
Zhang, D. (2014a). Policy suggestions on local government streamlining and the reform on administrative approval. *China Administrative Management, 8.*
Zhang, Z. (2014b). Credit system building: Hallmark of all-round advancement of the reform. *China Reform Daily, 7.*

Dual Transition and Incremental Reform on the Way Toward a Leaner Government

Qiuyun Zhao

Since the start of the reform and opening-up in 1978, China has enjoyed sustained and fast growth and created the "China miracle". However, the economy is still in a state of imbalance in terms of transformation and development. The Chinese economy entered the phase of dual transition in 1979. The most important reforms during the transition are about ownership and administrative power, and the reforms about ownership must be given top priority. This is because ownership reform is where breakthroughs and major achievements can be made in the transition of economic systems. A clear definition of ownership is also the driving force behind the transition of the development stage. There are two types of economic imbalance. The first type is characterized by an immature market, and the second also features the lack of real market players. Therefore, the key to move from the second to the first type of imbalance is to cultivate real market players with well-defined and clear ownerships. A learner government will, to some extent, push forward the dual transition whose progress relies on more reform measures in administrative streamlining.

Formation of a Highly Centralized System of the Planned Economy

In the early years of the People's Republic of China, the country's development level was quite low. Per capita GDP was only RMB104 in 1952 and was only 5% of the United States between 1949 and 1978. Low income suppressed capital accumulation. In 1952, China's per capita capital stock was only 1.77% of the US, 3.07% of the UK and 4.18% of France. It was only 2.06% of the US, 3.69% of the UK, 3.49% of France and 10.39% of Japan between then and 1978. The capital stock on infrastructure was also very small, which was only RMB 20.2 billion in 1953 at a constant price,

Q. Zhao (✉)
Guanghua School of Management, Peking University, Beijing, China

Y. Li and Z. Cheng (eds.), *The Chinese Path Toward a Leaner Government*,
https://doi.org/10.1007/978-981-19-6718-4_2

approximately 0.5% of that of 2008 (Jin, 2012). These figures all point to the low overall supply of the country's endowment.

The capital-intensive industry is generally characterized by a booming heavy industry, but it did not fit into China's economic reality at that time. The market was unable to drive the growth of the heavy industry that the government decided to develop first because the Chinese market was then unable to rebalance itself in the face of external structural shocks due to a lack of competitive market players. The only way is to artificially suppress the cost of heavy industry such as capital, foreign exchange, energy, raw materials, agricultural products and labor through institutional arrangement as a means to lower the threshold of capital formation for the heavy industry. Thus, a highly centralized macro policy environment took shape. It is characterized by all-round price distortion of products and productive factors, all for the strategy of putting the heavy industry first. The corresponding institutional arrangement was to exercise centralized and planned allocation and management of economic resources, put the industrial and commercial sector under state ownership, and make farms collectively owned and later owned by the people's communes. A regime was also set up to take away management autonomy from companies. This was how the highly centralized traditional economic system was formed in China in the context of its endowment structure and development strategies. The system had two pillars. The first was the state-owned enterprise (SOE) system, which tied government administration with business management with a blurred definition of ownership. The second was an urban–rural administrative system that separated cities from the countryside and restricted the flow of productive factors between them. The two pillars worked together to sustain the functioning of the planned economy. The policy of restricting the flow of productive factors aimed to keep farmers on land and in villages. It was the only way to keep the planned economy running. Chart 1 summarizes the chain of logics.

Characterized by national ownership and people's communes, the planned economy has the following manifestations.

First, industrial enterprises were nationalized. In a fully competitive market, private companies driven by profits tend to invest resources in the sectors that generate maximum profits. If companies are privately owned and managed, the right to profit distribution and choice of investment will both be in private hands, and the areas for resource accumulation may not always match the government's expectation for faster growth of the heavy industry. To obtain the right of profit distribution and invest resources in areas that met the state development goals, it was imperative to turn as many private businesses into SOEs as possible and ensure that companies with state ownership dominate the industrial sector. Guided by this thinking, the government set up the system of directive-based production plans for SOEs and the system of unified state control over revenue and expenditure. It then exercised direct control of SOEs by setting mandatory targets for them. In state-owned industrial companies, the goals of the government and those of management might not be the same. If SOEs were independent in production and management, the surplus value created might be held by the management. To prevent the scenario from happening, the autonomy of SOEs was completely deprived. This was how the institutional framework of SOEs

Chart 1 Formation of the two pillars of the planned economy

Social thinking	The "heavy industry first" strategy	Demand based on endowment structure	A twisted macro-environment	The planned economy	Economic imbalances
The history of being backward and bullied	Constraints in the way of accumulation for industrialization	Supply based on endowment structure	A low interest rate policy	A highly centralized financial system	The SOE system: government intervention in business affairs; blurred boundaries of property rights
Government invention capability	Constraints in global political and economic environment		A low exchange rate policy	A tightly controlled foreign exchange and foreign trade system	A divisive urban-rural governance system: restricting the flow of production factors between cities and the countryside
Collectivism	Factors of international competition		A low input price policy	A highly centralized material management system	Dual transition of the Chinese economy
Size of the country	An agricultural nation in shortage of capital		A low wage rate policy	The establishment of a unified purchase and distribution system of agricultural products	Building a leaner government
			A low daily necessities price policy	State owned industrial companies people's communes	

came into being. As a result, the state was responsible for the provision of production resources, distribution and transfer of products and unified management of revenue and expenditure. It was also responsible for labor and wages, profits, depreciation funds and costs for new product trials. Thus, a system was created that mixed government administration with business operations and failed to clearly define the property boundaries.

Second, agriculture was placed under the control of the people communes. According to the *Party's General Economic Guidelines and Tasks between 1949 and 1956*, farming practices that fit into the realities of the Chinese countryside after the land reform were family-based. During the farming seasons, ad hoc cooperative groups were set up, each with three to five households. As China advanced the economic strategy of putting heavy industry first in a macro policy environment of price distortion, the shift toward collective management of agriculture picked up speed. In this way, the government that controlled the purchasing and selling of everything could purchase more farm products at lower prices. The start of the "Great Leap Forward" in 1958 led to an upsurge in capital construction, a greater imbalance between saving and consumption and a disproportionate amount of grain levy compared to output. It was like an experiment to magnify the price distortion entailed by "the heavy industry first" policy. The microeconomic management system had to follow suit, leading to the fast growth of the people's communes and a divisive urban rural governance structure that restricted the flow of labor and resources between cities and the countryside.

Incremental Reform Toward a Leaner Government

"It does not matter whether the cat is black or white, as long as it catches mice." "(We are) crossing the river by feeling the stones." These are quotes from Deng Xiaoping, the man who started China's transformation from the planned economy to the market economy in 1979. In the early days, there was no blueprint, and the reform made its way forward bit by bit with many patch-ups along the way. The reform can be traced back to the 1960s with the goal of addressing inefficiency in the traditional economic system. However, it was bogged down to an endless cycle of cutting and delegating administrative power versus tightening control, accompanied by the expansion and contraction of government agencies. Power delegation and readjustment changed only the status of various localities and industries in resource allocation, instead of the old development strategies and twisted macro policies, resource allocation systems and non-independent management systems in SOEs. The economic reform launched in 1978 is an overhaul to the old economic regime, as the government explored new ways of meeting socialist targets. It is an all-around reform that gradually gathers momentum and penetrates the underlying issues. Its goal is to replace government orders with administrative guidance on economic development and transform China from the planned economy to a market economy.

The 1978 economic reform was initiated mainly because the long-held strategy of centering upon the heavy industry fell short of the expectation to catch up with advanced economies. Instead, China was lagging further behind its neighbors, especially the "Four Asian Tigers". The stark contrast formed a huge momentum for the reform. Moreover, the disappointing performance of SOEs and people's communes and lack of drive on part of the labor force only worsened under the traditional economic system. The newly elected state leaders hoped to carry out the reform for faster economic growth, better life for the people and ultimately greater support from the public. This is also a key driving force behind the reform in China. For decades, the macro policy environment created by the "catching-up and overtaking" strategy, the system of resource allocation and the non-independent business management mechanisms at the micro level were doing increasing harm to the economy and held back any improvement of people's welfare. Therefore, the opportunity cost of breaking away from the old economic system became increasingly smaller, and it also strengthened the resolution of the government to put the economy on a new track.

The reform in China started at the micro management level partly because macro policy distortion and centralized resource allocation were the underlying issue of the old economic system, and it was difficult to assess their negative impact. However, it was much easier to attribute the inefficiency of SOEs and people's communes to lack of motivation on part of the labor force. This explains why the 1978 reform began at the micro level, with the aim of raising enthusiasm for the workforce and productivity of the economy although a labor incentive scheme. The reform included a household contract responsibility system across the countryside and a number of integrated and industry-specific restructuring programs in cities to streamline administration and decentralize power.

Agriculture was organized by "production brigades" for over 20 years in the Chinese countryside between the launch of the cooperative movement in the 1950s and the adoption of the household contract responsibility system in the 1970s. The old system with few incentives hampered the initiatives of farmers. To raise farmers' incentives, the household contract responsibility system was established at the end of the 1970s. It had three main forms, namely, production assignment contracted to farming groups,[1] production assignment contracted to rural households[2] and a more flexible form of household contract[3] whereby farmers could keep more surplus in hands. The system went through a process of being outlawed, then being partially lawful and later being recognized nationwide. The CPC Central Committee issued documents to support the household contract responsibility system in September

---

[1] It means that the production brigade contracted the workload to each production group with a set timeframe, quality requirement and payment, and decided on awards and punishments based on how much the assignment was fulfilled.

[2] It means that the production brigade contracted land to rural households with a set production quota. After meeting the quota, the farmers could share the profits with the production brigade.

[3] It means that land was assigned to rural households according to the number of family members or labor force. The households were responsible for paying tax to the government and paying levies to the brigade as contributions to capital accumulation and welfare funds. They should meet the quota on government or contracted product purchase at set prices, and could consume or sell the surplus as they wished.

19,794,[4] December 1980[5] and September 19,806.[6] In 1984, it rolled out measures to consolidate and improve the household contract scheme by adding the top 4% production brigades into it, thus completing the microlevel reform in rural areas. The new system became the main contributor to agricultural development during that period. The success lies in the logic that output raised in excess of state and collective obligations was the reward to the household. This method of product distribution motivated farmers to produce more for higher income and displayed the comparative advantage of an abundant rural labor force in China. Later, the household contract responsibility system was further improved with the development of a double-tier agricultural management system. At the same time, new primary-level economic organizations in rural areas were established. Under the people's communes, rural primary-level organizations were more of an institutional arrangement than the choice of community residents. As a mandatory arrangement, there was naturally no exit clause in it. In the early 1980s, with the rollout of the household contract responsibility system, farmers quickly abandoned the people's communes. Almost at the same time, they looked for alternative cooperative organizations (rural primary-level economic organizations). These cooperative organizations opened the way for joint production and resource pooling with an output greater than working individually. They were welcomed by farmers because of the incentives they could generate.

At the same time, reform was carried out in the SOEs. It has gone through three phases. Between 1979 and 1984, the reform focused on less government intervention in exchange for better business performance. The policy of "greater autonomy and profit sharing" was adopted to enable SOEs to share profits with the government. It aimed to encourage managers and workers to work harder for more profits and income and raise the efficiency of resource utilization, with an ultimate goal of increasing both public wealth and personal income. Since October 1978, local governments have launched and later extended pilot programs with a number of measures[7] to expand business autonomy (Table 1). The policy of shared profits incentivized SOEs and their employees. The results showed that monetary incentives for SOEs and their employees helped mobilize the workforce and enhance business vitality. However, the unclear definition of "what power shall be cut and how much profit can be shared" and the dual-track pricing for resources and products opened the way for

[4] In September 1979, the CPC Central Committee adopted the *Decision on Matters Concerning Accelerating Agricultural Development*, which stated that the household contract scheme in rural areas should not be implemented except for special side-line production needs or the only household living in remote and mountainous areas with poor traffic access.

[5] Taking into consideration the role of the household contract scheme in improving farmers' life, the government decided to further relax restrictions on the scheme.

[6] In September 1980, the CPC Central Committee issued the *Matters on Further Accelerating and Improving the Agricultural Production Responsibility System*, which stated that "households in remote mountainous regions and poverty-stricken areas who wanted to join the household contract schemes should be allowed to do so. The farmers' wish for joining the household contract schemes in all its forms should be supported.

[7] The measures included higher wages, bonus, shared profits and more power in fiscal appropriation and resource allocation.

rent seeking. Some companies lowered the government production quota so that they could sell more by themselves. Some failed to follow government plans on transferring resources, and others competed in employee bonus issuance. The second phase was between 1984 and 1986, when the reform priority was to improve business vitality. The measures included decentralizing government power and establishing a new tax regime and a general manager responsibility system. During this period, nonstate-owned companies were more efficient in business operations, as they had no access to low-price resources reserved for SOEs and had to fight for survival in the market. The fact that an increasing number of rare resources flowed to them put pressure on SOEs to stay competitive and gain more vitality through the reform. The reform included turning business profit to corporate income tax, turning government appropriation to loans, launching contract management and the joint stock system. Two reform measures were carried out to boost the vitality of SOEs. One was cutting government directives in business management. The other was issuing a number of administrative rules facilitating the greater autonomy of SOEs. To sort out government-market relations, China embarked on a two-step reform from the 1980s to replace the government levy of business profit with corporate income tax. The first step was separating corporate income tax from profits. The second step was putting place a unified tax regime. The third phase of the reform started in 1987, and the focus was on reestablishing the corporate management system. All kinds of management responsibility schemes were launched during this period, such as contract schemes for large and medium-sized companies, leasing schemes for small businesses and trials on joint stock reform. By 1991, the keyword of the reform was "contract responsibility system". After 1992, the joint stock system was taken as the most effective way to clarify ownership, which was believed to be the root cause of industrial inertia. Joint stock reform became a new fashion. In reality, only the most efficient companies were allowed to issue stocks to investors and set up the joint stock system. The reform seemed to be successful, but competitive markets for products, resources and managers have not yet been established. The lack of autonomy suppressed the motivation of corporate managers, but autonomy would easily put management right above ownership right. This was an issue facing the joint stock reform, during which acts of management right encroaching upon the ownership right increased as ownership became less clear after the reform.

In general, SOE reforms targeted companies producing nonpublic goods. It had three goals – to make asset management more competitive and asset forms more fluid, and ensure the asset owners of their rights to check and supervise the managers. The main reform tasks were "adjusting interest relations between government and SOEs", "giving greater autonomy to SOEs", and "formulating a corporate system that fits into the market". Similar to the economic reform, SOEs also saw their reform goals evolve as the reform intensified. In the beginning, it was about addressing the unsatisfactory performance of SOEs. Then, it was about transforming the model of business management and later a market-oriented reform to make businesses more competitive. In this process, SOEs gradually increased their participation in market competition and enhanced their awareness and ability to improve resource allocation.

Table 1 Phases, time periods, focuses and policies of the SOE reform

Phase	Time period	Focus	Policy	Purpose
I	1979–1984	Narrowing power for higher efficiency	1. In October 1978, a pilot reform program to expand SOE's power was first launched in 6 *SOEs in Sichuan Province* 2. In May 1979, the Sate Economic Affairs Commission, the Ministry of Finance and 4 other central government agencies launched the pilot reform program in Beijing, Tianjin and Shanghai 3. In Autumn 1980, the central government extended practices of some pilot companies to over 6000 SOEs 4. In early 1980, Shandong became the first province in China to allow SOEs to take all the profits instead of submitting a certain proportion to the government	Incentivize workers and entrepreneurs, improve business vitality, and increase *social wealth and individual income*
II	1984–1986	Enhancing business vitality	1. On 1 June, 1983, the profit-to-tax reform began to be implemented 2. In September 1984, the phase II reform was launched 3. In September 1985, the State Economic System Reform Commission made it clear that companies could produce multiple products and engage in various operations to meet market needs 4. In 1988, the State launched the SOE pilot reform program of separating tax from profits and paying taxes before loan paybacks and profits taking 5. In 1990, only 58 kinds of products were under mandatory directive administration	Encourage SOEs to seek their comparative advantages, and make the government responsible for both social wellbeing and state assets owner

(continued)

Table 1 (continued)

Phase	Time period	Focus	Policy	Purpose
III	1987 onward	Rebuilding corporate mechanisms	1. In 1991, SOE contract responsibility system was launched 2. In 1992, the SOE joint stock reform was carried out	Shift operational mechanisms and let market rules drive SOE development

The previous analysis in this paper shows that China's economic reform started with the rural household contract responsibility system. It mobilized farmers to produce more and created conditions for the emergence of township enterprises and migrant workers. Its contribution to economic reform must never be underestimated. However, instead of addressing the dualistic structure of urban and rural areas in China, the household responsibility system only broke down people's communes, an extreme form of the dualistic structure. As a result, cities and the countryside remained cut off from each other, and the two household registration systems ran in parallel. After the third Plenary Session of the 12th CPC Central Committee, the focus of the reform shifted to cities, and SOE reform became the talk of the nation. There is no doubt that SOE reform was of great importance, but rural reform seemed to be forgotten. Moreover, there was no predesigned "reform package". Reform started at the microlevel by giving incentives to farmers and SOE workers instead of the macrolevel advocated by the Washington Consensus. The measures and intensity of the reform were tied to economic issues and the affordability of society. It carried the typical logic of "crossing the river by feeling the stones". The reform started with giving back greater autonomy and profits at the micro level to spur enthusiasm of the businesses and their employees to create new resources. The method of resource allocation was changed to reach the initial goal of faster economic growth and industrial restructuring for sectors suppressed by the traditional economic system. However, the lack of institutional support for the economic reform resulted in the doomed cycle between decentralizing power and tightening control, which added to the challenges the reform faced. The consequence was that the ownership reform in SOEs was stalled, and similar reforms in rural areas, especially the one to separate rural land ownership rights, contract rights, and use rights, barely started.

Separating Rural Land Ownership Rights, Contract Rights, and Use Rights—A Step Further

With surging urbanization and industrialization in recent years, rural labor has flocked into cities, and farmland has to be reallocated. This will enable land to be shifted to farmers with higher productivity and increase land use efficiency (Jin & Deininger, 2009). Farmland has become fragmented under the long-held household contract responsibility system with families as production units, and there was an urgent need to move toward specialized and appropriately scaled-up farming through land transfer and centralized management. A smooth transfer of the right to land is based on a set of well-defined and protected ownership and use rights. However, over the previous two decades, incomplete and unstable rural land ownership has increased the transaction cost, which is now a widespread issue in the farmland management regime. Although the central government has been trying to strengthen farmers' rights to contracted use of land, the rights are yet to be legally defined and generally acknowledged in terms of space and property attributes. Moreover, although the government claims that the term contracted land use is as long as several decades, in reality, contract relations are unstable. In many places, the size of the land may change with changes and movements of family members and land requisition. The unclear and unstable rights harbor unpredictable risks for land transfer, limit the size and scale of the transfer and ultimately suppress land use efficiency. As the need for farmland transfer grows, there is a rising urgency to determine land ownership and use rights to protect farmers' interests in transactions (Zhou, 2013).

In fact, since the launch of the household contract responsibility system in the early 1980s, the central government has always wanted a stable land contract relationship to encourage farmers' long-term investment in land. In 1984, it stated that "the right to land contract will remain unchanged for 15 years" and adopted the policy of "overall stability with minor adjustment".[8] In 1993, on the basis of the first round of land contract, the government launched the second round of contracting under a "30-year term". It also encouraged some regions to keep the original size of contracted land regardless of changes in rural family members. These statements on stabilizing land contract rights were later incorporated into the *Land Management Law* in 1998 and the *Rural Land Contract Law* in 2002. The latter also requires the village collective to issue land contracts and contract management certificates to farmers. The decision was made at the third plenum of the 17th CPC Central Committee held in 2008 that "the current land contract relationship shall remain stable and unchanged for a long time." The statement was frequently quoted by the annual No. 1 Document (on rural affairs) of the CPC Central Committee.

Despite all these efforts, land transfer under the current management system is still affected by the lack of clarity and stability in contracting rights. First, although maintaining the stability of land contract rights was written into law, there is no proper registration and management of the establishment, change, transfer and loss of land contract rights in the current system. The contract relationship was built on the first round of transfer. Frequent land readjustments have led to inaccuracy in the location and size of the land. In the early days, the value of farmland was quite low because contractors had to pay taxes and fees. Therefore, farmers did not pay much attention to ownership rights in land transfer. Later, the rising economic value of farmland triggered more disputes and pushed up transaction costs. Second, the land is owned by the village collective, and each villager in theory enjoys equal rights to land. That is why contracted land is often redistributed after changes in the family population of rural households or government land requisitions. The survey shows that since the establishment of the household responsibility system, 63.7% of the villages have made land adjustments in the second round of contract, and 34.6% of the villages made further adjustments after the second round. The main reasons are demographic change (64.5%) and land requisition (10.6%) (Ye et al., 2010). Land transfer will be constrained without well-defined land ownership and contract rights because the

---

[8] The "minor adjustment" means that the village collective can make readjustment according to the change in family members, namely, "more land for more family members and less land for fewer family members". "The major adjustment" in comparison means that the village collective takes back all the land and redistribute it among the residents currently live in the village. (Xu & Zhang, 2005).

lessor will be worried about whether he can get the land back in the future, and more importantly, the lessee will be concerned about the loss of his long-term investment once the land is reallocated.

As early as 2009, the Ministry of Agriculture conducted small-scale trials in selected townships of eight provinces, including Shandong, Chongqing and Sichuan. The purpose was to further protect farmers' right to land contract and use and facilitate land transfer. Chengdu of Sichuan Province was doing very well. Its reform goal was "rights restoration and farmers empowerment".[9] The land rights determination has made significant headway and gathered a lot of experience. The Ministry of Agriculture unveiled the pilot programs of land ownership and contract rights determination across the country in early 2011, marked by the release of the *Opinions on Pilot Programs of Rural Land Contract Rights Registration*. There were three tasks involved. The first was the accurate demarcation of the land boundary. The second was the establishment of a registration and management system to put registration, modification, transfer and loss of land contract rights on record for use as evidence when disputes occur in land transfer. The third is the issuance of land contract certificates to farmers as legal protection. The document also required local governments to carry out the pilot programs in a pragmatic and prudent manner. Trials could be held first in one to three "highly representative" counties (county-level cities or districts) before being replicated elsewhere.[10]

In summary, since the initiation of the rural household responsibility system in 1978, China's economic and administrative reforms have been going on for over three decades. In terms of the growth generated and the progress made, the reforms have been successful in breaking down the highly centralized planned economy and pushing forward an incremental reform on administrative streamlining. That said, with the dual transition of the economy, the determination of rural land ownership and contract rights has assumed more importance and requires more efforts in the reform.

Bibliography

Jin, G. (2012). China's infrastructure capital stock estimates. *Economic Research Journal, 2012*(4).

Jin, S., & Deininger, K. (2009). Land rental markets in the process of rural structural transformation: Productivity and equity impacts from China. *Journal of Comparative Economics, 2009*(4).

Lin, Y., Cai, F., Li, Z. (2014). *China's miracle: Development strategy and economic reform: Enlarged edition*. Shanghai People's Publishing House.

[9] Here the "rights" referred to property ownership rights. "Empowerment" covered the power derived from ownership. The goal was first raised during Chengdu's reform in coordinating development between urban and rural areas. It was later included in the land reform mobilization documents of other local governments and even the central government (Zhou, 2013).

[10] Interestingly, interpretation of "highly representative" varied among regions. Field studies showed that some regions chose townships featuring more people than land to gather ultimate reform experience, some chose townships with fair balance between land and farmers for easier initial progress, while many others chose townships of various characteristics.

Li, X., Wen, T. (2009). Evolution of China's rural land system in the past 60 years. *Impact of Science on Society, 2009*(3).
Li, Y. (1991). *The unbalanced Chinese economy*. Economic Daily Press.
Li, Y. (2013). *Dual transition of the Chinese economy*. China Renmin University Press.
Xu, Q., Zhang, Y. (2005). Land reallocation, contract rights stability and long-term investment incentives for farmers. *Economic Research Journal, 2005*(10).
Ye, J., Feng, L., Jiang, Y., Prosterman, R., & Zhu, K. (2010). Survey on Chinese rural land use rights 2008: Findings in 17 provinces and policy suggestions. *Management World, 2010*(1).
Zhou, Q. (2013). *Urban and rural China*. Citic Press.

Excessive Macrocontrol and Preventive Measures

Laijun Luo

Macrocontrol is called stabilization policies in advanced economies, where it is meant to be ***a public policy to offset short-term economic fluctuations so that output and price remain as close to their long-term levels as possible. However, in China, macrocontrol tends to be used as a tool to promote economic growth***. It is true that macrocontrol has made remarkable contributions to fast growth in China for decades, but inappropriate use of this policy tool in some cases has also triggered problems and side effects. The article focuses on the overexertion of macrocontrol and the logic, considerations and measures to correct the practice.

Key Manifestations of Excessive Macrocontrol

I. Resorting to macrocontrol when it should not be used

Macrocontrol policies tend to be used on economic issues that should be handled in a different way. Not every issue can be solved by macrocontrol in the economic governance of a country. Here is an example of weak investment demand. Liu (2016a, 2016b) said that the reason for weak investment demand is not that banks have no money to lend or that there is inadequate monetary supply. It boils down to a structural issue in which the real economy, the manufacturing sector in particular, lacks good investment choices. The issue becomes more prominent with large and super-large SOEs. Corporate financing is not a major issue now, as companies have the chance to be listed in domestic and overseas stock markets for direct financing. State-owned banks in general trust large and super-large SOEs and are very happy to provide them with indirect financing support. However, their weak capabilities in indigenous innovation and R&D have led to efforts to upgrade industrial structures.

L. Luo (✉)
National Academy of Development and Strategy of Renmin University of China, Beijing, China

Y. Li and Z. Cheng (eds.), *The Chinese Path Toward a Leaner Government*,
https://doi.org/10.1007/978-981-19-6718-4_3

Increasing investment without structural, technological and product transformation will only result in poor-quality investment in duplicated projects and exacerbation of overcapacity. Such investment practice seems unsustainable when all sectors are looking into ways of addressing overcapacity. Sluggish investment demand is the result of difficulties in upgrading the structure of the real economy, as there are few effective investment opportunities left. It ultimately becomes a structural issue of limited space for industrial upgrading due to the weak innovative capabilities of these companies.

How does China normally deal with sluggish investment demand? China regards investment as a major driving force for economic growth. Once investment slows down or slips, proactive macro policies will be adopted to stimulate the economy, such as raising credit supply, cutting interest rates or increasing government investment. ***Expansionary macrocontrol measures can stimulate investment in the short term, but they may also cause long-term concerns. For example, the weak momentum in industrial upgrading, massive overcapacity, and potential inflation are all closely associated with the expansionary macrocontrol policies that are created to stimulate investment. The tighter these measures become, the worse the structural problems will be.***

II. Replacing market role with macrocontrol

If macrocontrol is used to tackle a problem that can be easily settled by the market, it will, more often than not, worsen the problem instead of solving it. At the same time, the government will have to pay for the huge policy cost. For example, when there is a short supply of pork in the market, some local governments will provide subsidies to pig farmers in the hope that the pork supply will increase as a result. However, this seemingly reasonable macrocontrol policy will only lead to more serious problems because farmers are encouraged to raise pigs in excess of market demand, and oversupply pushes down the pork price. Then, farmers have to cut the number of pigs, which may again lead to a short supply in the market. Even worse, some companies and individuals hoard the pork when supply is short and sell it at a much higher price for exorbitant profit. They also anticipate a higher number of pigs under government incentives and further lower the purchasing price for marginal profits based on their monopolizing status and low price, thus inflicting heavy losses on farmers. The purpose of these companies is to repeat the short supply in the market, and when that happens, they will continue to hoard pork and raise prices for more profits. In this case, government incentives have, to a large extent, exacerbated the fluctuations. Subsidies offered to address a tight market have led to oversupply at a later stage. Removing subsidies in case of oversupply has made the second round of short supply even worse. The government measures have done nothing but to help speculators profit from the doomed cycle. To solve this problem, ***the government should crack down on hoarding instead of increasing the pork supply. At the same time, access to market information is also very important in smoothening out pork supply and demand at all stages***.

Another case concerns the "short supply" of monopolized goods, in which the government may be persuaded to take stimulatus measures to increase market supply.

However, does it work? Before answering this question, let me talk about hunger marketing, which means the suppliers deliberately lower the output to create a false impression of short supply. If the demand is one hundred units, then the suppliers will only ship to market 99 units and raise the price by a large margin. Consumers have to accept the price because of short supply. Hunger marketing is allowed in a non-monopoly environment, but if used for monopolized goods, it will become a tool for gaining unlawful interests at the expense of consumers and will be punished in advanced economies. Macrocontrol of hunger marketing behaviors at either the supply side or the demand side will be of no avail. In contrast, it may serve the interests of market cheaters. If efforts are made to stimulate the supply side through government incentives such as subsidies or tax cuts, it will further increase the profits for the suppliers and encourage them to continue with hunger marketing. If the government takes measures to cut demand, marginal demand will come down first, leaving behind only rigid demand. Then, the suppliers will further cut shipments and raise prices for higher overall profits with less cost. ***Therefore, no macrocontrol measures at either the supply or demand side will resolve economic issues*** caused by hunger marketing in a monopoly setting. ***It may even create more chaos in the market. The only effective measure is to punish acts of hoarding and let the market balance supply and demand on its own.***

III. Frequent use of macrocontrol

The fact that macrocontrol becomes a ready resort whenever the economy slips or faces challenges is in itself a problem. This is because efforts are made only to address symptoms instead of the root cause.

Addressing economic issues is like treating illness. It is more important to remove the root cause than to treat symptoms. Once the root cause is addressed, all its symptoms will go. The government needs to identify the root causes of economic problems and take targeted measures. To make an analogy, a person infected by a virus may have a fever. It makes him sometimes feel cold and sometimes feel hot. The feeling is the symptom, and virus infection is the cause. When antiviral treatment removes the root cause of the disease, the alternate cold and hot feelings will also disappear. However, if the treatment is only targeted at the symptoms by trying to cool down the patient he feels hot and keep him warm when he chills, the measures will have to change frequently, and the length of treatment will extend. The failure to identify the root cause will make the illness more serious instead of curing it. Macrocontrol in certain periods is more like treating symptoms and is frequently employed. Moreover, instead of addressing the root cause, habitually resorting to macrocontrol makes things even worse or creates more problems. This in turn often results in repetitive and frequent use of such measures.

IV. Costs associated with higher growth

Economic growth is accelerated at the expense of the following. First, less attention is given to resource conservation and environmental protection. Some local governments have approved projects of high pollution discharge and energy intensity that do not meet environmental standards. Economic growth targets are thus met at the cost of resources and the environment. The practice creates long-term problems, as resources and the environment have become the biggest bottleneck of sustained growth for China's economy. Second, the economic welfare of some population groups has been compromised. Monetary ease has diluted the purchasing power of the currency in real terms. It has affected the purchasing power and economic welfare of the people who have no way to keep the value of their savings from being compromised. Unequal access to investment has widened the gap in income distribution between social groups and worsened the economic benefits of people with less income. The low product and industrial standards have kept product quality at a low level. The domestic standards, which are lower than international standards, have given low-tech manufacturers a breathing space. However, their low-quality products have weakened economic performance and social welfare. Fourth, the government puts GDP growth before efficiency in resource allocation. Local governments in China are leading the efforts on economic development. Their single-minded pursuit of output value and economic growth, the lack of a market competition mechanism and the launch of poorly considered investment projects have all led to profound distortion of resource prices and inefficient resource allocation.

V. More short-term than long-term considerations

A key problem with China's macrocontrol is placing more emphasis on short-term effects without giving full consideration to the long-term consequences. The aforementioned weak investment demand is a case in point. Inappropriate investment stimulus in the past may help raise the investment demand at that time but has led to more sluggish investment demand in the future, an even harder problem to be resolved. In another case, the government made the proposal on energy price reform back in 2006, but the reform has since been put aside the concerns that it may increase energy costs for businesses and affect output and economic growth. This perfectly reflects the relationship between short-term and long-term considerations. The government must understand their underlying relations and develop policies on this basis. Putting investment before consumption in economic governance is another example. This is because the effect on the economy through increasing investment comes more quickly than through increasing consumption, and the push from the consumption side may not be as strong as from the investment side. That is why China's macrocontrol policy is more investment-based. This has caused imbalances between investment and consumption. In the long term, however, a higher consumption level in a country will contribute more to the economy and help create more vibrant economic institutions and stronger momentum of sustained growth. In this sense, investing before consumption is short-sighted. In China, income distribution policies give more consideration to capital returns and the investment needs of industries and the government. This has inevitably squeezed personal income and resulted in the underconsumption of individuals. Over the past years, the consumption curve in China has been going down instead of going up. The consumption to GDP ratio is approximately 60–70% on average globally. In China, it was above 50% in the 1980s, slightly over 45% in the 1990s and 45.2% in 2001. However, by 2008, the ratio dropped to 35.3%, only half the world's average. The government has been working hard to increase domestic demand, but only investment demand has been boosted, and the consumption demand is becoming increasingly weaker.

Solutions

I. Clarifying the roles of macrocontrol, development planning, market and social governance and their relations

Economic governance should not rely too much on macrocontrol because it cannot solve all the problems and may even make things worse in some cases. ***In the present context, China needs to make good use of a variety of policy tools of different natures, such as macrocontrol, development planning, market regulation and social governance. These measures can be mutually reinforcing when playing their respective roles, but they cannot replace each other.***

Sole reliance on macrocontrol is not enough to meet structural and technological challenges in areas such as industrial upgrading, balanced growth of urban and rural areas, integrated regional development, technological progress and income distribution. In these areas, macrocontrol can serve as a supporting measure, while the main policy tool should be development planning, such as those on industrial growth, urban and rural development, regional integration and technological progress. While there is a large controversy on the use of development planning, it is an important policy tool that should not be excluded since China is still in the development phase, to be more specific, the phase of faster industrialization and urbanization. There are quite a few development planning initiatives in China, but it is not easy to put them to good use. The key to success lies in giving full play to the role of the market.

Industrial plans or policies are good illustrations of development planning. The role of industrial policies in the economy has always been an issue of great controversy. They succeeded in helping the US catch up with the UK and in helping Japan and the ROK in their economic take-offs. However, almost the same policies suffered great setbacks when transplanted into Latin American countries. Paul Krugman (Krugman, 1997) and some other economists have little trust in industrial policies. Krugman holds that industrial policies cannot play a decisive role. Rodrik (2002) points out that industrial policies will distort resource allocation made by the market and open a huge space for rent-seeking. Lall (2001) even doubted the ability of the government to formulate sound industrial policies. All this shows that at issue is not whether industrial policies will produce good governance effect, but how to use it properly for expected results.

China values the role of industrial policies. However, the policy effect has been far below expectations. Instead of making great improvements to the industrial structure and competitiveness, they have resulted in overcapacity in quite a number of industries and the creation of many low-end manufacturing and processing businesses. However, it would be unfair to blame the policies because of failure to put them to best use. Taking funding for China's strategic emerging industries as an example, the amount of funding for such industries or technologies is determined by the companies' output or business scale. The bigger they are, the more funding they will receive. The government should change the practice by shifting the focus from output and business scale to the companies' support for R&D and product users. R&D requires huge investment, especially for key technology development, and the payback period is long. It cannot be done by companies alone and needs to be included in national science and technology development planning. In the production phase, the products may not sell well out of the concerns over unstable technologies. At this initial period, the government should offer product users buyers a subsidy to help nurture the market for the industry. Policies that support R&D and product users can also help avoid the malpractice of fraudulently obtaining government funding by simply expanding the business scale.

For any macrocontrol measures or development planning to be successful, the most important thing is to respect and give full play to the role of the market. The relationship between the government and the market must be clearly defined. The government cannot overreach its mandate, or even worse, stand in the place of the market. As a policy tool, the current supply-side structural reform should be a combination of development planning and macrocontrol measures. Its success hinges on the efforts of giving full play to the role of market, known as the invisible hand. According to the analysis made by Liu (2016a, 2016b), companies are among the first to feel the impact of supply-side structural reform. If the rights of companies as market players are not fully protected or respected by the economic or the legal regime, they will likely become the subjects of undue and arbitrary intervention by the government, or even worse, slide back to the time of the planned economy. A sound relationship between the government and the market holds the key to successful supply-side reform in China. The reform targets can be met only with the help of the market instead of administrative measures. Otherwise, it would probably lead to denial of the market economy, which would prove the reform to be a failure, a consequence no one wants to see.

Attention must also be placed on the relations between macrocontrol and social governance. When enforcing macrocontrol measures, the government should also take into consideration the environment, life quality, food safety, economic welfare, ethics and culture, and people's mindsets. Except for extreme cases, the government should refrain from disrupting these aspects just for the sake of meeting its macrocontrol targets.

II. Aligning growth targets with the law of economic development

The governments of developing countries need to take into consideration whether the growth targets should be based on national development goals or the real state of the economy. For them, keeping the economic growth rate above a certain percentage is probably necessary to resolve some issues. For some countries where the majority of people are still living under the poverty line, growth of higher speed but lower quality would be better than keeping growth at a low level, which makes poverty reduction more difficult. Another scenario where a higher growth rate with lower development quality might be a better choice is when unemployment is about to reach a level that will trigger serious economic and social problems unless growth is raised to a certain rate. For countries that have made some progress in national development, growth targets should be set by taking into consideration both national development goals and the state of the economy. If the growth targets deviate much from the economic reality, it will do big harm to the quality of development and increase barriers and costs for meeting the targets.

It is much suspected that China's growth targets are based on its national development goals. However, the government has taken into full consideration the economic reality. For example, the growth target is set at 6.5% between 2016 and 2020, a speed required for achieving the goal of doubling the GDP and per capita income of 2010 by 2020. At the same time, the government has also analyzed China's potential growth in the next five years. In drafting the thirteenth Five-Year Plan (2016–2020), the National Development and Reform Commission organized a study on China's growth potential during this period and drew reference from the research findings of international organizations and market analysts on its potential growth rates. Then, the drafters conducted modularized demonstrations for growth scenarios of 6.5, 7 and 7.5% under presumed values of indicators such as investment, consumption, fiscal arrangement, import and export to see whether the growth can also meet other national targets, such as revenue, employment, resource and environment affordability and the ability to adapt to external dynamics.

It has been proven that the Chinese government took into account both national development goals and the state of the economy when setting the average annual growth target between 2016 and 2020. However, further studies are needed on this subject to provide a more comprehensive policy basis for setting growth targets beyond 2020. For example, ***what will be the optimum growth rate for meeting the environmental, product and industrial standards, development quality requirements and benchmarks in resource and investment utilization if they are all higher than the previous years? Such consideration in setting the growth targets will help ensure quality growth and sustainable development of the economy***.

III. Shifting focus from economic growth targets to employment targets

According to Liu (2016a, 2016b), thanks to the reform and opening-up, China has maintained an average annual growth rate of over 9%, which is very high. It sets a new record in the contemporary world. The record was first set by Japan after the Second World War. It created a 20-year golden period of growth from the 1950s to the 1970s. It was followed by the ROK with thirty years of fast growth. Now, the record was broken by China. Statistics between 1978 and 2014 showed that the country's average growth was as high as 9.7%. It has transformed China's economic outlook and raised its global GDP from 9th place to second place and its GDP share in the world from 1.8% to approximately 13%. China is now the world's second largest economy, with a GDP of 63.7 trillion yuan by the end of 2014, an increase of nearly 28 times over the past 40 years.

Statistics showed that compared with Japan and the ROK, China has maintained a longer period of high economic growth. ***However, decades of fast growth have***

created challenges alongside huge wealth, such as environmental pollution, overcapacity and an industrial structure characterized by high energy consumption, pollution, low technology level, low added value and weak competitiveness. In this context, it would be harder for macrocontrol targets to meet the overall development imperatives compared with decades ago if they only promote quantitative growth. Given the size of the population in China, it will be more advisable to shift the focus to employment targets.

The growth targets are consistent with the employment targets in most cases. However, ***with the development of the economy, technologies and the service sector, the correlations between growth and employment have weakened. The gap has widened between growth target-based measures and employment target-based measures.*** Li (2014) described the correlations by saying that in the past, many people believed that only high growth could create more jobs, while low growth would lead to unemployment. However, it has been proven that not all jobs are necessarily created by economic growth. If the growth is high-tech driven, it may even lead to fewer jobs. Different types of growth or investment have different impacts on employment. High-tech investment may squeeze people out of jobs, while private funds, the growth of SMEs and the service sector may raise employment by a large margin. In the current context, it will make a lot sense both economically and socially if China's macrocontrol measures are employment-driven instead of growth-driven.

IV. Putting to practice the thinking that macrocontrol measures should target the real economy

The 2008 financial crisis may have shaken the underlying thinking behind monetary policies or disrupted perceived relations between the financial sector and the real economy. Blanchard (2013) pointed out that the evolution of the macroeconomy throughout the financial crisis triggered reflections on an old subject, namely, relations between inflation and output and lessons for monetary policy making. A controversial viewpoint is that "economic growth will approach its potential level so long as inflation remains stable." Central banks more or less accept this argument regarding the appropriateness of adopting a growth target that is pegged with an inflation curve, although they believe that the correlations may not be as precise. The analysis shows that ***to tie monetary policies with inflation targets is in essence to tie them with industrial output and the real economy.***

Since the outbreak of the financial crisis, however, relations between inflation and output in advanced economies have changed considerably compared with the precrisis period. As output in real terms went down against potential output and the unemployment rate quickly climbed up, most economists were of the view that inflation would come down or even give way to deflation. However, inflation has remained close to the precrisis level in most advanced economies. A plausible explanation is the weakening of the correlations between shortfall in output and inflation. ***If this trend continues, to tie the monetary policy with inflation will not necessarily bound it with output and the real economy. Therefore, the focus of monetary policy should be shifted more toward activities of the real economy because its ultimate goal is to serve the real economy.***

Concerning the Chinese economy, the challenge of virtualization has become more serious in recent years. It is a question of whether money has flowed into the real economy and to what extent it has affected the production, distribution and consumption of wealth. The slowdown of private financing and M2 supply in recent years proves that financial institutions have failed to provide strong support to the real economy and businesses still find it difficult to obtain financing. Instead of flowing into the manufacturing industry, the liquidity has flocked into the real estate and financial sectors, which have expanded rapidly due to the "asset-expenditure" effect. The added value of these two sectors has been growing in step with the growth of M2 supply, and their high growth rate is much related to disproportionate liquidity inflow. In addition, a lot of residential housing was bought not for home use but for investment sake. That is why China's real estate sector also demonstrates the features of the virtual economy.

What has happened in China shows that monetary and financial operations are at best loosely connected with the real economy. Therefore, it is highly necessary for monetary policies and actions to target the real economy. It is important to know where the money should go when exercising the monetary policy. It should enter the production and consumption sectors, and it is imperative to avoid massive liquidity flow into the virtual economy.

V. Restoring the functions of monetary policy and fiscal policy for price stability and public finance, respectively

According to traditional theories, macrocontrol serves four major goals, namely, economic growth, price stability, full employment and balance of international payments. In practice, most Western countries have to make choices among the goals according to their national priorities. Both the "staged goals" and the "dual goals" that they may choose place great importance on price stability. This is mainly because in advanced market economies in the West, price stability indicates effective resource allocation and healthy economic performance (Woodford, 2003). In addition, Western countries have an average consumption ratio of 70%, and their consumption is highly sensitive to price level. Price stability therefore generally ensures steady economic growth. According to some scholars, China does not have to focus on price stability as much as Western countries do in exercising macrocontrol because the weakness in its market mechanism makes it hard for the price signal to fully reflect what truly happens in the economy. China's past economic growth was to some extent driven by a relatively loose monetary policy instead of price stability. It has, however, a big downside as the policy that may stimulate the economy in the short term limits the growth in the long term and entails a twisted investment mechanism, misallocation of resources, distortion of income distribution, inability to move up the value chain and less motivation for technological progress. Such analysis highlights the significance of price stability for the growth of developing countries. Short-term growth without price stability may do more harm than good. In fact, the pros are much smaller than the cons. This is a matter that needs to be further reviewed and analyzed with specific cases.

Discussion on the aforementioned subject is not important thus far as China is concerned, as the country has been growing at a fast pace for nearly four decades and is no longer driven by monetary factors. Now, there is every reason for the monetary policy to play its traditional role as the price stabilizer. What remains unchanged amid dynamic circumstances is the basic law of economics. If the government and the central bank accept the view that restoring the role of monetary policy in stabilizing prices and providing a stable and predictable monetary environment and pricing system can generate more economic growth and social benefit than relying on monetary supply as an economic stimulus, they should consider taking moves in this direction or at least draw reference from this prudent policy thinking to a certain extent.

Much of the credit of China's economic growth goes to its proactive fiscal policy, which is still used time after time as a main tool in generating growth. Needless to say, proactive fiscal policy has achieved much, but its most apparent weakness lies in the restriction and exclusion of market behaviors. Its effects are waning as problems in the course of economic development gradually unfold. That is why the current fiscal policy considerations need to be revised. Returning it to its basic function of public finance is an important direction. This means that the focus of fiscal policies should shift as soon as possible from promoting economic growth to providing public goods. When supporting a proactive fiscal policy with more budget expenditures, the government should ensure that the majority is spent on health, education, social security, environmental protection and people's welfare.

On the other hand, the demand for China's public finance is huge. In the first three quarters of 2015, China's fiscal revenue grew only by 7.6%, but its expenditure on health, education, social security, and environmental protection increased by approximately 20%. Public expenditure will be under even greater pressure due to the aging of society and greater emphasis on public welfare, resources and environmental protection, as stated in the 13th Five-Year Plan. That is, the government needs to scale back the role of fiscal policies in macrocontrol and spend more on public welfare. The policy change will also reflect the government's philosophy of putting development quality and social benefit before the economic growth rate.

VI. Making job market stability and improved economic structure primary and secondary macrocontrol targets

This policy recommendation, based on the conclusion of the previous analysis, determines the target for macrocontrol as "ensuring a stable job market first and then improving the economic structure". Stabilizing employment can avoid a number of problems resulting from quantitative expansion triggered by the policy to maintain the growth rate. Macrocontrol can play a supportive role in facilitating technological, industrial and market measures for structural readjustment in the long term instead of carrying the burden of improving the economic structure all by itself. To be more specific, it is expected to provide an appropriate monetary and fiscal environment for structural readjustment or coordinate the efforts in this field.

Another problem connected with China's macrocontrol policies is that there are too many goals to fulfill, which makes it difficult to set the focus and may bring undue interruptions to economic development. Taking the current policy as an example, the targets include steady growth, improved structure, better life, social harmony, progress in reform and risk mitigation. It seems that macrocontrol can solve all problems, which is impossible. Macrocontrol can only play the role of a stabilizer. Making stable employment and structural readjustment as primary and secondary targets means that macrocontrol plays clear but limited roles and should not be employed at will to solve problems outside its scope of responsibility.

A Thought-Provoking Conclusion

A conclusion that may draw our attention and provoke our thoughts is that economy can be compared to a living creature. The health of an economy is similar to the health of a human body. Macrocontrol is used to treat short-term illness in a targeted manner, while making good health genuine and lasting relies on the appropriateness of such long-term factors as rest, diet, exercise and emotion. Since short-term measures generate effects much faster than long-term measures, too much value has been placed on macrocontrol instead of technological progress, market regulation, rule of law, education, quality, credibility and other long-term measures. Now, supply-side structural reform presents a large opportunity for us to shift our focus to long-term factors in economic governance. China must take the chance created by the reform to upgrade and improve its economic governance system in its entirety.

Bibliography

Blanchard, O., Dellariccia, G., & Mauro, P. (2013). Rethinking macroeconomic policy. *New Finance, 2013*(6).

Krugman, P. (1997). What ever happened to the Asian miracle. *Fortune, 136*(4).

Lall, S. (2001). Comparing national competitive performance: An economic analysis of world economic forum's competitiveness index. *Queen Elizabeth House Working Paper Series*, S61.

Liu, W. (2016a). China's economic growth and macrocontrol. *Journal of the Party School of the Central Committee of the CPC, 2016*(1)

Liu, W. (2016b). Reflections on China's macro economic policies 2009–2016. Speech at the 10th anniversary of China macroeconomic forum, 18 June 2016.

Li, Y. (2014). Will high growth bring high employment? A dialectical view. *Economic Daily*.

Rodrik, D., Subramanian, A., & Trebbi, F. (2002). Institutions rule: The primacy of institutions over geography and integration in economic development. *NBER Working Paper, 2002*(9305).

Woodford, M. (2003). *Interest and prices: Foundations of a theory of monetary policy*. Princeton University Press.

Streamlining Government Administration and Financial Regulation—Building Innovative Financial Regulatory Platforms Based on Data Science

Zhiyong Ding, Jie Ma, and Shilan Feng

With the faster growth of Internet finance, wider adoption market-driven interest rates, tightened capital control and mounting financial risks and pressure, financial regulators are confronted with the complexity of balancing administrative streamlining with financial regulation when the industry is stretching out in scope with apparently different focuses for each business line and a myriad of innovations. The success of delegating financial regulation power lies in a keen knowledge of what is meant by this policy, what administrative functions and powers should be streamlined, and on what grounds and for what purpose. It is important to address both the "first mile" and the "last mile" issues in streamlining government administration in the financial sector, namely, building a regulatory decision-making system and a strategic transmission system supported by smart technologies and data science. The systems will serve to integrate government streamlining with financial regulation and support big data-enabled regulation and direct service. Along this line of thinking, cutting government powers in financial regulation will truly enhance the performance, efficiency and competitive strengths of the financial sector and serve its globalization strategy.

Z. Ding (✉)
Guanghua School of Management, Peking University, Industrial and Commercial Bank of China Co., Ltd., Beijing, China

J. Ma
China Financial Magazine, Beijing, China

S. Feng
Guanghua School of Management, Peking University, Beijing, China

Y. Li and Z. Cheng (eds.), *The Chinese Path Toward a Leaner Government*,
https://doi.org/10.1007/978-981-19-6718-4_4

Relations Between Streamlining Government Administration and Financial Regulation

Thanks to the reform and opening up over the past 30 years, China has traversed the path of fast economic growth. Its sustained high GDP growth has created an economic miracle. As of the end of 2015, China's GDP reached RMB67.67 trillion, an increase of 6.9% over 2014, making China the second largest economy in the world. However, no one can ignore that the world economic and financial landscape is becoming increasingly complex in the general context of sluggish growth. Some regions have fallen behind in development due to the worsening of the geopolitical environment. A number of uncertainties in economic and financial development at home and abroad are bound to affect the Chinese financial market. Therefore, in the face of economic slowdown, fewer fluctuations in the financial sector and increasingly diversified new financial products, there is an urgent need to continue to cut government power and let the market play a decisive role so that the financial market can fully support the growth of the real economy through resource allocation.

Streamlining government administration aims to cut government powers while strengthening regulation in China's financial sector. Excessive intervention and control by the government over the financial market and putting review and approval before financial supervision will constrain the market and dampen its role in facilitating the growth of the real economy. On the other hand, if the government does not put much thought into streamlining administration, or simply delegating the power to the market, it will result in blind spots which will hamper the growth of the financial market instead of promoting it. This is the last thing the government wants to see when formulating the policy. The policy encourages the government to retreat from areas that should not fall into its responsibilities and play a better role within its mandate. There must be clear rules on what the government should take care of and in what way. Financial market regulation hinges on the mechanism of rights and responsibilities. To ensure healthy development and effective regulation of the financial market, continuous efforts must be made to streamline government administration and uphold the centrality of the market's role. Review and approval must be combined with the monitoring and regulation of financial activities during and after they are carried out to forestall any room for rent seeking in the market. The rule that the reviewers are accountable for their decisions must be enforced in financial regulatory bodies to make regulators accountable for market order and health.

The power taken away from the government must be truly shifted to the market and fully enforced by the market. It is only natural for the government to encounter various forms of obstacles and challenges while cutting its own power. Some are visible, others are not. They include the "first mile", the "mid-journey" and the "last mile" issues, which refer to obstacles in the phases of strategy and policy-making, trials and final execution. In the face of these difficulties, it is important for the government to free up the mind, take a new thinking and resort to big data and smart technologies for greater vitality and efficiency in building a regulatory model suited to China's financial market. To ensure a smooth power shift, government streamlining should be conducted according to laws and regulations, and a sound self-regulatory system must be set up in the financial market. Reform should be carried out in the review and management system that has thus far failed to catch up with the growth of the financial market in an effort to boost the dynamism of market players and serve the growth of the real economy. At the same time, the delegated regulatory power needs to be properly exercised to prevent a power vacuum. Otherwise, administrative streamlining will encounter more barriers or cause more problems afterwards. Therefore, it is important to make sound decisions concerning which financial regulatory items can be shifted from the government for the purpose of smooth delegation and efficient enforcement of these powers.

Regulation needs to be efficient and creative. Cutting red tape will give full play to the role of the market players, but it may give rise to unregulated market behaviors, low credibility of market players and infringements on customers' interests. Law-breaking activities in the financial market will cause distortion of the financial market, where bad money drives out good. These problems will significantly constrain the growth of law-abiding companies and entrepreneurs and cut back the effects of the reform. To make regulation more efficient, the government should focus more on supervision during and after the trading process to ensure healthy development of the financial market. It should also transform its philosophy of financial regulation and improve the awareness of the rule of law and fairness and its own sense of responsibility. Sound and effective financial regulatory rules, processes and standards must be adopted to set clear limits for market players and put them under law-based supervision. The government should serve as a good referee and maintain a level playing field. It should give enough space to those who play by the rules, give yellow cards to those who have committed minor fouls as a warning and red cards to serious rule offenders and remove them from the market.

To make regulation more creative, the government should adopt new financial regulatory mechanisms and methodologies. An integrated regulatory platform needs to be put in place, covering all regulatory items of the central bank and China's banking, securities and insurance regulating agencies. It will help form an integrated financial regulation mechanism across industries and sectors to build synergy and avoid overlapping and gaps in supervision. Efforts should be made to advance "smart regulation" by using big data, cloud computing, the Internet and other information technologies, exploring new models of "big data + financial regulation", and realizing the connectivity and sharing of financial regulation information between regulatory bodies and government departments at all levels. This will help break the information barriers between different departments, advance the building of a unified financial credit system and a sound information disclosure and credit record system to hold dishonest financial institutions accountable and improve financial regulatory efficacy.

Streamlining administration and strengthening regulation must go together. The government should transform its functions and improve services through reform and innovation. Freeing up mind and building consensus are required to carry out reform in the financial sector and adapt to the new normal in the financial market. The complex relations between financial regulation and government streamlining should be well managed, and these two important areas of work deserve the same attention. Financial regulatory power should not be simply delegated without overall consideration, and areas falling into the responsibility of market players should not be put under tight control. When shifting the power to the market, the government must have a keen understanding of which regulatory measures are effective and which are not. The history of China's financial market development shows that the power of approval concerning financial institutions is much sought after by government agencies. However, when problems occur, the buck passing among these agencies makes it difficult to define regulatory responsibilities, especially in novel financial markets and cross-cutting businesses. Regardless of what specific government arrangement is made, structural arrangements are needed in financial regulation to unleash the potential of market players. The global financial crisis tells people who relying solely on self-discipline and self-regulation of the market will end in nowhere. Instead, it will seriously undermine socioeconomic development and financial stability. The growth and stability of the financial market and sustainable socioeconomic development can only be ensured with a prudent regulatory system and a smart and integrated regulatory platform based on data science.

Global Comparison of Financial Regulatory Models

With the innovation-driven growth of Internet finance, faster globalization of the financial sector and lingering effects of the 2008 global financial crisis, all countries are facing the challenge of building a new financial regulatory system. The financial crisis was the result of a serious mismatch between government supervision and market roles in resource allocation as well as the failure of financial regulation. Upholding the basic policy of market-based resource allocation together with reforms in financial supervision, regulation, layout and eco-environment is imperative to catch up with financial market development. The following is the analysis of the financial regulatory models in the US, the EU, the UK, Singapore and Australia.

I. The American model

Before the outbreak of the financial crisis in 2008, the United States adopted a separate supervision model. Regulation was mainly carried out by the Federal Reserve (FR), the Office of the Comptroller of Currency (OCC), and the Federal Deposit Insurance Corporation (FDIC). After the financial crisis, the United States established a macroprudential regulatory framework led by the Federal Reserve and the Financial Stability Oversight Council. The Federal Reserve regulates holding groups, nonbank financial institutions, systemically important payment clearing systems and systemically important financial institutions and sets strict and prudent standards on capital requirements, liquidity requirements, stress tests and counterpart credit limits to ensure effective separation of decision-making from enforcement, prompt collection of information data of institutions under regulation, and effective monitoring supported by big data. The Financial Stability Oversight Council supervises the financial system's participants. It focuses on identifying systemic risks and systemically important institutions, such as systemically important banks, nonbank financial institutions and financial businesses, as well as various risk factors that threaten financial stability. The FSOC keeps the separate supervision model and pays more attention to vacuums in financial regulation.

II. The EU model

The EU is a major economy in the world. Euro is circulated in 17 EU member countries according to the single currency policy. With over 8000 monetary and financial institutions and a total asset of 50 trillion Euros, the EU has become a key driver of global financial development. There are a number of large banks and financial holding groups in the EU; 14 of them have been rated as the world's systemically important banks, and 7 countries are founding members of the Basel Committee. In terms of macroprudential regulation, the European Central Bank is responsible for macroprudential regulation, and the European Systemic Risk Committee (ESRB) is responsible for bank regulation. In terms of microprudential regulation, the European Banking Authority (EBA) is responsible for regulating the banking industry. The European Insurance and Occupational Pensions Authority (EIOPA) is responsible for regulating the insurance industry. The European Securities and Markets Authority (ESMA) oversees securities industry. The three agencies have established sound mechanisms for communication and coordination.

III. The UK model

Before the 2008 financial crisis, the Bank of England, the Ministry of Finance and the Financial Services Authority were responsible for the UK's financial regulatory framework. The Bank of England was responsible for maintaining financial stability. The Financial Services Authority was in charge of market entry approval of financial institutions and regulatory measures development and enforcement, and the Ministry of Finance oversaw of the legal and institutional framework. This architecture failed to include macroprudential regulation against systemic risks. In 2010, the UK reformed and upgraded the financial regulatory system by adopting an integrated supervision model, replacing the Financial Services Authority with the Prudential Regulation Authority (PRA) and the Financial Conduct Authority (FCA). The PRA is responsible for the prudent and micro regulation of the financial system. The FCA regulates the conduct of financial institutions in customer services. The Financial Policy Committee (FPC) was established under the Bank of England to be responsible for macroprudential regulation and systemic risks. The newly established Consumer Protection and Market Authority (CPMA) and Economic Crime Authority (ECA) regulate financial services and economic cases.

IV. The Singapore model

The Singaporean banking system consists of the Monetary Authority (MAS) and commercial banks. The MAS performs the duties of the central bank and the government financial agent under a sound financial environment and financial system and regulates full banks, offshore banks and wholesale banks. Singapore adopts a centralized and integrated supervision model, focusing mainly on maintaining financial stability, at the center of which is risk monitoring. The MAS conducts prudential regulation of the financial industry through regulation over banks, insurance companies, sectoral risks and complex institutions and prudent policy management. Its roles cover three aspects, namely, on-site inspection, off-site inspection, auditing and joint supervision; financial license issuance and prudential regulation; and giving full play to the role of the financial market in information disclosure and corporate governance. Regulation, risk-related regulation in particular, is carried out in accordance with the rules of the international financial market on the premise of controllable risks. The MAS focuses on corporate governance and internal control and implements prudent accounting and prudential regulation.

V. The Australia model

Australia enforces a twin-peak regulatory model. The regulatory power is shared among the Australian Prudential Regulation Authority, the Securities and Investments Commission, and the Competition and Consumer Commission. The Prudential Regulation Authority is responsible for setting standards to prevent, assess and warn of financial risks, ensure a dynamic balance among stability, efficiency and competition of the financial system, and protect the legitimate rights and interests of depositors, policyholders and fund investors. Eighty percent of the assets of the country's financial system are under regulation. The Securities and Investment Commission oversees corporate, market and financial services and targets financial services institutions, securities exchanges, futures trading institutions, pension funds companies, insurance companies and savings institutions, as it strengthens the prudential regulation of securities companies and supervises board directors and executives of listed companies on their performance, assesses the fairness, orderliness and transparency of financial market operations, and monitors financial services in an effort to ensure sound and sustainable development of the financial market. The Competition and Consumer Commission addresses unfair competition and consumer protection in the financial market and maintains market balance and order. The Australian Ministry of Finance, the Reserve Bank, the Prudential Regulation Authority, and the Securities and Investment Commission form the Financial Regulation Commission, which responds to various risks of the financial system in a timely manner through open information exchange, coordination and communication.

Among the financial regulatory models of major economies, the experience of the US, UK, EU, Singapore and Australia can be borrowed to replace the current separate supervision model driven by PBOC, CBRC, CSRC and CIRC, so that there will be no missing links in the regulatory process. Full consideration should be given to the ability of the new model to tackle financial and economic crises and establish a prudential regulation policy framework for overseeing systemically important financial institutions and coordinating key financial infrastructures.

Analysis of China's Financial Regulatory Model

With the slowdown of the Chinese economy and readjustment of its industrial structure, pressure on industries of overcapacity is mounting, and NPLs in the financial sector continue to rise. Policy makers should take into full consideration what kind of regulatory model is suited to China's financial sector to effectively mitigate the financial risks the country is facing.

I. Institutional regulation

With the growing trend of integrated business operations of financial institutions, traditional regulatory measures can no longer meet the needs of financial globalization. It is imperative to establish financial regulatory bodies according to the types of financial institutions. The current financial regulatory system is a typical specialized institutional regulatory model. The *Basel III* went into force on 1 January 2013, when the leverage rate began to be put under regulation. Liquidity Coverage Ratio was added on 1 January 2015. Regulatory requirements on global and domestic systemically important banks took effect on 1 January 2016. In a new economic normal with market-based interest rates, China took a solid step in implementing the *Basel III* by adopting the *Management Measures on Commercial Banks' Capital*. Regulation over banks aims more at maintaining a healthy system and fair competition in the banking sector.

Banking institutions are under the regulation of the China Banking Regulatory Commission. The roles of the CBRC include the regulation of banks, trust and investment companies, financial asset management companies and other deposit-type financial institutions; the adoption of development plans, policies and regulations and industry rules for the banking sector; the approval of the opening, registration modification, termination and business scope of banking institutions; and the formulation of prudent operation rules for banking institutions in accordance with laws and regulations. Consolidated supervision is carried out to maintain healthy performance and growth of the banking industry. Securities institutions are under regulation of the China Securities Regulatory Commission, which is responsible for regulation of the securities and futures market, maintenance of market stability and compliance, adoption of development plans, policies and regulations and industry rules for the securities and futures market, and supervision of the issuance, transactions, custody and liquidation of stocks, bonds and funds and the listing, trading and liquidation of futures contracts. Insurance institutions are regulated by the China Insurance Regulatory Commission. Its responsibilities include supervision of the insurance market, adoption of development plans, policies and regulations and industry rules for the insurance sector, lawful protection of the interests of the insured, stability of the insurance market, adoption of risk management, evaluation and early warning systems for the insurance industry to promote fair competition, sound operation and healthy growth of the insurance industry.

II. Functional regulation

As globalization characterizes China's financial industry, the corresponding regulatory system must adapt to the changes. The business model of financial institutions has changed from the original "separate business" to the "integrated business", which calls for changes in the model of financial regulation. Functional regulation is mainly based on the business nature of financial activities. For example, financial business can be divided into banking, securities, insurance, trust and fund businesses. Regulation is not differentiated among financial institutions offering such services. This can effectively avoid any vacuum in financial regulation due to a higher level of coordination and efficiency. Problems identified in this process can be promptly addressed, and the overall risk of the financial institution's asset portfolio can be estimated. It will help create a fair and competitive market environment for financial institutions.

The emergence of Internet finance has brought about tremendous changes to financial functions. A financial institution can now undertake a variety of financial functions. Functional regulation is a model designed according to the underlying roles of the financial system. It mainly focuses on the basic functions of financial products and identifies regulatory bodies and rules according to the business type to minimize conflict of roles and overlapping and vacuum in regulation. Functional regulation promotes financial innovation. The standards are easy to harmonize, and financial functions under regulation are relatively stable. This facilitates cross-regional and cross-country regulatory cooperation. As long as the regulatory approaches are precisely targeted at corresponding financial functions, effective financial regulation can be achieved.

III. Twin-peak regulation

China's financial market has become increasingly mature. It embraces globalization and adopts an integrated business model. Since the financial market is still underdeveloped and leaves room for improvement, the twin-peak model is needed to cover both the financial market and all important financial institutions. This model separates prudential regulation from behavioral regulation. It highlights the protection of the lawful rights and interests of financial consumers and builds a separate system for behavioral regulation. Prudential regulation is divided into macroprudential regulation and microprudential regulation. Macroprudential regulation aims to check the systemic risks of the financial system with tools such as countercyclical capital buffering, capital addition, liquidity addition, dynamic provisioning and dynamic loan value ratio. Microprudential regulation aims to limit the risks of individual financial institutions by using tools such as the capital adequacy ratio, leverage ratio, and liquidity ratio. Before 2008, the global financial regulatory model was designed to protect the entire financial system through the effective regulation of individual financial institutions. This was typical microprudential regulation. The bankruptcy of Lehman Brothers, however, reminded everyone that microprudential regulation failed to effectively prevent the systemic risks of the financial system, and macroprudential regulation was needed to manage the systemic risks of financial institutions and the markets. Therefore, an effective financial regulatory system must be an effective combination of macroprudential and microprudential regulation.

Behavioral regulation is a kind of financial regulation aimed at high regulatory efficacy and efficiency. It regulates financial institutions' business behaviors and information disclosure to help financial consumers obtain sufficient information, uphold fairness in financial markets, and foster ethics and culture that honor credibility and integrity among financial institutions. Because of the status of financial market players and the intrinsic characteristics of financial products and services, such market disfunctions as anti-competitive acts, improper market behaviors, information asymmetry and system instability in the financial markets cannot be curbed by minimum financial regulation, and a special behavioral regulator—financial conduct authority—is needed to protect consumers, intervene in advance of financial risks and deviations, promptly address behavioral risks, and adopt effective regulatory strategies to ensure that these risks are within control. Behavioral regulation includes three aspects: institutions, product lines and responses. Institutional regulation focuses on the evaluation of consumer protection by individual financial institutions. Product line regulation focuses on the functional monitoring of the services and products involved, and response regulation focuses on market conduct based on consumer feedback and risk events reported.

IV. Regulatory models

The global financial crisis that broke out in 2008 dealt a heavy blow to the financial system and the real economy and constituted an unprecedented challenge to traditional financial regulatory theories, models, methodologies and tools. It exposed both the vacuum and overlapping areas of regulation under the multiauthority financial regulatory model. The current model of regulatory responsibility shared by the PBOC, CBRC, CSRC and CIRC has led to fragmentation of regulation and problems in policy coordination, which may easily give rise to regulatory vacuums and rent seeking. The financial regulatory framework can no longer adapt to the needs of financial globalization and business diversification. It is imperative to remove the unchecked spots of financial regulation, stop rent seeking and maintain stable growth of the financial market by improving the monetary policy system and the financial regulatory system. A macroprudential and microprudential regulatory system must be installed. Based on the models and history of financial regulation, China should avoid drastic short-term changes in its financial regulatory framework. Instead, it should adopt a step-by-step approach to promote innovation and transformation of the financial regulatory model.

An effective "multilayer + twin-peak" model should be put in place that relies on the data science-supported decision-making system to strengthen joint supervision among financial regulatory agencies.

First, while holding onto the separate supervision model, it is important for financial regulatory agencies and the central bank to move in tandem through mechanisms of regulatory coordination and law enforcement.

Second, a "China Financial Stability Regulatory Commission" should be established on the basis of all the financial regulatory bodies to form a joint regulatory system featuring a clear division of responsibilities and functions to make regulation in the financial sector more effective.

Third, this "China Financial Stability Regulatory Commission" should set up an organizational framework for financial regulation and spell out responsibilities on macro- and micro-prudential regulation. The PBOC is responsible for monetary policies, macroprudential regulation, regulation of systemically important institutions and financial eco-environment and infrastructure improvement. The CBRC, CSRC and CIRC are responsible for the microprudential regulation and behavioral regulation of financial institutions. The regulatory responsibilities of local government authorities should also be defined. The CBRC, CSRC and CIRC should be merged into a single "Financial Regulatory Commission".

Fourth, a new "multilayer + twin peak" regulatory model with Chinese characteristics should ultimately come into being. The first layer of this model is the "China Financial Stability Regulatory Commission". The second layer is the CBRC, CSRC and CIRC. The third layer is the corresponding local governments and regulators. Twin peaks refer to prudential regulators and behavioral regulators. The CBRC, CSRC and CIRC are responsible for prudential regulation. The Financial Consumer and Investor Protection Authority should be responsible for behavioral regulation. An administrative framework should be established encompassing the China Financial Stability Regulatory Commission, the central bank, the Financial Regulatory Commission and the Financial Consumer and Investor Protection Authority.

The global financial crisis reminded us that regulation by specific regulators on selected financial markets can no longer adapt to the needs for financial regulation supported by big data. The ongoing innovation of the financial market and fast growth of IT have brought unprecedented challenges to the entire financial regulatory system, which lacks effective regulatory platforms and tools for the prompt solution of problems in the financial market even if it has spotted financial risks.

Innovation of Data Science-Based Financial Regulatory Platforms

With the advent of Internet finance and big data, reforming the financial regulative bodies alone can no longer fully adapt to the needs in the age of Internet finance. There is an urgent need to build a "data science-based financial regulatory platform" to support their regulatory models. This will be an intelligent and integrated regulatory platform that serves the development of the financial markets.

In recent years, a revolution has taken place in the financial regulatory system triggered by theoretical improvements in big data value discovery, collaborative self-organization, property rights definition, capital factors, large-scale collaborative innovation and management decision making, integration of the theories on multi-source heterogeneous data integration and mining and personalized value measurement, and particularly broad application of big data in the financial regulatory system in the twenty-first century. Financial regulators conduct value mining of big data on institutions, functions, business and personnel through a data science-based regulatory platform to improve the promptness, accuracy and dynamics of their decision-making. This will adapt the financial regulatory system to a panoramic management model driven by big data. Participants in management and decision-making use diverse and interactive information flows to establish a scenario statistical prediction model and use big data mining technology to construct a multisource heterogeneous and unstructured platform for data connection, integration and analysis.

Financial regulatory platforms driven by big data are in the phase of exploration and development both globally and in China. Extensive practical research on the platform has been conducted abroad, mainly in the banking, insurance, securities, trusts and other sectors. Powerful enterprise-level databases have been set up for both structured and unstructured data. They feature classified management and cluster analysis through big data mining technologies. Drawing upon management application theories and models in various fields, the platform contains an intelligent management decision-making model to meet financial regulatory needs and offers a real-time display of the regulatory data of financial institutions. Thus laying the foundation for the development of the financial regulatory system. The application of big data in the financial regulatory system in China has taken its initial shape. Data science is used more in building enterprise-level databases in different sectors and regulatory fields and collecting statistics and data from financial institutions than in big data integration, interaction and intelligent mining in all regulatory areas.

Financial regulatory agencies must put all the main business data in the enterprise-level database and install a series of applications, such as data breakdown, comprehensive statistics, intelligent screening, regulatory models, and problem diagnosis, in the form of an independent dataset. The financial regulatory platform serves management and decision making in various regulatory fields. It facilitates financial regulation and the healthy growth of financial markets by combining data science with regulatory models.

Three things are important in this process. The first is regulatory technologies. There is a need to apply data science to the regulatory manual and procedures to build synergy between off-site and on-site regulation. Regulatory models supported by data science will be more effective in removing information asymmetry and identifying the best practice. It will improve the quality and efficiency of financial regulation and promote the healthy and steady growth of lawful financial institutions. The second is regulatory methods. Regulators should continue to make improvements in risk monitoring, model application and pricing management, build a financial market risk monitoring architecture with big data technologies and monitoring models, improve regulatory approaches of financial holding groups, and reflect industrial realities by putting in place a financial risk rating system. The third is consolidated regulation. Under the current regulatory conditions, it is important to consolidate statements of various institutions under regulation driven by big data, especially for those of financial holding groups. In this process, high-value credit risk exposure and standards and requirements for loan regulation should be made clear. In this way, a sophisticated and science-based financial regulatory system can be put in place to maintain stability of the financial market.

With changes in the landscape of the financial industry and regulatory requirements, the existing financial regulatory model is under challenge. To improve the effectiveness of financial regulation in all respects, a top-down data science-based regulatory platform needs to be built following the principles of integrated supervision and functional and twin-peak regulation driven by big data and a management paradigm that supports value creation of the financial sector. A big data-driven financial regulatory system needs information technology as well as management and decision-making tools for building a simple and convenient financial regulatory platform and making 7×24 financial regulatory services a norm with improved reporting frequency and timeliness. A visual, mobile, intelligent and integrated big data financial regulatory platform will thus be set up to provide regulatory solutions for the banking, insurance, securities and trust sectors and serve the national strategy of integrated financial regulation.

With growing conflicts between the application of data science and information security and higher requirements on the professional ethics of people working in the financial sector, it is important to ensure openness and integration of the financial regulatory system while maintaining information security. Interaction and innovation will feature the future financial regulatory platform. Internet thinking and big data management will create a sound environment of "equality between big and small institutions" and "equal rights for regulators and the regulated". As the internal and external boundaries of financial regulatory bodies become more blurred, financial regulation will become increasingly integrated. With the faster application of big data and standardization of regulatory disclosures, financial regulation will become ubiquitous, covering strategy formulation and policy execution in all industries, businesses and institutions. Financial regulation supported by data science will be carried out under clearer guidance.

This platform will put together new theories on management, value creation, strategic planning, decision making, organization and system. It will set the course for financial regulatory integration, support innovative regulatory approaches and construction of an integrated and intelligent platform in this area. With the aim of creating a world-class financial market, China is trying to enhance its market's international competitiveness by promoting integrated finance, fostering corporate groups and pursuing global development. To achieve this goal, China needs a big data-driven financial regulatory platform that is science-based and appropriately designed to effectively keep the progress on track. This platform must serve the financial regulatory reform and innovation and the growth of financial business, move in tandem with development of the financial system and institutions, and reflect the regulatory philosophy featuring division of responsibilities, coordination and cooperation for mutual benefit.

The platform will aim to solve problems in the financial market through the problem analysis of specific business offerings, especially those with unique characteristics. The regulatory gap is a fact to be considered in the financial sector. No single regulatory agency has the responsibility or ability to oversee the entire financial system. The dominant role of indirect financing in the financial markets of developed countries is gradually declining. Direct financing is on the rise. The complexity, vulnerability and opacity of financial markets will inevitably affect economic growth. Big data is therefore required for the collection, classification, analysis and evaluation of the data and information for all-around regulation over the financial market. As required by the financial regulatory system, big data can display and integrate all sorts of information on this platform, give an all-round and truthful account of all regulatory data and provide a comprehensive evaluation of the performance and activities of financial institutions. It can in this way support financial regulators at all levels in decision-making and promote the general improvement of financial regulation.

The platform has a five-in-one structure that integrates management, decision-making, data, system and business.

Management integration establishes an intelligent and integrated financial regulatory system by collecting data on various business lines on the platform, including the organizational structure, job categories, functional division and staffing of the financial regulatory agencies as well as resource allocation and relations among business lines and main regulatory participants. Management integration can be supported by mechanisms of integrated, functional and twin-peak regulation. An interconnected analysis and management system based on financial regulation and a strategic transmission system based on big data-enabled financial regulation can thus be set up to meet the needs of all sectors and all levels and serve the healthy development of the financial industry.

Decision-making integration is used to build a big data network composed of all business lines under the regulation of financial regulatory agencies. It collects, organizes and processes information on financial regulatory decision-making concerning various business areas to help regulators at all levels make proper decisions and conduct effective regulation. Big data-enabled decision-making helps overcome inefficiency resulting from segmentation by coordinating and integrating all regulatory areas. What matters most in decision-making integration is to converge as much as possible the overall interests of financial regulation and the interests of individual business lines and build a regulatory decision-making support system based on data analysis to meet the need for future financial regulation.

Data integration is composed of big data information of all business lines under regulation of the financial regulatory agencies. Data collection, transmission, processing and storage help regulators pool local data into a big dataset and transform accumulative data into specific information. All-round data will replace sample data to make financial regulatory decisions less subjective and more balanced and better informed. Financial regulators will thus achieve integration of regulatory data through real-time transmission with Internet technology, large-volume data processing and calculation with computer technology and low-cost operation with cloud storage technology.

System integration integrates different regulatory business system modules to break functional segregation and data fragmentation and achieves connectivity and information sharing between systems. It technically integrates structured and unstructured information such as business systems, regulatory systems, reporting systems and databases to address the long-standing issue of data source dispersion, duplicated system development and inconsistency of data standards. It aims to achieve intensification, automation and intelligence of system data and ensure that financial regulatory demand is adequately met.

Business integration supplies data and integrates business models according to financial regulatory needs. Regulatory needs are viewed from a holistic perspective, and regulatory lines are integrated through division of responsibility and coordination to reduce redundant steps and processes of financial regulation, avoid artificial segmentation of financial regulation and overlapping in regulation, and cut the cost and expenses of the regulatory agencies. When meeting the need for financial regulation, it also helps minimize regulatory input and build an integrated service support system based on interim and ex post financial regulation. It can also promote reforms on process management and regulatory improvement and the establishment of a financial regulatory support system aimed at offering better services to the financial sector.

Bibliography

Ba, S., Jin, L., et al. (2015a). *Implementation of Basel capital accord III—In A financial structure perspective*. China Renmin University Press.

Ba, S., Zhu, Y., Jin, L., et al. (2015b). *Basel III and transformation of financial regulation*. China Financial Publishing House.

Basel Committee on Banking Supervision. (2014). *Basel III*. China Financial Publishing House.

Bian, Z., Mao, Z., Liu, M., et al. (2011). *Financial regulation*. People's Publishing House.

Chen, E., Qi, Z., Han, J., et al. (2015). *Upgrading China's economy—Documentary review of administrative streamlining by the central government*. China Yan Shi Press.

Deng, W. (2015). *Pressing ahead with streamlining of government administration*. China Yan Shi Press.

Ferren, A., Moloney, N., Hill, J., Coffey, J., et al. (2016). *Regulatory change in the post-financial crisis era*. Law Press.

Guo, T. (2009). *Financial regulation*. China Financial Publishing House.

Kellerman, J., Dehan, J., & Devries, F., et al. (2016). *Financial regulation in the 21st century*. CITIC Press Group.

Liu, C. (2015). *Deciphering Basel—A Brief analysis of the international banking regulatory framework*. China Financial Publishing House.

Liu, S, Zhou, X., Liu, X., et al. (2011). *Introduction to financial regulatory reforms in the United States*. China Financial Publishing House.

Ma, J. (2016). *The great simple truth—Theory and practice of streamlining government administration and power delegation*. People's Publishing House.

Wan, F., et al. (2013). *Regulation over financial groups—Global comparison and China's choice*. China Financial Publishing House.

Wu, Z. (2015). *Evaluation report on the effectiveness of the US banking industry and its regulation*. China Financial Publishing House.

Yong, J. (2015). *Research on banking behavioral regulation: Analysis of the practice of FCA policy in the UK*. China Financial Publishing House.

Capital Market Reform: Administrative Streamlining, Institutional Building and Regulatory Enforcement

Hanping Xiao

The role of the capital market in economic growth and structural change continues to increase along with economic development, but its impact on the real economy depends on the efficiency of resource allocation in the financial system. As an important part of China's capital market, the stock market has grown fast into the world's second largest market, driven by the top-down approach of the government in the process of China's economic transformation. Despite its size, however, China's stock market is weak and vulnerable. It has been troubled by low efficiency in resource allocation and high volatility. As the economy enters the "new normal" phase, the importance of the stock market in China's economic transformation and upgrading and in promoting innovation continues to increase. Therefore, a critical issue to be addressed in developing the stock market under the "new normal" is how to improve the efficiency in resource allocation and ensure market stability.

A Review of Past Development and Reforms

Since 1979, China has embarked on a transition from the traditional planned economy to the socialist market economy. Characterized by a clear definition of ownership, the joint-stock system has been gradually recognized as the best choice for creating independent market players and reforming SOEs as the reform progresses. Introducing the joint-stock system into state-owned enterprises and nurturing new joint-stock companies laid a solid foundation for the development of China's stock market.

I. Capital market development in the context of institutional transition

China's stock market was created with government support top down during the economic transition. In 1984, SOEs and collectively owned companies of smaller

H. Xiao (✉)
Hunan Financial and Industrial Vocational-Technical College, Hunan, China

Y. Li and Z. Cheng (eds.), *The Chinese Path Toward a Leaner Government*,
https://doi.org/10.1007/978-981-19-6718-4_5

sizes in some cities were the first to try the joint-stock system. This was when China's first stock shares came into being. An increasing number of companies, including major SOEs in China, conducted pilot programs on joint-stock systems in 1986. The primary and secondary stock markets with over-the-counter trading appeared in Shenyang and Shanghai in the same year. In 1990, the government allowed some eligible large cities to open stock exchanges. They were opened in Shanghai and Shenzhen in December 1990. In 1991, there were 8 stocks listed in Shanghai and 6 in Shenzhen. China's stock market has thus far been divided into two development stages since the opening of the stock exchanges.

The first stage (1992–1999) is a government-led exploration stage. The decision was made at the 14th CPC National Congress that the goal of economic reform is to establish a socialist market economic system. In 1993, the *Decision on the Financial System Reform* issued by the State Council stated that the issuance and listing of stocks should be regulated on the basis of the joint-stock reform of enterprises. In 1992, the State Council Securities Committee and the China Securities Regulatory Commission were established. In 1993, the National People's Congress promulgated the *Company Law* to regulate the establishment and operation of companies, and the State Council Securities Committee began to draft administrative regulations on the management of the securities market. In the same year, the State Council issued the *Provisional Regulations on the Administration of Stock Issuance and Transactions,* and the State Council Securities Committee issued the *Implementing Rules on Information Disclosure of Publicly Listed Companies*, the *Interim Measures on Prohibiting Securities Fraud*, and the *Notice on Prohibition of Manipulating the Securities Market*.

The government decided at the National Financial Work Conference in 1997 to conduct separate management and regulation of the financial sector and establish a national securities and futures management system for better coordination between the central and local regulatory authorities. In 1997, the State Council issued the *Interim Administrative Measures on Securities Investment Funds* to regulate the operation of securities investment funds. It added penalties into the country's 1997 Criminal Law (revised) on insider trading, leaking internal information, fabricating and disseminating false information and stock price manipulation to strengthen regulation on securities. In 1998, reform was carried out on the securities management system. The State Council Securities Committee was dissolved. Regulatory bodies on securities intermediaries and investment funds under the People's Bank of China were merged. Stock exchanges and local securities regulatory agencies were put directly under the administration of the CSRC. The goal was to put in place a CSRC-led centralized regulatory system. The Securities Law promulgated in 1999 gave legal status to the capital market.

The quota system for quota management was set up in the primary stock market where the underwriters could determine the issuance price for companies according to specific standards. In the secondary market, some shares were tradable, while others were non-tradable. Tradable shares were divided into A shares and B shares. Both could trade freely in the market. At this stage, the choice of issuers was in the hands of the government, which also regulated the stock index in the secondary market through administration, taxation and public opinion.

The second stage (2001–2013) is the stage of market transition. During this stage, institutional and structural deficiencies in the stock market included lack of investor protection, separation of shares into tradable and non-tradable ones, weak corporate governance, listed company scandals, poor management of securities companies and inadequate institutional investors. These problems landed China in a bear market that lasted for four and a half years starting from June 14, 2001. The sluggish stock market was in sharp contrast to the country's vibrant economic growth.

To restore investor confidence and promote healthy development of the market, the State Council issued the *Opinions on Promoting Reform, Opening-up and Steady Growth of the Capital Market* in 2004, which set the tone for capital market reform. As the reform and liberalization of the capital market progressed, positive changes appeared in the following fields. (1) The IPO quota system was replaced by the approval system, which went through the "channel phase" and the "sponsorship phase". The IPO pricing inquiry system was installed to place trading more under the market rules. (2) The reform to turn all non-tradable shares into tradable shares made good progress, and a multitiered capital market system took initial shape, encompassing the main-board market, GEM, NEEQ and regional equity markets. (3) Institutional investors were initially created in China, including securities investment funds, the National Council for Social Security Funds, insurance companies, QFIIs, enterprise annuities and RQFIIs. (4) Securities margin trading and stock index futures were launched. Structural changes such as the private equity fund registration system and the trend toward mixed business models of the financial industry also appeared.

With the implementation of the Securities Law and relevant laws and regulations, a market law enforcement system gradually came into being. In 2002, a government agency responsible for investigating and punishing market manipulation and insider trading was set up. The Ministry of Public Security established the Securities Crime Investigation Bureau to be co-located with the CSRC for investigation into securities-related crimes in an effort to strengthen enforcement against illegal activities such as insider trading and price manipulation. To enhance the protection of minority shareholders' rights, revision of the Securities Law and the Company Law began in 2003. The revised laws took effect in 2006. An independent board director system, the fiduciary duties of board directors and controlling shareholders, cumulative and proxy voting rights, related party transactions and restructuring were added to the revised Company Law. The personal liability of company managers for embezzlement and criminal responsibility for misrepresentation were also added into the 2006 Criminal Law.

II. Achievements and problems

Thanks to over two decades of development, China has gradually established a multi-tiered capital market system. The ownership of listed companies has diversified, and the number and market value of these companies have grown quickly. China has initially put in place a system of laws, regulations and rules for the multilevel capital market based on the Company Law, the Securities Law, the Securities Investment

Fund Law and the Criminal Law by drawing upon the experience of other countries. A securities regulatory enforcement system has been established that is led by the administrative law enforcement of the CSRC and supplemented by self-disciplines of trade associations and stock exchanges. However, path dependence in institutional reforms has resulted in an obvious dual structure in the existing legal system and regulatory policies. More specifically, features of planned and market economy exist side by side, undermining the efficiency and stability of the market.

At present, China has the world's second largest stock market, only after the United States. Despite its size, the Chinese stock market is typically weak and vulnerable. It is highly speculative and volatile, and stock prices change synchronously. The role of the market in the allocation of financial resources has been suppressed. The main regulatory challenges for the capital market are ill-conceived regulatory philosophies, weak law enforcement, institutional imbalances and mounting law-breaking cases. In recent years, a growing number of these cases have been observed. They increased by 14% year-on-year between 2009 and 2012 and grew by 21% in 2012 and 40% in the first half of 2013. Now, more than half of the cases concern insider trading, and cases of fraudulent issuance and false information disclosure are soaring. Increasingly, insider trading cases involve groups of people from different sectors and multiple layers of transactions with hidden names. Market manipulations in short-swing trading began to increase in multiple transactions across markets. Some cases involve people with complex connections, including senior executives of listed companies and intermediaries and officials of financial institutions and CPC and government agencies.

The development path of China's stock market is a path supported by the government from the top down in the context of reform and opening up. It plays an important role in the reform of state-owned enterprises, the development of the private sector and the transition of China to a balanced market economy. As a product of China's economic reform, the capital market itself has also experienced role changes of the government and the market in the process of administrative streamlining. In this period, the functions of the government and the market were gradually adjusted through continuous institutional innovation for the development of the stock market. However, the capital market is facing difficulties in adapting to the "new normal" of the Chinese economy, and there is a need to further improve its functions through institutional innovation and reform.

Importance of the Capital Market in the "New Normal"

The financial system apparently plays different roles in different stages of economic growth. In the early stage of economic development, capital accumulation and formation propel the growth of the financial system, and the banking sector plays a major role in it. When the economy reaches a certain stage, however, the goal of the financial system shifts from capital formation to productivity improvement. The role of the market in resource allocation continues to increase, and the capital market, stock market in particular, becomes more important to the financial system.

I. Stages of economic development and financial choice

The financial system impacts economic growth mainly through resource allocation, deposit mobilization, risk management and corporate governance. More specifically, the impact is made with two distinct but complementary mechanisms, namely, capital accumulation and total factor productivity (TFP) improvement. The capital accumulation mechanism helps the financial sector provide capital for investment projects in the productive sector by mobilizing deposits and overcoming barriers of investment indivisibility for the purpose of capital accumulation and output growth. Through innovative financial technologies, the TFP mechanism helps the financial system address information asymmetry that would make allocation of financial resources less effective, monitor investment projects and promote the development of new technologies and industries that require large investments.

In the early stage of economic development, capital accumulation and capital formation are the key drivers of economic growth. Factor-intensive investment and scale expansion characterize economic growth at this stage. Later, access to cutting-edge technologies makes innovation and higher productivity the main drivers of economic growth. The role of the financial system differs at each stage of economic development. In the low-income stage, the financial system drives economic growth mainly through capital accumulation. In the middle-income and especially high-income stage, however, the financial system mainly plays its role through improved productivity. The middle income stage is the critical point of change in the role of the financial sector in the economy. As the economy grows, the banking and securities markets become more mature. However, the two markets are changing all the time. In the financial system, the securities market becomes more important, and the financial architecture is more based on market rules.

II. China as a middle-income country

As China shifts its economic system from that of a highly centralized planned economy to that of a socialist market economy, the country is rapidly transformed from a traditional agricultural society to an industrial society. According to the latest definition by the World Bank, China has joined the rank of middle-income countries since 2010, and its economy has moved into the "new normal" under which China has to wrestle with challenges for all middle-income countries and issues facing its own development model in the new round of global economic and technological transformation. They include geopolitical conflicts amidst the rise of a major power, the path dependence of institutional and socioeconomic transformation, indigenous innovation on frontier technologies, overcapacity in production, high debt leverage, an aging society, wealth gaps and corruption.

To adapt to the "new normal", China must shift its growth driver from production factors to innovation to catch up with leading technologies. Moreover, China needs to develop frontier technologies through indigenous innovation and generate new technologies never seen before in human history through original innovation to expand the boundary of existing growth potential. Characterized by a high level of uncertainty, innovation of frontier technologies is the trial and error of the unknown, in which SMEs can play a greater role. To encourage innovation by SMEs, institutional support is needed in the financial sector to help them "match risks with returns". Experience in other countries shows that venture capital has a greater role to play in the growth model driven by frontier technologies, but venture capital needs support from a vibrant stock market. The dynamism of the IPO market in the United States has been the main factor behind the success of its venture capital.

III. Reform of the financial system as the key driver of the current economic transition and supply-side structural reform

Thanks to more than 30 years of reform and development, China has established a huge financial system. The system has played an important role in the fast growth of China's economy over the past three decades. However, the incompatibility of the financial system and the development of the real economy has become more apparent as the economy further grows. It is reflected in the following three aspects. First, the financial system is not fully market-based. The role of the market in resource allocation is significantly suppressed, resulting in low efficiency in resource allocation. Second, the Chinese financial system is currently an indirect financing system dominated by banks, and the proportion of direct financing is low. For example, in 2014, the proportion of direct financing for nonfinancial enterprises only made up 17.2% of the total financing. The consequential impact on the availability of the external funding source for innovation-driven SMEs is not conducive to sustainable economic growth. Third, while the overall leverage ratio is high, economic and financial risks are mainly concentrated in the banking sector. According to the latest findings of the National Finance and Development Laboratory on June 15, 2016, as of the end of 2015, China's total debt was RMB 68.48 trillion, and the total leverage ratio was 249%. The indebtedness of the nonfinancial sector was quite serious, with a debt ratio of 156%.

It is true that China has a huge financial sector, but it is highly dominated by banks. The weight of the capital market is low, and the role of the market is suppressed. As the economy enters the "new normal", its future growth will depend more on innovation. It is obviously difficult for the existing bank-led financial system to adapt to the needs of the "innovation-driven" development model. Therefore, it is imperative to reform the existing financial system. The experience of other countries emphasizes two important areas of financial system reform. First, the market must play a decisive role in resource allocation for the gradual realization of liberalization of the financial system. Second, stock markets should be multitiered to offer external financing for companies in various development phases and help strengthen the role of the market in the structure of the financial system.

Applying Market Rules to the Capital Market When Building a Leaner Government

The experience of other countries shows that the protection of investors' rights, efficiency of stock market resource allocation and market stability depend on not only the ability of the market to play a decisive role but also the availability of effective institutional arrangements and enforcement capabilities of regulators. To establish a relatively stable capital market with efficient resource allocation, the focus of the reform should be letting the market play a decisive role in the allocation of financial resources while streamlining government administration. Breakthroughs should be made in the reform path through institutional or legislative innovations. Power, responsibility and negative lists should clarify powers and responsibilities of the government and correct any misalignment between them in securities regulation. Market information asymmetry should be addressed through better and fairer information disclosure. Market behaviors of intermediaries, listed companies and investors should be regulated within the institutional framework. Law and rule breakers must be held accountable through strengthened supervision, law enforcement and industry self-discipline during and after trading to improve the efficiency and stability of the market and protect the lawful rights and interests of investors.

I. Primary market: a transition to the registration system

The primary market is the market for stock issuance where investors pay a large amount of money to buy the stock that carries with it intangible rights entirely based on the quality of the information provided by the issuer. Since there is a clear information asymmetry between the issuer and the investor in stock trading, the most important thing in this market is making appropriate institutional arrangements to avoid "adverse selection" caused by information asymmetry and protect the lawful rights of investors.

1. Issuance system

There are four types of participants in the primary market: issuers, investors, intermediaries, and regulators. Issuers refer to listed companies. Investors include both institutional and individual investors, and intermediaries include accounting firms, investment banks, law firms, and stock exchanges. A country has its own institutional arrangements and regulatory enforcement to mitigate information asymmetry in the issuance market. This has resulted in different issuance systems, including the approval system based on substantive review and value judgment and the registration system based on information disclosure review. In terms of issuance efficiency, the registration system is apparently better than the approval system.

Substantive review is used in the approval system. Issuers are obliged to disclose all information related to them and meet the issuance requirements stipulated by the law. The government judges the issuers' qualifications and the value of the stocks they issue. Only qualified issuers can issue stocks after obtaining approval from the regulatory body. The United Kingdom follows a typical approval system, where companies are required to go through the review process if they want to be listed. The issuer must tell the truth and meet some hard conditions to be allowed to issue stocks and go public. Hong Kong implements the same system, but starting from early this century, it began to shift from a substantive review model to an information disclosure model. The strategic plan of the HKEX 1998–2001 set the goal of shifting the stock issuance regulatory system to a further (complete) information disclosure model. It holds that Hong Kong now adopts a "highly market-based approval system." In Taiwan, as the local securities market evolves, stock issuance has gone through three phases, namely, the approval system phase, the approval system phase and the registration system phase running in parallel and the registration system phase.

The registration system is more market-based than other types of stock issuance systems. It adopts a formal review process with information disclosure at its core. The regulatory agency does not impose specific conditions on the issuer beforehand. The issuer needs to fully and accurately disclose all important information for investors to judge the nature and investment value of the securities. The competent authorities check whether the disclosed information is comprehensive, truthful and accurate during the review. The role of the securities regulator is to ensure that information is fully disclosed instead of authorizing issuance. Once losses are incurred to investors due to false information or concealment of negative information in the registration documents on part of the issuer, the regulator will hold the issuer and the intermediary legally responsible, which includes criminal and civil liabilities.

Unlike the approval system that heavily weighs on pre-issuance substantive review, the registration system aims to ensure that the disclosed information is truthful and credible by linking it with the issuer's reputation in the trading and his or her scope of liability when frauds occur. Unqualified and dishonest companies are thus removed from the market. Therefore, if there are no institutional arrangements to ensure the truthfulness, completeness and accuracy of information disclosure and heavy punishment for fraud, the registration system may lead to serious "adverse selection" or create "the Market for Lemons".

2. Issues and reforms

China had implemented the "quota system" for stock issuance before 2001, when the government played a decisive role. It was replaced by the "approval system" in 2001. The role of the market has been strengthened compared with the quota system. However, the government still has a significant influence on the pricing, scale and timing of stock issuance. Generally, the market role is limited in China's approval system. Many companies have been listed by falsifying documents on their performance to attract investors or even resorting to serious fraud. After one year of fast growth, their business often slackens. Losses may occur in the third year, followed by bankruptcy reorganization in the fourth year. The new system has failed to meet its expected goals. Despite several rounds of reform to boost the role of the market, the result was not satisfactory due to tussling among competing interests.

The *Decision on Major Issues Concerning Comprehensively Deepening the Reform* released at the Third Plenary Session of the 18th CPC Central Committee calls for "promoting the reform of the stock issuance registration system." The experience of other countries shows that the success of the registration system first and foremost hinges on a relatively complete legal and regulatory system set up by those who know the securities market well. Second, intermediaries with good reputation and professional expertise are needed to ensure the quality of the issuer's information disclosure. Third, well-known self-discipline organizations should be there to check the behaviors of intermediaries through a credibility mechanism to ensure that they act in accordance with professional ethics. Fourth, legal and regulatory institutional arrangements should be made to penalize false or misleading information disclosure. Fifth, regulatory bodies must have strong credibility. They need sufficient budget and staff with good knowledge of securities trading to investigate into cases involving false or misleading disclosures. Sixth, the judicial system must be honest, and its staff should be able to handle these cases and make decisions quickly to prevent capital flight.

3. Policy recommendations

The transition from the "approval system" to the "registration system" is an important institutional innovation that plays a decisive role in the allocation of financial resources. However, the smooth introduction of the registration system requires changes in the issuance system in the existing laws, regulations and rules. Second, an effective accountability system and a strong public law enforcement system must be in place to deter fraudulent issuance. Finally, the timing must be right for the launch of the new system. Given the current market environment in China, it takes time to transform and improve valuation structure and investment philosophies accumulated over the years. Therefore, it is advisable to move from the "approval system" to the "registration system" step by step, starting with institutional building and law enforcement.

The shift to the "registration system" is a major institutional reform based on the current market structure. It involves the adjustment of various interests and the renewal of market philosophies. Taking institutional building and law enforcement as the first step will provide necessary mechanisms and foster market integrity for the registration system. The shift comes in phases such as gradual readjustment of the current system and incremental implementation of the new system, leading to full coverage of the "registration system" in the market.

II. Secondary market: better structure and operational efficiency and a crisis response mechanism

An efficient secondary market is a market with accurate stock pricing and enough liquidity, where information affecting the value of a listed company can be truly and quickly reflected in its stock price and investors can complete the transaction without any delay. An efficient market improves the allocation of economic resources and helps form a well-functioning market for companies to exercise their controlling power for the benefit of corporate IPOs and refinancing.

1. Market structure and correction mechanism

The essence of accurate pricing is the full integration of information into stock prices to make them consistent with the basic values of companies. This covers information about specific companies and general market information. The former includes the competency of the management team, corporate business plans and historical records, financial status, research and development potential, etc. The latter refers to information on competitors, the industry and the local and global economy. In reality, the effective integration of information into stock prices generates information search and verification costs and requires specialized information analysis skills.

Stock market prices are the result of interactions between different types of traders. There are four types of participants in the secondary market, namely, insiders, information traders, liquidity traders and noise traders (speculators). Among them, information traders mainly include institutional investors and analysts. Institutional investors include mutual funds, pension funds and insurance companies. Insiders and information traders usually calculate corporate value based on the information they have, determine stock prices and correct deviations between price and value. The "buy and hold" strategy or an arbitrage trading strategy adopted by liquidity traders makes them insensitive to and uninterested in information, and their impact on prices is relatively neutral. In contrast, noise traders with irrational investment strategies will distort market prices. Therefore, the accuracy of market prices depends on the ability of insiders and information traders to balance noise traders' distortions and set prices on new information.

Insiders and information traders are the ones to set accurate pricing in the market, but whether they can make pricing accurate hinges on three factors. The first is the power balance of market players. If the size and strength of the noise traders is stronger than that of insiders and information traders, the market price will be inaccurate, which makes the market less efficient. The second is the availability of information. Information is the basis of pricing. It includes explicit information and implicit information. Information traders need to invest resources into information verification. Explicit information verification is relatively easy, but it is prone to repetitive investment, and it is difficult to verify implicit information on price manipulation. Third, information disclosure must be fair. Due to differences in information ownership between insiders and information traders, insiders enjoy monopoly in the ownership of specific information, putting information traders at a disadvantage. If it continues, the market may be inefficient, as information traders find it hard to grow in strength. Because of this, insider trading, market manipulation and securities fraud are prohibited in all countries and have been the main targets of regulatory enforcement.

The error correction mechanism in an efficient market prevents serious deviation of the stock price from the true value. However, if the size and influence of noise traders far exceed those of information traders, there will be serious price-value deviations. In the case of bubbles and crises, the balance of power between stock market participants will not serve market stability. The size of the noise traders, driven by the herd mentality, will keep expanding, resulting in serious imbalances in the traders' structure. This will lead to the failure of the market error correction mechanism and ultimately to a stock market crisis after the bubble bursts.

2. Crisis and bailout

The stock market crisis consists of two phases. In the bubble phase, the stock price continues to deviate from the true value determined by the fundamentals. Experience shows that stock market bubbles are often caused by overconfidence and herd behavior. Emerging markets and retail investor-led markets are more likely to generate herd behavior due to lack of transparency, high costs of information collection and weak regulatory enforcement. At the same time, in a market where noise traders are active, professional traders also tend to follow the herd behavior for short-term gains. They choose to live with the bubble instead of piercing it. Then, comes the crash phase. Stock market crashes are always caused by bubble bursts. No bubble, no crisis.

Low efficiency in pricing, massive speculation and high volatility are typical of an emerging transitional market such as China. Since the beginning of this century, China's stock market has seen three rounds of violent fluctuations, in the early 2000s, between 2007 and 2008 and between 2014 and 2015. The first two were caused by both factors at home and abroad. The most recent crisis was a serious "stock market crisis" mostly driven by domestic factors. Since mid-2014, China's A-shares entered a new round of bull markets. In 2015, China's A-share market prices witnessed an astonishing surge. By mid-June 2015, the Shanghai Composite Index was up to 152% over July 2014 and 59.7% higher than in the beginning of the year. The SME board and GEM rose by 138% and 165%, respectively, from the beginning of the year. From June 15 to July 8, 2015, however, the Shanghai Composite Index, Shenzhen Stock Exchange Index and GEM Index fell by 32%, 38.9% and 39.4%, respectively, in less than 20 trading days, hitting 2850 on August 26, down 45%. The fall of the SME board and GEM was 44.6% and 51.8%, respectively. During the crisis, the rise and fall of stock prices were generally huge in volume. The range of weekly and daily fluctuations and the frequency of abnormal fluctuations are also much bigger than before. During the global financial crisis, the range of fluctuations in the A-share market was as high as 7.66%. However, the figure was even higher after June 2015, reaching 7.90%, reflecting a more extreme state of the market.

This round of the stock market crisis can be attributable to the following factors. (1) Expectations. Misinterpretation of reform, transition, and capital market policies led to an outburst of bullish sentiment. (2) Leverage and liquidity. High leverage of private investment, structural financial products, bank wealth management funds, umbrella trusts and margin financing accelerated the formation of the bubbles and amplified the effects of the crisis. (3) Media and public opinion. The "bull market" ecstasy hyped by official and commercial media created herd behavior. (4) Financial technologies. Program trading has a role to play. It includes quantitative investment, high-frequency trading, the Homs trading system and Internet finance. (5) Regulatory factors such as regulatory misplacement, delays or laxity in supervision and poor adaptation of the regulatory system. The above factors played an important role in the stock market bubble and crisis, but in the final analysis, the problem lies in the flawed market investors' structure. Profound imbalances in the market traders' structure led to failure in the market correction mechanism, which resulted in a serious stock market crisis.

At present, investors in China's stock market are predominantly natural persons instead of institutional investors. Among institutional investors, nearly 50% are from overseas, whereas only approximately 13% are from China this decade on average. At the start of the current cycle, domestic institutional investors accounted for nearly 10% of the stock market value, and individual investors accounted for 37%. According to the *2014 Statistical Yearbook* of the Shanghai Stock Exchange, institutional investors (including public funds, national social security funds, QFII & RQFII, insurance companies, corporate annuities and securities companies) accounted for 14.58% of the market value. Institutional investors, represented by mutual funds, pension funds and insurance companies, are dominant forces in the US stock market, accounting for 20.5%, 13.8%, and 5.8% of the market share, respectively.

The investor structure of China's stock market makes the market inherently unstable, which was magnified in the last round of the stock market crisis by factors such as high leverage, regulation, expectation, financial technologies, media and public opinion, which caused quick bubble bursts and market collapse. Among these factors, the magnifying effect of leverage on market volatility has caused widespread concern. Leverage as a tool has been widely and excessively used in the market. At the same time, as many companies have multiple business operations, leverage entailed chain effects, amplified volatility in the market, and even triggered a systemic financial crisis. To avoid the spread of the stock market crisis leading up to systemic financial risks, it was necessary for government regulators to take bailout measures. However, the lack of effective crisis response and bailout mechanisms made government measures inadequate, and the government was under criticism at home and abroad for adopting too many bailout measures through administrative means. The crisis in 2015 laid bare the apparent weaknesses of the government in addressing emergency crises due to a lack of effective crisis response plans or coordinative bailout mechanisms. Therefore, it is important to study the roles of the central bank, Ministry of Finance and CSRC in response to the stock market crisis.

3. Policy recommendation

To improve market efficiency, the following measures are needed. First, the size of long-term funds with sound basis and rational growth trajectories should be steadily expanded, the number of information traders should increase, and the price correction ability should be enhanced. In addition, efforts should be made to improve the performance rating system and curb short-term investment behavior. Second, given the limited number of institutional investors, the stock market stabilization fund needs to be established on the basis of bailout funds to suppress irrational noise traders. Third, fair disclosure of information should be strengthened to crack down on insider trading, securities fraud and market manipulation and regulate the secondary market trading behavior of insiders and major shareholders. Fourth, media of all types need to be regulated in their ways of information dissemination concerning the market and listed companies so that their role as a watchdog will be given full play to improve market order and curb noise trading and herd behavior. Fifth, efforts must be made to strengthen the management of credit trading in the stock market and regulate the behavior of investors to control risks associated with leveraged trading. Sixth, it is important to work out an effective crisis response plan and a bailout mechanism and define the roles of the Central Bank, the Ministry of Finance and the CSRC in crisis response. In addition, there is a need to strengthen the tracking of the impact of new technologies and financial innovations on stock market trading behaviors.

IV. Administrative streamlining and regulatory reforms

It was decided at the third Plenary Session of the 18th CPC Central Committee that economic reform is at the center of all reforms. The core of the reform is handling the relationship between the government and the market, and the goal is to let the market play a decisive role in resource allocation and let the government play its role better. To let the market play a decisive role in resource allocation and transform government functions, the 18th CPC Central Committee decided at its fifth plenary session that efforts should be made to "deepen the reform of the administrative system, further transform the government functions, continue to streamline administration and delegate power, and improve regulation and services, in order to create a more effective government and stimulate market vitality and public creativity." On 10 September 2014, Premier Li Keqiang stated at the 8th Summer Davos Forum that the government must work out "three lists", namely, the power list, the negative list and the responsibility list, to define the powers and responsibilities of the government and the boundary between the government, the market and society. The list will also help solve the issue of misplacement, absence and overstretching of government roles in the market economy.

1. Theory, experience and reality

The stock market is a market of rights that relies on information. Asymmetry or poor quality of information weakens the protection of investors' lawful rights and market efficiency and stability. According to Prof. Bernard Black, in a robust and dynamic market, laws and relevant systems allow minority shareholders to believe that they can obtain accurate and complete information about the company's value in a timely manner and that the company's managers and controlling shareholders will not deceive them and infringe on their equity interest. According to Zohar Goshen and Gideon Parchom Ovsky, securities regulation includes disclosure of responsibilities and minimizing fraud, manipulation and insider trading so that regulators can create a competitive market for information traders. The IOSCO believes that a viable securities regulatory system has three core objectives: to protect investors, to ensure that markets are fair, effective and transparent, to reduce systemic risks and to create a fair, effective and credible market on this basis. The above viewpoints show that the philosophy on the development, regulation, and law enforcement of the securities market system aims to achieve adequate information disclosure, reduce transaction costs, and create an effective, stable and dynamic market to protect the lawful rights and interests of investors.

Practice around the world shows that the fundamental goal of securities market regulation is to protect the rights and interests of investors. The roles of the investors' rights protection system include (1) maintaining market integrity and protecting the rights of individual investors by prohibiting market abuse (insider trading and market manipulation) and securities fraud; (2) regulating intermediary agencies in their investment consultancy, asset management, transaction matching and other services and conducting investment promotions based on the market code of conduct; and (3) determining the mandatory information disclosure obligations of listed companies.

The Chinese capital market has been developed top-down by the government in transitioning from a planned economy to a market economy. Due to "path dependence" in the reform, the thinking of the planned economy and administrative authority are quite apparent in China's securities legislation and regulation. Despite the enhanced roles of the market as reform continues, the market still relies mainly on regulatory agencies for its growth. Regulators are still at the center of the market, and their policies and behaviors have a huge impact on the market, leaving a deep "policy-based" imprint on the market.

2. Policy recommendation

In the context of streamlining government administration, the key to the success of the regulatory reform is to break the "path dependence" in securities legislation and regulation and find new legislative and regulatory approaches in support of the decisive role of the market in the allocation of financial resources. At the heart of the regulatory reform are efforts to adjust the role of the regulators, correct regulatory misplacement, promote regulatory transformation, improve the regulatory enforcement regime, and let market decide resource allocation, improve efficiency and maintain stability of the market. To this end, reform needs to be carried out in the following fields:

First, the role of regulation should be clear. It is important for the market to play a decisive role in resource allocation in the context of building a leaner government. Securities regulation aims to make up for resource mismatch and low efficiency caused by market misfunctions in terms of information asymmetry, market monopoly and negative externalities of public goods to protect individual investors to the utmost extent.

Second, the mindset with regard to legislation, law revision and regulation needs to be transformed to correct regulatory misplacement. There are still significant legacies of the planned economy and too many administrative measures and approvals in market regulation. The *Report on China's Rule of Law Development (2014)* issued by the Chinese Academy of Social Sciences holds that regulators rely too much on administrative punishment for those who have violated laws and rules in the Chinese securities market, while the ratio and intensity of criminal punishment is low, let alone civil liability, which is a fact known to all. It is necessary to break such inertia and change the mindset in revision of securities law and market regulation, clarify the boundaries of the regulatory authorities with lists of powers and responsibilities, address misplacement, absence and overstretching of regulatory powers and improve the market regime.

Third, it is important to broaden the definition of securities and shift to functional and behavioral regulation. As an increasing number of companies have multiple business operations in a market that is under industry-specific regulation, it is necessary to broaden the definition of securities, expand the coverage of securities regulation and transform to functional and behavioral regulation to forestall systemic financial risks caused by regulatory vacuum or regulatory arbitrage.

Fourth, it is imperative to establish a new type of regulatory system composed of the CSRC, industry associations and stock exchanges with a clear division of responsibilities. In the new regulatory system, the main function of the CSRC is to protect the legitimate rights and interests of investors through regulatory enforcement, delegate its market and industry development functions and part of its administrative approval functions to self-disciplinary institutions. For example, securities exchanges and industry associations are responsible for market and industry development. Securities intermediaries are established under the registration system, and their senior management and employees must go through examinations and certifications. The reputation mechanism must be used to strengthen the self-disciplinary checks of securities intermediaries. Securities exchanges must undergo corporate transformation to become true market entities responsible for market development, stock listing and delisting and market management with a view to improving market functions and efficiency.

Fifth, a market-driven crisis prevention, response and bailout mechanism comprising the central bank, the Ministry of Finance and the CSRC must be established. Under normal circumstances, the CSRC, as a market regulator, should focus on crisis prevention. Once a crisis occurs, the central bank or the Ministry of Finance should be responsible for policy response and bailout according to the nature of the crisis.

Last but not least, effective deterrence must be in place by strengthening regulatory enforcement in both mechanism and intensity. A good law is worse than no law if it cannot be effectively enforced. Former SEC Chairman Christopher Cox believes that the focus of China's securities law should be on the enforcement rather than the appropriateness of the text. In the quantitative analysis of law enforcement of the CSRC since the implementation of the Securities Law in 2005, Zhang Wei and Li Xiang found that except for reputation punishment, the overall enforcement of penalties concerning property and qualification fines and market bans made by the CSRC is inadequate, which makes it difficult to effectively deter law breakers. Therefore, regulatory enforcement must be enhanced by strengthening criminal penalties, civil litigation and administrative punishment for violations of laws and regulations. A group litigation system should be introduced in due time, and there should be a special tribunal or court comprising professional experts to deal with securities-related crimes. In this way, an effective regulatory enforcement system will be formed to raise the efficiency of regulatory enforcement.

Bibliography

Allen, W. T., Shen, H. (2010). Assessing China's top down securities markets. In *Capitalizing China*. National Bureau of Economic Research Project.

Allen, F., et al. (2011). *China's financial system: Opportunities and challenges*. University of Chicago Press.

Bikhchandani, S., & Sharma, S. (2001). Herd behavior in financial markets. *IMF Staff Papers, 47*(3).

Bhattacharya, U., Daouk, H. (2009). When no law is better than a good law [OL]. Retrieved April 2009. http://ssrn.com/abstract=558021.

Ba, S., et al. (2016). Stock market crisis and bailout: Systematic risk prevention. *China Financial Risk & Stability Report*.

Black, B. S. (2000). The core institutions that support strong securities markets. *Stanford Law School John M. Olin Program in Law and Economics Working Paper, 200*.

Black, B. S., & Gilson, R. J. (1988). Venture capital and the structure of capital markets: Bank versus stock markets. *Journal of Financial Economics, 47*.

Chen, S., & Chen, J. (2012). Efficacy analysis and reconstruction of the securities law. *Global Law Review, 5*.

China Finance 40 Forum, Shanghai Finance Institute. (2014). *China financial reform report 2013*. Economic Press China.

China Securities Regulatory Commission. (2008). *China capital market development report*. China Financial Publishing House.

Daron, A., Philippe, A., & Fabrizio, Z. (2002). Distance to frontier, selection, and economic growth [OL]. NBER working paper series. Retrieved July 2002. http://www.nber.org/papers/w9066

Documents compilation of the third plenary sessions of CPCCC since reform and opening-up. People's Publishing House (2013).

Emilios, A. Cognitive biases and investor protection regulation: An evolutionary approach [OL]. http://ssrn.com/abstract=1133214

Goshen, Z., & Ovsky, G. P. (2006). The essential role of securities regulation. *Duke Law Journal, 55*.

Gu, L. (2014). *Research on the evolution of China's stock issuance regulatory system*. Economy & Management Publishing House.

Kaizoji, T. A behavioral model of bubbles and crashes [OL]. http://ssrn.com/abstract=1572367.

Li, L., & Tian, H. (2014). *China's rule of law development report (2014)*. Social Sciences Academic Press.

Li, Y. (2013). *China's economy in dual transition*. China Renmin University Press.

Li, Y. (2015). We have improved our understanding of building a leaner government. *Beijing Daily*.

Li, Y. (2012). On the "middle income trap". *Economics Perspectives, 12*.

Li, Y. (2009). *China's unbalanced economy*. Encyclopedia of China Publishing House.

Liu, Y. (2015). The power list system and the securities law amendment. *Journal of Gansu Political Science and Law Institute, 4*.

Rioja, F., & Valev, N. (2004). Finance and the sources of growth at various stages of economic development [OL]. *Economic Inquiry*. Retrieved January 2004. https://www.researchgate.net/publication/5211467

Research Group of National Finance Research Institute of Tsinghua University. (2015). *Improving system design, enhancing market confidence, and building a long-term healthy and stable capital market*.

Wang, G., Ying, Z., & Jiang, S. (2008). *China's financial reform: Historical experience and transitional model*. China Financial Publishing House.

Wang, X. (2013). Analysis of the reform toward the registration system: Issue-targeted thinking and exploration. *Securities Market Herald*.

Wang, X. (2015). Four challenges in the US registration system and lessons for China's capital market reform. *Securities Market Herald*.

Wu, J., Li, Y., Lin, Y., et al. (2016). *Understanding the new normal: Great changes and new dynamics*. CITIC Press Group 2016.

Wu, X. (2016). Stock market crisis: Logical structure, multi-factor analysis and policy recommendations. In *20th China capital market forum*.

Xiao, G. (2013). Regulatory enforcement: The cornerstone of a healthy capital market. *Qiushi, 15*.

Xiao, H. (1999). Development of China's venture capital investment. *Journal of Renmin University of China, 4*.

Xiao, H. (2007). Research on financial system reform and institutional investor development. *Securities Market Herald*.

Xin, T., Jun, W. (2016). Registration and approval models of public offering of stocks: Comparison and reference. *Securities Market Herald*.

Zhang, W., & Li, X. (2016). An empirical analysis of the law enforcement intensity of the securities regulatory commission. *Modern Law Science, 38*(1).

Zhang, Z. *Law and finance: The case of stock market development in China*. School of East Asian Studies, University of Sheffield.

Zhou, X. (2015). Deepening the reform of the financial system. *China Finance, 22*.

A Leaner Government and Reform of the Fiscal System

Er Che and Si Zhang

Introduction

I. A lofty mission

"The Chinese path", as we see, contains two elements—China's unique development path and its unique reform experience. China's unique development path refers to the one leading to higher productivity, overall national strengths and living standards in the socialist market economy. Its unique reform experience refers to the market-oriented reform in the country that started from streamlining administration and delegating power with regard to the fiscal system.

"Streamlining administration and delegating powers is essential in China's transition from a planned economy to a market economy and in the efforts to improve the country's socialist market economy." The observation made by Prof. Li Yining in the preface of the book boils down to the fact that a leaner government works for the market economy and fiscal system reform is conducive to the creation of a single market.

China, however, cannot simply replicate the fiscal systems of advanced market economies such as the US and the European countries because the political and fiscal power-sharing regimes, which are stable and mature in these countries, do not suit China, a country in social, economic and political transition. It is fair to say that building a learner government in China is by no means an abstract concept or indiscriminate replication. In contrast, China's reform in this area offers rich practical experience and follows the law of history. Streamlining administration in the early days of the reform and opening up did not mean that the power was delegated to the

E. Che (✉)
China International Economic Consultants, Beijing, China

S. Zhang
China International Economic Consultants, CITIC Reform and Development Research Institute, Beijing, China

Y. Li and Z. Cheng (eds.), *The Chinese Path Toward a Leaner Government*,
https://doi.org/10.1007/978-981-19-6718-4_6

market because market players that could react to price signals were nonexistent, let alone a market regime. In those circumstances, the reform was basically meant to adjust relations between governments at higher and lower levels, as they were most directly linked by fiscal ties politically and economically. The reform of government streamlining therefore started in the fiscal relationship between different levels of government. It is known as the reform of the fiscal system.

The reform and opening-up spearheaded by the reform of the fiscal system has brought continuous prosperity to China with fast GDP growth and remarkable infrastructure construction in such a short span of time. However, local governments' decisions on infrastructure investment are aimed at achieving short-term economic growth instead of improving redistribution. This has given rise to and even exacerbated a myriad of sustainable development issues since the beginning of this century, including uneven social distribution, environmental pollution, and shortages of public resources, such as inadequate access to high-quality education and healthcare. At this point, people started to turn their eyes again to the sustained and healthy growth that streamlining administration and delegating power may bring to the economy and place great importance on the reform of the fiscal system.

II. Regaining attention

The *Decision of the CPC Central Committee on Major Issues Concerning Comprehensive Deepening of the Reform* (hereinafter referred to as the Decision) adopted at Third Plenary Session of the 18th CPC Central Committee highlighted the importance of the fiscal system reform by putting it in a separate paragraph[1] which said, "The fiscal resource is the foundation and major pillar of state governance. A well-established fiscal and taxation system ensures sound resource allocation, a single market, social equity and long-term peace and stability of the country."[2]As we understand, this was the first time for China to expand the roles of finance and the fiscal and taxation system beyond the scope of the economy to the height of state governance and modernization process, in the hope that its impact will be more foundational and overarching.[3]

This is because state governance encompasses social, political, economic, cultural, ecological, party building, diplomatic and military fields. The notion transcends the philosophical debate of whether finance belongs to economic or political sciences or whether. The fiscal system is more responsive than the monetary system to macro regulation. Governance is broader in scope than administration. Administration refers to relations between government agencies at different or corresponding levels and

---

[1] Fiscal system reform was mentioned in Paragraph 5 of the 16-paragraph Decision.

[2] p. 19, The *Decision of the CPC Central Committee on Major Issues Concerning Comprehensive Deepening of the Reform*, People's Publishing House, 2013 edition.

[3] The most widely used finance textbook has the following definition for the roles of finance. "State finance is part of economy. It is a balance of payment activity of the government of allocating part of the national revenue for public needs and can be defined as state-dominated distribution activities."(Chen Gong: *Finance*, China Renmin University Press, 2012, p. 12). This definition obviously puts state finance and fiscal and taxation system in the economic category.

is related to the government itself, whereas the government can exercise governance or be subject to it. The subject of governance can also be extended to social groups, businesses and individuals. The difference between the two words means that China's fiscal system must serve the reform of the entire state governance system. One should appreciate the importance of fiscal system reform in driving and sustaining the national economy in the course of building China into a socialist market economy.

It is not a coincidence for the Decision to place such high importance on the fiscal system. A consensus that may have been reached since the start of China's economic reform in 1978 is the goal of building a market economy, and the strongest support for the goal comes from finance and the reform of the fiscal system. In fact, fiscal reform has advanced along with China's economic reform in the past four decades. It is an important part of China's overall economic reform agenda and even the main focus of the reform of China's political institutions. The fiscal reform has been keeping with the momentum of the market reform, rendering full support to it for greater vitality of the Chinese economy.

The key factor to the success of the market reform is that China began to readjust relations within the government at the very start of the reform and followed through in the entire process of reform policy implementation. The government tends to approach the relations it has with the market by reforming the relationship inside the government. Fiscal relations are at the core of this relationship. They include arrangements between government authorities on revenue division (both tax and nontax revenue division), division of expenditure responsibilities, transfer of payment and budget management (such as creditor's rights allocation).

After a brief introduction to the contribution the fiscal system reform has made to China's economic reform and its historical status, we need to conduct a literature review on why a leaner government and reforms on the fiscal system can offer a sustained driving force to power China's economic growth.

Literature Review

The planned economy stifled China's national economy, while the market-oriented reform freed up the productivity that had been suppressed. Based on this experience, a widely accepted view has been developed in the academic community that China's planned economy between the completion of socialist transformation in the 1950s and the start of the reform and opening-up in 1978 was a copycat of the Soviet model, as if the reform would naturally deliver benefits once the Soviet model was removed. This view cannot stand up to the test of history, as evidenced by the disintegration of the Soviet Union in the 1990s and the failure of the economic transition of Eastern European countries. Nor can it withstand examination with basic historical facts because it is easy to find the essential difference between the planned economy in China and the Soviet model. For example, the Soviet model is characterized by a highly centralized planned economy, with administrative directives covering all aspects of the national economy. In China, however, it was almost impossible for state directives to reach the vast countryside outside the cities. In reality, national plans were implemented in a case-by-case manner through hard bargaining between various levels of administration. Room for maneuver remained in policy implementation, and there is a doomed cycle whereby power delegation led to market disorder, which, in turn, resulted in tighter control. In China's unique planned economic system, neither planning nor the market succeeded in playing its due role under the interference of the government's power (Liu, 1987).

As Political Scientist Wang (1997) puts it, the cycle of delegating and tightening administrative power and case-by-case bargaining demonstrate that China originally did not follow the Soviet model in real sense since it was not an economic system Mao Zedong himself wanted to have for China. In the eyes of Economist Zhang (2008), "China's planned economy was branded with separation of powers from the very beginning." The views are so influential in the academic world that they have developed into a main theoretical framework for interpreting the country's economic takeoff in the past decade. It should be noted that in academic works, the separation of power often refers to the decentralization of power. It is the opposite of the act of the central government of taking back power from local governments and disproportionate involvement of the government in the economy. Decentralization includes the delegation of administrative responsibilities by the central government to local authorities and exit by the government from fields where the market has an effective role to play. In other words, streamlining government administration and delegating its power in the right fields and sequence based on the theoretic framework of Wang Shaoguang and Zhang Jun is the fundamental factor behind China's fast growth since the start of the reform and opening-up. The literature under this theoretical framework often concentrates on economic reform without giving due consideration to the question that the growth generated by the division of government power is obviously unsustainable (leading to such issues mentioned above as social inequities and environmental pollution). Inadequacies in the inclusiveness and scalability of this theoretical framework make it even more difficult to guide China's growth in the future. A theory that can better explain the past but provide no guidance for the future is bound to be less valuable.

Gao (2008) was the first to point out that the reform of the fiscal and taxation system is an integral part of the reform of the economic system. It was where breakthrough was made in guiding the historical transition of extending the reform from a few areas to all dimensions. Transforming the fiscal system of the planned economy to the one featuring public finance in line with the market economy is a powerful guarantee for the success of China's economic reform. This judgment gives a good answer to the aforementioned question from the perspective of the government's governance capability building. We will follow this extended framework and conduct a more detailed analysis.

Analysis of Streamlining Administration and Fiscal Contract

Streamlining administration in China's fiscal system started on the revenue side. Three major adjustments have been made to budget management. Now the reform is about restructuring the expenditure side. The author tries to take the readers although the reform in this field in a time sequence.

In addition, we believe that it is more helpful to approach the reform from the perspective of contract theory for a better understanding of the way to streamline administration in the fiscal system. This is because the fiscal system itself is an elastic institutional arrangement and, in essence, a grand contract between the central government and local governments. It includes side contracts on fiscal revenue, fiscal expenditure and budget management that connect both the revenue and expenditure sides. The interaction and evolution of these side contracts has pushed for China's economic development.

I. From concentration to division of power: the 1950s–1978

In 1950, the *Decision on the Unified Administration of Financial Revenue and Expenditure of 1950* issued by the then Government Administration Council (the predecessor of the State Council) adopted the fiscal system of centralized administration and unified collection and expenditure, and local governments had no fiscal power at all. In 1951, the Government Administration Council promulgated the *Provisional Regulations on Budgeting and Final Accounts*, which for the first time stipulated the basic principles, drafting, approval and implementation of government budgeting, and review and approval of final accounts. In the same year, the Government Administration Council issued the *Decision on the Division of the Financial Revenue and Expenditures System in 1951*, which revised the centralized administration model of 1950, and local governments began to have budget revenues. In 1954, the Constitution gave the National People's Congress the power to review and approve budgets and final accounts, but this system did not operate normally for a long time due to various historical reasons.

In 1956, China's central government decided to delegate much of the administrative power over SOEs to local governments after recognizing that local governments were able to protect their own interests. However, it resulted in a loss of control by the central government of the national economy, as local governments launched the "great leap forward" campaign after securing the control of SOEs, causing serious economic disorder and even significant depression of the economy.

The depression that lasted from 1959 to 1961 coincided with a mass scale of famine. The central government had no other choice but to take the power back. At an enlarged central work conference attended by delegates of five levels of government or the famous "7000 people conference", centralism was restored with the central government coordinating all affairs across the country. After the conference, much of the fiscal power of local governments gradually returned to the central government.

This round of fiscal power centralization was a temporary measure for China to eliminate economic difficulties. When the economy improved, the central government began fiscal decentralization again. In 1968, the central government started the reform of separating fiscal revenue from expenditure. However, because of the Cultural Revolution, the reform failed to produce any results. It was not until 1971, the first year of the fourth Five-year Plan period, that the central leadership again decided to shift the control of most of the state-owned enterprises to local governments. This was the first time that China had a "fiscal package contract" system whereby the central government set a fixed revenue and expenditure target for local governments, and the local governments promised to turn in a certain proportion of fiscal surplus to the central government and keep what was left. It could mobilize local governments to increase fiscal revenue while securing fiscal revenue for the central government. However, as the budget management system was unable to run properly, most local governments found it hard to make ends meet, let alone fiscal surplus. Therefore, this round of the "fiscal package contract" system was not actually carried out.

In 1974, the central government separated revenue from expenditure in the "fiscal package contract", partially removing local governments' fiscal autonomy. In 1977, the central government conducted pilot fiscal reforms of the "proportional package contract" in Jiangsu Province, which was later extended to 10 provinces and municipalities in 1978. The aim was to improve fiscal balance among local governments and encourage them to increase fiscal revenue through better economic performance.

The fiscal reform from 1950 to 1978 focused on the revenue side. Repeated adjustments were made to fiscal power and resource allocation between the central and local governments. It was proven that the state monopoly of revenue and expenditure in the planned economy could cause a number of problems because as a kind of fixed rent contract, it required local governments to turn in all its fiscal revenue to the central government and then receive funding from the central government according to the production plan. In this relationship, the central government could take all the surplus value, and there were few incentives for local governments to increase revenue.

II. Power decentralization and interest sharing: from 1979 to 1993

The Communiqué issued by the 11th CPC Central Committee at its third plenary session on 22 December 1978 stated that a serious shortcoming of China's existing economic system was the disproportionate centralization of power, which should be delegated boldly with proper guidance. Li Xiannian, then vice president of China and vice premier of the State Council, pointed out at a work conference of the CPCCC on 5 April 1979 that administrative power was in general too centralized in China's economic system. On 4 October of the same year, Deng Xiaoping, then vice chairman of the CPC Central Committee, said at a meeting with the first secretaries of provincial, municipal and autonomous regional CPC committees that the fiscal system was too centralized and that some fiscal powers should be delegated to local governments. It is therefore fair to say that the fiscal reform once again spearheaded the economic reform that was launched at the historical juncture in 1978. The fiscal reform in this phase was characterized by "power delegation and interest concession".

In the late 1970s, ravaged by the Cultural Revolution, China's economy was at the brink of collapse. The country was also in a heated political debate on "two whatevers". The chaos suppressed production and stifled the economy. In this context, the power that could be delegated by the central government was in fact only concerned with fiscal management, and the interests that it could give away were basically the share of fiscal revenue in national income distribution.

Traditionally, in China, the fiscal system was almost entirely at the service of the sector of public ownership. The nonpublic sector was not to be reckoned with and far from active. This held back the vitality of the national economy. As the central government gradually "delegated power and gave away interests" in the fiscal system, initial progress was made in the country's market-oriented reform, represented by rising national strengths and a more dynamic economy.

These steps, however, were in essence part of a one-off game. The central government devolved some of its fiscal power to local governments. In other words, "the central and local governments ate from separately bowls". The government also allowed SOEs to keep more profits for themselves, which was termed "cutting taxes and giving away profits". The fiscal readjustment was crucial in securing recognition of the major reform policies from all interest groups early on as well as the steady progress of the overall reform. However, the balance was fragile and unsustainable, as power delegation and interest transfer were achieved at the cost of lower fiscal revenue and more expenditure. It is difficult for this model to secure steady operation of the fiscal system because although the concession made may have succeeded in carrying out the reform in the short term, the fiscal imbalance it entailed was unsustainable and may even pose a significant threat to the national economy.

In 1987, the central government decided to allow SOEs to sign responsibility contracts with their respective administrative authorities. It was accompanied by corresponding "fiscal package contract" reform. This was the second time China launched the "fiscal package contract", and the reform made progress. The government could collect revenue in a variety of forms, including on a fixed amount, proportionate to corporate income or through sharing the additional profits with SOEs. The practice cased the disruption of the policy of "power delegation and interests concession" on the fiscal revenue for the central government and gave incentives to local authorities to grow the economy and seek financial resources.

According to contract theory, the fiscal responsibility contract system implemented between 1980 and 1993 was a share contract with certain elements of the agent levying contract.[4] With a share contract, the central government gives a percentage of the revenue back to local governments as commission. The share contract enables the central and the local government to share the "residual claimants" identity and revenue risks, which may lead to diminishing marginal incentives for local governments in revenue collection. In reality, due to the lack of a full-fledged budget management system in those years of fiscal responsibility contracts, local governments mainly focused their efforts on extrabudgetary revenue collection for their own use instead of increasing budgetary revenue under the framework of the share

[4] With an agent levying contract, a local government hands over a set amount of tax revenue to the central government and claims for the residual. It is unique in a way that local governments can be full residual claimant of the revenue they collect after paying their quota to the central government. However, they have to bear revenue risks by themselves (Lv, 2009).

contract with the central government. In the early 1990s, extrabudgetary income even amounted to 90% of the budgetary revenue levied by local governments.

The fiscal responsibility contract system gave a further push to the market economy, but it also had serious flaws, such as regional blockade, local protection, invisible market barriers between regions, market segmentation and lack of flow of resources. Consequently, resistance to the economic reform built up. Local governments increased extrabudgetary revenue collection to offset their fiscal quotas handed to the central government. The gap in financial strengths between the central and local governments gradually widened and posed a threat to the long-term stability of China. In response, the central government initiated the reform of building a tax-sharing system.

III. Institutional innovation: 1994–2014

The fiscal responsibility contract system driven by power decentralization incentivized the local governments, but it also squeezed the financial pool of the central government.[5] The ability of the central government to regulate the macroeconomy and conduct social governance was under severe challenge, which would eventually damage the health and order of the local economy. In this context, the central government decided to overhaul the country's fiscal system. In 1991, the State Council issued the *National Budget Management Regulations*, which took effect on 1 January 1992, to replace the 40-year-old *Provisional Regulations on Budget Management*. A five-tiered government budgetary system was set up to separate central and local budgets. At the third Plenary Session of the 14th CPC Central Committee in November 1993, the *Decision of the CPC Central Committee on Matters Concerning the Establishment of a Socialist Market Economy System* was adopted. In December, the State Council released the *Decision on Adopting the Tax-sharing Fiscal Management System*. The reform toward a tax-sharing system was launched. The *National Regulations on Budget Management* were replaced by the *Budget Law*, which took effect on 1 January 1994. Zhu Rongji, then vice-premier of the State Council, said, "I take (the Budget Law) which will take effect on 1 January next year (1994) as a foundation for long-term stability and the socialist market economy. It will ease or even solve the current difficulties and ensure a sound momentum of economic growth by keeping the growth at a relatively high level".[6]

In essence, the tax-sharing system is a system in which the central government and local governments share taxation power. As a new round of fiscal reform on the revenue side, it is also called the division of revenue power. The reform aimed to further straighten the relationship between the central and local governments by dividing the revenue of central and local governments according to tax categories. In the following 20 years, the tax-sharing system has played a fundamental role in China's economic transformation and ensured fast growth of both the economy and fiscal revenue.

[5] By the end of 1993, approximately 60% of the central government's expenditure had to rely on the borrowing from local governments or foreign governments.

[6] Zhu Rongji: *Transcript of Zhu Rongji's Remarks* (volume 1), People's Publishing House, 2011, p. 329.

According to contract theory, the tax-sharing system in China is a combination of share contracts and tax-sharing contracts.[7,8] As set in the tax sharing contract, both the central and the local government have full rights of collection and earnings of their respective categories of tax. This means that the central government completely delegates the power of collection and the right to earning some taxes to the local government. It ensures adequate financial resources of the central government and, at the same time, keeps the incentives for local governments to cultivate tax sources, expand the tax base and strengthen coordination with the central government.

While acknowledging the crucial importance of the fiscal and taxation reform of 1994, one should not overlook its historical limitations, as it mainly focused on the fiscal revenue distribution and adjustment of interest relations between the central and local governments. Little was done on the government expenditure responsibility and the payment transfer mechanism between different levels of government.[9] In addition, reform on fiscal expenditure was lagging behind, and local governments took advantage of the Budget Law to borrow heavily through the financing platforms they built. Despite the public assets produced, fiscal and financial risks were on the rise due to the absence of budget supervision and insensitivity to pricing. In addition, the tax-sharing system only covered relations between the central government and provincial governments. No corresponding system was in place between governments at the provincial, prefecture (municipal), county (district) and township levels. In fact, the local fiscal system was still characterized by "package contract" and "case-by-case bargaining". In short, the tax-sharing reform was not carried through to the end. Moreover, the 1994 fiscal reform did not try to solve the issue outside the system, namely, the relationship between government and market. As a result, industries and companies enjoying government funding support are running with overcapacity, while SMEs with no government credit endorsement still have little access to affordable financing[10].

[7] The tax-sharing contract strictly follows the tax-sharing system, by which the central and local governments are fully entitled to tax revenue of certain categories, respectively, and do not have to share revenue with each other. The general practice is that minor tax categories like real estate, land and charges are levied by local governments and major tax categories such as corporate tax and personal income tax are collected by the central government.

[8] Currently in the tax-sharing system, the share of VAT between the central and the local government is 75:25, and 60:40 for both corporate income tax and personal income tax. These three categories of tax are covered by the sharing contract, and the remaining belongs to the tax-sharing contract.

[9] Zhu Rongji, then vice premier of China, had such comments: "There is a small 'tail' left untouched in the tax-sharing reform. The Ministry of Finance gives all ministries a funding package to be allocated to local governments. This is exactly the revenue that was turned in by the local governments. The practice only makes things more difficult...and must be changed." Quoted from *Transcript of Zhu Rongji's Remarks* (volume 1), People's Publishing House, 2011, p. 365.

[10] After over three decades of fast growth, China is now in a medium to high growth trajectory. During the economic restructuring aimed at cutting excess capacity, corporate merger, restructuring and even market withdraw have become the price that has to be paid.

IV. Stronger reform since 2015

Government streamlining and power delegation in the fiscal system since the beginning of the reform have generated enormous economic benefits, but they are more in terms of stimulating the short-term growth of local governments' economic performance than improving the industrial structure, regional economic balance and fairness in income redistribution. Following the third Plenary Session of the 18th CPC Central Committee, the *Overall Plan for Deepening the Reform of the Fiscal and Taxation System* was adopted by the Political Bureau of the CPC Central Committee on 30 June 2014 to address this issue, and the revised Budget Law was adopted by the National People's Congress on 31 August 2014 and took effect on 1 January 2015.

The new round of the fiscal reform took place in a special context. China was progressing toward a market economy with increasingly diverse forms of ownership, which led to wider and more diverse sources of government revenue. This naturally helped distribute fiscal expenditures to more social sectors. This trend further instilled a public nature to fiscal policies. The all-around fiscal reform involved power devolution on fiscal expenditure to give play to the role of government funds as a leverage and guide in support of the supply-side reform.

A revisit of the reform of China's fiscal system over the past six decades proves that the country's fiscal system contributes to social production and the market economy. The reform has raised productivity, but on the other hand, it has created a number of issues that have forced the central government to continuously modify its relations with local authorities. There is a view that it was local government's noncompliance with the fiscal and taxation contracts that has driven institutional innovation and stimulated economic vitality. Such a view fails to recognize the unsustainable nature of the development model featuring identical projects between regions, high energy consumption and high pollution of industries, and inadequacies in education, health and other public services. Is there a better way of improving governance than policy swings of the central government between decentralizing and tightening control with its absolute authority? The answer is "yes".

Putting Equal Emphasis on the Rule of Law and Rule by Virtue

I. Limitations of contractual governance

The premise for the success of China's fiscal reform is the absolute political authority of the central government. Unlike western countries where the power of the central government comes from local governments, the power of local governments in China is bestowed by the central government. The central government has full power and ability to initiate changes in fiscal and taxation contracts with local governments as the economy grows, but this practice has also heightened the alert of both central and local governments against each other. One could feel the estrangement when reading documents issued by the central government. A number of documents released by the State Council in 1988 repeatedly stressed that "comrades in people's governments at all levels must develop the economy and strengthen fiscal management in strict accordance with state policies by taking into account the overall interests and the difficulties of the central government." This implied significant frictions between the central and local governments at that time. Another example is that in 2012 and 2013, the National Audit Office released audit reports on local government debt on behalf of the central government twice. This shows that the Ministry of Finance, as the government's executive department of fiscal affairs, could not have a full picture of the indebtedness of local governments through regular oversight. To obtain relevant information on local governments, interim audits and other unconventional measures had to be employed.

It was proven that the absolute political authority of the central government may not result in the economic obedience of local governments. The central government often changed its fiscal relationship with local governments and frequently used additional administrative resources to supervise them, which made them more opportunistic. After all, no contract is perfect. Just as the central government can revise it on its own, local governments can also take advantage of its flaws to engage in speculation. As in game theory, in the first-order game, the central government has the rule in its favor and can make full use of it. In the second-order game, the local government can give full play to its strengths on information collection. The fiscal system, which may look flexible, is actually quite costly and inefficient.

II. Moral strengths as a third force

The logic of Mansel (1995), a key advocate for public choice theory, actually provides a good explanation for the obstacles faced by China in the process of streamlining government administration and competition between the central and local governments in fiscal reform. However, the school of public choice tends to approach this phenomenon only from the perspective of relations between the market and the government, and the solution proposed is privatization.

China is a country under the guidance of Marxism and Leninism and practices socialism with Chinese characteristics. A feasible solution may be drawn from the speeches that Mr. Li Yining has made in recent years where three regulators of the economy are frequently mentioned, namely, market, government and moral strengths. In his opinion, the market is the first regulator. As an invisible hand, it plays a decisive role in resource allocation according to the law of nature. The government represents the second regulator. Like a visible hand, it charts the course through planning, laws, regulations and policies. Morality is the third regulator. It represents a seemingly invisible but actually visible hand and is the oldest regulating tool among them.

According to Li Yining, the market came into being only a few thousand years ago, but trade of goods between tribes occurred with the disintegration of primitive communes long before the appearance of the market, and the government appeared even later than the market. What helped sustain human society in between without the regulative roles of the market or the government? The answer is moral strengths.

As the third form of regulation, it was actually the only regulatory tool available when there was no market or government and remained essential after the latter came into being. The conclusion he made was that market regulation is intangible, government regulation is tangible, and moral strengths are both tangible and intangible because they rely on self-discipline and culture to reach their effect.

The emphasis on moral strengths can be traced back to *The Theory of Moral Sentiments* written by Adam Smith, the founder of economics, before the publication of *The Wealth of Nations*. Adam Smith taught "moral philosophy" for a long time at the time-honored University of Glasgow in northern England. His research in this field was as deep as his studies on economics, and the relevant works were published even before his economics classics. He lived in a time a few hundred years ago when ethics and even economics were all part of moral philosophy for both the academic and the economic communities of Britain. When he was writing *The Wealth of Nations*, he was also revising *The Theory of Moral Sentiments* more than five times until the last years of his life. This testified to the importance Adam Smith placed on the role of morality in social and economic governance. Human emotions were analyzed from the perspectives of morality and individual and social welfare. He also talked about compassion, justice and benevolence and other widely recognized virtues in his book.

We are living in an era where wealth creation depends more on skills than labor, but not yet on intelligence. There are still over one hundred million farmers in China trying to make a living through hard labor, which is a harsh reality that requires the attention of people who study the relationship between intelligence and wealth. Democracy and freedom are of course important today, but on top of that is fairness and justice. They all need to be regulated and supported by morality to achieve social harmony.

III. Beyond the contractual theory

Adam Smith highlighted moral self-discipline as the "soft approach" in balancing the market economy and social ethics. Later, Jeremy Bentham put forward the "hard approach", or law, as punishment to correct mistakes in the market economy. That is, anyone who fails to have self-discipline will be subject to external constraints that may include other people, society, or conventional social ethics, as mentioned by Li Yining. Without a unified norm, society would be in chaos.

To build a sustainable society, a wise government must try to avoid creating social gaps. It should keep the majority of people away from the sense of despair. On this note, we need compromise, tolerance and sympathy instead of revolution, violence and indifference. The role of moral strengths is essential even in a full market economy with a good government. As Li Yining puts it, humanity needs moral regulation, which has a longer history than other regulating tools.

The 18th CPC Central Committee at its third plenary session raised the role of state finance from the level of government revenue and expenditure activities to the level of national governance and placed it in the state governance system under the framework of the rule of law after the rule of law was put forward at its fourth plenary session. Decentralization of the fiscal system should transcend the doomed cycle of loosening and tightening the fiscal power top down, lower the frequency of unilateral modification of the fiscal rules by the central government, and strengthen fiscal discipline on local governments in accordance with the law. This will set a good example for further promoting the tax-sharing reform below the provincial government level. Such an exemplary role can, to a large extent, urge local governments to comply with the principle of ensuring the public and nonprofit nature of their fiscal arrangement and provide high-quality public goods for market players of all ownerships in the process of building a modern people-centered fiscal system.

A law sets strict boundaries and red lines that no one can cross. That said, it is a more often a contract with loopholes because people are allowed to maximize their self-interests so long as they do not cross the lines. Policymakers in local governments tend to exploit these loopholes from the position of strength in information, and the central government tends to revise the contract as it deems necessary. This results in institutional inefficiency, waste of social, economic and political resources and disservice to the people. We already know that intangible moral strength is stronger than law. Officials of both the central and local governments should not only follow the rule of law but also emphasize political integrity and governance ethics. Therefore, a well-prepared contract and sound political integrity should be the basic form of fiscal reform in the new era.

In other words, in handling the boundary between the government and the market, it proves unfeasible to allow the government to take care of everything and leave nothing to the market. It is also wrong to practice "market economy fundamentalism" by completely turning to the laissez-faire approach.

Conclusion

On the journey from the planned economy to the market economy, managing the relationship between the government and the market is of primary importance. If the government exercises governance with cities as basic units mainly through fiscal investment in state-owned enterprises, it will be difficult to nurture market players that take care of their own profits and losses, and the market will be unable to play a crucial role in resource allocation. The economic stagnation in the later period of the planned economy was a telling case. If the government had retreated to the role of the "night watchman" advocated by Adam Smith, then China would not have seen such remarkable growth in infrastructure or have the ability to serve as a powerhouse to pull the world economy out of doldrums amid global economic uncertainties as well as challenges brought by the financial crisis.[11]

[11] It will be hard to imagine how China can avoid various financial crises without strong government regulation. It would also be inconceivable that China could remain unaffected by the financial quakes triggered by the Asian financial crisis in 1997, the US subprime mortgage crisis in 2008 and the European debt crisis in 2009 without proper government intervention.

What are the goals for fiscal reform? We are of the view that the reform should take into account the market, society and government and highlight respect for law and moral strengths.

First, the market shall play a fundamental role in resource allocation. Fiscal reform aims to give better play to the role of the market and make up for its shortcomings, rather than encouraging the government to compete with the market for resources. In other words, streamlining government administration and delegating power in the fiscal system is a market-oriented reform.

Second, taxation reform should go further. Tax collection should be moved further toward the consumer end. Tax categories should be expanded in the phase of redistribution and accumulation of national income to promote social equity. The tax-sharing system should take a firm hold to offer incentives to local governments in building a single national market to ensure that the reform brings enough social benefits.

Third, new ways should be explored to include the fiscal system in state governance. As the reform progresses, the state's fiscal system needs to exit from nonpublic and for-profit fields and enter the political, cultural, social, environmental and other fields of state governance in accordance with the law. Building a leaner government through fiscal reform should be carried out under state guidance.

Bibliography

Chen, G. (1965). The nature and scope of the socialist fiscal system. *Economic Research Journal*, (8).

Department of fiscal and taxation system reform, ministry of finance. *The decade of fiscal and taxation reform*. China Financial & Economic Publishing House (1989).

Gao, P. (2008). Public finance: Conceptual definition and evolution context—Footprints of China's 30 years of fiscal reform. *Economic Research Journal*, (12).

Liu, G. (1987). Dual models of China's economic transition. *China Economic Studies*, (1).

Lv, B. (2009). Institutional structure and financial impact of the tax-sharing system. *Economic Research Journal*, (6).

Liu, X. & Guo, Q. (2016). 300 years of finance analyzed in the perspective of state governance. *Finance and Trade Economics*, (3).

Liu, Z., et al. (1998). *Fiscal and taxation reform and development in China*. China Financial & Economic Publishing House.

Liu, Z. (2014). Establishing a tax-sharing system during the reform and opening-up. *China State Finance*, (1).

Mansel, O. (1995). *Logic of collective action*. Shanghai People's Publishing House.

Wang, S. (1997). *Limits of the power sharing system*. China Planning Press.

Xiang, H. (1994). *Reform of China's fiscal system*. China Financial & Economic Publishing House.

Zhang, J. (2008). Power sharing and growth: A Chinese narrative. *China Economic Quarterly*, (1).

Taxation Reform Practice in Building a Leaner Government

Shunkui Huang

Building a leaner government is essential in modernizing the state's governance capacity and plays an important role in improving the socialist market economy, promoting the transformation of the growth model and further advancing the reform in all aspects. At the core of these efforts is to balance three pairs of relationships—government and market, government and the public, and central and local authorities. The market should play a crucial role in resource allocation. Intervention in business management should be reduced as much as possible, and market and local governments must be given the power to do things that are they are more capable of doing. The continuous high growth China has enjoyed since 1978 is largely attributed to the power delegation from the central government to local governments and the market. Tax is the most important source of revenue for the government, and the taxation system reflects the economic relations between the central and local governments and between government and market. A modern taxation system features institutional simplicity, a broad tax base and a low tax rate. Cutting red tapes as is required by the modern taxation system serves to galvanize market players of all sorts of ownership. It can bring more vitality to the market, guide and regulate economic activities more effectively, push for economic transformation and promote the shift of the growth model.

The Importance of Taxation Reform to Building a Leaner Government

I. Promoting modernization of national governance

The 18th CPC Central Committee made it clear at its third plenary session that the aim of comprehensively deepening the reform is to promote modernization of

S. Huang (✉)
Guanghua School of Management, Peking University, Beijing, China

Y. Li and Z. Cheng (eds.), *The Chinese Path Toward a Leaner Government*,
https://doi.org/10.1007/978-981-19-6718-4_7

the state governance system and capacity.[1] Finance is the foundation of a nation, and a country's fiscal and taxation system plays an extremely important role in state governance. The ruler of the Tang Dynasty (618 A.D.–907 A.D.) replaced the traditional "headcount-based" taxation system with a property-based system to make tax burden fairer with fewer tax categories and easier procedures. The system gave more incentives to the working people. In the Ming Dynasty (1368 A.D.–1644 A.D.) The taxation system was further consolidated to give more freedom to farmers. It stimulated commodity trading at that time. As the complexity of state governance increases with the expansion of government functions, it is imperative to set up a taxation system compatible with modern state governance. This institutional improvement will help define the functions and responsibilities of the government and clarify the scope of responsibilities and fiscal relations between governments at all levels. It will also regulate the behavior of the government or the "visible hand", promote the free flow of resources and market growth, and make the government more of a regulator and watchman of the market.

II. Incentivizing market players of all types

Before 1978, China was under a highly centralized fiscal and taxation system that had suppressed the incentives and creativity of local authorities, government departments, public institutions and business communities. The 11th CPC Central Committee stated at its third plenary session that too much power concentration was a serious defect of China's economic system. Local authorities and companies should have more freedom under the guidance of national plans to generate incentives, initiatives and creativity for central government agencies, local authorities, companies and the workforce. Economic reform should start with the expansion of the fiscal power of local governments and companies. In other words, the fiscal reform spearheaded the economic reform. The decision was made at the 3rd Plenary Session of the 12th CPC Central Committee that the reform would follow the principle of separating government roles from business management and streamlining administrative functions to revitalize SOEs and the national economy. The reform of the fiscal and taxation system shall aim at strengthening the dynamism in SOEs, managing well the relations among the government, SOEs and their employees and increasing the autonomy of SOEs. Greater vitality of SOEs and higher incentives among all market players are crucial to the success of the overall reform agenda and faster growth and better performance of China's economy.

III. Building a single national market

A fair and unified market calls for the removal of all covert barriers that stand in the way of building a single national market and fair competition. In the phase of "eating from separate bowls" when fiscal responsibilities were divided between the central and local governments, power delegation and the fiscal contractual relationship between the central and local authorities pushed local governments to maximize

[1] The Decision of the CPC Central Committee on Several Major Issues concerning Comprehensively Deepening the Reform (2013).

their fiscal revenue. Preferential policies on taxation and nontax revenue were rolled out for the government to make undue intervention in the economy. As a result, the local economy was booming at the expense of a unified tax code and fair competition. The role of the market in resource allocation was undermined, and the national economy was fragmented. The tax-sharing system can help break such economic fragmentation, as it divides revenue according to tax categories and thus loosens the revenue bonds between local governments and business communities. As tax is no longer collected from companies according to their administrative relations with the central or local governments, companies have become independent market players. Fair competition is enhanced for the common development of businesses of all ownerships. Revoking local tax concessions, removing local protectionism and putting an end to unregulated taxation competition of various types between regions are conducive to the unity and regularity of the taxation system, fair competition in the market, and mutual complementarity and coordinated development between regions.

IV. Shifting the growth model

The government regulates the economic structure and social distribution by budgeting and taxation.[2] The taxation system is an important part of macro control of the socialist market economy. Strengthening the regulatory functions of taxation helps push forward the reform in all fields. A proactive fiscal policy involves the reduction of taxes and fees and lowers the burden on small and micro businesses in particular. The central government exercises macro control by adjusting the rate in key tax categories, and the local governments regulate the economic activities of their respective regions through revenue collection. A two-step "profit to tax" reform has shaped a better-regulated relationship between the government and SOEs in corporate income distribution and given more autonomy to SOEs. Taxation policies for the banking sector have been adjusted in support of the reform and development of the financial system and fair competition. Tariffs and import taxes are exempted for equipment used for investment projects encouraged by the government among a wider tariff cut in support of inbound investment and imports of advanced technological equipment. The business tax to VAT reform introduced in 2012 prevents double taxation and lowers corporate burdens. It also promotes industrial transformation, growth of the service sector and creation of new business models. To secure the transformation of the growth model and readjustment of the economic structure, it is imperative to strengthen the role of the taxation system in economic regulation and social development and adopt a sound taxation regime and relevant policies to shift the growth model and upgrade the industrial structure.

[2] The Decision of the CPC Central Committee on Matters Concerning the Establishment of the Socialist Market Economic System (1993, pp. 1286–1303).

Power Delegation in China's Taxation System Since 1978

Since the beginning of the reform and opening up, China's taxation system has gone through two phases. The first was between 1978 and 1992, and the second began in 1992. Taking into account blurred boundaries of responsibilities between the government and SOEs and the direct management of SOEs by the government under a highly centralized planned economy, the 11th CPC Central Committee decided at its third plenary session to delegate power for the sake of more business vitality and greater autonomy of companies. Given its critical importance in resource allocation under the planned economy, the fiscal system was an area where breakthroughs could be made in the reform. In the reform of dividing fiscal power, or "eating from separate bowls", the central government has given away part of its power and interests to local authorities, narrowed the scope of administrative intervention, and gradually enhanced the role of the market. Thus, little by little, the government delegated its power on resource allocation to the market.[3] To drive the economy and improve revenue, local governments have been working hard to build a pro-business environment, support the growth of the nonpublic sector and promote the diversification of market players. In 1992, the goal of building a socialist market economy was set for the reform. In 1994, the fiscal framework of a tax-sharing system featuring separate economic responsibilities between governments at different levels gradually took shape as required by the market economy. Efforts were also made in unifying the tax codes, concentrating taxation power, evening out the tax burden and simplifying the tax rules to make the taxation system compatible with the socialist market economy. Since 2004, the taxation system has been further finetuned in the principle of "simplified rules, broad base, low rate and strict management".

I. Gradual establishment of a tax system under the socialist market economy

In the fiscal system of 1985 featuring different tax categories, verification of revenue and expenditure and stratified taxation responsibilities, there were a myriad of taxes. To address issues such as overlapping product taxes and industrial and commercial taxes and different tax rates for businesses of different ownerships that hampered the division of responsibilities among market players and market-based production, business tax reform was introduced in 1994, and a modern taxation system took its initial shape. The VAT was launched in 1979 to remove dual taxation. Reform on the structure of turnover tax started in 1985, and tax categories were narrowed from 270 to 96. VAT expanded coverage from only a few products in a few industries to most of the industrial products except tobacco, alcohol, petrochemical products and electricity, and the dual collection of turnover tax was cut by a large margin. In 1994, VAT replaced production tax and salt tax on all goods as well as all processing and repair services. The VAT coverage was further expanded in 2012 to harmonize taxation for goods and services and eliminate double taxation. It was part of an effort to promote division of labor, growth of the service sector, transformation of the manufacturing industry and business vitality. Between January 2012 and August

[3] Kang and Houquan (2008, pp. 5–23).

2014, thanks to the VAT reform, tax was cut by RMB 307.5 billion.[4] The consumption tax was introduced in 1994 on 11 categories of goods, and its scope was readjusted in 2006. The *Regulations on Consumption Tax* were revised in 2008, followed by the tax and fee reform on oil products. A total of 14 items of goods are now covered by the consumption tax.

The business tax initially covered only petroleum, hardware, electronic equipment and chemical products. In 1985, its coverage was expanded from 11 to 14 categories to help with economic regulation. In 1993, the number of categories was reduced to nine. The resource tax was levied on crude oil, natural gas and coal in 1984 based on sales revenues of taxable goods as well as the progressive tax rate determined by the profitability of sales. It was changed to a quantitative quota-based tax in 1986 and covered 7 categories in 1994. However, in 2007, the resource tax on goods such as crude oil and natural gas began to be price-based to discourage the practice of concentrating on resource-rich mines only and make resource tax and fees fairer. Regarding specific item-based taxes, construction tax was shifted to regulatory tax on fixed assets investment to strengthen guidance on investment and was halved in the second half of 1999 and suspended in 2000 to encourage investment. Reform was carried out on the real estate tax to improve urban development and property market regulation. The tax coverage was expanded, tax rates adjusted and criteria simplified. In 1988, the banquet tax was launched to encourage rational consumption. In the same year, land use tax was also added as an economic means to control and properly manage urban land, harmonize price differences of land between and inside cities, and encourage land users to conserve land. In 1987, the government began to collect taxes on farmland occupied for nonfarming purposes and scrapped the agricultural tax and farm produce tax after 2004. There were 34 main tax categories in China in 1992. The number was reduced to 24 after the tax-sharing reform and further decreased to 20 and 18 in 2004 and 2014, respectively.

II. Giving full play to the incentives of the central and local governments

During the fiscal and taxation reform in the period after 1978, the central government devolved to the local governments more fiscal and administrative power by moving from "eating in the same bowl" to "eating in separate bowls". After the tax for profit reform, companies began to pay taxes to the governments where they were registered. The fiscal power of local governments was expanded together with their economic responsibilities. This added impetus to their ability and motivation to push for social and economic development. In 1983, the decision was made that the central government should collect industrial and commercial taxes on tobacco and alcohol, a measure to curb the ill-advised expansion of relevant industries by local governments for high profits and tax revenues. In 1988, a fiscal contract responsibility system was launched that devolved the administrative power of 13 local tax categories of diverse sources to local governments as an incentive to improve their fiscal income and ease the long-standing issue of the absence of a proper reward mechanism. The tax-sharing reform in 1994 strengthened the macro control capabilities of the central

[4] Jiwei (2015, p. 165).

government by putting in place a regime for the stable growth of tax-based fiscal income and improving the tax structure. The share of such direct taxes as income tax and property tax in the total tax revenue has increased, and the revenue structure with transaction tax and income tax as the main tax categories has become more balanced. Tax category-based revenue is useful in restraining local governments from the single-minded development of industries such as tobacco and alcohol for high profit and revenue and launching duplicative projects. It has also broken regional segmentation by establishing a single market. The incentives of both the central and the local governments were raised in the process of industrial structure improvement.

III. Fairer distribution among the government, businesses and individuals

Income distribution among the government, businesses and individuals has been better regulated through the income tax regime. First, the corporate tax regime was reformed to give more power and profits back to SOEs. The two-step tax for profit reform has helped SOEs retain more after-tax profits for the sake of business growth and employee benefits, thus adding more vitality to SOEs. Pilot programs on government-SOE tax and profit relations have been carried out in the principle of raising business vitality, improving its management and self-discipline and strengthening regulation of the tax regime. In pilot areas, all SOEs running with profits are subject to a 35% corporate income tax, which facilitates corporate mechanism improvements and fair competition. In the new turnover tax regime with VAT at its core after the tax-sharing reform, corporate income taxes for companies of different ownerships have been merged into a single corporate income tax. It has provided a level playing field for companies of all ownerships and straightened out relations between the government and the businesses in the field of distribution. Second, personal income tax has been streamlined. In 1988, the personal income regulatory tax was levied on the income of private business investors gained from their companies. A 40% personal income regulatory tax was levied on corporate profits used for personal consumption by private business investors, and no tax would be levied on profits used for business development to protect the lawful interests of private businesses and give incentives to their managers. In 1986, the tax was expanded to all individuals with two tax rates according to the sources of income. Income generated from wage, contracting and subcontracting, service and property leasing were merged into general income and were put under an excess progressive tax rate. Income generated from technology transfer, author remuneration, and interest rates was subjected to a 20% tax ratio. The 1993 *Personal Income Tax Law of the People's Republic of China* further streamlined individual income adjustment tax and consolidated it with personal income tax for foreigners and self-employed individuals. The government then made five revisions to the law and raised tax deductions for wage incomes.

IV. Better regulation of extrabudgetary funds and gradual steps to include them in the budget

Tax revenue is the main stable source of public revenue for a market economy. In the years before the reform, when companies were dominated by public and collective ownership, it was hard for people to see the importance of taxation as a way of revenue generation and economic regulation. In 1980, tax revenue accounted for only 50% of the government's fiscal income. The share gradually increased with the progress of the tax reform, as charges, compulsory fee items and extrabudgetary income collected by governments at various levels were either revoked or put under budgetary management. In 2014, tax revenue rose to 88.1% of the national fiscal income. The share of nontax revenue in the government's fiscal income was 50.7% in 1980. It decreased to 19.8% in 1994, further decreased to 6.1% in 2000 and climbed to 15.1% in 2014. The largest part of nontax revenue is administrative income, which stood at 24.6% in 2014.

The reform includes the following. First, extrabudgetary funds were gradually consolidated into fiscal funds. The economic reform in 1979 expanded the autonomy of local governments and companies and resulted in a drastic increase in both budgetary and extrabudgetary funds. Between 1982 and 1992, extrabudgetary funds increased by 3.8 times, with an annual growth of 17%, almost 6% higher than the growth of budgetary income in the same period. Regulations on the management of extrabudgetary funds were issued in 1986, 1996 and 2010 to make the funds better regulated. Second, the tax-and-fee system was reformed to regulate government behaviors. Between 1998 and 2004, 1913 items of government charge were removed, and rates were lowered for the other 479 items, easing public financial burden by RMB149 billion.[5] In 2008, the government replaced highway maintenance fees and five other kinds of fees with a higher consumption tax on refined oil and gradually removed tolls of Class II roads for government loan payment. On 1 August 2013, 33 items of administrative charges at the central government level were removed or exempted, followed by 314 items of administrative charges at the provincial level on 1 November 2013.[6] In 2014, coal companies in Shanxi Province saw their fee burden cut by RMB10.85 billion or 27.5% to a ratio of 10.6% in real terms, 4% lower than in the years before 2013.[7]

V. Putting tax code formulation and tax collection under the rule of law

Economists such as Adam Smith and Adolf Wagner all stressed the importance of simplicity in tax codes and procedures for the convenience of tax payers. The cost of both collection on the part of the tax authorities and compliance on part of tax payers must be as low as possible. As the share of taxation in fiscal revenue continues to rise, strengthening tax collection and management was crucial in raising the government's income. The *Law on Tax Collection and Management of the People's Republic of China* and the *Implementing Rules on Tax Collection and Management of the People's Republic of China* adopted in 1992 put the practice under the rule of law. The 1994 reform of the industrial and commercial tax regime set strict criteria on policy-based tax reduction and exemption to curb arbitrary, excessive and unauthorized tax reduction and exemption practices. The authority of the tax law was established, which gave

[5] Kang (2008, pp. 2–20).

[6] Lihui and Qiuyu (2013).

[7] Chaoyang (2014, pp. 6–7).

full play to the market role and nurtured a favorable environment for fair competition. As the tax reform was carried out in 1994, the functions of taxation policymakers and tax collection and management authorities were separated. The Ministry of Finance was responsible for formulating and interpreting part of the general regulations and implementing rules on taxation, and the tax bureaus were responsible for tax collection and management. They were divided into central and local tax bureaus that collect taxes separately to strengthen tax collection and management.

After the 1994 reform on the industrial and commercial tax, the Gold Tax Project, a national computer-based tax collection and management project, was launched to fight crimes such as falsifying, reselling and stealing invoices and strengthening the regulation of VAT. A tax declaration system based on self-verification and payment by tax payers was set up. Declaration forms and payment sheets were simplified and standardized. Procedures were made easier for tax payers. In 2014, the General Administration of Taxation (GAT) released 87 tax items that were subject to review and approval and began conducting list-based management on each item. The *Rules on Taxation Service for Tax Authorities at the County Level* took effect on 1 October 2014, which set 1120 rules on 212 service items of 9 major categories and 72 subcategories in terms of data provision, procedures and time frame. According to GAT, starting from 1 April 2016, small-scale VAT payers can make tax declarations on a quarterly basis in principle. The Henan provincial branch of the State Taxation Bureau has delegated approval power for 16 items from provincial and municipal tax bureaus to those at county and district levels, raising the number of approval items for county and district bureaus to 44, or 69% of the total items for approval in Henan. Since August 2015, national and local tax bureaus in Shanxi Province have explored new methods of cooperative tax services to ensure "seamless connections" for tax payers. The local branch of the State Tax Bureau in Ningxia Hui Autonomous Region scrapped 57 or 65.5% of the tax approval items, consolidated 206 services, removed requirements on 185 types of declaration materials, cut the ratio of materials submitted by tax payers for routine tax-related services by 52.6% and narrowed the processing time by over 30%. In addition, services for 118 items, such as tax registration and collection, invoice keeping and tax reliefs, can be accessed at the government tax service center.[8]

Problems with the Taxation System in the Context of Building a Leaner Government

I. Tax policies are not fully backed by laws.

First, the legal system on taxation is incomplete, and the laws are adopted by legislative bodies at lower levels. Only three of the current 18 tax categories, namely, personal income tax, corporate income tax and vehicle and vessel tax, are enacted

[8] Yang (2016).

by the National People's Congress. The legal system on tax collection and management and law enforcement remain weak. Second, there are too many improper local preferential tax policies. To stimulate growth, local governments have expanded the scope of such policies without seeking legal mandates and offer covert tax credits and incentives for businesses and individuals such as proportional tax rebates, subsidies, supports and rewards in violation of the principle of law-based taxation and unified tax codes.

II. The tax sharing regime between the central and local governments is not well conceived.

Tax categories are unevenly divided between the central and local governments. The ratio of VAT revenue between them is 75:25, which to some extent boosts the quantitative growth of the local economy but overlooks structural problems such as duplicated projects and overcapacity. The fact that local authorities bear 7.5% of the tax rebate on exports has dampened the enthusiasm of entry port cities in foreign trade and hinders the flow of production resources and goods across regions. Local taxation systems remain weak. For example, local tax categories are mostly underdeveloped, which affects the stability of local revenue sources. Nontaxable incomes are disproportionally high in some regions, and a few primary-level governments face financial difficulties. Progress is slow in the tax-sharing reform under the provincial level.

III. Obstacles remain in building a single market.

The policy of "eating from separate bowls" places too much emphasis on local interests. It allows local governments to control SOEs and collect fiscal revenues from them under the segmented administrative relations between them. Local governments therefore favor industries that can generate more tax revenues and opt for market segmentation. This has resulted in impeded cross-regional trade, lower economic efficiency, tax credits abuses and poor-quality and duplication of development projects. The tax-sharing reform has failed to remove tax incentives in the form of rebates and unfair policies aimed at attracting investment in some localities. The problems of redundancy in development projects and market segmentation among regions remain to be solved. All this has seriously violated the principles of the tax codes and fair competition on the market to the detriment of the structural improvement of the tax regime and the creation of a unified market.

IV. Socioeconomic needs in the new era cannot be fully met.

The layout of tax categories is unbalanced, and regulation is either nonexistent or overlapping. Value-added tax and business tax are separately levied on goods and services, and double taxation exists, which is not conducive to industrial upgrading. VAT revenue is shared by the central and local governments based on the sources, which to some extent has quantitatively boosted the growth of the economy. Resource tax collection is volume-based, and the scope of collection is narrow, which does not help with resource conservation and ecological protection. The high proportion for indirect tax and the unreasonably low proportion for direct tax have, to a certain extent, eroded the role of taxation as an automatic economic stabilizer.

V. Irregularities in replacing tax with fees persist.

China's fiscal system was under frequent change before the tax-sharing reform. In this context, local governments tend to put their own interests above others. This resulted in a segmented economy, poor management of extrabudgetary funds and a huge increase in extrabudgetary funds mainly through fee collection. The central government also relied on extrabudgetary funds for fiscal expenditures. The rising share of extrabudgetary funds in fiscal revenue of both the central and local governments made it more difficult to properly manage the national economy and could easily breed corruption. After the tax-sharing reform, the central government gradually moved extrabudgetary funds into the budget to further improve fiscal management and increase revenue. However, impulse remains for local governments to expand the size of the extrabudgetary funds. Between 1994 and 2013, the proportion of tax revenue to fiscal income nationwide fell from 98.25% to 85.54%, and the share of nontax revenue in fiscal income increased year by year. In a number of regions, there are just too many fee items that have squeezed out the tax base and encroached upon the role of tax as the main source of the government's fiscal revenue. At the same time, serious problems remain in fee collection, including unauthorized fee items, mounting fee burden on businesses and farmers, replacing tax with fees, misappropriation of fees collected, relying on fees for wage payments and institutional expansions.

Tasks and Suggestions

I. A law-based taxation regime

A law-based taxation regime underpins the reform of administrative streamlining in this field.

The principle of law-based taxation must be established and respected. A sound taxation regime must be in place to regulate the behaviors of market players and coordinate the taxation relationship between the government and the market and between the central and local governments. Legislation should speed up to strengthen the legal framework of taxation. Provisional tax regulations need to be codified, and legislations on taxation should be elevated to higher levels. Taxation should be managed in strict accordance with law to uphold unity, integrity and authority of the government. The scope of discretion should be narrowed, and tax relief policies should be better regulated.

II. Adequate incentives for all relevant parties

The reform will not succeed under too much government intervention. Therefore, the government must transform its functions by cutting or giving away the power that does not fit into the market economy, making best efforts in areas of its responsibility and letting the market take care of what it should. Unequal treatment placed by the existing taxation code on different market players must be gradually removed. The government should withdraw from the direct allocation of resources as much as possible. Local authorities should be discouraged from the single-minded pursuit of the economic growth rate and lavish spending on project investment. They should also rectify the practice of distorting resource prices, market mechanisms and resource allocation through tax relief policies and fiscal subsidies. Steps should be taken to promote free competition and an unimpeded flow of resources, invigorate market players and improve the socialist market economy. Mao Zedong was right in saying that "initiatives taken by both the central and local governments are much better than those coming from either side."[9] The success of the 1994 tax-sharing reform was attributed to the establishment of an incentive mechanism through which everyone got what they earned and a nation-wide synergy was forged. The new taxation system should strengthen the power of the central government to exercise macro control and push forward important reforms for coordinated development among regions. Local governments must conscientiously uphold the authority of the central government by aligning their own development plans with the national plan. At the samc time, the central government must allow more flexibility when issuing policies to unleash creativity and protect the interests of local governments, give them more leeway and initiatives in the reform and boost the economic and social vitality of all localities.

III. A unified and simplified tax regime

The future taxation regime will be characterized by a single tax rate, a simplified system and a broader tax base. The goals of the streamlining administration in taxation include a better tax structure to prevent double taxation, a higher ratio of direct taxes and a strengthened position of tax revenue as the main channel for government fiscal income.[10] Direct taxes should serve as an "automatic stabilizer" and "income adjuster". Price on goods and services should be less distorted by indirect taxes, and the market should play a larger role in resource allocation, as local governments are encouraged to shift the growth model. The government should improve VAT by simplifying the rates, removing undue concessions, promoting legislations, ensuring full coverage on eligible goods and services and putting an end to double taxation. The sales tax should play a better role as its coverage extends to products of energy-intensive and high-pollution industries and some luxury goods. It will be collected at the wholesale or retail end instead of when goods are produced or imported. The tax base will be expanded, and the tax source will be evenly distributed among regions. The relations between natural resources and related fees and taxes should be straightened out. A price-based resource tax should be introduced. Reforms will be launched on taxes and fees of coal, crude oil and natural gas. Administrative charges and government fund management should be better regulated. Administrative charges may be converted to business charges levied by the state. Fees that help fulfill

[9] Zedong (1999, p. 31).

[10] Zhang (2014).

government responsibilities and carry the features of taxes should be replaced by corresponding taxes. In this way, fees and taxes will perform their due functions to ensure good order of the market, cut business cost and encourage market investment.

IV. Reviewing and regulating preferential tax policies

Placing preferential tax policies under check helps ensure fair competition[11] in a unified market, creates a level playing field for market players of all kinds and allows the market to play a decisive role in resource allocation. The measure is part of the government's effort to improve macro-regulation and promote economic transformation. Policies that disrupt fair competition should be removed. Other preferential policies should also be placed under check to establish a long-term regulatory system. A whistle-blowing system must be in place to strengthen supervision. A better revenue distribution relationship should be set up between the central and local governments. The impulse of the local authorities to issue tax relief policies for revenue generation purposes should be discouraged. All kinds of preferential tax policies in effect should be placed under review. The mandate for issuing such policies should be given to a single authority. Nontax revenue and fiscal expenditure should be subject to strict regulation. Efforts should be made to gradually move regional-based preferential policies to sectorial-based ones in accordance with the industrial growth guidelines to nurture a single market and promote the free flow of goods and resources.

V. Capacity of modernized tax collection and management

Tax collection and management should meet the needs of the socialist market economy. The layout and functions of government departments, especially tax authorities at all levels, should be improved. Tax procedures should be simplified. The front desk of the taxation center shall be responsible for handling all tax-related matters instead of simply directing taxpayers to go to different rooms according to service types. New ways of tax management should be employed in which taxpayers are divided into different categories based on the results of the risk analysis, tax payment evaluation and tax inspections. The focus may shift from overall fraud prevention to targeted monitoring. A sound tax service system and platform with more efficient processing capabilities must be set up. The internal information management system should promote the integrity and sharing of tax data. The tax authorities should give a full mandate to the front desk and define the rights and responsibilities of tax collectors and payers. Tax collection should be law-based and IT-supported. All taxes payable should be collected. Excessive tax and fee collection must be banned. A fair and equitable environment that covers all areas of taxation is needed to promote tax reforms, welcome new technologies and adapt to various tax sources. Taxation and compliance costs must be lowered, and powerful data support should be available to serve taxpayers as well as tax collection, management and relevant decision-making. Big data should be used to address the inconsistency of standards and fragmented information and reduce institutional uncertainties, information asymmetry and labor input. Fairness in taxation and legislative support in this

[11] Notice of the State Council on Reviewing and Regulating Preferential Policies for Taxation and Other Matters (2014, pp. 22–24).

area should be raised to promote administrative streamlining of the taxation system and socioeconomic development of China.

Bibliography

Jia, K. (2008). Three decades into China's fiscal and tax reform, a brief review. *Public Finance Research*, (10).

Jia, K. & Zhao, H. (2008). Three decades of China's fiscal reform: Policy implementation and institutional evolution. *Reform*, (5).

Li, L. & Wu, Q. (2013, November 2). Fiscal and taxation reform: Promoting China's economic transformation. People's Daily.

Lou, J. (2015). *Deepening the reform of the fiscal and taxation system*. People's Publishing House.

Mao, Z. (1999). *Works of Mao Zedong* (Vol. 7). People's Publishing House.

Notice of the state council on reviewing and regulating preferential policies for taxation and other matters. *State Council Gazette*, (35) (2014).

Shen, Y. (2016). Addition and subtraction have multiplying effect in cutting red tapes. *Gongchan-cangren*, (5).

The decision of the CPC central committee on matters concerning the establishment of the socialist market economic system. *State Council Gazette*, (28) (1993).

The decision of the CPC central committee on several major issues concerning comprehensively deepening the reform. *People's Daily*, (2013, November 16).

Xue, C. (2014). Tax for fee reform of the Shanxi government saved RMB 17 billion or more for coal companies. *Shanxi Cai Shui*, (12).

Zhang, R. (2014). A new round of fiscal and tax reform is launched to strengthen state governance—Interpretation by Lou Jiwei, minister of finance on deepening the fiscal and tax reform. *China State Finance*, (14).

Administrative Streamlining and Mixed Ownership Reform

Yang Hao and Zhe Liu

Administrative streamlining and mixed ownership reform have been two important reform measures taken since 2013. They are pressing reform tasks at the forefront of all the reform programs and were included in the five key reform areas determined by the State Council at its meeting in 2014. Administrative streamlining and mixed ownership are mutually supporting and reinforcing instead of moving on parallel tracks. They both aim at balancing relations between the government on one end and businesses and the market on the other. In this article, the author discusses the relations between administrative streamlining and the mixed ownership reform in the context of the progress made thus far, puts forward policy recommendations and analyses legal issues concerning the reform.

Mixed Ownership Reform is an Important Propeller for Administrative Streamlining

I. Administrative streamlining characterizes the SOE reform.

The mixed ownership reform has been viewed as a major strategy of the SOE reform since the third Plenary Session of the 18th CPC Central Committee in 1978, the one that pushed the SOE reform into a new phase. As key pillars of China's planned economy, SOEs were seen as an extension of government agencies rather than independent economic entities before 1978, since their production plans, wages, awards and profit distribution were all arranged by the government. Their efficiency proved to be very low under the planned economy. As a Chinese saying goes, when all means are exhausted, changes become necessary; once changes are made, things will

Y. Hao (✉)
State Administration of Foreign Exchange Investment Center, Beijing, China

Z. Liu
State Food and Drug Administration, Beijing, China

Y. Li and Z. Cheng (eds.), *The Chinese Path Toward a Leaner Government*,
https://doi.org/10.1007/978-981-19-6718-4_8

improve. SOE reform naturally asserts as the main battlefield of China's economic reform.

Issues coming out of SOEs originally were around undue intervention by the government in their management, so the reform for that period was more about the delegation of government power back to enterprises. Administrative streamlining and power delegation fully characterized the reform of SOEs in the early days. In October 1978, six SOEs in Sichuan Province were the first to try the policy of delegating power and transferring profit from the government to enterprises. The first shot of China's SOE reform was fired. (Wenkui & Dongming, 2008). However, this policy gradually gave rise to a serious imbalance in profit distribution. Later measures such as the "economic responsibility system" (whereby the SOEs turned over a fixed amount of profit to the government and kept what remained), "profit to tax" (whereby corporate tax for large and medium-sized SOEs took up 55% of their profit) and "contract system" (whereby a fixed baseline of profit was set, and companies kept the excess and made up for the deficiencies). However, these measures bore a huge cost of bargaining and contained many loopholes.

The early period of SOE reform lays bare the difficulty in power delegation. Giving away all administrative power over SOEs (such as the contract system) could stimulate vitality for the time being, but the lack of a long-term business strategy due to absence of specific corporate owners led to quite a few moral hazards for business operation. This period of SOE reform was haunted by the doomed cycle in which power delegation led to market disorder, which, in turn, resulted in tighter control.

It was not until the mid- and late 1980s that the joint stock reform on enterprise ownership dominated the SOE restructuring. The reform was the best way to define ownership and cultivate independent market players and ultimately create a proper incentive mechanism (Yining, 1991). The performance of SOEs gradually improved with the joint stock reform, but the reform was unable to straighten out the relations between the government and SOEs. This was because in companies dominated by state capital, decisions were mainly based on opinions made by the state assets administrative bodies who also held final decision-making power on key appointments, while the board was more ceremonial. Compared with private businesses, SOEs were less flexible in management models and less effective in remuneration incentives. It was in this context that the mixed ownership reform gradually stepped into the front stage.

Mixed ownership was developed spontaneously in the ownership reform of SOEs. The joint stock reform produced a large number of state-holding companies of mixed ownership, as some of their stocks were held by employees and local private businesses. In 2013, the *Decision of the CPC Central Committee on Certain Major Issues Concerning Comprehensively Deepening the Reform* (hereafter referred to as the *Decision*) was released at the third Plenary Session of the 18th CPC Central Committee. According to the *Decision*, China will encourage companies to set up mixed ownership. Mixed ownership, which allows integration and crossing-holding for state capital, collective capital and non-publicly owned capital, is an important form of the basic economic system. Thus, the concept of mixed ownership became widely known, and the reform in this direction was established as the forefront of the SOE reform.

Corporate governance can establish mixed ownership through the participation of private capital. In mixed ownership companies, the government exercises the rights of state-owned shareholders through the board of directors without conducting direct management. By doing so, the role of the government shifts from managing corporate employees and business to capital management. The essence of mixed ownership reform is to clarify the boundary between the government, enterprises and the market. Cutting government administration and shifting management power to SOEs is the guiding principle of the reform.

II. Mixed ownership reform forces state asset regulators to delegate power.

Cutting power is a "self-initiated reform" of the government, which in itself is not easy. Our field study shows that only mixed ownership of equity can push for the transformation of the government's role in SOEs.

The field study was carried out in 2014 on companies of mixed ownership in Ma'anshan, an important industrial city in Anhui Province that saw the creation of several "mixed ownership" enterprises during the last round of SOE reform. We asked the executives of these companies a question: "If the corporate governance of private companies is a better choice, why did you go an extra mile by only attracting private capital instead of shifting directly to its corporate governance?" The answers were almost the same. "The structure of capital determines the way of governance. In other words, private capital would not work with us if the newly established mixed-ownership enterprises retain the old SOE governance model." In this sense, mixed ownership not only forces companies to set up a corporate governance structure but also compels state assets regulators to cut and delegate their power.

The most effective regulators competent authorities, SASAC, employees' representatives meeting, tax authorities, CPC organizations within enterprises, board of directors, shareholders' meeting, board of supervisors.

Chart 1 Mixed ownership reform and transformation of industrial regulators (research findings in Ma'anshan)

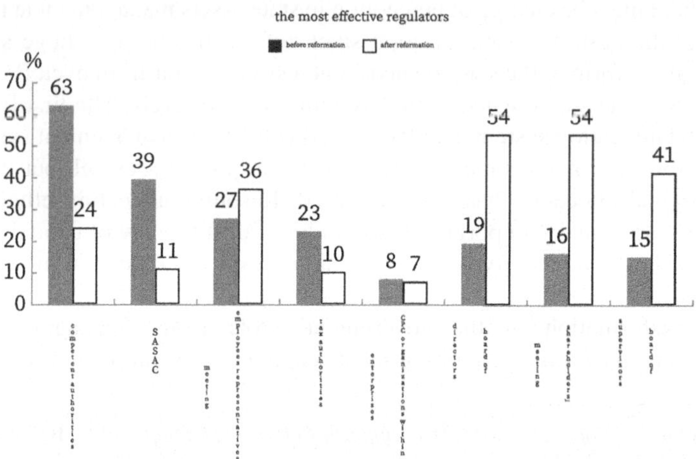

We conducted a questionnaire survey in Ma'anshan. A total of 102 questionnaires were distributed, and 99 valid questionnaires were collected, including 36 from the government, 14 from SOE executives and 49 from company employees. The findings show that after the reform, the most effective supervisor of the companies changed from "the government" and "state assets administrative commissions" to "board of directors" and "shareholders' meeting". This shows that transformation of the ownership structure has indeed improved corporate governance and forced the role shift of state assets administrative bodies.

The release of the *Decision* was soon followed by reform plans adopted by various localities for local SOEs focusing on the development of mixed ownership. In Beijing, companies with less than 50% state ownership may no longer follow the SOE regulatory system.[1] As the original management measures taken by the government for SOEs are not necessarily applicable to mixed ownership companies, the reform pushed for change of measures on part of state assets administrative bodies to streamline administration and delegate power.

Power Delegation Underpins Mixed Ownership

I. Perception change in the government is crucial to the success of the mixed ownership reform.

Changes in the government's perception of SOEs and state assets are crucial for the mixed ownership reform to succeed. The reform will not come through unless the government redefines the power boundary and revises the management mode of state assets. It is a self-targeted reform of the government focusing on furthering streamlining administration and delegating power. When the power is partially transferred to companies and the market, certain interest groups will feel upset, and vested interests are a barrier hard to overcome. Therefore, the change of perception is fundamental in the reform. Misunderstanding of state asset management must be addressed, and the first, there must be change of perception in state assets management at the macro level. Over the past 30 years, the joint stock reform has brought huge success to SOEs, but the reform of the state-owned capital system is far from over. Professor Li Yining divides the state-owned capital system into two levels. The first level is the state capital allocation system, and the second is the SOE management system. The reform of the SOE management system has been quite successful, but the reform on state capital allocation has not yet started. Resource allocation efficiency and productivity are equally important. It would be against the law of capital to merely focus on raising productivity instead of making resource allocation more efficient. (Yining, 2013).

The transformation of the government's role from "managing corporate employees and business" to "monitoring the capital" helps improve the efficiency of

[1] The *Guidelines on Comprehensively Deepening the Reform of Municipal SOEs*, Beijing Municipal Government, August 2014.

state asset allocation by channeling them more to areas in need. Research findings (Shanwen, 2016) show that the average proportion of state-owned capital in industries of overcapacity[2] was as high as 50.5%. The higher the proportion of state-owned capital is, the faster the performance declines, as has been the case in recent years. The survey raised two issues. First, the efficiency of state-owned capital allocation is low. State-owned capital is unable to be promptly transferred to industries with higher economic performance when the economic cycle changes. Second, the high proportion of state-owned capital blocks or delays proper functioning of the market exit mechanism because when SOEs see their performance deteriorate, they will go all out to seek support from local governments instead of following the market rules. The evaluation of state asset management should not be based on the performance of certain companies. Instead, it should be carried out at the macro level of capital allocation to better facilitate its flow into areas that generate better performance.

Second, management philosophy on SOEs at the micro level should also change. The government can no longer apply the traditional management methods for SOEs to companies with mixed ownership. The traditional system of personnel management must be replaced by a new system based on the *Company Law* under the principle of one share for one vote and an equal right for an equal share. The original management thinking should also give way to corporate governance whereby the government exercises its shareholder's rights as the owner of the state capital by participating in the corporate governance of companies of mixed ownership. That is how its role changes from "management" to "governance".

It is particularly important to stress that in companies with mixed ownership, the government should not set limits on remuneration incentives. In the past, executives of SOEs had administrative titles, and their salary was determined accordingly. This practice has been under criticism for failure to tie how much work they do with how much they earn. The arrangement might seem reasonable in those days when there were too many SOEs for state assets administrative bodies to allow each one to have its own renumeration system. The government had no other way but to adopt a "one-size-fits-all" approach on the total amount of the salary. According to some surveys, the greater the government intervenes in businesses, the weaker the measurement and evaluation role of accounting performance. This means that the "one-size-fits-all" approach hurts the vitality of state-owned enterprises. In mixed ownership companies, the government as a shareholder should participate in remuneration setting through the board of directors and the remuneration committee.

In addition, the principle of equal rights for equal shares should apply to government and private shareholders alike in mixed ownership enterprises. Provisions on special interests of state capital should be limited. In competitive industries, caution is needed in setting up golden shares and other preferred shares. At the current stage, private investors still hold a relatively conservative attitude toward the reform out of concern over the inadequate protection of private capital in mixed ownership

[2] Industries of overcapacity include coal mining and washing; ferrous metal smelting and extended pressure processing; nonferrous metal smelting and extended pressure processing; ferrous metal mining and nonferrous metal mining.

enterprises. Provisions on special rights of state-owned equity will only increase the worries of private investors and clear the way for the government to intervene, which is against the reform plan of cutting government power in businesses.

Third, cutting government power is not the end in itself. The ultimate goal is not to make the government smaller but to make it more efficient and make sure that it concentrates on its due responsibilities. In the mixed ownership reform, the government needs to carry out top-level design and explain in advance a number of important issues. For example, which industries are suitable for promoting mixed ownership reform? Is there a minimum proportion requirement of state-owned shares in mixed ownership companies for different industries? How can the loss of state-owned assets be addressed during the transfer of state-owned shares?

II. Managing the board directors should be on the duty list of state assets watchdogs.

State-owned asset supervision and administration commissions (SASAC) at all levels take the main responsibility for administrative streamlining and power delegation in the mixed ownership reform. It is important to produce a duty list for SASACs to check the progress of moving from "managing corporate employees and business" to "managing assets". As their current list of administrative powers is short, the room for having a shorter list is limited. Therefore, the reform will focus on the list of duties.

According to the power list published by 47 departments of the State Council in 2014, SASAC only has one item for review and approval. It is about the professional titles of political and ethical work staff of central enterprises in the category of non-administrative license approval. The administrative power lists of most local SASACs are also short. For example, the list of administrative powers and responsibilities of Shanghai municipal SASAC only contains supervision of ownership transactions of state-owned assets and two other items. This means that reform of SASAC at all levels should focus on adjusting and improving their supervisory functions, or in other words, cutting red tape in performing specific duties.

According to the *Field Study Report on Adjusting and Improving Local SASACs Supervisory Functions for a Better System of Sate-owned Assets Supervision* released by the SASAC of the State Council in July 2015, SASACs in Tianjin, Shanghai, Jiangsu and 13 other localities had prepared the list of duty items by the end of April 2015. Items outside the list shall be determined by companies on their own. This has helped shift some power from SASACs to businesses.

However, we noticed that the current reform measures are not enough for establishing a sound supervision and selection mechanism for the board directors of SOEs. In a company of mixed ownership, the board director or chairman appointed by SASAC will participate in the business management of the company on behalf of SASAC under the framework of corporate governance. Therefore, when the SASAC delegates more power to enterprises, it also needs to assign equally important duties to board directors acting on their behalf to ensure a balance of power and responsibilities.

The following three issues on board directors need to be addressed. First, how can board directors be selected to represent state-owned shareholders in mixed ownership companies? Are directors selected from government agencies or the companies themselves? Second, how can their performance be evaluated? Third, do they keep their administrative rankings?

Expectations on Reform Results Are Met Through Legal Improvement

The *Decision* calls for the development of a mixed ownership economy. It is a policy document that sets the goals and program of action for further deepening reform in an all-around way. The rule of law is indispensable because the right policy goals and program of action need to be achieved through concrete measures. The guidance and support from the rule of law will push the reform to move forward on the right track. General Secretary Xi Jinping has repeatedly stressed that all major reform programs must be law-based. The rule of law must serve to guide and propel the whole process of reform. Efforts must be made to strengthen the coordination of legislative work to ensure that reform is carried out under the legal framework. Legislative improvement is fundamental to the success of the mixed ownership reform driven by administrative streamlining and power delegation.

I. Necessity

Despite progress made in China's mixed ownership reform, there are still many challenges to overcome. The greatest challenges include complex relations between state assets supervisors and SOEs, weak corporate governance, and unequal treatment between state-owned capital and private capital. These have added to the uncertainties of private investors who are thinking of joining the mixed ownership reform, making them less enthusiastic and more hesitant. The key to securing further progress of the reform lies in the right approach and solution to the abovementioned challenges.

The solution lies in the rule of law. Laws are needed to draw up measures and set expectations for the reform. The legal system can define the boundary between the government and the market and set the code of conduct for the government and market players. The rule of law aims to promote the freedom of market transactions and guarantee their security. It restrains the power of the government and ensures that the government plays its due role. Laws, properly conceived and implemented, will help the government better streamline administration and delegate power to boost the growth of industries with mixed ownership. It will further strengthen the controlling power and weight of a more vibrant state-owned sector and improve its abilities to mitigate risks, all in an effort to meet the goal of national prosperity.

II. Better institutional protection for property rights

A leaner government is essential in facilitating mixed ownership reform. In building a leaner government, state asset supervisors need to focus on capital management instead of managing personnel and business matters. The success hinges on how the corporate governance structure and the relevant legal system can better protect property rights and interests of investors representing various ownerships in the mixed ownership enterprises and provide incentives for their participation in sectors of mixed ownership.[3]

1. Different descriptions in law

It must be admitted that there are differences between the legal provisions of public property and private property. Their descriptions are different in the *Constitution*, the fundamental law of the state, which emphasizes that "public property is inviolable" and describes private property as being "protected by law".[4] Like the *Constitution*, other laws and regulations also differ in their descriptions of public property and private property and relevant rights protection. The *Criminal Law* provides special protection for state-owned assets. For example, the provision on "quasi-government functionaries" in Article 93 of the *Criminal Law*[5] reflects special protection for state-owned assets. The *Criminal Law* of China puts state employees under stringent oversight. It also provides for strict control over state-owned companies and their leaders appointed by the government as "government employees", with the purpose of strengthening the protection of state-owned assets. Those who commit crimes specified in Article 165–169 and the crime of "unauthorized division of state-owned assets" in Article 396 of the *Criminal Law*[6] are narrowed to persons working in

---

[3] According to the *Guidelines of the State Council on the Development of Mixed Ownership in State-owned Enterprises* (Guo Fa [2015] No. 54), one of the basic principles of developing mixed ownership is "institutional improvement and property protection. This includes property and contract protection, a single market, equal exchange, fair competition and effective regulation. In this way, property rights and interests of investors of mixed ownership enterprises will be fully protected, and enthusiasm of investors of all kinds of ownerships to participate in the development of mixed ownership sectors will increase".

[4] Article 12 of the *Constitution* stipulates that socialist public property is inviolable. The state protects socialist public property. Appropriation or damaging of state or collective property by any organization or individual in whatever means is prohibited. Article 13 states that a citizen's lawful private property is inviolable. The state protects the right of citizens to own and inherit private property in accordance with the law. The state may, in order to meet the needs of the public interest, expropriate or requisition a citizen's private property in accordance with the law and make due compensations.

[5] The "scope of state functionaries" in Article 93 of the *Criminal Law*: the term "state functionaries" as used in this law refers to those engaged in public service in state organs. Public servants in state-owned companies, enterprises, institutions or people's organizations and those assigned by state organs, state-owned companies, enterprises or institutions to nonstate-owned companies, enterprises or public organizations for public service, as well as other persons who perform public service in accordance with the law, shall be regarded as state functionaries.

[6] Crimes listed in Article 165–169 are: the crime of illegally engaging in the same business area as the one he is employed to work in; the crime of making illegal gains for friends or relatives; the crime of fraud inducing dereliction of duty in entering or performing a contract; dereliction of duty by personnel of state-owned companies, enterprises and institutions; the crime of abuse of power by

state-owned organizations such as government organs, SOEs and public institutions. This aims to protect the interests of SOEs and public institutions.

In private laws such as the Property Law, the Contract Law and the Company Law, emphasis is laid on equal treatment and protection to both public and private property. In reality, however, the treatments are far different because of the differences in the identity between public and private property. It is easier for state-owned enterprises than private companies to obtain government projects or loans from commercial banks. Moreover, when economic disputes arise between state-owned and private businesses, SOEs are better protected, while private companies often end up losing the case no matter how hard they try. The reality seems just the opposite of the vision set for protecting property rights and developing mixed ownership.

2. Protecting property rights of all kinds of investors

Public property has a public nature, as it involves the legal interests of the public. Unlike private property, however, it does not have a specific protector. As a result, it is more vulnerable to infringement. In this sense, it is justifiable to place it under special protection by the law. The mixed ownership reform must not lower the protection of state-owned assets as public property, affect returns of state-owned assets, or allow losses of state-owned assets to occur. That said, it is more important at this stage to highlight the concept of equal protection. The *Decision* explicitly states that "the property rights of the public and nonpublic sectors are both inviolable." The expression is clear, as is the commitment of the CPC to changing the status quo. For the socialist market economy to take shape, China must fully understand, respect and apply the basic rules of the market economy and let the market play a decisive role in the allocation of resources. The country's economic environment has changed, but the laws have not been updated, which has given rise to mounting issues relating to inadequate regulation and protection of the mixed ownership sector.

To nurture the mixed ownership sector, a well-developed modern property rights system must be codified. The system of property rights protection should be improved to properly protect the rights and interests of all kinds of investors and grant them equal access to resources and a level playing ground. The market should also be given clear and reasonable expectations. It is important to achieve the following: first, the law should spell out equal protection and equal regulatory treatment for public and private property to meet the needs of further development of mixed ownership. Second, specific measures should be taken to ensure law enforcement and prevent unequal treatment in practice. Third, special treatment for state-owned assets out of consideration of national security and national interests should be made public in the form of laws to prevent under-the-table dealing that might weaken the protection of state-owned assets. Transparency will boost investors' confidence in joining the reform and help them make informed decisions.

It is worth noting that protecting state-owned assets is not bound to conflict with providing equal protection and regulatory treatment to public and private property.

---

personnel of a state-owned company, enterprise or institution; the crime of converting state-owned assets to shares at low prices or selling them for personal gains.

The clause on special protection of state-owned assets in the Criminal Law is a case in point. Similar to the Criminal Law of 1979, the current Criminal Law also divides companies into state-owned and nonstate-owned companies based on their ownership (Xiaoping, 2008). The shift to the market economy over these years has resulted in profound changes in the ownership structure. With the emergence and development of mixed ownership companies, a business model has taken shape featuring diversified investment, mutual penetration and integration of state-owned, collective and private capital. The Criminal Law currently in effect repeatedly emphasizes the protection of state-owned assets in "state-owned companies and enterprises" but fails to provide for the protection of state-owned assets in the mixed ownership sector, which has weakened the protection of state-owned assets. In contrast, providing equal protection and regulatory treatment to both public and private property means protecting property rights of all investors and ensures that property rights in both public and nonpublic sectors are equally inviolable. Protecting all investors and property rights in both public and nonpublic sectors on an equal basis and punishing infringements will, on the contrary, expand the much-needed legal coverage of state-owned asset protection in mixed ownership companies. What undermines state-owned asset protection is not the concept of equal protection or integration of the legal framework for both state and nonstate-owned assets. Rather, efforts should be made to prevent the loss of state-owned assets during the mixed ownership reform.

3. Preventing the loss of state-owned assets

Preventing the loss of state-owned assets is an issue of keen public interest in both mixed ownership reform and government power delegation. Openness and proper regulation are both critical to the success of this task.

First, there should be an open process in setting the rules. Social intermediaries and individuals need to have a role in the drafting of government policies and SOE reform plans to mitigate the risk that policies and reform plans only serve the interests of those who draft them as well as concerns over inadequate sincerity or even fair play in the SOE reform (Yue, 2015). Rules before action are essential in the reform of mixed ownership. The reform will not be fair if the rules are not fair.

Second, reform measures should be based on laws and regulations. It is important to follow such laws and regulations as the *Company Law*, the *Bidding Law*, the *Securities Law*, the *Law on the State-Owned Assets of Enterprises* and the *Measures for Supervision and Administration of the Transactions of State-Owned Assets of Enterprises*, especially their clauses on public disclosure. Internal and external oversight must be strengthened to forestall under-the-table dealing and insider trading. It will help prevent the loss of state-owned assets as much as possible and ease concerns over the loss of state-owned assets in the process of reform. On 1 July 2016, SASAC and the Ministry of Finance jointly issued the *Measures for Supervision and Administration of the Transactions of State-Owned Assets of Enterprises*, which specified rules on the corporate transactions of state-owned assets and explicitly required that additional equity offerings and asset transfer of SOEs should be carried out openly in the property rights trading institutions. All these measures help foster and expand a well-regulated property rights market and facilitate the reform process.

Third, price assessment of state-owned assets should be based on sound judgment. The qualification, service quality and independence of the evaluation institution are very important, and standard procedures must be followed to ensure reasonable pricing. To avoid insufficient assessment of intangible assets and profitability of the companies, the source of assessment information should not be limited to tangible assets. Finally, the impact of other factors on prices, such as equity, total assets and profitability, should be noted. As equity and profitability vary significantly between companies, asset prices reflect their real value instead of being miscalculated (Jide & Bingyao, 2015). In addition, independent evaluation and audit should be strengthened in the reform process to prevent shady operations in the mixed ownership reform of SOEs.

Conclusion

As two important reform measures launched in 2013, administrative streamlining and mixed ownership reform have been mutually supportive and reinforcing. The reform of mixed ownership is a new chapter of the SOE reform, and administrative streamlining, which characterizes the SOE reform, is a natural part of the mixed ownership reform. Measures taken by the SASAC to cut government power are crucial steps in pushing forward the mixed ownership reform. These reform measures are the result of the transformation in the thinking of the government. Policy goals and action plans are materialized through concrete measures, and the rule of law is essential. We must bear in mind the reality, build a sound legal system, keep a reasonable expectation of the reform and make steady progress.

Bibliography

Gao, S. Keeping to the right direction and waiting for the right time. Essence Securities 2016 Medium-term Strategy Meeting.

Li, Y. (1991) *The unbalanced Chinese economy*. The Economic Daily Press.

Li, Y. (2013). *Chinese economy in dual transition*. China Renmin University Press.

Li L. & Xiong, Q. (2014). Actively, steadily and orderly promote the pilot reform of the judicial system. *Qiushi*, (16).

Wu, Y. (2015). Issues and the rule of law in the SOE mixed ownership reform. *Tribune of Political Science and Law*, (33).

Zhu, X. (2008). Research on the criminal law protection of state-owned assets of mixed ownership enterprises. Unpublished doctor's dissertation, Shandong University.

Zhang, W. & Yuan, D. (2008). *30 years of economic reform in China (on SOEs)*. Chongqing University Press.

Zhang, J. & Wu, B. (2015). How to avoid the loss of state-owned assets in the reform of mixed ownership—A case study of Sinopec's mixed-ownership reform. *Friends of Accounting*, (19).

SOE Restructuring and Streamlining Administration: Incentives and Constraints

Yuanfeng Zang

As an important part of the reform of state-owned enterprises (SOEs), restructuring creates new forms of governance for SOEs and represents a transformation of the economic system. It aims to ensure that "production relations" are attuned to match "productive forces". It is also a process of building a modern enterprise system. The efforts generally bring about changes in three areas. The first concerns the form of the company that includes the way corporate capital is organized and how corporate governance is structured. The second area is the company's ownership structure. The third involves reforms of the company's internal system. SOE restructuring is important as it helps to put in place a modern corporate system and transform government functions toward the goal of building a sound socialist market economy.

Remarkable progress has been made in SOE restructuring since the late 1970s. However, while playing an important role in introducing market rules to SOEs, it has also encountered quite a few challenges, such as the loss of state-owned assets and higher corporate debt ratio. The core issues include change or transfer of ownership. "Taking orders from the government" makes the company less competitive, but "cutting government's control power" would result in rapid loss of state-owned assets. That is why little progress was made in the transformation of government functions, especially in administrative streamlining, and the restructuring of SOEs was put on hold. The decision was made after the 18th National Party Congress in 2012 to take the shifting of government functions as a central task in the reform of the country's administrative system. The commitment to build a leaner government with streamlining administrative review and approval as the first step has opened new possibilities for SOE reform. It brought the reform into the phase of institutional innovation. The following is an analysis of the state-owned capital system, corporate governance structure, ownership transaction and internal management in

Y. Zang (✉)
Guanghua School of Management, Peking University, Shenhua Guohua Electric Power Research Institute, Beijing, China

Y. Li and Z. Cheng (eds.), *The Chinese Path Toward a Leaner Government*,
https://doi.org/10.1007/978-981-19-6718-4_9

the process of the corporatization (joint-stock system) reform of SOEs in the context of streamlining administration and delegating power.

Reform of the State-Owned Capital System

As the focal point of China's economic restructuring, the restructuring of SOEs is closely related to the reform of the state-owned capital system. Both hinge on the success of transforming government functions. Since the late 1970s, notable changes have taken place in the basic structure of China's corporate system. The dominating status of state ownership was gradually given way to the creation of multiple ownerships. The government, as the owner of state-owned assets, began to shift its roles from business management back to social and economic governance. The establishment of the State Administration of State-owned Assets in 1988 was highly symbolic. From then on, the government began focusing on economic and social governance while putting state-owned assets in the hands of one specific department instead of many. The department responsible for the administrative oversight of SOEs was revoked in the 1998 reform of government institutions. State-owned asset supervision and administration commissions (SASAC) were set up at the central and local levels in 2003. Thus, the government's identity as the state capital investor was established, representing a large step toward separating government administration from business management in SOEs and applying market rules to these companies.

The establishment of SASAC has been instrumental to the growth of the state-owned economy. It promotes the separation of government administration from business management and the separation of ownership rights from management rights. SOEs began to make business decisions on their own and take care of their own profits and losses. The SASAC guarantees the maintenance and increment of state-owned assets. On the other hand, however, it tends to follow a highly administrative work process due to inadequate knowledge of the responsibilities of an investor. For example, it often acts as an intermediary for government departments at all levels by giving orders to SOEs. Offices at higher administrative levels are responsible for regulating those under them. These are undoubtedly redundant functions that do not match the status of an investor. The rights, obligations and roles of SASAC have not been harmonized.

In addition, there are challenges in the property relations of SOEs. Although decisions were made at the third Plenary Session of the 14th CPC National Party Congress to separate investor ownership from the corporate property rights of SOEs, which laid a solid foundation for the joint-stock reform of SOEs, the line between ownership and corporate property rights and relevant rights and responsibilities remains too blurred for a modern corporate system. Under the current system whereby the SASAC's mandate covers state-owned assets, core personnel and key business decisions, there is no strict definition of the "corporate property rights" for SOEs. Therefore, SOEs only have "business management rights" rather than "corporate property rights" as enjoyed by other types of businesses.

Since SASAC's core mission is still supervision and administration of SOEs, the government has not fully retreated from corporate business management. Instead, it has a direct hand in the day-to-day operations of SOEs through project approval, administrative monopoly, market lockdown, credit intervention and price control. As a result, SOEs have not become genuine market players. They can only be called "semi-market players". Government intervention limits the role of the market in allocating resources. In some SOEs, the problem of "insider control" remains. In other words, the role change of the government is not complete. What the modern market economy needs is companies that make independent business decisions and assume responsibilities for their own profits and losses, or in other words, market players and corporate entities in real sense.

The restructuring of SOEs is a complex and systematic undertaking that requires compatibility between the institutional arrangements of SOEs and the general legal and policy environment. Full restructuring of SOEs hinges on progress in the institutional reform and transformation of government functions. A preliminary suggestion is to strengthen the power of SASAC and allocate state-owned capital based on a three-tier capital management structure encompassing SASAC, state investment fund corporations and SOEs. Under this structure, the SASAC is responsible only for allocating state-owned capital and maintaining and increasing its value. It allocates state-owned equities to state investment fund corporations that supervise and evaluate the capital management of SOEs in the capacity of their shareholders and decide whether to increase or reduce the investment of state-owned capital. These institutional reforms will further clarify corporate ownership as well as the rights and responsibilities of all relevant parties. A broad sense of state "ownership" is replaced by "ownership" narrowed to investors of SOEs, which is a notion different from the company's "property rights". The move will ensure that the investors will be able to effectively perform their duties, and the property rights of SOEs will be fully protected. More companies will then embrace market rules because they are open and fair. It will also fully mobilize SOEs, enhance its vitality and make them real market players. Moreover, it will improve the corporate governance structure of SOEs. To become real market players, SOEs must have a sound corporate system that includes shareholders' meetings, boards of directors, general managers and boards of supervisors and perform their rights of control and management effectively and properly. This will provide a strong institutional guarantee for further deepening of the SOE reform.

A Diverse Corporate Governance Structure

The main purpose for SOE restructuring is to break away from a monotonous governance structure. In this process, a diverse corporate governance structure is needed for SOEs to gain more vitality.

The ownership system is the basis for allocating and exercising limited resource management rights and an important factor in corporate organization and decision-making. It determines the motivation and decisions on resource allocation as well as the standard costs of business transactions, through which the structure of economic activities is established. There are basically two ways to determine the corporate governance structure on the basis of business ownership. One is to determine the form of enterprises under a given environment, such as the monotonous form of SOEs under the planned economy. The other is to limit the choice of corporate governance structure within the "assets portfolio" under the management of SOEs allowed by the ownership system. For example, the mixed ownership governance structure is formed under the system of joint development of all ownerships with public ownership as the mainstay. In other words, different ownerships set different rules and result in different corporate governance structures. Corporate ownership determines a company's governance structure.

The governance system of SOEs in China follows the trajectory of "proprietorship–partnership–corporation". Corporate transformation and the governance structure of SOEs are designed and guided by the government "in a reverse course". While the old governance system remains, SOEs have transitioned from traditional factories to corporations. They have gone through reforms such as transferring power and profits from government to enterprises, tax for profit, contract responsibility system, and establishing a corporate property system and governance structure that separates government functions from business management and distinguishes investors' ownership from corporate property rights. The government has played a major role in all these steps of the reform.

Traditional SOEs have their unique governance structure fit into their form of organization. They have specific ownership and corresponding supervision, incentive and restraint mechanisms. They belong to a single owner. There is only one property owner, one ownership structure, and one source of investment returns. As a result, there is only one governance system for these companies. Since the launch of the reform and opening-up, due to the effect of "path dependence", the traditional factory-like governance structure of SOEs has had a profound impact on the governance structure of SOEs during their transition to corporations, which has prolonged the above singularities that characterize SOEs.

It was decided at the third Plenary Session of the 14th CPC Central Committee held in the early 1990s that the goal of the SOE reform was to establish a modern enterprise system, in which the corporate governance structure was basically defined as a unilateral one under the control of constant capital. In other words, governance structure is based on equity ownership. A company, however, is a combination of multiple interests driven by constant and variable capital. Its governance structure should therefore be determined by both constant and variable capital. However, the absolute domination of corporate capital, constant capital in particular, no longer meets the need for a company's growth. Too much emphasis on the importance of shareholders in corporate governance while ignoring the desire of employees and creditors to engage in corporate governance has left a myriad of "gaps" in the process of restructuring with corresponding consequences. This has given rise to problems such as "insider control" and management corruption in building a modern enterprise system.

The root cause of "insider control" in SOEs is the absence of owners or difficulties in conducting effective supervision over management. Although the law has made it clear that SOEs are owned by the state, two issues remain. First, there is not yet a complete system on the property rights of SOEs that matches the system of state ownership. Second, the division and transfer of state ownership are difficult to carry out in both paper and practice. In this context, SOEs are unable to have a sound and effective corporate governance structure and thus inevitably fall into "insider control". In addition, in the process of corporate restructuring, SOEs are trying their best to be listed. This has exposed a number of weaknesses on part of China's state-owned capital structure and the capital market in choosing and incentivizing corporate management.

In other countries, the separation of corporate ownership and management takes a long time to complete. Governance structure varies in countries that are different in types and availability of organizational and market resources. However, countries with successful experience are common in one aspect. They all have mature financial markets and full-fledged legal systems. In the case of China, the priority is not a fixed governance structure paradigm but a good corporate property rights system and clear rules of the market economy. The most urgent imperative is to improve the financial market and relevant laws and regulations. In addition, as governance structure may vary significantly depending on the business environment for the company, the corporate governance structure and supervision mechanism are unique, diverse and ever-changing. A competitive market environment is the precondition for building an effective corporate system based on the separation of ownership and management.

Ownership reform is a necessary step to improve the governance structure of SOEs in China. Corporate restructuring entails a number of reform measures to address the key challenge of imbalance between the right to benefit and the right to control. The basic idea is to give full play to the role of the market and gradually push for transformation from state or collective ownership to diverse and mixed ownership. The growth of China's capital market and its institutional investors and better performance of SOEs will help more SOEs become market players with diverse ownership structures. It should be emphasized that improving the corporate governance structure is not limited to ownership reform. It also implies changes in the way of governance. The change of ownership may bring more development funds and opportunities to SOEs, but it does not necessarily mean improvement of their governance mechanisms. Therefore, further restructuring of SOEs should not take place through the traditional method of administrative power sharing. First, legislation is needed to improve the ownership system and define property rights and the power and responsibilities of stakeholders. This is fundamental to the transformation of corporate management mechanisms and paves the way for the free transfer of property rights and better resource allocation. Second, SOEs' state ownership and property rights must be clearly distinguished and defined. State ownership can be converted to ownership by SOE investors through the establishment of state investment fund corporations. This is the way to determine the corporate property rights that fit into the modern enterprise system so that SOEs are able to transfer property rights to some extent and become full market players that operate on their own and bear due responsibilities for profits made and losses incurred. Third, corporate property rights must be separated from management rights. A diverse corporate governance structure should be set up with a sound system encompassing shareholders' meetings, boards of directors, general managers and boards of supervisors.

Market for Corporate Property Trading

The property trading market is an important place for capital operation and exchange. It provides a fair, open and well-regulated platform for the transfer (sale) of state-owned property. In the restructuring of SOEs, corporatization (turning SOEs into joint-stock companies) is completed mainly through property sales, and this directly involves the value of state-owned assets. The value of the assets can be discovered most directly, efficiently and conveniently by the property trading market. As an essential part of the capital market, the property trading market can help prevent the dilution of state-owned assets or improper asset allocation.

Starting from the late 1970s, large changes have taken place in the way capital is allocated as China began to move from the planned economy to the market economy. Fiscal allocation by the government has gradually given way to market financing, and companies have been yearning for financing through the capital market. This calls for the creation of a property trading market. In addition, with the massive structural adjustment and development of the high-tech industry in recent years, the need for a property trading market has continued to rise.

In a market economy, funds and resources are allocated and redistributed mainly through the capital market. Companies raise funds on the capital market for business launch and growth. However, they do not rely on a single market for financing. A multitiered capital market should be created for companies of different sizes, performance and development phases. A property trading market can help address the uneven development of capital markets in eastern and western China and significantly promote the establishment of capital markets at various levels featuring mutual complementarity and reinforcement as well as coordinated development.

The property trading market should also be set up because of its importance to China's economic transformation and SOE reform. There is an urgent need to nurture a property trading market for strategic adjustment of the distribution of state-owned capital in different sectors and for SOE reforms. The market is also imperative to meet the funding needs for revitalizing China's Northeast, developing the western regions, and shifting government functions. It can also prevent the loss of state-owned assets and curb corruption.

Pulling state-owned capital out of competitive sectors is a long-term and arduous undertaking that involves consolidation, mergers, divestment, joint ventures and many other forms of restructuring. The property trading market will provide information, transaction rules and price evaluation for these economic activities to enhance the success rate and transaction efficiency. At present, the reorganization, ownership transfer, mergers and property transactions of SOEs are still the government's responsibility. This government-led reform model carries strong authority and can avoid disputes on rights and responsibilities to some extent, but the intensity and scope of this reform model are highly limited. "One-on-one" negotiation over the counter implies asymmetric information, a low success rate and loopholes and risks. If the role is given to the market, it will create more possibilities and provide an open and well-regulated trading place to prevent the loss of state-owned assets. Such a move will also promote the transformation of government functions.

The property trading market in China is beset with the following problems. First, the lack of macro regulation and policy guidance from the government and the absence of relevant laws and regulations have resulted in the uneven development of property trading markets between regions and ill-regulated transactions. Second, the functions of the property trading market need to be further improved. Third, a single national property trading market has yet to take shape. Incomplete market mechanisms have constrained property transactions to some extent.

To advance the SOE reform, efforts must be made to nurture the property trading market, particularly in the following three areas. First, a unified property exchange should be set up in each economic functional zone to bridge regional and industrial division. With the concentration of resources and information and unrestricted price bidding, transaction efficiency will be enhanced, and capital and resource imbalance among regions will be narrowed, thus creating a "unified, open, competitive and orderly" property trading system. Second, the property trading market should feature sound regulation and innovative mechanisms. Such a mechanism should tally with the modern market system to facilitate the shift of government functions from administration to supervision. The property exchange can act as a corporation and an investor in diverse sectors that operates on its own and bears responsibility for its profits and losses under the principle of a fair and open market. Third, explorations on new ways of property transaction should be made. In addition to fixed assets, transaction of equity, creditor's right and intellectual property should also be encouraged. Fourth, the self-discipline of the property trading market should be tightened. Based on industrial self-discipline practice, the regulatory regime of the property trading market should be strengthened to protect the lawful rights and interests of both sides of the transaction. Institutional building of industry associations should gather pace to ensure proper order of the market, improve efficiency in industrial regulation and protect lawful rights and interests of the property exchange.

A Sound SOE Internal Management System

The essence of SOE restructuring is to give them more growth incentives through the transformation of the systems in organization, management and distribution and push SOEs for self-improvement based on market rules and a corporate mechanism of independent operation and self-discipline to achieve better economic performance and maximum profits. This is the conclusion from our research and the analysis from the perspective of ownership, rights, responsibilities and property transactions of SOEs. The issue of internal governance follows SOE restructuring. A sound governance system is also key to a modern enterprise system that facilitates the building of a socialist market economy.

What comes first is the organizational and governance structure of the company. In August 1980, Deng Xiaoping delivered an important speech entitled *Reform of the Leadership System of the Party and the State* at an extended meeting of the Political Bureau of the CPC Central Committee, in which he explicitly proposed that the leadership system of SOEs should be transformed in a prepared and orderly manner to further straighten out SOEs' internal relations. In the early 1960s, the government issued the *70 Industrial Rules* (*Regulations on the Industrial Work of SOE*), which set preliminary rules on the leadership system of SOEs and their relationship with the government. The management structure was defined as the collective leadership of the SOE's party committee over political work and the chief executive responsibility system on business operations. In the 1980s, however, the autonomy of the chief executive increased, while the power of the Party committee was weakened. The *Law of Industrial Enterprises of Public Ownership* promulgated in 1988 codified the responsibility system of SOEs' chief executives. As the reform progressed, SOEs gradually changed to joint-stock companies. The shareholders' meeting, the board of directors and the board of supervisors were set up in accordance with the Company Law. The new governance structure contradicted the old structure, which was composed of the party committee, the employees' representatives meeting and the trade union. In September 1999, the 15th CPC Central Committee adopted the *Decisions of the CPC Central Committee on Major Issues Concerning Reform and Development of State-owned Enterprises* at its fourth plenary session, which stated that the corporate governance structure is the core of the corporate system, SOEs are ultimately controlled by their owners, and the board of directors, board of supervisors and management shall bear their respective responsibilities. It also set clear rules on appointing individuals to concurrently serve as chairmen or party secretaries of the companies. Later, the ownership and management of SOEs were gradually separated through measures such as establishing state-owned assets administration and supervision commissions. This completed the transformation of SOE's leadership system.

As one can see, the governance structure described above is not consistent with the modern enterprise system in the real sense, nor has it created a structure of check and balance between the shareholders meeting, the board of directors, the management and the board of supervisors. The boundaries of powers and responsibilities in corporate governance should be further clarified between the power organ, the decision-making body, the executive branch and the supervisory body. To be more specific, as the highest power authority and decision-making body of the company, the shareholders meeting should be composed of all shareholders. The board of directors should be elected by the shareholders meeting to perform the functions of corporate governance and strategic decision-making and report to the shareholders meeting. Management should be appointed by the board of directors to manage the company's business. The board of supervisors should be composed of supervisors elected by the shareholders meeting and the employees of the company to supervise the conduct of the board of directors and the management. It must be noted that, following the vision on the state-owned capital management system, the "state ownership" exercised by SASAC in the past should be transformed into the "investor ownership" to be exercised by the state investment fund corporation. This can ensure that the state's control over state-owned capital is not weakened.

The selection, incentives and discipline of professional managers should also be taken into consideration. The selection of management for restructured SOEs now remains a highly administrative process, as most senior managers are appointed directly by the companies' administrative authorities instead of the board of directors. As a result, it is difficult to create a mature market of professional managers or put in place a competitive regime or an incentive and self-restraint mechanism for them. With the deepening of the SOE reform, there will be an increasing number of market-driven companies of mixed ownership, and the creation and expansion of the system and market of professional managers will only come naturally. In the corporate governance structure under the modern enterprise system, the board of directors and its chairman, who act on behalf of the shareholders, are both responsible for the strategic decision-making and supervision of the management, while the general manager is responsible for the company's business operations. Market-based selection of professional managers will provide them with incentives, help them to develop a sense of crisis and urgency and improve their work efficiency. What is also essential is a diversified renumeration structure and equity incentives, which will fully mobilize the enthusiasm of professional managers, align their interests with those of the company, and thus ensure long-term and stable growth of the company. Sound corporate disciplines are also crucial. They can put professional managers under supervision through internal and external monitoring mechanisms.

Last but not least is the human resource management and remuneration system. Human capital no doubt plays an important role in the growth of a company with an ever-improving modern enterprise system. However, corporate human resource management currently needs to address issues such as obsolete management philosophies, inadequate staffing, backward training and lack of incentives. In addition, the design and reform of the renumeration system has produced little effect despite the commitment made in this field. Problems of disproportionate income gaps and weakness in income distribution regulation and structural design have surfaced. To solve this issue, it is important to take the following steps. First, philosophies of human resource management should be updated. Employees should be guided to rediscover their roles in the company and cultivate a greater sense of belonging to it. Second, a well-conceived human resource development and management plan should be developed. Efforts should be made to attract and nurture experts and professional managers to realize the growth strategies of the company. Human resource development and management should be carried out while the needs of employees should also be met. Third, the performance evaluation system should be improved. Effective performance evaluation underpins human resource management. It can strengthen team building, improve management efficiency, promote two-way interaction between the company and its employees and enhance their drive and enthusiasm. Fourth, vocational training for employees should be improved. Well-targeted employee training programs are needed, including courses outside the workplace and lectures given by external trainers. Measures such as job rotation and making training part of performance and salary assessment can be adopted to encourage employees to train for self-improvement. The corporate remuneration system should be better designed as part of the wider reform to cater to the needs of management and employees. For example, market rules can be used to diversify renumeration packages for management, which can include both short-term and long-term incentives. Renumeration for ordinary employees can be designed by taking into consideration the basic salary, performance-based income and welfare benefits. On this basis, efforts should be made to gradually roll out and improve a remuneration scheme that fits into the modern enterprise system featuring clear target groups, well-designed rules, proper relations, adequate incentives and strict disciplines.

Bibiliography

Chi, W. (2011). *Research on theory and practice of state-owned enterprise restructuring*. Beijing Normal University Publishing House.

Enterprise survey team of the national bureau of statistics. *Research on state-owned enterprise reform and hot issues*. China Statistics Press (2001).

Li, X. (1994). Relationship between state ownership and SOE corporate property right. *Reform*, (1).

Liu, Y. (1998). *Research on the reform of state-owned enterprises and related issues*. Dongbei University of Finance & Economics Press.

Li, Y. (2013). *China's economy in dual transition*. China Renmin University Press.

Li, Y. (2014 March 18). Reform of state-owned capital allocation system is at the heart of SOE reform. Wenhui Daily.

Li, Y. (2015). A leaner government and independent market players. *Administration Reform*, (9).

Ren, H., ed. (2004). *Interpretation on reform of state-owned enterprises*. China Financial & Economic Publishing House.

Shao, N., ed. (2014). *Records of SOE reforms*. Economic Science Press.

Wei, Y., Bian, W. & Zhou. B. (2003). *Research on strategic adjustment of the state-owned sector and state-owned enterprise restructuring*. Economy & Management Publishing House.

Streamlining Government Roles in Land Transfer and Confirmation of Land Rights

Ke Xu, Wei Dai, Chengming Li, and Haomin Li

The theory of economic imbalance proposed by Professor Li Yining divides economic imbalance into two categories.[1] (Yining, 1990). China is in the second category. A mature market is not yet in place, and the number of market players in the real sense is too small. A land ownership reform[2] aimed at fostering true market players is at the heart of China's economic restructuring. Over the past three decades, the reform on corporate ownership in China has made enormous headway. SOEs and private companies have basically become market players. The number of companies with mixed ownership is growing. The transformation of ownership in collectively owned businesses has been successful. However, property ownership reform in rural areas has long been neglected for historical reasons, and progress in this field has been slow.

The household contract responsibility system established in 1979 was a major reform initiative but fell short of a rural property ownership reform. The failure of the existing laws to fully protect farmers' right to property is part of the reason behind farmers' rejection of land requisition and forced demolition of their houses as of today. Farmers lack property-induced income, as it is difficult to pursue economies

[1] In the first category, the market is yet to play a decisive role, where prices are not flexible and imbalance in supply and demand is a normalcy. However, individual businesses are run by independent commodity producers. They are market players in real sense who bear responsibility for all profits and losses. They have the right to choose areas of investment and ways of management and bear their own investment and operational risks. In the second category, the market conditions remain the same, whereas individual businesses are not run by independent commodity producers, and therefore cannot be recognized as true market players. They have to bear investment and operational risks but don't have the right to choose areas of investment and ways of management.

[2] The land ownership reform defines land ownership and cultivates independent market players.

K. Xu (✉) · H. Li
Guanghua School of Management, Peking University, Beijing, China

W. Dai · C. Li
School of Software and Microelectronics, Peking University, Beijing, China

Y. Li and Z. Cheng (eds.), *The Chinese Path Toward a Leaner Government*,
https://doi.org/10.1007/978-981-19-6718-4_10

of scale, as land is scattered in smallholder farms and efficiency is low in land use when farmers flock to cities in search of better income jobs. Confirmation of land rights in the context of streamlining government roles will be the focus of China's rural reform going forward. Land rights confirmation entails three rights and three certificates for farmers[3] (Yining, 2013). This will assure farmers of their rights and consequently raise their work incentives and efficiency in land use and transfer. It will elevate China out of the state of imbalance featured in the second category as farmers become market players with a new identity as family farm owners whose property rights can be clearly defined. As the market further improves, China will gradually shift from the state of economic imbalance featured by the first category to the state of economic balance. The transformation will carry great significance.

The paper will review the evolution of China's rural land system, highlight the importance of the confirmation of land rights and its relations with streamlining government roles, and prove how land transfer and the confirmation of land rights promote China's economic and social progress with empirical models. The author, in conclusion, will put forward policy recommendations for China's rural land reforms by taking into account reforms and relevant practices in other countries.

Evolution of China's Rural Land System

The current land system is unique to China out of the country's historic origins. A review of the history of China's rural land system can offer a valuable reference for the current rural land reform. The system can be divided into three phases starting from 1949 according to changes in relations between land ownership and management rights (Sui, 2004).

I. The phase of individual ownership and independent management (1949–1953)

The rural land system in the early years of the PRC was a continuation of the policy that the CPC enforced before 1949.

In September 1949, *the Common Program*[4] of the Chinese People's Political Consultative Conference replaced the system of land ownership for the semi-feudal and semi-colonial society with a land system of farmers' ownership and set the course for the reform. Later, the *Law on Land Reform*[5] effective in June 1950 codified farmers' ownership of the land.

During this period. The land belonged to farmers, and ownership was closely combined with land management rights. The land reform raised incentives for farmers as never before as they became owners of the land they worked on. As

[3] The three rights refer to farmers' right to manage their contracted land, use their homesteads and build houses on their homesteads. The three certificates refer to certificates for farmers to manage their contracted land, use their homesteads and build houses on their homesteads.

[4] The *Common Program* refers to the *Common Program of the Chinese People's Political Consultative Conference.*

[5] The *Law on Land Reform* refers to the *Law on Land Reform of the People's Republic of China.*

a result, rural productivity was improved together with farmers' lives. According to the National Bureau of Statistics, between 1949 and 1952, grain production increased from 113.184 million tons to 163.931 million tons, and unit yield grew from 1029.33 kg/hectare to 1322.25 kg/hectare, up 44.8% and 28.5%, respectively.

II. The phase of collective ownership and unified management (1953–1978)

In 1953, the CPC adopted the *General Guidelines of the Transitional Period*. With the progress of agricultural cooperatives, the land system was adjusted correspondingly to a collective ownership of rural land that carried unique features of the time. The changes were as follows.

Individual ownership and mutual assistance—individual ownership and unified management—collective ownership and unified management.

During this period, land ownership and management rights were again merged after a short period of separation at the collective level. The failure of people's communes to provide incentives to farmers resulted in lower productivity, leaving a heavy toll on rural development, despite progress made in rural development.

III. The phase of collective ownership and contract-based management (1978-now)

The 11th CPC Central Committee decided to embrace economic development as the central task at its 3rd Plenary Session. The *Interim Regulations Governing Rural People's Communes* adopted at the session marked the beginning of a new round of land reform as it encouraged the expansion of autonomy for production brigades, which was a crucial step of the reform. Key policies in this period are as follows.

Land contract for rural production groups—land contract for rural households on trial basis in selected regions—land contract for rural households nationwide.

In January 1983, the rural land system centering on the household contact responsibility system was officially established with the release of the relevant document.[6] In the following three decades, reform has been pushed forward with the extension of the tenure of land contracts and the legislative protection of parties to land contracts. The rural land system has been improved and has become more stable.

In this period, changes have taken place again in the land system. While the land is collectively owned, the management rights belong to farmers. It has provided more autonomy and incentives to farmers and promoted agricultural modernization. Farm yields have increased quickly.

The chart below lists China's policies and regulations on the reform of the land system since 1949 (Dan & Maohua, 2009) (Table 1).

Importance of Land Rights Confirmation

Land is the essential means of livelihood for farmers and has long been their immediate concern. Disputes on rural land transfer, requisition and compensation are at

---

[6] *Issues Concerning Current Rural Economic Policies.*

Table 1 Policies and regulations relating to China's land system reform

Time	Name of regulation	Content
September 1949	*Common program of the Chinese people's political consultative conference*	"Replace the land ownership system of the semif-eudal and semi-colonial society with the land ownership system for farmers"
June 1950	Law on land reform of the PRC (draft)	Recognize that land is owned by farmers who have the right to land management, trading and lease
November 1950	Instructions on issuing land and property ownership certificate	Annul land contracts signed before the reform and replace them with land and housing ownership certificate
February 1953	Decision on mutual assistance and cooperation in agricultural production	Foster mutual assistance groups and primary-level agricultural production cooperatives nationwide
December 1953	Decision on developing agricultural production cooperatives	Launch advanced agriculture cooperatives
June 1956	Charter of advanced agricultural production cooperatives	Complete the transformation into advanced cooperatives and move collective ownership from farmer-based to collective-based
August 1958	Decision on building people's communes in rural areas	Launch the people's communes
June 1961	Regulations on the work of the rural people's communes (revised) (or "the 60-article rural regulations"	"Brigades are entitled to land within their scope of production"
September 1979	Decision on issues concerning accelerating agricultural development	"Tasks can be contracted to work groups and production brigades are responsible for accounting and distribution. Renumeration is calculated according to the amount of production. Reward is given to those who overfulfill the production target."
January 1982	Minutes of national rural work conference	Recognize household production contract
January 1983	Issues concerning current rural economic policies	Officially establish the household contract responsibility system
January 1984	Circular on rural work for 1984	Extend the land contract period "The land contract period is generally no shorter than 15 years"
April 1986	General principles of the civil law of the PRC	Protect the right of management on contracted land "Rights and obligations of contract parties shall be specified in the contract in accordance with the law"

(continued)

Table 1 (continued)

Time	Name of regulation	Content
June 1986	Law on land management of the PRC	Provide legislative protection to land ownership and contract management rights
April 1988	Constitution of the PRC (amended)	The constitution stresses that "the land use right can be transferred in accordance with the law"
March 1993	Constitution of the PRC	Write into the constitution that "rural collective economic organizations follow a dual management system combining unified and separated operation based on household contract"
November 1993	Policies and measures concerning development of agriculture and rural economy	"Extend contract period by thirty years after expiration of original farmland contract"
June 1997	Circular on further stabilizing and improving rural land contract relations	Set the land contract policy featuring "overall stability with minor changes"
August 1998	Law on land management of the PRC	"Land use right can be lawfully transferred"
August 2002	Law on rural land contract of the PRC	Uphold long-term stability of land contract management right
June 2003	Decision of the CPC central committee and the state council on accelerating forestry development	Launch trials on collective forestry rights reform
June 2008	Guidelines on advancing the reform of collective forestry rights system	Nationwide launch of collective forestry rights reform
February 2008	Measures on land registration	Promote and regulate land rights registration and certification to protect land right
October 2008	Decision on issues concerning advancing rural reform and development	State for the first time that land contract relations will remain unchanged for a long time, require smooth progress in rural land right confirmation, registration and certificates issuance

the heart of farmers' complaints in their fight for rights protection and have seriously threatened rural stability and development in recent years. The *Decision of the CPC Central Committee on Major Issues Concerning Comprehensive Deepening of the Reform* adopted at its 3rd Plenary Session asked for "the improvement of a modern property system with clear definition and rigorous protection of ownership, rights and responsibilities and smooth transfer of property rights". The goal of building a sound property protection system sets the course for rural property system reform.

China will become a strong and prosperous socialist economy only when its farmers secure their land rights and become market players in real sense (Yining, 2013). As a breakthrough in China's rural property system reform, the confirmation of land rights is highly significant to the country's economic and social development.

I. Confirmation and transfer of land rights and improvement of land quality

Confirmation of land rights helps better protect farmers' interests, encourages economies of scale as appropriate and increases farmers' income. In recent years, confirmation of land rights has been rolled out in the countryside of China but has fallen short of creating a regulated land transfer market. The fundamental cause was the lack of clearly defined property rights and the weak position of farmers as land owners. Therefore, farmers are less willing to transfer their land for fear of poor protection of their interests and ultimate loss of ownership of the transferred land.

Confirmation of land rights will ease the abovementioned concerns and encourage more farmers to trade their land, ultimately raising land use efficiency. It will also offer relief to rural collectives and local governments away from issues of entangled interests and help them focus more on regulating the market and service for land rights transfer. Thus, the market can play a decisive role in resource allocation and facilitate trade in land rights.

According to a survey conducted by Liu Tao and others on land transfer in Nanjing, land transfer in the context of poorly defined land trading rights led to the degradation of soil fertility in rural areas to some extent (Tao et al., 2008). After the land rights were confirmed, farmers saw their rights protected and thus raised expectations on long-term investment in their land. The degradation of soil fertility caused by frequent changes in land use was reversed, and crop yields increased.

II. Confirmation of land rights and farmers' income

The most obvious benefit generated by the rural land reform is the growth of farmers' income. With land ownership well defined and confirmed by the government, farmers are fully motivated to increase productivity. Property-based income is also on the rise, bringing extra benefits to farmers in the form of land and house rent. Land rights transfer also encourages farmers to expand production on larger pieces of land with more specialized operations to realize economies of scale. Raising food production and farmers' income is what the reform aims to achieve.

III. Confirmation of land rights and social stability

Social unrest throughout Chinese history has its roots in the poor protection of the basic rights and interests of farmers, as farmers had no other choice but to rebel once their land plots were taken away. Land is always essential to social stability. Recent years have seen frequent occurrences of farmers protesting against land requisition and filing complaints about village collectives. The failure to offer proper compensation to farmers' fundamental interests or legal protection to their rights has added to instability in rural areas. The root cause lies in the blurred definition of property rights. Confirmation of land rights can protect farmers' interests to some extent, and contracts provide a legal basis for matters related to land requisition and house demolition. Protection of farmers' interests will reduce the number of land disputes and promote social harmony and stability.

Relations Between Confirmation of Land Rights and Streamlining Government Administration

Confirmation of land rights serves the purpose of identifying the ownership, contractual and management rights of rural land and restoring its full property rights to farmers. This is the top priority of rural land reform and a prerequisite for the smooth transfer of land (Quanbao, 2011). What the law can do is to uphold farmers' lawful rights to land, which has been poorly protected due to ambiguous regulations. Under the current system of collective land ownership, farmers "are owners of land in name but have no land under their names". Land is transferred in a restrictive manner to serve the interests of village committees, township governments and even property developers instead of those of farmers. The current system has also led to mounting cases of land-related corruption in recent years. Some local governments have taken advantage of inadequate regulation on land requisition, house demolition and relocation of villagers to get compensation by cheating. Therefore, the government should streamline functions and delegate power to the market for rural land transfer to improve regulation and service and let the market play a decisive role.

I. Clarity in land rights helps build a leaner government.

Since land-related property rights are ambiguous and unconfirmed in law, the government has to act as both the regulator and the referee in the face of problems that occur in land transfer due to a lack of relevant legal provisions. As a result, the administrative process is prolonged, and more seals are needed to complete the transaction. The consequent higher cost in time and money has seriously eroded the efficiency of rural land transfer. In addition, since it is difficult for the government to always maintain a sound balance between responsibilities and interests, the roles of local governments as both the regulator and the referee have led to a large number of cases involving land-related corruption. This has held back the progress in land trading under the policy of building a leaner government.

When land rights are confirmed, land-related property rights will be spelled out, the role of the government as a regulator will be better defined, and the rural population will have more autonomy in land transactions. It will help reshape the government's role and image and serve the goal of building a leaner government.

II. A leaner government will maximize the benefit from confirmation of land rights.

Confirmation of rural land rights aims to regulate rural land transfer, promote market vitality and ultimately increase farmers' yields and income. Building a leaner government aims to straighten out relations between the government and the market by streamlining administration and improving regulation and service while letting the market play a decisive role. It is imperative for the government to improve its due functions and delegate power that ought to be exercised by the market. The responsibilities of agricultural authorities at all levels should be reshaped for the coordinated development of the rural economy.

Strong measures in building a leaner government will raise the efficiency of government regulation and administration (Chen, 2015). Laws and regulations concerning land transfer will be improved, and disputes will be settled through judicial means. The rising number of land disputes will force the legislature to introduce legal instruments that confirm land rights with a clear definition of ownership. In a market economy, agricultural authorities at all levels must ensure that the market decides resource allocation in the countryside to foster a vibrant rural economy. Moreover, village collectives and township governments, once streamlined, will shift their functions away from bureaucracies on land transfer. As owners of land, farmers will be more willing to trade their land and make better choices for themselves in so doing based on well-informed judgment. Consequently, farmers' property-based welfare will improve. The income gap will narrow, and urban–rural integration will be enhanced, which constitutes the greatest benefit of land rights confirmation.

Case Study on the Benefits of Land Rights Confirmation

I. Philosophy

Confirmation of land rights and restoration of ownership to farmers serve the government's aim to raise farmers' income and food production. Farmers can indeed become owners of land through land rights confirmation, but it remains to be seen whether land transfer is a good incentive to encourage farmers to protect their land ownership and raise efficiency in land use. Agricultural insurance thus came into being. How willing farmers are to buy insurance reflects, to a large extent, the effects of land transfer policies. The following is an analysis into factors that affect the result of land transfer policies based on the willingness of farmers to buy agricultural insurance.

II. Research Methodologies

What are the factors that affect farmers' willingness to buy agricultural insurance? Support from the national government on agricultural insurance expands the awareness of its importance among farmers, but challenges remain in securing farmers' recognition and readiness to buy the insurance. Therefore, it is important to understand the main factors affecting their purchase willingness.

We visited 1018 households, 56 cooperatives and family farms in typical rural areas of Anhui and Jiangsu in a survey that covered five areas, including disaster impact, risk management strategies, and recognition and acceptance of agricultural insurance. A logit model was set up with data collected in searching for the factors.

III. Contents

1. Demographic features
2. Economic features:
   field planting: growth areas, disposal of farming land and reasons, agronomics (means of production and irrigation);
   family income: annual household income, main source of income, agriculture-generated income, main reasons for selecting crop species; channel of distribution, and market price for main crops; and
   family expenditure: annual household expenditure (the item of the highest spending) and the method of purchasing farming resources.
3. Disaster impact and risk management strategies:
   daily risks that are of the greatest concern to rural households;
   agricultural disasters that farmers worry about most;
   knowledge of how agricultural disasters occur and how to prevent them;
   access to pre-disaster information and access channels;
   perception of rural cooperatives;
   measures taken before agricultural disasters to mitigate risks and those;
   measures taken during the disasters;
   post-disaster means of livelihood; and.
   suggestions for government disaster relief.
4. Recognition and acceptance of agricultural insurance:
   knowledge and experience of agricultural insurance products; and.
   compensation of agricultural insurance (such as speed of loss assessment and claim settlement, and procedures and amount of claim settlement by insurers).
5. Survey on demand for agricultural insurance and affordability

IV. Model building

A retrogression analysis is performed with a logit model. Independent variables are shown in Table 2.

A logit model is then established with SAS software. Step one is the result that contains the intercept term only and not variables, as shown in Table 3.

Step two: put Variable X10 into the model and arrive at Table 4.

The result of an overall test of the model is shown in Table 5.

The original presumption is that all variables have a parameter of 0. The test results reveal the overall relevance of the model.

−2 Log L and Score are used to examine whether the variables are significant. L in −2 Log L means Likelihood Ratio. The p value of both likelihood ratio and score was less than 0.05. Therefore, X10 is a significant explanatory variable.

We add other variables into the test in the same way and arrive at a maximum likelihood estimation, as shown in Table 6.

Table 7 shows the estimates of the model parameters. For X10, 95% of the confidence interval excludes 1. It shows that X10 is a highly significant explanatory variable (the confidence interval of the ratio excludes 1).

Table 2 The values of explanatory variables and explanations

Variables	Symbol	Value	Explanation	Expected impact
Age	X1	1: 11—20 years 2: 21—30 years 3: 31—40 years 4: 41—50 years 5: 51—60 years 6: > 60 years	Farmers more senior in age with richer farming experience are less acceptive to agricultural insurance	Uncertain
Gender	X2	0: female 1: male	Women in the survey are less aware of the importance of agricultural insurance. However, in households where men work elsewhere as migrant workers, women become the main workforce in the farms and have a decisive role to play in insurance purchase	Uncertain
Household size	X3	1: 1 person 2: up to 4 persons 3: up to five persons	Household size also has potential impact on insurance purchase. We put it in the regression formula for examination purpose	Uncertain
Years of farming	X4	1: < 20 years 2: 20—30 years 3: 30—40 years 4: 40—50 years 5: > 50 years	The survey reveals that the older the farming age, the less enthusiastic farmers tend to be about agricultural insurance. Elderly farmers tend to believe that farming relies on natural climate and farmers' efforts. They do not trust or count on other's help	Negative

(continued)

Table 2 (continued)

Variables	Symbol	Value	Explanation	Expected impact
Number of family members as migrant workers	X5	1: 0 2: 1 3: 2—3 4: > 4	In fact, the number of family members as migrant workers has both positive and negative impact on the willingness of purchasing agricultural insurance. In the survey by Yaohua (2007), the variable value of "migrant workers or not" has positive impact on demand for agricultural insurance. A possible explanation is that rural migrant workers know more about insurance and can afford to buy it because of higher income. On the other hand, as more family members work in the cities, the size of farming workforce goes down together with the area of farmland. The need for insurance consequently will also come down	Uncertain
Educational level	X6	1: no schooling 2: primary school 3: junior high school 4: senior high school 5: vocational school 6: university	Yuehua and others (2007) conclude that the higher the educational level, the better the ability to understand the role and features of insurance. Experience shows that the higher the educational level, the greater the cognitive abilities, acceptance for novelties and sense of self-protection farmers will have. These are factors that play a direct role in the willingness of purchasing insurance	Positive

(continued)

Table 2 (continued)

Variables	Symbol	Value	Explanation	Expected impact
Household income from farming	X7	1: < 30,000 2: 30,000—50,000 3: 50,000—100,000 4: > 100,000	The variable measures the total farming income of a household. Generally, the *higher the income from farming*, the greater the appreciation of risks, and vice versa. Moreover, higher income rural households are more able and willing to spend on insurance with their disposable income	Positive
Total household income	X8	1: < 5000 2: 5000—7500 3: 7500—10,000 4: 10,000—20,000 5: > 20,000	Like income from farming, the higher the total household income, the greater the tendency to buy insurance. In contrast, the lower the income, the more difficult it becomes to afford insurance premium	Positive
Household expenditure	X9	1: < 4000 2: 4000—5000 3: 5000—7500 4: 7500—10,000 5: > 10,000	The greater the household spends, the less the likelihood to buy insurance, even if the income is high	Uncertain
Knowledge of agricultural insurance	X10	1: none 2: a little 3: quite some 4: a lot of	Questions include "Have you ever heard about agricultural insurance?", "Do you have access to insurance, loss assessment and compensation settlement information?", and "Do you know that agricultural insurance is subsidized by the central and local governments?" There are four options under each question	Positive

(continued)

Table 2 (continued)

Variables	Symbol	Value	Explanation	Expected impact
Knowledge of risk mitigation measures	X11	1: none 2: a little 3: quite some 4: a lot of	Questions include "Do you know anything about the formation and prevention of agricultural disasters?", "Have you taken measures to mitigate the effect of disasters on farm yield?", "What measures will you take to minimize the risks of agricultural disasters?" There are four options under each question	Positive
Area of household's own farmland	X12	1: < 3 mu 2: 3—5 mu 3: 5—10 mu 4: > 10 mu (1 hectare = 15 mu)	The survey shows that many big farming households are clients of insurance companies. Policy terms for some of them are more stringent than small holder farms, which reflects that big farms are easy to get compensated. This is a noticeable factor in the decision on insurance purchase	Positive
Agronomics	X13	1: pure manual work 2: partial mechanization 3: pesticide, pest and disease control 4: full mechanization	The options for the question about means of production include pure manual work, partial mechanization, pesticide and pest and disease control, and full mechanization. They reflect the technical levels of farmers and may affect the farmers' decisions on insurance purchase	Positive
Disaster relief efforts of governments	X14	0: no 1: yes	The greater the government invests in disaster relief, the less the initiative of farmers, and vice versa	Positive
Willingness to buy agricultural insurance this year	X15	0: no 1: yes	The question helps understand whether farmers who have bought insurance are ready to renew the policy and explore the bottlenecks for agricultural insurance	Positive

Table 3 Index values of intercepts

Chi-square value	Freedom	Probability
64.1663	15	< 0.0001

Table 4 Index values of AIC, SC and −2 Log L

Index	Intercept only	Intercept and covariate
AIC	398.636	342.667
SC	403.159	351.715
−2 Log L	396.636	338.667

Table 5 Model test

Test	Chi-square value	Freedom	Probability
Likelihood ratio	57.9680	1	< 0.0001
Score	52.6366	1	< 0.0001
Wald	41.4332	1	< 0.0001

Table 6 MLE results

Variable	Freedom	Estimate	Standard error	Wald Chi-square value	Probability
Intercept	1	−1.1607	0.5017	5.3524	0.0207
X10	1	1.4142	0.2197	41.4332	< 0.0001
X11	1	0.3667	0.1282	4.3262	0.0375
X12	1	0.4532	0.1643	5.3457	0.0453

The survey shows that the area of family farms, to a large extent, affects farmers' purchase of agricultural insurance. When farmers obtain more land through land transfer, they will pay more attention to their land. In the past, farmers did not care about insurance for a small piece of land of one to two *mu*. However, now as the farming area may expand into five to six *mu* through trading, they have become more interested in it and more willing to buy agricultural insurance to guarantee the yield and returns, as it may bring changes to their life. Quite a few farmers are also considering transferring their land to large farms under more specialized

Table 7 Odds ratio estimates

Variable	Estimate	95% Wald confidence interval
X10	3.677	[2.414, 5.601]
X11	1.306	[1.016, 1.679]
X12	1.406	[1.124, 1.734]

management to secure the yield. Currently, organizations and individuals such as farming cooperatives and large farming households have become the main focus of agriculture, as advanced management models, mechanized farming, and economies of scale on large farmlands can drastically cut costs and raise yields. They are taking proper measures, such as buying agricultural insurance to reduce their exposure to natural disasters and other risks. The head of a large farming household surveyed is a graduate of an agricultural university. His family has contracted the land of all other villagers. Because of the use of advanced farming and irrigation techniques, the family's annual income from farming rose to over RMB 500,000. It proves to be a good way to improve family welfare. Obviously, land transfer is a sound approach to facilitate agricultural development.

Land Resource Transfer Practices Abroad and Inspirations

I. Land transfer in developed countries

1. The United States

Unlike other developed economies, in the United States, the basic farming unit is the family farm. Thanks to its advanced economic system, land trade is highly market-driven. Its full-fledged legal system on land effectively protects the lawful rights of farm owners in land inheritance, mortgage and lease. The American Farm Bureau Federation, a nongovernmental organization, plays an important role as a critical voice for interest claims in protecting the rights of farmers and farm owners during land transfer. The US practice provides inspiration in the following two areas: first, China's rural land system reform should aim at the improvement of laws and regulations and their effective enforcement to ensure the law-based transfer of rural land. Second, nongovernmental farmer organizations should be created at a faster pace to represent farmers in their claims and protect farmers' interests.

2. Japan

After WWII, the land reform was carried out in Japan, which banned corporations' involvement in agriculture-related sectors as well as the purchase and holding of land by nonagricultural entities. The policy was not changed until the enforcement of the *Rural Land Revision Act* in 1970. The latter granted agricultural corporations the freedom to buy and lease farmland jointly established by farmers. Farmland resource management companies were set up to facilitate the lease of farmland. In 1993, the government again revised laws and policies on land to attract young people to the agricultural sector. Plans on the dissemination and training of new farming technologies were released. As a large number of farmers reached retirement age in the late 1980s, farmland was gathered and transferred on a large scale, creating a fast-rising number of large farm owners. To draw on Japan's experience, China should recognize the importance of a well-defined land ownership to land transfer and push forward confirmation of land rights. Moreover, the prompt release of effective pro-agriculture policies from the government is a key guarantee for raising agricultural production and rural productivity.

II. Land transfer in developing countries: India's experience

There was a time in India when farmland management was too fragmented to generate an economy of scale and productivity was low. Later, the government carried out land reform to address this issue through legislation that forced the merger of small pieces of land. The practice led to widespread land monopoly. Land distribution was unfair, and the interests of smallholder farmers were not protected. Weak legislation and administrative intervention on land transfer at various government levels prevented the formation of an inclusive and efficient land transfer system. Like India, China has many people but limited farmland. Compared with farmland, the population is disproportionately large. Promoting rural productivity and protecting farmland is a top priority in promoting steady growth of the agriculture sector. Government departments at all levels in the countryside have the responsibility to protect farmland and strengthen land use administration. In particular, efforts must be made to prevent transferred land from being converted to nongrain-producing land to ensure the food security of China.

Further Improving the Confirmation of Land Rights During Land Transfer in the Context of Building a Leaner Government

As reform intensified on all fronts, the central government decided to build a leaner government. This idea has since been widely appreciated with the implementation of a number of policies of delegation and cancellation of administrative approval powers. Because rights and interests related to land resources are unclear, agricultural departments are confronted with issues such as inappropriate or excessive administration, low farming productivity and serious waste of land and other natural resources. Confirmation of rural land rights helps define rights and responsibilities in relation to land resources, encourages agricultural authorities at all levels to shift administrative functions and priorities for higher efficiency, and ultimately advances the building of a leaner government in the agricultural sector. The author believes that in this context, improvement should be made in the following areas for confirmation of land rights and land transfer.

I. Improving laws and regulations on rural land transfer and confirmation of land rights

Laws and regulations concerning rural land transfer and land rights confirmation are divided into three categories: before, during and after land transfer. The first category refers to the land ownership system, namely, laws and regulations on the confirmation of land rights that define the rights and responsibilities of land owners and users. Confirmation of land rights protects farmers' rights to manage, benefit from and transfer the land or use it as collaterals. The second category refers to the system of transferring land management rights or laws and regulations related to rural land transfer. They aim to better protect the lawful rights and interests of farmers and other parties to land transactions during land transfer in the form of law. The third category refers to the land dispute settlement framework, an important mechanism to protect farmers' interests after the transaction is completed. A variety of measures are needed to settle disputes that include consultation, mediation, arbitration and litigation. The establishment and improvement of the land ownership system, the mechanism for transferring land contract management rights, the land dispute settlement regime and relevant laws and regulations will form a sound legal basis and an effective institutional guarantee for land transfer and confirmation of land rights.

II. Creating a market-driven platform for transfer of rural land

The rural economy is an essential part and indicator of the socialist market economy. A market-driven platform is much needed to improve the land transfer of the rural economy. By reviewing the study of Tingjun (2013), the author suggests that efforts be made in four areas. First, the government should establish local databases through digital technologies for rural land transfer that connect supply with demand to minimize information asymmetry. Second, nongovernmental organizations should be encouraged to play the role of intermediaries in the land transfer market to ensure that transactions are market driven and well-regulated and made through intermediaries, thus paving the way for land transfer on a larger scale. Third, an appropriate land transfer pricing regime is needed that can fully reflect the intention of both parties of transactions and market supply and demand to forestall price manipulation. Fourth, the government should give full play to the regulatory role of agricultural departments at all levels to ensure sound progress of land transfer and balanced and sustainable development of the rural economy.

III. Putting in place and improving the rural social safety net

The weak rural social security system has seriously affected the progress of rural land transfer. As a result, farmers have no choice but to rely more on land, the only source for their survival. They worry about losing the means of livelihood once the land is lost during transfer. Consequently, rural land transfer has been significantly held back. A full-fledged rural social safety net is imperative to address this issue and free farmers from old thinking. It must be more comprehensive with broader coverage. The benefits of urban social security schemes can be gradually expanded in view of the unified management of social security schemes nationwide. A rural social security scheme should at least include health insurance, pension and minimal allowance and should address education, health and other major concerns of farmers. Only when these concerns are resolved will farmers rest assured, and the rural land transfer market gradually expands.

IV. Strengthening regulation over the use of transferred land

The issue of willfully converting farmland to grow nongrain crops or using it for nonagricultural purposes is widespread during land transfer. The former refers to the practice of growing fruits and other cash crops on the transferred farmland. The issue arose due to differences in the market prices of various farm products. The large regulatory cost makes it almost impossible to exercise full regulation. To solve this issue, the government must provide farming households corresponding subsidies and explain the policies patiently to dissuade them from the practice. Turning farmland to nonagricultural land is more serious in nature, but it is easier to solve through measures such as tightening regulation on rural land transfer approval and punishing in accordance with the law those who have converted the transferred land unlawfully to other purposes.

Bibliography

Chen, L. (2015). The importance of streamlining administration and delegating power to confidence building in government. *Theoretical Observation*, (3).

Chen, D. & Tang, M. (2009). Review of China's rural land reform in the past 60 years. *City*, (10).

Feng, S. & Zhang, G. (2016). Obstacles to the transfer of management rights of contracted rural land in China and their solutions—In the perspective of farmland property right system. *Guangxi Social Sciences*, (2).

Gao, T. & Zhang, G. (2015). Reflections on the confirmation of land rights. *China Market*, (17).

Hu, S. (2004). Evolution of rural land policy of the communist party of China: In the perspective of rural land ownership and management rights. Unpublished doctor's dissertation, Hunan Normal University.

Li, Y. (1990). *Unbalanced Chinese economy*. Economic Daily.

Li, Y. (2013). *China's economy in dual transition*. China Renmin University Press.

Liu, T. & Qu, F, et al. (2008). The impact of land fragmentation and land transfer on farmers' land use efficiency. *Resource Science*, (10).

Wang, Q. (2011). Rights confirmation opens the way for new land reform. *Land and Resources Herald*, (10).

Yan, T. (2013). Research on current rural land transfer in China—A case study of Ningyang county, Shandong Province. Unpublished Master's dissertation, Shandong University.

Zhang, Y., Shi, Q. & Gu, H. (2007). Theoretical study and empirical analysis of demand for agricultural insurance. *The Journal of Quantitative and Technical Economics*, (4).

Household Registration System Reform and Administrative Streamlining

Weixuan Zhao, Junyang Zhou, Zhongwen Zhang, and Ping Zhang

According to Prof. Li Yining's theory of the dual transition of the economy, China is transforming itself from a planned economy to a socialist market economy and from a traditional agricultural society to an industrial society. Over the past three decades, the dual transition of the Chinese economy has shaped a unique path of reform and opening up and paved the way for the country's sustainable development. In this process, reform has been carried out in all aspects of China's economic and social endeavors. It has continued to add impetus to the sustained growth of the economy.

Today, as the socialist market economy continues to improve, the administrative model under the planned economy can no longer catch up with the economic model of all-round opening-up and full mobility of production resources. Administrative streamlining has thus become a major reform agenda in building socialism with Chinese characteristics. Urbanization in China is in full swing as the country shifts from an agricultural society to an industrial society. How can the orderly movement of hundreds of millions of rural surplus laborers[1] into cities be ensured? How can the sound development of cities and towns of various sizes be promoted? How can equal access be provided to public welfare? These questions concerning "people-centered urbanization" are all closely related to the household registration system reform. It has placed the household registration system reform and administrative

[1] Measured by the current mechanization level, rural surplus labor is estimated to be 105 million (joint research team of the DRC, State Council and the Word Bank).

W. Zhao (✉)
Guanghua Management School, Peking University, Beijing, China

J. Zhou
Financial Research Institute, CASS, Beijing, China

Z. Zhang
School of Economics, Peking University, Beijing, China

P. Zhang
School of Chinese Language Education for Foreigners, Peking University, Beijing, China

Y. Li and Z. Cheng (eds.), *The Chinese Path Toward a Leaner Government*,
https://doi.org/10.1007/978-981-19-6718-4_11

streamlining at the core of the dual transition. As was thoroughly explained by Prof. Li Yining in the preface, administrative streamlining is part of the institutional reform of the government in step with the progress in economic reform. Reforms in the government roles and the household registration system are mutually complementary and reinforcing.

The author intends to analyze the past and present of China's household registration system reform from the perspective of administrative streamlining and analyze the crucial role that the household registration system reform plays in China's economic development. The interconnectedness among the household registration system reform, the land reform and the fiscal reform and their contribution to a new type of urbanization in China will also be discussed. The final part is policy recommendations for China's reform and development.

The History of China's Household Registration System and its Reform

China's household registration system currently in place still separates urban residents from rural residents, a practice unique in China. The marked line between urban and rural populations has also gone through some changes alongside the socioeconomic development of the country. In general, the system is divided into four phases.

I. The phase of free movement (1949–1957)

Population migration was relatively free in the early years of the People's Republic because the central task for the government was collecting national demographic data, a full-fledged household registration system was not in place, and the urban–rural line was not defined nationally. In July 1951, the Ministry of Public Security issued the *Provisional Regulations on Urban Household Registration Administration*, the first ever regulations on household registration for the PRC. Based on the national demographic data, the regulations had a big impact on the movement of the population. During this period, a person could submit applications to both the police station that kept his household registration information and the one in charge of the neighborhood that he would move into, so long as the reason for doing so was fully justified. Free intercity and urban–rural population flow during this period was not restricted.

II. The phase of strict control (1958–1979)

The *Regulations on Household Registration of the People's Republic of China* was officially promulgated by the NPC Standing Committee in 1958. It codified for the first time the household registration system in a relatively comprehensive manner to ensure law and order, protect the lawful rights and interests of citizens, and better contribute to socialist development. To accelerate growth and remove poverty, the

CPC Central Committee adopted the first Five-year Plan that gave top priority to the growth of the heavy industry. The plan focused on the strategy of "city first" and included policies of putting industrial development and cities before agriculture and the countryside, increasing funding for industrialization in urban areas and easing pressure for resource competition by restricting massive population migration from rural to urban areas. This was the start of China's household registration system featuring urban–rural segmentation and population control through compulsory measures.

III. The phase of moderate relaxation (1979–1997)

Since the start of the reform and opening up in 1978, as the role of the market in resource allocation became more obvious, the readiness and chances of labor flow have gradually increased. The *Circular on Household Registration of Farmers in Townships* issued by the State Council in October 1984 was the first breakthrough made in China's household registration system reform. In 1992, the Ministry of Public Security issued "valid local urban residential household" certificates to the aforementioned farmers to attract human resources into small towns, special economic zones and development zones designated by the government. The certificates were called the "blue household certificates" because the covers were made of blue leather. In addition, the State Council formulated rules on the registration administration of three types of residents—permanent, temporary and boarding—based on the economic and social reality of the country at that time. Despite some relaxation of population flow, migration was still under tight control to ensure social stability in the early years of the reform and opening-up.

IV. The phase of new progress in reform and opening-up (since 1998)

As China made more progress in the reform and opening-up and urbanization, cross-regional migration from rural to urban areas increased in both frequency and scale. "Farmer workers" came into being as a large and highly representative group. The flow of funding, jobs and products, together with the possibility of property ownership and entrepreneurship, has created extensive and frequent migration of the population across cities and between cities and the countryside. Instead of meeting the need for social development, the current system has somewhat held back the urbanization process. Therefore, it is imperative to draw on the experience and lessons of other countries, take into consideration the ever increasing size of population flow in China, and accelerate the household registration system reform to break policy barriers against population flow and replace segmented residential policies with a new type of household registration administration system.

The following tables are policies and regulations on household registration system reform since 1949 (Table 1).

Table 1 Policies and regulations on household registration system reform

Time	Policies and regulations	Content
1949	Common program of the Chinese people's political consultative conference	Descriptions of the freedom of movement of citizens was made for the first time
July 1951	Interim regulations on the administration of urban household registration	The regulations provided for freedom of migration and unified household registration for citizens. It was China's first government regulation on household registration administration
June 1955	Directive on the establishment of a permanent household registration system	The household administrative and registration departments and their competent authorities shall be the civil affairs departments of the people's committees at or above the county level and the ministry of internal affairs
1958	Regulations of the People's Republic of China on household registration	It was the first time for China to adopt the household registration system in the form of legislation. Household registration was divided into "rural" and "nonrural" categories. It was the first time to artificially divide citizenship
August 1964	Provisions of the ministry of public security on handling household registration transfer (draft)	More stringent restrictions were made on migration from countryside to cities. Farmers living in cities were under tighter checks
January 1975	The 1975 constitution	The "freedom of citizens to reside and migrate" was revoked. People were confined to the current place of residence. Urban and rural areas were artificially divided, and the household registration system featuring urban–rural segmentation officially came into being
1984	Circular of the CPC central committee on rural work in 1984	Some farmers who worked for or started their own businesses in the service sector in cities were allowed to settle down in cities, but they had to provide for their own food rations
July 1985	Interim provisions of the ministry of public security on the administration of temporary urban residents	Temporary residential system was launched. The household registration system was further improved

(continued)

Table 1 (continued)

Time	Policies and regulations	Content
August 1992	Circular on the implementation of valid local urban household registration system	Restrictions on rural to nonrural household registration was further lowered. Farmer were able to shift their identities to urban dwellers with money
The end of 1992	Decision of the state council on reform of the household registration system	The 1958 criteria that separated "rural" from "nonrural" status was revoked. New household registration criteria were adopted based on places of permanent and temporary residence
October 1998	Circular on strict control of excessive growth in rural to nonrural households	Guidelines on curbing excessive growth in rural to nonrural households were made. Specific quotas were set for quantitative control with corresponding policies to put the number of rural to nonrural households under strict control
2013	Decision of the 18th CPC central committee at its third plenary session	The Decision drew a better-thought roadmap for the household registration system reform. The unprecedented expansion of megacities calls for proper control and guidance of population flows. Policies would be more flexible to support the growth of small and medium-sized cities by encouraging farmer workers who met the criteria to settle down there. Sound household registration policies and criteria would be made to promote coordinated development of megacities and small and medium-sized cities. Efforts would be made to reach the household registration system reform goals in two phases, a decade for each
July 2014	Guidelines of the state council on further promoting the reform of the household registration system	Freedom of migration was further stressed. General guidance was made on polices relating to personal rights and interests of citizens. The Guidelines called for quicker pace in the household registration system reform, steady progress in formulating and implementing supporting policies and proper distribution of public resources to ensure equal treatment between urban and rural areas

Progress Analysis of the Household Registration System Reform

I. Population administration in developed countries

1. USA: life registration + social security number

The United States implements a life registration system on its people. The government has a complete registration handbook on the birth, death, marriage and family of every citizen and basic information of their parents and social contacts of them and their children. The corresponding social security number system is the cornerstone of the country's population administration. All US citizens and foreign nationals long residing in the US have unique social security numbers that work as certificates for access to education, employment and housing services. People can move freely with SSN. Instead of the migration registration system, the government links migration registration with the tax payer's address. A US citizen can enjoy local social security service so long as he pays tax to local authorities. Although people are allowed to move around the country, there are laws to restrict population migration to minimize disruptions to local residents.

2. Europe: civil registration + post-migration registration

The population administration system in European countries is different from that in the United States. Most of them follow the civil registration system, which records the birth, death, marriage and children of each citizen as well as detailed information concerning the income and profession of their parents and spouses. The system is protected by law in Europe through codification of the civil registration system. Given differences in national conditions, administrative systems and legislations, there are three models of civil registration, namely, concentrated, dispersed, and concentrated + dispersed models. The administration of population migration in Europe is based on a post-migration registration system under which people are allowed to move freely between countries but are required to register at the government departments afterwards.

3. Japan: "household register + resident certificate"

Population administration in Japan is based on a "household register + resident certificate" model that combines Western and Asian governance features. The household register is widely used in Asian countries, which regard a family as a basic unit. It contains residents' ID information and their relations with family members. Resident certificates take individuals as basic units and place of residence as the main content. A certificate records changes in place of residence, information of migration and tax payment and qualifies an individual's access to public service. Japan allows freedom of population movement. It sets up a creative system of "register household information as you go", but there is a strict set of laws and regulations on household changes. Before moving out, residents must go to the local government to give reasons for leaving and the intended place of residence for obtaining the permit for cancelling the household registration. In addition, he has to register with the local government of his new place of residence within 14 days. With the application of information technology, citizens can now complete online migration registration with their personal registration number.

Population administration in developed countries highlights three combinations. It combines market rules with the rule of law in terms of institutional setups. It combines civil registration with dynamic demographic statistics with regard to population registration and combines free movement with post-migration registration.

II. Household registration system in China

The household registration system reform is one of the key reform initiatives of the Chinese government. Control in small towns has been basically lifted where "rural households" and" nonrural households" are merged into "residential households". In large and medium-sized cities, criteria for urban household registration have been eased. However, reforms in megacities such as Beijing, Shanghai and Guangzhou are more cautious. The government stated in 2016 that "all localities shall issue policies and measures to implement the household registration system reform initiated by the State Council". By 25 April 2016, with the release of the *Guidelines on Further Advancing the Household Registration System Reform* by the municipal government of Shanghai, 29 provinces had issued reform plans. Through population size control in large cities, integrating rural with nonrural household status and lifting restrictions on urban household registration, the reform has picked up pace and delivered massive benefits. The following is an analysis of the reform progress in various localities.

The current household registration system in general still functions in terms of population control, social management, resource allocation and welfare distribution. Analysis shows that it has the following weaknesses.

First, identity discrimination. Different household registration types in China correspond to different public services. There is now a large disparity for residents in social security, education and employment opportunities between urban and rural areas, eastern and central and western regions, and different cities, resulting in identity discrimination.

The second is poor legal protection. Population administration in China is based on the household registration system, which relies more on administrative decrees than laws. As a result, it is difficult to identify the rights and responsibilities of residents. The *Regulations on Population Administration* issued over 50 years ago are still in effect but no longer meet the current needs.

Third, outdated population administration. The population is registered in China as households, which is a static method of management that only reflects the size of the household population. As economic and social progress accelerates, the labor movement becomes more frequent. Household-based registration fails to record a significant volume of information on population movement, resulting in huge discrepancies between registered and actual populations and their residences, which poses a great challenge to modern population administration.

Fourth, restricted movement of the population. Recent years have seen massive population movement across China. However, people have to obtain prior approval from destination authorities before relocation. Such household registration arrangements restrict population movement, especially the free flow of the labor force from the countryside to cities or between cities. In terms of the administration of migrants, many large cities have set exorbitantly high standards on household registration for migrants, making it impossible for them to enjoy the same treatment as is offered to local residents in access to public services. It has also made freedom of population movement impossible to realize.

Importance of the Household Registration System Reform

The latest statistics[2] show that China's urbanization rate reached 56.10% by 2015 and is expected to rise to 70% by 2030 (joint research team of DRC, State Council and the World Bank, 2014). Approximately 1 billion people will by then live in cities and benefit from China's economic modernization. The steady progress of urbanization is crucial in meeting China's development and transformation targets.

Nevertheless, the current urbanization rate in China is based on the number of permanent urban residents. It will be only 39.9% if based on the household population, which is 16.2% lower.[3] In recent years, the growing number of migrants (shown in Table 2) has not only led to the redistribution of production resources but also posed challenges to China's economic reform. The large number of rural migrants who live in cities without urban household registration are unable to have equal access to welfare enjoyed by registered urban residents. The resulting unfair distribution of public service poses risks to social stability. From this perspective, rapid progress in household registration system reform will generate a great impetus for China's all-around economic and social development.

I. Raising economic productivity

According to the theory of development economics, in the process of integrating urban and rural governance structures, surplus rural labor will flock from the traditional farming sector to the modern industrial sector as a low-wage demographic dividend for economic growth. However, the binary economic structure created by the segmentation of the urban–rural household registration system limits the freedom of migration and employment to a great extent. The free flow of production resources is essential to building a unified resource market across China for the efficient allocation of resources. Therefore, household registration system reform is of great importance to raising productivity, as it unshackles the migration of the labor force. This is also what scholars often refer to as the benefits delivered by the reform.

---

[2] *China Statistical Yearbook 2015*, National Statistics Bureau of the PRC.

[3] National Development and Reform Commission: *Report on China's New Urbanization 2015*, China Planning Press, 2016.

Table 2 Number of migrants and number of people not living in place of registered household

Year	No. of migrants (100 million)	No. of people not living in place of registered household (100 million)
2010	2.21	2.61
2011	2.3	2.71
2012	2.36	2.79
2013	2.45	2.89
2014	2.53	2.98
2015	2.46	2.92

Data source China Statistical Yearbook 2015, National Statistics Bureau of the PRC

A survey conducted by the joint research team of the DRC, State Council and the Work Bank in 2014 showed that based on the productivity gap between traditional industries and modern urban industries, every 1% population migration from rural to urban areas will raise China's GDP by 1.2 percentage points. Du Yang and Cai Fang found in their studies (2014) that according to the population migration goals set in the *National New Urbanization Plan 2014–2020*, at a presumed economic growth rate of 5.5%, the net annual returns created by the nation-wide household registration system reform will top RMB 1.2 trillion. This means that the reform will improve China's labor market, continue to unleash the country's growth potential and promote healthy and sustained development of the Chinese economy.

Meanwhile, there is a large gap between urban and rural areas of China in consumption level. As indicated in Chart 1, China's urbanization rate has increased from 27.46 to 56.10% since the 1990s, but the consumption level in urban areas has been 3 times that of rural areas.

Chart 1: comparison of the urban–rural consumption level in the urbanization process

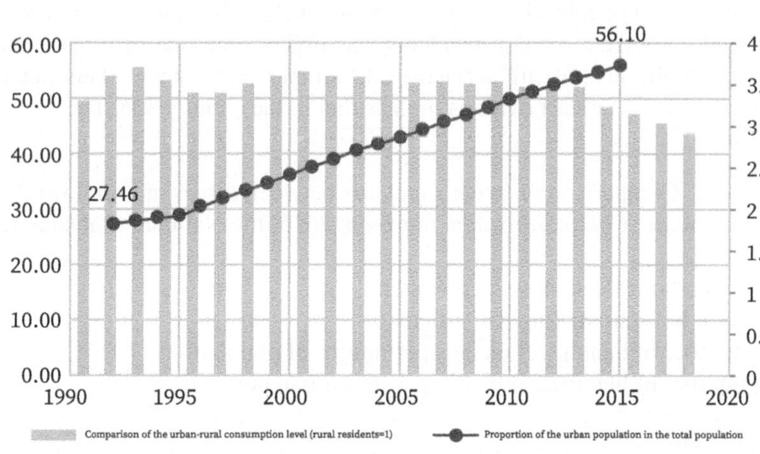

Comparison of the urban–rural consumption level (rural residents = 1) proportion of the urban population in the total population.
Data source: *China Statistical Yearbook 2015*, National Statistics Bureau of the PRC.

Because of restrictions in the household registration system, a large number of rural migrants are unable to have their identity genuinely changed to "urban residents". With different welfare, social security benefits and consumption habits, they find themselves alienated, although they live in the same city as urban residents. A comprehensive household registration system reform aims to help migrants integrate into cities. The government should include them in the social safety net and fully tap their consumption potential to create a larger market. Providing them and their children access to employment, health care, education and other public services is also a long-term investment in human capital. It may not produce economic returns in the short term but will transform China's inefficient growth model in the long run and ultimately promote industrial upgrading and global competitiveness of the country.

II. Narrowing the urban–rural income gap

According to data released by the National Bureau of Statistics, the Gini coefficient of household income in 2015 was 0.462, still higher than the international redline of 0.40. The per capita income difference between urban and rural residents decreased slightly to 2.73 but remained high. According to the *Report of China Labor Dynamic Survey 2015*, the average per capita income in China in 2014 was RMB 29,394. The figure for eastern China was RMB 34,980, higher than that for the central and western regions, which were RMB 26,408 and RMB 23,897, respectively.

Over the years, China has been struggling with serious income inequality between urban and rural areas and between the eastern and western regions. The household registration system, which severely restricts the flow of population, is a major contributing factor to such inequalities. There is a large gap between urban and rural areas in terms of people's living standards and welfare benefits. As shown in Chart 2, the Engel coefficient of rural residents was higher than that of urban residents. In terms of public health care services, the number of health workers per thousand people in cities is at least twice as high as that in the countryside. The gap continues to grow.

Chart 2: Comparison of living standards between urban and rural residents.
Data source: *China Statistical Yearbook 2015*, the National Statistics Bureau of the PRC.
—urban households Engel coefficient.
—rural households Engel coefficient.
—number of health technicians per unit rural population.
—number of health technicians per unit urban population.

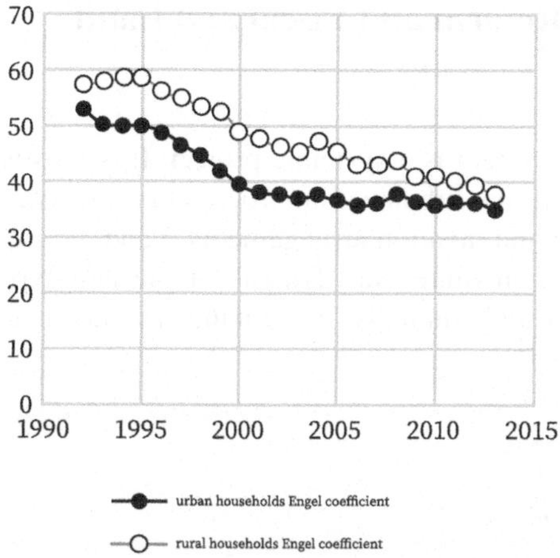

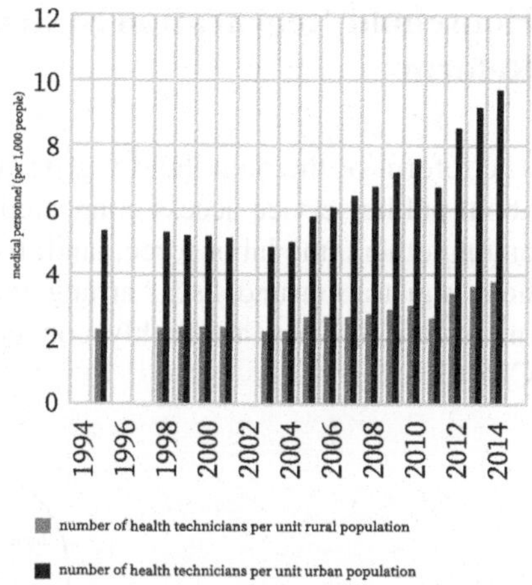

The household registration system causes serious institutional barriers, making it impossible for the surplus rural labor force to move into cities in an orderly way and share the benefits created by economic growth. For those who have come to cities and contributed to the growth of the local economy and tax revenues, the system prevents them from enjoying the same welfare treatment that urban residents enjoy. The lack of access to public goods such as employment, children's education, health care, housing and social security makes it difficult for these migrants to fully integrate into the city life, and their income level is lagging further behind the registered urban residents. Therefore, only by gradually stripping away the privileges tied to the urban households and various political, economic and cultural interests attached to the household registration system can the government ensure that every hardworking citizen in the city is entitled to equal public welfare. Only by decoupling labor, personnel, wages, prices, education, health, social welfare and other institutional arrangements linked to the household registration system can China create a level playing field and mitigate the hidden risks caused by inequality.

In addition, according to Professor Cai Hongbin of Peking University, social mobility underpins long-term economic growth. Equal opportunity and full social mobility hinges on the implementation of rules on fair competition and removal of the imbalance in human capital investment in the fields of education and health care. Therefore, the reform of the household registration system, the full elimination of institutional discrimination and the construction of a fair labor market of equal opportunities are essential in avoiding the middle-income trap and achieving long-term healthy economic growth for China.

Household Registration System Reform and Fiscal and Land Reforms

The reform of the household registration system is a systemic project. It is mostly about public service access connected with the urbanization process that involves, among others, the labor force, land, fiscal and taxation arrangements. Land, household registration and fiscal arrangement constitute the "Trioka" of the new-type urbanization. They are highly connected and mutually influencing, as shown in Chart 3.

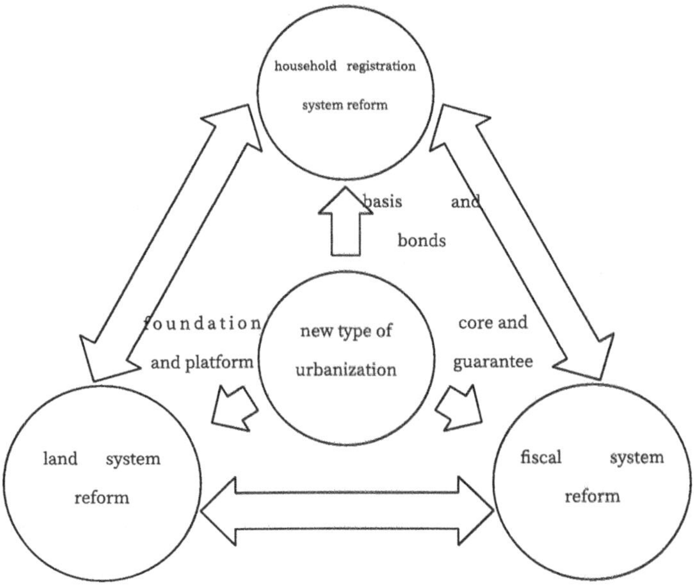

Chart 3: Relations among the household registration system reform and land and fiscal reforms
Household registration system reform; new type of urbanization; land system reform; fiscal system reform; basis and bonds; foundation and platform; core and guarante.

Land is crucial to urbanization and survival of the rural population. As local governments deliver public service and promote household registration system reform, they must function within the limit of the fiscal system. Both the household registration system reform and the fiscal reform aim at fair distribution of public services for attracting rural population into the cities. The purpose of the land reform is to make better use of land by turning it into capital resource on the basis of well-defined ownership and right to use. In this way, farmers moving into cities will see their livelihood basically secure and stop worrying about making ends meet. The question is now how to adapt policies to local realities and make the best of the Trioka to transform the growth model and build synergy in propelling a new round of economic reform and development in China.

I. Household registration system reform and fiscal reform

The essence of household registration is public service related to housing, minimum allowance and education, and its reform is about adjustment of the rights and interests of households. The basic goal of government expenditure is to provide non-discriminatory public services to market players. However, due to the current tax sharing system, it is difficult for local governments to have fiscal power that is commensurate with their administrative duties. Therefore, they tend to take the household registration system as a necessary barrier to avoid budgetary spending on migrants. In this context, success of the household registration reform hinges on balancing the fiscal relations between the central and local government and between different localities so that fiscal power can be shared properly through the budgetary system, and incentives are in place for the government to offer public services for migrant workers.

The main challenges for migrant workers in their urban integration include employment, social security, children's education and their own education and training. The government's fiscal functions include resource allocation, income distribution and public goods supply. These functions require enormous financial resources. Studies conducted by the research team of DRC, the State Council (2011) in the cities of Chongqing, Wuhan, Zhengzhou and Jiaxing found that the cost of transforming migrant workers to urban residents is approximately RMB 80,000 per person. Assuming that 15 million new urban residents are added every year, the annual increase in China's public expenditure will reach RMB 1.2 trillion. The *China Urban Development Report* and the *Urban Blue Paper* concluded that the per capita public costs of rural-turn-urban population in China's eastern, central and western regions are RMB 1,76,000, RMB 1,04,000 and RMB 1,06,000, respectively, or a national average of RMB 1,31,000. The total cost nationwide will climb to RMB 51.1 trillion by 2030. Undoubtedly, the huge cost has brought enormous burden to local governments and seriously hindered the household registration system reform. It is agreed that the solution may lie in the policy of "pay as you go", which means that pubic service funds for a person can be allocated to the new administrative area where that person migrates to for unification of the government's fiscal and administrative power. At the same time, some public services will be put under the unified management of the central government, and budgets will be allocated to local authorities according to national population statistics.

In addition, to address the issue of unclear payment responsibilities under the tax sharing system, efforts are required to improve the payment transfer system both top down and across regions to cover the needs of a large migrating population. Under the current system, the decision-making power of most public services lies with the central government. Local governments are responsible for executing the order of payment, and their decision-making power is very limited. A top-down payment transfer can remove asymmetry of power and financial resources between the upper and lower levels of government. The mismatch between fiscal revenues and expenditures of local governments caused by population flows calls for wider application of IT across the country to enable cross-regional payment transfers between local governments. Liu and Gan (2013) put forward a highly valuable suggestion that there should be two models of payment transfer in China, one vertically from the central to the provincial governments and another both vertically and horizontally between governments below the provincial level.

II. Household registration system reform and land reform

Two issues need to be addressed in completing the identity change for rural migrants in cities. One is to peel off the welfare benefits attached to the household registration, and the other is to separate social security from the land. A binary arrangement that divides China's social security benefits into household-based and land-based benefits must be scrapped to break China's economic structure of urban–rural segmentation. Only in this way can China succeed in transiting from the planned economy to the socialist market economy and from a traditional agricultural society to an industrial society.

During the reform, the government, businesses and individuals may share the cost of integrating rural migrants, and the household registration administration model can be replaced with the residence administration model through a transitional residence permit system. In addition, the current land system should be modified to allow farmers to retain land rights when they give up farming and become urban citizens. Zhang (2011) found in his survey that nearly 90% of the farmers are reluctant to move into cities if it means giving away their contracted land. The "land for urban household identity" approach seems unrealistic. Liu et al. (2015) drew the same conclusion from the jurisprudential perspective that the nature of the "land for social security" approach is to exchange what farmers have in hand for what they are entitled to by repackaging the cost of welfare delivery as compensation for land loss. The practice violates the principle of equity.

The current rural land ownership system has grown out of the "production brigade-based three-tiered land ownership" system of 1962. The *No. 1 Document of the CPC Central Committee* in 2014 pointed out that on the basis of the implementation of collective ownership of rural land, the government should protect farmers' right to their contracted land and ease restrictions on land management rights. In July 2014, the State Council issued the *Guidelines on Further Advancing the Household Registration System Reform*, which stressed that farmers are entitled to the right to contract and manage the land and the right to use their homestead in accordance with the law. Farmers are also entitled to their shares of collective benefits as members of the collective economic organizations. These are their lawful property rights and cannot be revoked as a precondition for granting them urban citizenship. Therefore, the reform of the household registration system should be carried out in tandem with rural land reform, as the latter aims to protect the legitimate rights and interests of farmers by converting rural land ownership to the property rights of rural residents and nurturing the market for trading rural land-related property rights.

The essence of rural land system reform is the confirmation of land rights. Confirmation and certification of land rights will define ownership and facilitate reform in other fields. According to Xinhua News Agency,[4] ownership of over 90% of the collective land in China's rural areas has been confirmed and certified, and confirmation of land contracts and management rights will be largely completed within five years. The establishment of a property rights trading system is at the center of rural property rights system reform. The "land-to-stock share" reform will ensure the orderly and well-regulated transfer of rural property rights. Rural property rights trading centers can be established with new-type farmer cooperatives. Land trading can be stimulated with further improvement of land transfer guarantees and other supporting policies. It is agreed that the new land system featuring land capitalization and urban–rural integration can provide farmers with initial funding for their non-agricultural businesses. More importantly, it will lend a strong impetus to the household registration system reform and urbanization in China toward the ultimate urban–rural economic and social integration.

Policy Recommendations

I. Coordinated development among the eastern, central and western regions and faster growth of small and medium-sized cities

There are two kinds of urban welfare in China, namely, household-based welfare and nonhousehold-based welfare. Nonhousehold-based welfare mainly includes urban infrastructure, informal jobs and other non-competitive public goods such as information, environment and cultural atmosphere. Differences in nonhousehold-based welfare between cities based on their gaps in the economic and social development level are a key factor behind population migration. The economic and social development gaps between cities in China are now too wide, and therefore the nonhousehold-based welfare in large cities is even higher than the household-based and nonhousehold-based welfare in small cities. As a result, rural migrants would rather stay in large cities without registered status than go to small cities as registered residents. The resulting overconcentration of the rural population in large cities makes it difficult for the reform to produce any substantive results in delivering nondiscriminatory welfare there. Zou (2014) of China Renmin University drew a similar conclusion that China is facing imbalances in terms of both the development level between cities of different sizes and the welfare between registered and unregistered urban residents in the process of urbanization. This has gravely diminished the success of the household registration reform.

With this in mind, while pursuing the reform for equal access to welfare within the city, efforts should be made to narrow the gaps in the development level between cities, guide the flow of population, investment, and social resources more to small

[4] http://www.jjckb.cn/.

and medium-sized cities, promote balanced growth for all cities and create a sound basis for further reform of the household registration system.

II. Pressing ahead with IT application and the rule of law

Improvement of laws and regulations is crucial to the success of the reform. Provincial and municipal authorities have issued plans on household registration system reform based on the *Opinions on Further Promoting the Household Registration System Reform* of the State Council. However, they still need to further improve the implementation rules. There are quite a few laws and regulations related to rural land ownership, such as the *Law on Rural Land Contract*, the *Administrative Measures on Transfer of Rural Land Contract Management Rights*, the *Law on Property Rights* and the *Implementing Rules of the Land Administration Law*, but they mostly contain general principles that need to be further elaborated. Laws and regulations regarding the exit mechanism, compensation standards and social security for farmers still need to be improved.

As part of the national IT application program, the government should conduct accurate, complete and timely administration of the population on the basis of general management of population information. To this end, national household registration authorities should establish and improve their population information database to put an end to the state of segmentation of administrative bodies and their roles, institutional redundancies and overlapping mandates. The national information management system must be straightened out. Greater efforts are needed in the database building of the national population information center. Joint development on advanced population information technologies should be carried out so that population information management will cover all aspects of society to better serve the socialist cause.

III. Cutting back government roles and building a service-oriented government

Minimizing government roles is the general principle of this round of the reform of building a leaner government. Premier Li Keqiang stressed in the report on the work of the government in 2015 the importance of streamlining government administration and setting the limit of government power, which was welcomed by the delegates to the National People's Congress. Streamlining government administration is essential in building a sound socialist market economy. The vitality, creativity and productivity of the economy and society will be maximized when the power of the central authorities is delegated, as it should, to the market, public, businesses, social organizations and local government, whose rights and roles must be fully respected. This principle should be upheld in the household registration system reform, including replacing the pre-registration review with post-settlement registration and simplifying the process of registration to promote population movement. The approach of the government should also change correspondingly from administration to service delivery by providing more equal access to public service for residents and pursuing a new type of urbanization.

There is every reason to believe that under the guidance of building a leaner government, China will successfully meet its household registration system reform target, complete the dual economic transition, achieve long-term and steady development, and ultimately create a path to success with unique Chinese features.

Bibliography

Chen, X. (2015). Solving the difficulties of getting urban resident identity for farmers: Household registration and land management system innovation. *Jiangsu Social Sciences* (3).

Deng, Z. (2014). Land, household registration, fiscal and taxation reforms are key to the new-type of urbanization. *Economic Review Journal* (8).

Du, Y., Cai, F., Qu, X., & et al. (2014). Continuing the Chinese miracle: Reaping dividends from the reform of the household registration system. *Economic Research Journal* (8).

Gan, X., & Liu, D. (2015). Household registration system, equal access to public services and reform of the financial system. *Public Financial Research* (3).

Huang, G. (2012). Comparative study and enlightenments of the legal systems on household registration in other countries. *Hebei Law Science* (12).

Huang, Y. (2013). Fiscal constraint and institutional advancement of public service supply in the process of turning migrant workers into urban residents. Unpublished master's dissertation, Ocean University of China, 2013.

Jie, D. (2008). Enlightenment and reflections for China from the population administration measures of developed countries. *Population and Economics* (4).

Joint research team of DRC of the State Council and the World Bank. (2014). China promotes efficient, inclusive and sustainable urbanization. *Management World* (4).

Li, Y. (2013). *China's economy in dual transition*. China Renmin University Press.

Liu, D., & Gan, X. (2013). Choice of transfer payment model for equal access to public services in the perspective of population flow. *Journal of Zhongnan University of Economics and Law* (4).

Liu, Y., Xie, H., & Lu, G. (2015). A study on laws concerning rural land property rights in the perspective of household registration system reform. In *Research on real estate law of China* (vol. 12). Law Press China.

Qu, X., & Cheng, J. (2014). Continuing China's miracle: Reaping dividends from the reform of the household registration system. *Economic Research Journal* (8).

Research team of DRC, the State Council. (2011). The overall trend and strategic orientation of the process of integrating migrant workers into cities. *Reform* (5).

Wang, Q. (2014). Household registration reform and population information management in China. *Contemporary Economic and Management* (12).

Xing, D. (2016). A study on the measures of the integrated reform of household registration system and rural land property rights. *China Agriculture Information* (2).

Zhang, S. (2015). The experience of urban population administration in developed countries: Case study 10. *China Development Observation* (11).

Zhang, Y. (2011). Willingness of migrant workers to settle down in cities and the choice of China's urbanization path. *Chinese Journal of Population Science* (2).

Zhu, Z. (2014). Research on the mechanism of the interconnected reforms on the household registration system and the rural land system. *Qiushi* (12).

Zou, Y. (2014). Dual imbalance of urbanization and reform of household registration system. *Economic Theory and Business Management* (2).

Zou, Y. (2015). Logics and policy choices in the reform of the household registration system. *Economist* (4).

Educational Reform and a Leaner Government

Ning Liu

China's economy is in a new normal. The growth has changed gears. Changes have been made in the economic structure, and the effects of the previous stimulus packages have yet to be absorbed. The world has seen years of sluggish growth since 2008. Negative interest rates appear for the first time in human history. In this context, stepping up the reform holds the key to addressing the underlying economic problems at home and abroad. The focus of this round of the reform is to delegate government powers and put them under checks to inject vitality into the market and local authorities. Thanks to over three decades of reform, an all-around market system has taken its initial shape in China. Businesses have become more vibrant and sensitive to prices as their ownership is clarified through joint stock reforms. Private companies have become the main players in the market.

That said, the planned economy has left a deep imprint on education. The government plays multiple roles. It provides and manages education and at the same time develops the educational system and evaluates the quality of teaching. Often, educators have to take orders from government officials. If students are taken as the products of education, then what and how many shall be produced and how to produce are all subject to government decisions. Privately run schools or educational institutions do not have much confidence in themselves, as their role in China is trivial in both legal sense and practice. Such an educational model, characterized by a blurred government role and close-door operation, easily gives rise to insider control, as evidenced by mounting cases of corruption. While the quality of education in China calls for urgent improvement, the appeal of international education is increasing with a rapidly growing number of young students studying abroad. From July 2014 to February 2015, the number of Chinese students receiving basic education in the United States increased by 23.5%, and the number receiving high school education increased by 50%. China has become the world's largest source of international students. The huge contrast between the lack of progress in educational reform and

N. Liu (✉)
Qingdao International Academy, Qingdao, China

Y. Li and Z. Cheng (eds.), *The Chinese Path Toward a Leaner Government*,
https://doi.org/10.1007/978-981-19-6718-4_12

the huge success of economic reforms makes it all the more necessary to reform China's current educational model.

The world is in the new round of technological revolution. Breakthroughs in information, energy and biotechnology have created favorable conditions for China's economic transformation featured by innovation and entrepreneurship. High-tech keeps improving. Traditional manufacturing industries have been upgraded. With the application of information technologies, IoT, AI, 3D printing and new materials, products can be made quickly and in small quantities at a time. Thus, "made in China 2025" characterized by industrial revolution 4.0 can be realized. This is a key step for China as a major industrial country to seize the historical opportunity to catch up and overtake advanced economies and become an industrial power by means of new technologies. The very foundation of the endeavor is human resources, including various kinds of technology researchers and professionals of special skills. To pursue economic restructuring, China's needs to foster consumption and the service sector as new growth drivers of the economy. The service sector is now powered by mobile Internet, cloud computing, IoT, big data, artificial intelligence, virtual reality and other new technologies. In the field of mobile Internet, for example, online technologies can help locate precisely idle resources and match them with the demand side for the first time in history. Thanks to the precise match of information and the use of mobile phone terminals imbedded with GPS, offline efficiency has been significantly enhanced. It has made online ordering plus offline delivery and the shared economy a possibility.

Education providers need to adapt to changes in economic and technological development and train people for our future. New technologies should be employed to meet market changes in education. The educational reform focusing on streamlining government functions will become a main part of the country's economic transformation and the Chinese national renewal. Following this philosophy, the CPC Central Committee and the State Council issued the *Outline of the National Program for Medium and Long-term Educational Reform and Development (2010–2020)* in 2010, which stressed the need to "advance the reform of the educational management system, focusing on streamlining administration and transforming government functions, delegating power from the central government to local governments and from the government to schools, and clarifying the responsibilities of governments at all levels. It also says that schools shall be regulated, and school management and performance evaluation shall be separated from government regulation. A well-coordinated and well-organized educational management system shall be established in which government administration is separated from school management, each with its clear mandate." The Outline also calls for the government to "grant, expand and ensure decision-making powers to universities in accordance with the law and improve service to universities by adopting sound administrative systems and measures, cutting administrative approval items and improving regulation in the review process." In 2013, the *Decision of the CPC Central Committee on Major Issues Concerning Comprehensively Deepening of the Reform* required "further separation of government administration from school management and performance evaluation, greater authority of provincial governments in overall planning of education, more autonomy for universities, and better internal governance structures of universities". These documents charted the course for streamlining administration in the field of education.

Understanding the Meaning of a Leaner Government in Connection with Educational Goals

All reforms have goals to serve. Setting the goals for education is the key to defining government roles and designing the reform framework. Education is a process participated in by students, their parents, schools and the government, each making contribution in their own ways. A clear target for education will help the government decide how and where to roll back its role and to whom powers are delegated.

Countries may have different understandings in different periods about the goals of education and the role of the government in this field, which can determine the course of development and even the fate of a nation. Education reflects a country's will. It is the way for the government to cultivate human resources for nation-building. From this perspective, education is defined as "a social phenomenon to train people and a necessary means to pass on experience in work and life." The goal of education places more emphasis on training the future workforce in large numbers, as students are taught to acquire the skills that society needs. That is why the government needs to be part of it in terms of setting the knowledge system, choosing the way of teaching and regulating the educational process. As the government represents the overall interests of the people, it can easily set a unified goal for education. Education also represents individual processes that tap into the potential of different persons. If this is also taken as the goal, the government should take into consideration the diversity of individual needs and complexity in meeting such needs and give more play to the role of the market while focusing on macrocontrol. Education providers, on their part, should design courses and develop ways of teaching to cater to the needs of different students to fully unleash their potential. The government should do more to encourage the people to vote with their feet and choose whatever education they suit themselves or their children.

With diversification of human skills triggered by fast growth of new technologies and the service sector and a variety of vocational skills needed for Made in China 2025, more consideration should be given to the individuality of education, which is taken as an approach to unleash people's hidden potentials. Alfred Whitehead, a renowned educator of the twentieth century, once said to the effect that the students are humans, and the purpose of education is to inspire and encourage them to pursue self-development.

Modern education theory holds that the purpose of education is to tap human potential and respect individual capabilities. What is important is to develop students' cognitive structures and display the possibilities of their potential in invention and development. As Piaget put it, the goal of education is not to feed knowledge or train people to do things that are being doing now but to create the possibilities for a child to invent, discover, criticize and prove and to create men who are capable of trying something new. When this goal is respected, the role of the market or the invisible hand will become a main focus of the reform. Therefore, it is important to determine the goal first. The following are interpretations of the educational goals in Taiwan and the Chinese mainland.

The goal of education interpreted by the law of education in the Taiwan region is to foster integrity, awareness of democracy and rule of law, humanistic character, healthy body and abilities to think, judge and create, promote respect for basic human rights, protection for eco-environment, and understanding of and care for different countries, ethnicities, genders, religions and cultures so that students will become modern citizens with national identity and global perspectives.

In the *Law of Education of the People's Republic of China*, the goal of education is to serve socialist modernization. Education must be connected with physical work to train undertakers and successors of the socialist cause who are developed in an all-around way in the moral, intellectual and physical perspectives.

Clarifying the Aim of Building a Leaner Government Based on the Role of the Government in Education

The government's participation in education and the formation of the public educational system and its role as the main provider of education are vital to the industrialization and modernization of the country. It reflects the national interests and responds to the development needs of a country in the process of industrialization.

Humanity has witnessed two major role shifts in education providers. The first was replacing home education with religions and communities. It was not until after industrialization that the state became the main provider of education. In the process of national modernization, the US and industrialized countries in Europe began to regard education as part of national powers and developed the system of public schools with administrative means. Education was offered through public channels that led to the creation of a new social system to serve the public and ultimately a public school system. The educational system has thus been gradually established, which mainly relies on public schools with the government as the primary driver. Its basic goal is to provide educational services to the public.

The purpose of government participation in education is consistent with its efforts to balance efficiency and equity in national development. The government hopes that education will reflect the public will of raising the educational level of citizens and the caliber of researchers. As industrialization progresses, the wealth gap has widened. As urbanization continues, access to education has become more unbalanced between urban and rural areas and among regions. Active participation of the government will definitely help improve fair access to education.

The US data show that government participation has not improved the quality of education.

Chart 1: Comparison of US government spending on tuition and the results of education for students aged 17 at the primary educational stage (K12) at constant prices since 1970

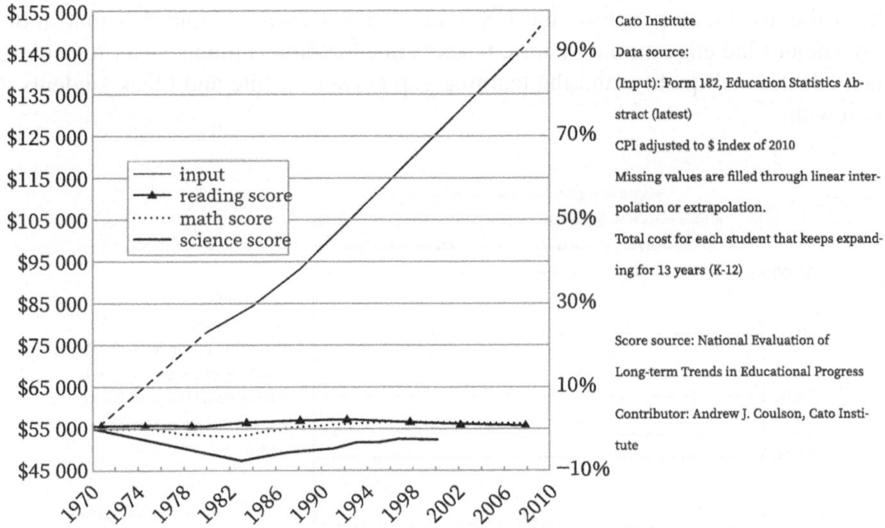

—input,
—reading score,
—math score,
—science score.
Cato Institute
Data source:
(Input): Form 182, Education Statistics Abstract (latest)
CPI adjusted to $ index of 2010.
Missing values are filled through linear interpolation or extrapolation.
Total cost for each student that keeps expanding for 13 years (K–12).
Score source: National Evaluation of Long-term Trends in Educational Progress.
Contributor: Andrew J. Coulson, Cato Institute.

The above table indicates that in 2011, the government spent $1,51,000 on primary education (K12) for every student through the public educational system, more than three times that of 1970 at constant prices. However, the reading and math capabilities of students did not improve much, and there was a drop in their science scores. This is directly related to their ways of learning and the lack of innovative capabilities, but the underlying cause is the change in the nature of learning from capability building to obligations and responsibilities because of government participation in education, in which citizens are in the subordinate state. They are at the receiving end with no say at all. Public education institutions, on their part, pay too much attention to undue formalities and compliance mainly for the purpose of meeting government requirements. Because of government monopoly, public schools have been strictly following government plans, giving little consideration to the choice of learners and competition from private schools.

Likewise, the conclusion based on the data available regarding the gap between the white and black people in the US in education shown in Chart 2 is that in the government-led educational system, fairness in education is much easier to achieve than educational quality, and the learning gap between white and black students is narrowing.

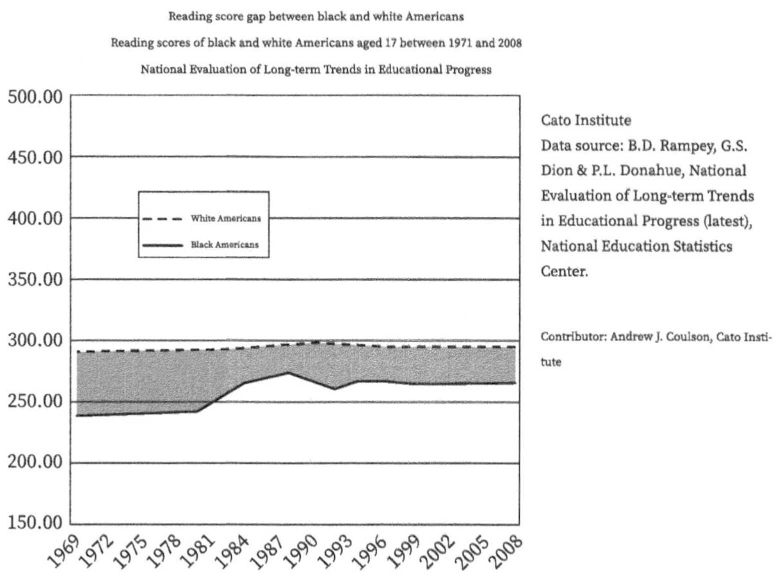

Chart 2: comparison of reading scores between black and white Americans at the age of 17 from 1971 to 2008

Reading score gap between black and white Americans.

- Black Americans
- Bhite Americans

Reading scores of black and white Americans aged 17 between 1971 and 2008.
National Evaluation of Long-term Trends in Educational Progress.
Cato Institute.
Data source: B. D. Rampey, G. S. Dion and P. L. Donahue, *National Evaluation of Long-term Trends in Educational Progress* (latest), National Education Statistics Center.
Contributor: Andrew J. Coulson, Cato Institute.

In the course of national modernization, the government has gained a dominating power over education, which is mainly as follows.

Fiscal and appropriation power. As a public service product, education requires large fiscal spending. Modern civilization is characterized by ensuring citizens' rights to education through government budgetary appropriation. However, the government must ensure, through streamlining administration and delegating power, that the power is properly exercised to maintain fair distribution of educational resources and raise efficiency in their response to educational needs and corruption. Some of the powers include setting rules on managing and distributing the government educational funds, deciding the share of educational funds between the central and local governments, encouraging educational institutions to seek funding autonomy, designing incentives, regulating types and amount of scholarships, and adopting taxation rules on education.

Planning power. This covers two aspects. (1) The state authorizes relevant government institutions through law to make regional plans on education similar to zoning in urban development to ensure equal access to education in step with urbanization. (2) The government decides on planning, goals and standards of education to reflect the will of the country or a region for development and maintain consistency in educational quality. It also sets rules and qualifications regarding market access for educational institutions, such as the number and types of educational providers, information collection and technology use.

Ownership. The government is the owner and the manager of educational institutions. It also plays a part in the routine operation of educational institutions. However, as it does not have the ability or experience in managing education as a business, it needs to delegate its ownership and authorize and regulate those who have good knowledge of education to run schools.

Evaluation power. The government evaluates the result of education by itself or through a third party and decides on rewards or punishments to educational institutions accordingly. Relevant information shall be promptly published.

Bearing in mind the government's power in education, we need to push for the improvement of educational quality by bringing in market forces and private sectors in the new round of government streamlining. The government will instead focus on fairness in education. The *Decision of the CPC Central Committee on Major Issues Concerning Comprehensively Deepening of the Reform* requires "further separation of government administration from school management and performance evaluation, greater power of provincial governments in overall planning of education, more autonomy for universities, and improved internal governance structures of universities". The goal of separating the roles is forward-looking and sensible. The power list can help the government withdraw from specific and meticulous management and focus more on macro planning and regulation. It is an important step to check the government's power and advance educational reform. To delegate educational ownership, incentives must be given to education providers to protect the interests of schools. Power delegation in the evaluation system is needed so that third-party institutions and professional education providers can be brought in to address the ineffective evaluation of education due to the asymmetry of information.

Rolling Back Government Administration in Education in the History of China's Educational Reform

Rolling back government administration in education is an incremental process that should move in tandem with economic and social reforms. A study of the major educational reform initiatives in the past three decades and their impact today will help navigate the efforts to build a leaner government in the new round of reform. The *Decisions on the Reform in the Educational System* released by the central government in 1985 (hereafter referred to as the *Decision*) has a far-reaching impact on educational reform and government streamlining in China.

The *Decision* sets a clear goal for the educational reform: "the central government deems it necessary to carry out fundamental and systematic reforms. The government shall reform the management system by strengthening macro control, streamlining administration, raising the autonomy for schools and reforming the personnel system. Philosophies, contents and methods of education that do not fit into socialist modernization shall also be changed accordingly." "Streamlining administration" is an important part of the *Decision,* and the following steps were taken in this direction.

1. Delegating administrative power. The central government delegated power and responsibilities to local authorities and focused on general policies and guidelines. The local authorities were responsible for working out and putting in place specific policies, systems and plans. They could exercise leadership, administration and inspection power over schools. Governments at the provincial level (including autonomous regions and municipalities under the direct administration of the central government) divide responsibilities among provincial, municipal (prefectural), county and village administrative bodies.
2. Promoting diversity of educational providers. Local authorities should encourage and guide SOEs, social groups and individuals in running schools and seek funding from organizations, collectives and individuals into educational services on a voluntary instead of mandatory basis. Local governments should keep down fees collected from schools and relieve schools of their financial burdens.
3. Giving more autonomy to schools. The *Decision* stresses autonomy for schools, especially institutes of higher learning. This was the first time that school autonomy was included in a government document. It gave universities the right to admit students of contractual programs and self-financed students, adjust the service scopes of academic programs, formulate teaching plans and syllabi, and compile and select textbooks. According to the *Decision*, schools also have the right to be commissioned or partner with other organizations to conduct scientific research and technological development and form consortiums with other schools, research bodies and businesses. They can also appoint and remove officials up to vice presidents and nominate vice president candidates, dispose of capital investment and funding from the government, use self-raised funds, and carry out international educational and academic exchanges.

In 1993, the CPC Central Committee and the State Council promulgated the *Guidelines on China's Educational Reform and Development* (hereinafter referred to as the *Guidelines*), which set the goal of the educational reform. It says "a wholistic and step-by-step approach is needed to push for the reform toward building a new educational system that fits into China's socialist market economic system and its political and technology systems." The *Guidelines* once again define the relations between the educational reform and the overall reform of the national economy. Taking into account how the market economy affects the efforts of building a learner government, it calls for a greater role of market players and regards education as both a public good and a market commodity. Under this philosophy, the *Guidelines* put forward new measures for delegating government powers.

1. Putting in place a system of diversified bodies of educational service, where the government plays a dominating role and other sectors join in the efforts. Basic education is mainly run by local governments. A new approach to higher education should gradually take shape where the central and provincial governments (including provinces, autonomous regions and municipalities under direct administration of the central government) play a major role and nongovernment sectors participate in running schools. Vocational and adult education should be mainly offered by industrial organizations, businesses and public institutions or through joint efforts of various social sectors.
2. Further delegating power to educational providers. The school personnel and distribution systems must be reformed. On the basis of proper staffing arrangement, a work post responsibility system and a recruitment-appointment system should be established to widen wage scales. The reform aimed to break egalitarianism and give more incentives to school staff and ultimately transform the internal operation mechanism of schools and improve their educational performance and returns.
3. Giving better play to the market role. Market competition should be first introduced to the school's logistic department. It should also be used to reform and improve the educational investment system to increase educational funding and establish a more market-based fee-collection system for noncompulsory education. Educational funding should be raised through various channels, with government appropriation as the main source, supplemented by educational taxes and fees, tuition and fees for noncompulsory education, income from businesses run by schools, private donations and fund raising, and educational funds. The minimum tuition fees should be raised for noncompulsory education, and the standards and measures should be determined by governments at the provincial level and central authorities in charge of school administration, while the affordability of the public should also be taken into consideration. Students of poor families should enjoy tuition and fee deduction or exemption or be granted student loans.
4. Strengthening oversight of school fund raising activities. The government should facilitate funding for schools through financial and credit means, support school-run businesses, high-tech companies affiliated with schools and work study

programs. It should also help them launch educational deposits and school loan services.
5. Exiting from routine school management roles and focusing on macro administration. The government should define rights and obligations for universities through legislation and help them enjoy true autonomy in running public education.
6. Implementing classified management of budget appropriation. The government should set up different standards and measures of appropriation for schools of different levels and categories. It should encourage schools to raise funds in accordance with laws and market rules.

However, due to a weak market mechanism and imbalance between fairness and efficiency, schools remained dependent on the government despite some newly gained autonomy, and their actual status was not changed substantially.

In 1995, the National People's Congress adopted the *Education Law of the People's Republic of China*, which for the first time made clear the status of public schools as legal persons as well as their lawful rights to put the autonomy of schools on solid legal ground. According to it, "a school or any other institution of education that meets the requirements for a legal person shall acquire the status of a legal person from the date of approval and registration of its establishment", "a school or any other institution of education shall, in civil activities, enjoy civil rights and bear civil liabilities according to law", and "businesses run by schools or other institutions of education shall bear separate civil liabilities".

To advance the reform, there is a need to tap into the market players that have grown in number since 1995, respect spontaneous bottom-up reforms, make up for market misfunctioning through legislation and institutional improvement and spell out the goals for educational reform. The need for better and individualized educational services for people with improved living standards should be taken into consideration. The supply-side reform should be intensified to raise the quality of education. The government should rely more on the market to deliver diversified educational products to serve different needs, while public schools should aim more at fairness in education. Measures for delegating government power should be specified for both public and market-based education.

Recognizing Education as Tradable and Profit-Making Commodities in Government Power Delegation

Education has been included in the 12 services sectors on the GATT (later transformed to WTO) sectoral classification list since 1994, where it has been recognized as tradable goods and a sector likely to be privatized, higher education in particular, with the market playing a dominant role, the same as goods for import and export. According to the World Bank, 1.42 million people of medium–high income countries studied abroad in 2012, up 160.9% from 5,40,000 in 2000. They were followed by India, Indonesia, the Philippines and other medium–low income countries, where the number of students studying abroad increased from 3,40,000 in 2000 to 7,50,000 in 2012, up 120.6%. In comparison, OECD and non-OECD countries of high income saw a relatively stable outflow of students with an average annual growth rate of under 10%.

By 2013, there were 718 private universities in China (including 292 independent colleges) with 5.5752 million students, accounting for 29.5% of the total number of universities and 22.5% of the total number of students. However, education has not been fully recognized as a tradable and profit-making commodity. According to the *Law on Promoting Private Education* of 2003, investors may obtain a fair share of the school profit returns after deductions of necessary costs and fees in accordance with government regulations and funding reservations for school development. Measures for obtaining the returns shall be set by the State Council. However, it also stresses that "private education shall be nonprofit making and is a part of the socialist educational undertaking."

The revised *Educational Law* of 2015 replaced the wording "no organization or individual may set up schools or other educational institutions for profit" with "schools or other educational institutions wholly or partially financed by government funds or donations shall not become profit-making organizations". The *Guidelines of Educational Planning* make it clear that "efforts shall be made to classify schools into profit and nonprofit ones". However, in reality, education is not regarded as something tradeable because of the following factors.

1. Private educational institutions are unable to get listed and therefore unable to have access to direct finance. According to Article 3 of the *Law on Private Education Promotion*, "private education belongs to the nonprofit undertaking". They can only register with civil affairs authorities as noncorporate legal persons, which is different from corporate legal persons registered at the industrial and commercial administration departments, a precondition for getting listed. As nonprofit and noncorporate organizations, private educational institutions cannot become listed companies.
2. Private educational and tutoring institutions must report to a number of authorities and face complex approval and registration procedures. Article 11 of the *Private Education Promotion Act* stresses that "privately run schools engaged in diploma education, preschool education, self-taught examination, etc., shall subject to review and approval of the government departments for education at or above the county level in accordance with their mandates defined by the state. Private schools mainly engaging in training of professional skills and vocational qualifications shall be subject to review and approval of the administrative departments of human resources and social security in accordance with their mandates and shall submit a copy to the educational administrative departments for record-filing purposes." Educational, labor and social security, and industrial and commercial departments are in charge of review and approval of matters related to private educational and tutoring institutions, and civil affairs and industrial and commercial departments are responsible for their registration.

3. Private schools are under restrictions for public fundraising. According to Article 8 of the *Implementing Rules on Private Education Promotion Law*, "when establishing a privately funded school, the founder(s) shall not collect money from students or their parents, or raise funds through public financing." However, it is not clear whether "no public financing" means these schools cannot raise funds for starting school operations or they cannot be listed on the stock market for fund raising.

Globally, the trend of educational reform includes privatizing public schools by delegating government power to the market, providing public service and encouraging competition among service providers through building public–private partnerships between the government and schools and other market-based initiatives.

1. Most of the universities in the US, including Ivy League members such as Harvard and Yale, are run privately. In terms of basic education, approximately 20% of primary schools and 10% of high schools are privately funded. "Charter schools" have emerged in recent years as a new type of public school under market rules. In the 1990s, under the *No One Left Behind Act*, a public school would be ordered to shut down if it failed to pass the state's standard tests for three years in a row, and a nongovernment institution, a company or even individuals could take over it and change it to a charter school. The charter schools receive their initial funds from the state government and receive over 2 billion dollars of funding every year from the federal government, including the *No One Left Behind Act*. Local governments pay for students' annual tuition subsidies the same as they provide for students in public schools. School runners may apply to the government for taking over such public schools based on their own educational specialties and school programs. To date, there are 5673 charter schools in the US, accounting for 4% of total student enrollment.
2. Only about 7% of students in Britain go to private schools, which are generally better-run than public schools. "Free schools" have appeared in recent years and are similar to after-school programs in the US. These schools enjoy full autonomy. They are out of the control of local governments, enjoy greater budgetary power and almost complete freedom in staff recruitment, wage and syllabus setting, and even in semester length and curriculum. In 2013, the government approved 102 "free schools" that enrolled over 100,000 students, meeting the full admission quota. The government says that businesses, individuals and social organizations can apply for opening "free schools" and run them according to their wishes, so long as they are willing to promote the idea of equality and democracy, respect individuals, care for the environment and commit themselves against violence and racism.
3. In Japan, the ratio between public and private universities is 20:80. The proportion of public universities is falling, and state-run universities have been transformed to corporations responsible for their own profits and losses.

Defining the nature of education as tradable goods helps determine the scope of authority for the government and brings the following reform benefits.

1. The commodity nature of education and the status of school runners as market players will reduce willful intervention by the government in school affairs and ensure school autonomy legally and economically. Hence, the current phenomena where the head of the educational authorities can summon heads of schools for meetings as he wishes and is involved directly in the daily affairs of the schools will be fundamentally changed.
2. Market forces will raise school efficiency and ensure the quality of education. It is the same as economic reforms that use the market mechanism to protect the rights of market players and minimize government support to nonperforming SOEs that have wasted national resources. The market will encourage private entrepreneurs to provide goods and services and entrust services through contracts, franchises and vouchers to private companies and individuals who are engaged in market competition.
3. The market protects consumers of education of their rights to choose and seek quality goods. Fiscal, personnel and policy-making powers are delegated to all sorts of educational institutions. Educational service providers and consumers are also reminded of their obligations and responsibilities. The right to choose, in particular, maximizes the opportunities of individuals in the educational market. Transforming public schools to charter schools and free schools will help them better engage in market competition, optimize the allocation of educational resources and encourage them to provide the best services to educational consumers.
4. Fairness in education is ensured. Educational reforms in a number of countries show that the market force and privatization of education will expand access to education for ordinary people and promote fairness in education. Because of fierce competition, educational service providers will try their best to lower the price and raise the service quality. Learners will have more decision-making power and the right to choose in terms of quality, form and price of educational service. The schools will pay more attention to learners' needs, make up for deficiencies as demonstrated by traditional public schools and try to meet various needs of consumers in a more flexible way. Ultimately, learners will gain more autonomy and the right to choose.

School Vouchers Can Promote the Delegation of Government Power in Terms of Educational Funding Appropriation

American economist Milton Friedman proposed the concept of school vouchers based on the idea of "free to choose" for students and their parents and full market competition. The idea of school vouchers is to provide each student educational funding that the government originally allocates to public schools in the form of school vouchers based on the unit cost of each student. It will give parents more freedom to choose and force public schools to raise funding by themselves by collecting tuition fees. They will have to compete not only among themselves but also with private schools. The right to funding appropriation means that the government will have more administrative power over schools. School vouchers are good because they can shift the power of funding from the government to the market and thus lower the possibility of power abuse and confusion in other areas. To show fairness in education, citizens with vouchers have the right to choose educational suppliers according to government regulations and personal needs. If they choose private schools because of limited choice from the government-run schools, the vouchers can compensate for part of the tuition fees of the private schools to reflect fairness in education. Otherwise, those who send their children to private schools with no subsidies would have paid twice for education, one in the form of taxation and the other tuition.

It is quite difficult to put the idea to practice. Only two cities and one state in the US are practicing the school voucher system. Given educational imbalances and operational complexities in China, the voucher system will face great challenges. Nevertheless, the idea offers new inspirations in advancing educational reform and delegating government power by respecting market forces and giving play to the roles of different entities to improve educational equity and quality. Thus, more power shifted from the government can be transferred to the market.

The Theory and Practice of Enterprise Reforms will be Used to Address Issues Involving Investors and Managers of Public Schools

The enterprise reform in China follows the policy of clarifying business ownership. In the early days of the reform, we hoped to let SOEs take care of their own losses through contracts and property mortgages of enterprise heads. Later, state assets administration authorities were entrusted to define obligations and enhance the regulation of investors. Later, a multitiered joint-stock system was put in place to link business ownership to specific organizations or individuals. As schools gain more autonomy, relations between the government as investors and school managers remain unclear. Blurred management power has given rise to a number of issues, such as insider control by school principals.

Public schools implement a system by which the head of school takes responsibility under the leadership of agents of public assets. The education bureau is the government agency that exercises the rights on behalf of the public assets owner. However, the practice fails to provide full institutional protection to the assets. For example, SOEs were under the control of the National Planning Commission (NPC) before the economic reform. It would be unrealistic to keep the NPC away from SOEs without the establishment of the State Assets Administration Commission, which acts on behalf of the pubic assets owner. Public schools have legal person status according to law, but they lack corresponding governance structures. There is a reason to believe that transferring the power of school management from the government to schools themselves will lead to more autonomy for school principals.

Allowing school principals greater autonomy in school management carries significant "institutional cost", as the power will be concentrated without any checks on a person who plays decision-making, administrative and supervisory roles all at the same time. This will lead to inefficient use and even loss of public assets as well as abuse and rent-seeking of public power in the field of public education.

There have been cases of corruption in a number of provinces, such as Guangdong, Hainan, Zhejiang and Jilin, in recent years, involving the construction of school buildings, textbook selection, project bidding, the purchase of school uniforms, teaching and enrollment and campus improvement. In 2015, 49 educational officials in Haikou were caught violating laws and discipline. The head of the municipal disciplinary commission said that it was mainly because leading officials, especially heads of schools, have overriding and unchecked power. According to a municipal court official in Haikou, schools often ask equipment providers for specific equipment information when inviting a bid. So long as the head of the school sets "technical requirements", it will be easy to lock in the winner, and the bidding will be nothing but going through the formalities.

Administrative streamlining and power delegation are the aims of educational reform. At the center is how the government positions itself and checks its own powers. A thorough understanding of the goal of education and full respect for the uniqueness of education in the new era are crucial to redefining the roles of different parties when separating the government administration from school management and evaluation. Analysis of the reason and history of government involvement in education and defining the government's rights of participation in four kinds of education will improve the mechanism of power distribution. Reform is an incremental process, and building a leaner government has been our goal since the reform began in 1984. What have we learnt over the past 30 years? What are the features and challenges for the reform in the new era? To answer these questions, we need to revisit the reform over the past decades and improve our understanding of what it will bring in the new era. In the new round of the educational reform, we should move education out of the range of public service products and recognize it as market commodities. The application of some theories and practices of SOE reform in China can be applied to the delegation of government power in the field of education in the new era. Freidman's theory about school vouchers will help us set the framework of separating government roles as both the funding party and the school manager. Education carries the attributes of both public goods and market commodities. Schools are places to both cultivate collective national will and ideology and keep to the essence of education by promoting the self-improvement of individuals and tapping into their potential. Power should be separated and delegated to meet the needs of the central and local governments, the market, schools, students and their parents. The endeavor will determine China's long-term economic and educational development, the educational level of citizens and industrial upgrading and ultimately keep China away from the mid-income trap.

Bibliography

Coulson, A. J. The Impact of Federal Involvement in America's Classroom [OL]. http://www.cato.org/publications/congressional testimony/impat federal involvement americas classrooms.

Center for China and Globalization (CCG). (2015). *Blue paper on international talents: Report on the trend of studying abroad*. Social Sciences Academic Press.

Encyclopedia of China: Education [Z]. Encyclopedia of China Publishing House (1985).

Friedman, M. (1982). *Free to choice: A personal statement*. Commercial Press.

Hurun Research Institute. (2014). *Special Report on Overseas Education*, May, 2015.

Lao, K. (2009). 200 Years of public schools: Problems and transformations. *Peking University Education Review* (10).

Marshall, J. A. (2011). Effects of the federal role and intervention in education [OL]. http://www.heritage.org/Research/Testimony/2011/03/Effects-of-the-Federal-Role-and-Intervention-in-Education.

Ministry of Education of PRC. (1999). *50 Years of education in the PRC*. Beijing Normal University Publishing House.

Pu, R., & Xu, L. (2015). Reflections on the reform of educational decentralization. *Journal of Educational Studies* (5).

Urban, W. J., & Jr. Wagoner, J. L. (2009). *American education: A history* (4th ed.). Routledge.

Zhu, Y., & Ma, G. (2014). *Restarting educational reform: 18 Lectures on China's educational reform*. SDX Joint Publishing House.

Streamlining Institutions and Staffing is Crucial to Building a Leaner Government

Huimin Tian and Zuojun Li

Building a leaner government is a major decision for the reform of government institutions and the transformation of government functions. It is of great importance to improve the socialist market economy and the governance system and maintain the healthy and sustainable development of the economy and society. Advancing the institutional reform of streamlining administration and transforming government functions is a major task set at the 18th CPC National. The *Decision of the CPC Central Committee on Major Issues Concerning All-round Deepening of the Reform*, adopted at the third Plenary Session of the 18th CPC Central Committee, stresses the need to deepen institutional reform and improve the government's organizational structure. Since the founding of the People's Republic of China, a number of government institutional reforms have been carried out to address overstaffing. However, these reforms have failed to break the cycle of institutional downsizing and expansion and even worse have resulted in overlapping functions, low operating efficiency and weakened governance capabilities. China has made great efforts to cancel and delegate administrative reviews and approvals. However, the effects are lower than expected, as government institutions and staff have not been removed. The key to building a leaner government is to cut institutions and staff, which is a difficult but also an urgent task for the government.

H. Tian (✉)
Center for Financial Research and Development, China Development Bank, Beijing, China

Z. Li
Institute of Resource and Environment Policy Research, Development Research Center of the State Council, Beijing, China

Y. Li and Z. Cheng (eds.), *The Chinese Path Toward a Leaner Government*,
https://doi.org/10.1007/978-981-19-6718-4_13

The Effect of a Leaner Government on Implementing the Government's Reform Initiatives

I. Streamlining administration and delegating power is an important measure to accelerate the transformation of government functions.

The transformation of government functions is the core of the reform of the administrative system and an important part of improving government efficiency and modernizing the country's governance system and capacity. Streamlining administration and delegating power is essential to all-round deepening of the reform and building a sound socialist market economy. As a self-reform of the government, it holds the key to building a government with modern governance capacity.

Cutting down government agencies and staff and delegating their power to the market and society will solve issues such as buck-passing due to blurred responsibilities of bureaucracies that are too large and complicated. It will also help speed up the transformation of government functions, provide sound governance under the rule of law, and create a favorable environment for economic and social development. The consequential shifting of government roles will push for greater vitality of market entities and economic transformation and upgrading in China.

II. Streamlining administration and delegating power is an important aspect of improving the administrative operation mechanism.

The administrative operation mechanism refers to the specific procedures, rules and actual state of action for ensuring normal functioning of the government under a certain administrative system. Building a clean government is what both the government and the people want from the reform. An efficient, fair and transparent administrative system is needed to develop a sound administrative operation mechanism.

Streamlining administration and delegating power is essential to a sound administrative operation mechanism. It is a major institutional innovation that drastically cuts and restricts the government's power of review and approval and redefines public power to improve the government's credibility. More specifically, the government assumes the roles of the rule-maker and the judge while shifting the roles of athletes to market players to stimulate their vitality and momentum for growth. A long-term stimulus can thus be created to improve business performance and give the market more maneuvering space on the basis of the list of government powers and responsibilities and an open and convenient service platform. The administrative mechanism of a leaner government will thus be more coordinated and adaptive with better incentives and restraints.

III. Streamlining administration and delegating power is an urgent requirement for raising administrative efficiency.

More efficient administrative operations bring higher efficiency and productivity to the government, which is very important to social progress. When the role of the government is streamlined, its organizational, management and working efficiency will increase, leading to better performance at the levels of decision-makers, management and working staff. It will also promote fairness in government administration, equity in the government administrative procedures and administrative system, and ultimately social justice.

Parkinson's Law states that the operational efficiency of an administrative organization has nothing to do with the number of staff, and the levels of management have nothing to do with the work itself. Therefore, reducing the levels of government administration will not cause inefficiency. It is therefore necessary to redefine government functions, improve government structures and transform the way of governance. This requires power devolution and institutional downsizing.

Before the cancelation and delegation of review and approval powers, overstaffing was a serious problem for the government. The problem may only worsen as more powers are removed or delegated. Institutional and staff downsizing is therefore a crucial step to address overstaffing and promote reforms, improve the work style and raise and administrative efficiency of the government.

IV. Streamlining administration and delegating power is an important measure to break the existing setup of power and interests.

Administrative power is in nature self-expansionary. The power associated with the "big government" system gives rise to rent-seeking and corruption. Every single power relates to interests, and its cancellation and delegation are connected with fights for interests.

Therefore, a continuous effort to build a leaner government, transform its functions, and roll back and regulate its power will significantly reduce rent-seeking and curb corruption at the source. It will also break the inherent structure of interests by moving out powers that have been concentrated in the government and relieve the "pains" brought by the government reform. The government will take a long-term view, strengthen its credibility and execution capacity, and project an image of a clean and efficient government. A better future will be created thanks to the reform.

Main Issues in Institutional and Personnel Downsizing

I. There is a lack of overall arrangements for institutional and personnel downsizing.

Over the years, making administrative order has been a norm of government actions. The lack of overall coordination in the reform of administrative streamlining has the following manifestations. The supervision mechanism of the party and government at all levels is inadequate. Personnel arrangements are made arbitrarily without a fair and serious restraint mechanism. There is a lack of supporting arrangements for institutional reform. Government agencies and roles are established for the purpose of accommodating functionaries without any legal basis. Budgetary allocation and support increase with the rising number of institutions and personnel without proper checks. The approach of the government to administrative streamlining is more on the conservative side. Administrative personnel lack the courage to target reform at themselves, make necessary sacrifices or shoulder greater responsibilities. The government is unable to make sound predictions, conduct systematic thinking or find effective measures.

II. The reform is trapped in a cycle of institutional downsizing and expansion.

China's government agencies have long faced the issue of low efficiency caused by overstaffing, excessive hierarchies and undivided responsibilities. There are too many government posts and personnel in institutions that are arbitrarily set up and difficult to consolidate. The consolidations and upgrading of institutions are made without due consideration. Despite several rounds of reform, including four with an explicit goal of building a smaller government, progress has been slow. The size of the government has inevitably rebounded after repeated efforts of downsizing, and the number of people on the government payroll has surged instead of falling. The structure of government personnel is twisted with more bosses than working staff.

According to statistics, from 1978 to 2009, China's population increased by 39.6% from 960 million to 1.34 billion, while the number of officials in the administrative departments increased by 2.5 times from 4.67 to 15.53 million. To date, there are more than 7 million civil servants in China, and more than 30 million people work for the government and public institutions. That adds up to nearly 40 million. Taking into account other personnel on the government payroll, the total size of staff requiring budgetary support is close to 60 million.

III. There are many strata and authorities of administration in the government.

The government administration is divided into five strata in China, namely, the central government, provincial government (province, municipality directly under the administration of the central government, autonomous region and special administrative region), prefectural government (prefecture-level city, prefecture, autonomous prefecture and league), county government (municipal district, county-level city, county, autonomous county, banner, autonomous banner, special region and forest region), and township government (township and ethnic minority township). This further adds to the existing multiple layers of administrative organization and leads to distortion of information going up from the primary level and misinterpretation of policy passing down from the central government. It fails to motivate governments at lower levels to play their roles diligently, improve the performance of the government, or modernize government institutions.

In addition, there is an issue of overlapping authorities. Some powers are too spread out and overlap among departments of the central government, while others are too concentrated without proper checks and balances. There is also a power imbalance between the central government and local governments. Most of the personnel and fiscal power is held by the central government, while the burden of policy execution falls onto local governments. Overstaffing will, instead of raising efficiency, add to administrative burden and lower the efficiency of the government.

IV. Government officials are hesitant to push through the reform.

Reform means readjusting existing interest structures. It will inevitably hurt the vested interests of certain sectors and personnel. The institutional reform is no exception.

During the reform, some administrative personnel "may regard the change as a real or potential threat to their power, positions and influence, and develop a negative attitude toward the reform" (Mill, 1997). Out of self-interest, they tend to guard their own vested interests, and their reluctance has affected policy implementation. When gives and takes the reform into account, they will choose to sit back and take a wait-and-see attitude out of the perception that those who are the first to reform will be the first to lose.

When they are pushed by the central government to make adjustments during the reform, they often set barriers and bargain on the reform policies. Some departments only consider their own interests instead of the overall economic and social development or the need to maximize public interests. Some departments, localities and interest groups even go out of their way to resist and obstruct the streamlining efforts for rent-seeking purposes or for the protection of their own interests.

V. It is not easy to divert personnel from the overstaffed government.

After several rounds of institutional reform, there are still 25 ministries and commissions under the State Council (not including the General Office of the State Council). Local governments have as many administrative and political organs. For example, each locality has its own party committee, people's congress, people's political consultative conference, commission for discipline inspection, trade union, women's federation, communist youth league and department of the armed forces with separate institutions and working staff. The size of government leadership is too large. In contrast, some cities in western countries have only one mayor and few deputy posts, compared with more than seven or eight deputies as in China. Their offices and functional bodies are also much smaller. In China, the number of government agencies is too large, with too many subdivided and overlapping functions. The self-expansion of government departments leads to a bloating number of agencies and leadership positions and results in massive administrative costs and a heavy burden on fiscal expenditures.

There are three main issues in diverting surplus personnel. One is the "backflow" of diverted staff. There have been several major downsizing initiatives in the past, but there are an increasing number of people in the government because many have returned through the "backdoors" left in the reform. Another issue is shifting surplus staff to lower levels of the government. Those in the provincial governments are sent to prefectural governments, and those in prefectural agencies are shifted to county and township offices. In other cases, people are diverted to SOEs and public institutions. Nothing has changed in essence.

VI. Government officials are reluctant to push forward the reform.

It is natural for government agencies and their staff whose interests are at stake to develop reluctance toward the reform. This includes delays in taking action, a wait-and-see approach and bargaining. The underlying reasons are, first, that government positions are connected with high social status in the eyes of many. There are concerns about uncertainties brought by the reform, and it is not easy to break away from old perceptions and habits. Second, ideas and forces developed under the old system over the years are deeply entrenched. Third, government officials enjoy life tenure and do not have to worry about pensions. The government can recruit as many people as the budget allows. Government agencies can guarantee a decent life for their employees in both good and bad times. Fourth, government officials can only be recruited and promoted, not in the other direction. Fifth, obsession for higher government posts and ranks is widespread. These mentalities are the biggest obstructions to institutional reform.

Underlying Barriers to Institutional and Personnel Downsizing of the Government

I. Lack of top-level design and system incompatibility.

Building a smaller government, especially cutting down on agencies and personnel, needs to keep in step with the institutional reform in the political, economic and cultural fields. The management system of social organizations must be changed for greater vitality before government functions can be safely transferred. A sound mechanism for restricting the size of government bodies is needed, and laws and regulations should be in place to consolidate the achievements of the reform. We need to adopt the law on the staffing of state institutions as soon as possible to put decision-making and procedures of staffing administration under the legal and budgetary framework. The reform of the social security system should pick up speed for building a unified and sound social security system. This is an essential step to ensure the smooth implementation of policies on institutional and personnel streamlining.

II. Constraints on the existing government payroll system.

People whose salaries and work-related expenditures are covered by the government budget are called people on the government payroll. They are divided into three categories in China—people who work in the Party, government and mass organizations' organs; staff of public institutions, and retirees from these two types of workplaces. The structure and function of people on the government payroll is still facing grave challenges. Despite several reform initiatives, the size of this group has continued to grow, although at a moderate rate, putting greater fiscal pressure on the government. The number "exceeds the staffing limit" by nearly 20 times compared with the United States. The findings revealed by a top research institution show that the expansion and contraction of the size of government payroll in China are highly consistent with the cycle of expansion and contraction of fiscal expenditure in China. In addition, the power concentration in the government has given rise to an increased number of government staff and soaring budgetary expenditures, which will eventually lead to lower wages for those on the government payroll.

III. Too much power and resource concentration as a result of slow progress in transforming government functions.

Since reform and opening-up began, the focus of the government has shifted from economic development to public service. The lack of progress in transforming government functions is mostly caused by half-hearted reform in building a market economy. The size of the government depends on its power and resources at its disposal. On the other hand, supervision of government agencies with huge power is not in place, resulting in rent seeking and poor effects of the reform. The experience of these years of government reform shows that it is much more difficult for departments with approval authority to do streamlining than those without. The reasons are, first, the government needs people to do reviews and approvals, and second, because of the associated interests, people with such powers are reluctant to be diverted.

IV. Entrenched restrictions, powers and interests for the government.

As a government-led reform, streamlining administration and delegating power are in nature subject to constraints originating from the roles, interests and awareness of the government. In addition, defects in the design of the supporting system of the reform have added to such constraints to a certain extent. In essence, building a smaller government is a process of institutional transformation and innovation to ensure that the power structure of the government meets the need for economic and social development. As the government decreases, institutional streamlining will not only reduce the number of agencies and staff and delegate more power to businesses and society but also transform government functions and administrative philosophies. Aimed at readjusting and redistributing power, interests and resources, the reform will change the existing structures of power and interests in the government, which will inevitably hurt the vested interests of certain departments and people. The departments of vested power and interests will thus try to strengthen their functions as much as possible and form a community of interests to solidify their positions, expand their power and maximize their interests instead of conducting reform on themselves. This will only make the reform more difficult to succeed. The existence of government departments with vested interests has become the underlying cause of the sluggish progress of the reform.

V. Ill-designed institutional staffing arrangement and loose management of diverted personnel.

To build a smaller government, efforts should be made to not only transform government functions but also address the issue of overstaffing. To transform government functions and define the responsibilities of each department, consolidation is needed, and government functions should be straightened out. The problem of institutional staffing and management of diverted personnel must also be solved. Government functionaries should be moved to other positions or out of the government as needed. This step is crucial to the smooth progress in government consolidation. This requires the government to offer people diverted from the government different types of training and education with resources available and create opportunities for their career development.

VI. Impacts of the traditional administrative culture on government staff.

As an underlying layer of the administrative system, administrative culture is a kind of "collective will" in the government and has an impact on governance through the will of the government staff. The reform is directly affected by the traditional administrative cultural barrier, the inherent worship for officialdom, reluctance to make changes, and psychological reactions to uncertainties brought by the reform among government staff. This constitutes the internal constraints on the reform. The long-held worship for official ranks and the concept of an omnipotent government has had a great influence on government functionaries and obstructed the smooth progress of institutional reform. Under such a culture, government agencies and staff tend to develop a bureaucratic style of work and regard themselves as a privileged group. Highly centralized power leads to unclear government functions, and the traditional administrative culture creates a government that values public administration more than public service.

Thoughts and Measures on Advancing Institutional and Personnel Downsizing

I. Strengthening the top-level design of the reform and improving relevant supporting systems.

Strengthen the top-level design on institutional and personnel downsizing. The reform is by no means simple or easy and needs rules at the top level and coordinated efforts among all departments. They are also needed to ensure success in building a leaner government. A good top-level design on administrative streamlining requires the State Council to coordinate efforts between various government departments and local authorities.

First, we must free up the mind and embrace novelty. Freeing up the mind is critical to top-level design and must be embraced as the first step. What we need is the courage of targeting reform at ourselves, giving up what we have had and imposing pressure on ourselves. Second, we should be forward-looking in our judgment of institutional reform. Third, there should be a systematic arrangement and plan for the institutions and personnel that have been streamlined. Fourth, proper methodologies need to be found for the management of streamlined institutions and personnel. Fifth, a sound statistical analysis must be conducted on the streamlined institutions and personnel.

The reform is a systematic one and needs a sound supporting system. Coordination must be made across departments to support reforms of the political, economic and cultural systems.

II. Establishing a proper government payroll system and advancing the reform of government consolidation.

The issue that repeated streamlining efforts result in more serious overstaffing needs to be addressed through the reform of consolidating administrative strata and government departments of the existing administrative system.

A sound budgetary payroll system should be put in place. People on this payroll play an extremely important role in government operations, and payroll size bears on social stability and public well-being. Therefore, we should improve the social security system, the government performance evaluation and supervision mechanism, the budget supervision function of the people's congress, and the division of responsibilities among government agencies and optimize government strata and administrative regions. Issues relating to the diverted staff must be addressed. It is necessary to expand the coverage of the reform from "government officials" to "personnel on the budgetary payroll" so that state-owned enterprises and public institutions will no longer be the "safe haven" for diverting government functionaries. In addition, consolidation of government agencies is needed to raise efficiency and cut costs where similar functions and responsibilities are integrated under one department. Top-level designers should consider setting up dedicated supervision departments and creating a supervisory system of checks and balances with separate roles. This will help break the power concentration and vested interests among government departments and push for the creation of a leaner and more unified and efficient government.

III. Faster transformation of government functions and proper designation of government roles.

In the reform of government departments, the government should delegate some of its powers and functions, clarify the scope of its responsibilities, transform its functions, focus more on market supervision and public services, exercise the power within institutional restraints, and gradually turn itself from an administrative regulator to a public service provider. To this end, we should accelerate the transformation of government functions and ensure their proper distribution. The central government should drastically cut the number of administrative review and approval items and replace review and approval with record filing. Otherwise, the institutional reform will be dragged for too long.

First, we should formulate more specific measures to improve government structures and functions, foster a system of checks and coordination, and strive to solve the problems of overlapping institutions and responsibilities. Second, we should, following the requirements for government function transformation, determine the roles of different departments to solve problems such as unclear or overlapping responsibilities, overstaffing and buck passing. Third, we should set pilot programs of putting counties under the direct jurisdiction of the provincial government. Fourth, we must strengthen the reform of government institutions at all levels, strive to reduce administrative costs and improve administrative efficiency.

IV. Breaking through vested interests and restoring efficiency to government institutions.

It is imperative to remove the inherent constraints on government roles and break the entrenchment caused by vested interests.

Government Streamlining in essence is about the redistribution and adjustment of interests and powers. It should be pursued in accordance with the law. Those who resist and obstruct the reform must be subject to legal sanctions. The reform of local government in particular should aim at building an efficient administrative framework despite opposition from the vested interests.

V. Improving the structure of government institutions and placement of diverted personnel.

Continuous efforts should be made to improve the structure of government institutions and the placement of diverted personnel to address the challenges arising from institutional overstaffing and the diversion of government employees.

We must establish a long-term mechanism to support the reform of government institutions. The *Report of the 18th National Congress of the Communist Party of China (CPC)* stressed the importance of controlling the size of administrative organs, cutting government positions and raising their efficiency. To achieve this goal, staffing quota management should be strengthened, and a cap should be put in place. New measures are needed to address the root cause of increased government staffing and keep the government payroll from expanding. A "rigid" approach should be pursued, and a sound constraint should be exercised in managing institutional staffing. Strict discipline in this regard must be upheld to build synergy. A restraint and supervisory mechanism should be set up to match institutional staffing with the fiscal budget. Legislation on government staffing must pick up speed to include relevant changes in legal procedures.

To improve the resettlement of diverted staff, we should adopt supporting reform measures in terms of personnel organization, income distribution and social security. Great efforts should be made to help them find jobs and obtain loans and other financial concessions and support. The government can also use resources out in the market to offer them vocational training and career orientation.

VI. Transforming government administration philosophies and establishing a sound personnel mechanism.

Government streamlining is a revolution that profoundly changes people's thinking and perceptions. The progress of the reform in government institutions has been seriously hampered by the traditional administrative culture featuring "rule by man", seclusion, bureaucratism and worship for officialdom. Therefore, it is imperative to break away from such thinking and embrace the vision of reform and development. Cultural progress must be stressed in the reform to remove hesitation from the government and gather motivation for advancing the reform. A sound personnel mechanism should be in place through which comprehensive and fair evaluations of government staff are carried out to decide who should stay. Meanwhile, a sound official appointment system featuring strict supervision and merit-based selection is needed to make it easier for the government to promote, demote, recruit and dismiss its employees.

In conclusion, building a leaner government spearheads the nationwide reform and the transformation of government functions in China. The key to success lies in institutional and personnel streamlining. The government must free up its mind, raise its awareness, make overall planning and advance all supporting reforms. It should push for progress in the reform of the administrative system and reach the goal of turning itself into a clean and honest service-oriented government with well-designed functions and a sound structure to gain greater satisfaction from the people.

Bibliography

County Administration System Reform Research Group. (2005). Difficulties and outcomes of the streamlining of county-level government agencies. *Journal of Chinese Academy of Governance* (3).

Gao, N., & Liang, P. (2015). Why are government institutions expanding? In the perspective of diverse departmental interest. *Economic Research Journal* (9).

Li, J., & Zhao, E. (2007). Government streamlining in China in the perspective of Parkinson's law. *Today, Hubei (Theory Edition)* (1).

Li, Y. (2015). *Research on the Internal constraints on government's streamlining and power delegation since the reform and opening-up.* Unpublished master's dissertation, Shandong University, 2015.

Li, Z. (2006). Rethinking on the streamlining of government agencies. *Journal of Shanxi Normal University* (9).

Liu, L., & Song, G. (2004). Multi-interest game in government budgeting. *Finance and Trade Research* (5).

Liu, Y. (2013). The fundamental solution to organizational streamlining. *Phoenix Weekly* (10).

Mill, J. (1997). *Representative government.* The Commercial Press.

Qin, P., & Huang, J. (2008). Diversion of surplus personnel during government streamlining and consolidation. *Trade Unions' Tribune* (11).

Tan, Y. (2008). Analysis on the game theory in defining functions of government departments: reflection on overlapping authorities. *Academic Forum* (7).

Wang, W. (2008). *Construction and transformation: 30 Years of Chinese government reform and development.* Zhengzhou University Press.

Wang, X. (2013). Streamlining administration and delegating power: A new round of government institutional reform in perspective. *Journal of Hunan Administration College* (6).

Xue, X. (2006). The number of civil servants per unit GDP in China is 20 times that of developed countries. *China Reform News.*

Zhang, Y. (2014). Streamlining administration and delegating power: Warning against the phenomenon of "streamlining organizations instead of staff" [OL]. <China.org.cn>. Retrieved October 17, 2014.

A Leaner Government and a Better Administrative Accountability System

Dawei Yan and Bo Fan

A leaner government has political, economic and legal implications. In the context of advancing the reform and the rule of law as decided by the central government, government streamlining will significantly promote efforts in these fields and ensure that the reform is carried out under the rule of law. The rule of law requires that the reform set a clear limit of power for the government, businesses and society in legislation and that the fundamental principles of the rule of law be fully executed. The rule of law plays an important role in promoting and ensuring the implementation of the reform on government streamlining, and its role should be appreciated and upheld in the course of the reform. As the rule of law in China deepens, the administrative accountability system plays a more obvious and direct role in promoting and ensuring a successful reform of administrative streamlining. Improving the administrative accountability system in China has theoretical importance. It will also help solve practical issues in China's government administration.

The Administrative Accountability System in the Context of Building a Leaner Government

I. The emergence and development of the administrative accountability system

Academics and practitioners may differ in their understanding and definition of the administrative accountability system. Nevertheless, it is generally recognized as an important part of political accountability.

D. Yan (✉)
Disciplinary Inspection Commission of the CPC Henan Provincial Committee, Beijing, China

B. Fan
Emergency General Hospital, Beijing, China

Y. Li and Z. Cheng (eds.), *The Chinese Path Toward a Leaner Government*,
https://doi.org/10.1007/978-981-19-6718-4_14

Since the 1980s, reform of the public administration system has gathered momentum in many countries. A historical trend has taken shape to strengthen the administrative accountabilities of government employees and build responsible governments. Many countries and regions have established administrative accountability systems. On 17 April 2002, the government of the Hong Kong Special Administrative Region proposed a specific plan on senior officials' accountability to the Legislative Council, and the plan took effect on 1 July in the same year. Then, the administrative accountability system started to be implemented in Hong Kong. In recent years, the CPC Central Committee and the State Council have placed high importance on the institutional building for administrative accountability. The term was frequently mentioned in the 2004 Report on the Work of the Government, the Reports of the 17th and the 18th CPC National Congresses, and the report of the third Plenary Session of the 18th CPC Central Committee. At the executive meeting of the State Council held on 13 May 2015, decisions were made on administrative accountability. In January 2016, the work report of the sixth Plenary Session of the 18th CPC Central Commission for Discipline Inspection made it clear that administrative accountability should be institutionalized under the rule of law. The *CPC Accountability Regulations*, which was adopted at a meeting of the Political Bureau of the CPC Central Committee on 28 June 2016, aims to regulate and strengthen the Party's accountability and provides important guidance to the country's administrative accountability system. The move was followed by similar efforts of local governments at all levels. For example, the government of Hunan and other provinces introduced interim regulations and measures on administrative accountability.

II. Basic functions of the administrative accountability system

1. Punishment and education. In essence, administrative accountability is a legal system to hold relevant persons accountable. It can be considered a negative evaluation of illegal administrative acts by the State. Administrative accountability includes not only moral condemnation but also the imposition of some adverse consequences on the party held responsible, namely, administrative organs or civil servants who have committed illegal administrative acts or have failed to perform administrative duties, so that the persons responsible will suffer certain losses in the political, economic or other aspects. The educational function of the administrative accountability system is realized in the process of imputation. First, there is a need to determine whether the subject bears legal obligations for its administrative act and whether its behavior is in violation of its statutory obligations. Then, the legal consequences for such acts will be determined accordingly. Through the identification and investigation of responsibility, the government and its staff will understand the standards and measurements for legal administrative acts, take lessons and avoid the recurrence of illegal administrative acts. To hold relevant personnel legally responsible as stipulated in the Regulations can be a solemn reminder to the law breakers themselves and other administrative organizations and their staff as well, who will stay alert and more conscientiously put their own administrative acts within the legal framework.

2. Warning and prevention. In reality, the number of administrative organs and public servants held accountable for committing illegal administrative acts is not high. However, letting them bear legal responsibilities is not enough; administrative accountability should cover all administrative organs and their staff. In this sense, the system plays the role of warning and preventing law-breaking acts for all administrative organs and their staff in addition to those held accountable.
3. Consolation and compensation. The victims, whose lawful rights and interests have been violated by such illegal administrative acts, may develop resentment or even retaliatory mentality against the administrative organs and their staff that have committed such acts. The establishment of the administrative accountability system to hold the wrongdoers accountable in accordance with the law will provide consolation and compensation to the victims by restoring their reputation and eliminating the negative impact that the illegal acts may have caused.

III. Basic relationship between administrative streamlining and administrative accountability

Streamlining administration is naturally linked to administrative accountability. The administrative accountability system is an important guarantee for the smooth progress of government streamlining, which, in turn, offers a good opportunity for the implementation and improvement of the administrative accountability system. The administrative accountability system is of special significance in the efforts of building a learner government.

1. The administrative accountability system is an important institutional guarantee for advancing the reform of government streamlining. A leaner government needs to be supported by the administrative accountability system. To make the government leaner and more effective, those who fail to perform their duty of government streamlining must be held accountable. As the government rolls back its functions, the role of the market will be given a better play, but it may also lead to government inaction. A sound administrative accountability system will not only prevent undue government intervention in the economy and subsequent distortion of the market but also hold the government accountable for inaction to curb such malpractice to some extent.
2. Government streamlining provides an important opportunity for the implementation and improvement of the administrative accountability system. Government streamlining will give a better focus to the administrative accountability system by scaling down a large number of unnecessary administrative interventions. In addition, it will also expand the coverage of administrative accountability beyond traditional "arbitrary administrative acts" to include administrative inaction. This, to some extent, broadens the scope of the administrative accountability system and enriches its content.

In other words, government streamlining is of great importance to China's administrative system reform, and its success is inseparable from the support of the admin istrative accountability system. Meanwhile, it has also offered a good opportunity for the improvement of the administrative accountability system. Government streamlining and administrative accountability must advance in tandem. This is how they relate to each other.

The Main Challenge for the Administrative Accountability System and the Underlying Causes

In China, the administrative accountability system is relatively young, and there is still room for improvement in both theory and practice. The main challenge for the system is the lack of substance, which is reflected at both the macro and micro levels.

I. Challenge at the macro level and its underlying causes

1. Absence of specialized laws. Here, "specialized" is emphasized because legal provisions in our laws on administrative accountability are fragmented instead of being systematically and theoretically organized. For example, the inclusion of "take responsibility and resign" into the *Law on Civil Servants* is a big step toward the codification of administrative ethics in China but falls short of realizing law-based governance on administrative accountability in China.
2. More policies than laws. The existing administrative accountability system is mainly reflected in such central government documents as the *Report on the Work of the Government* at the second Session of the tenth National People's Congress and the *Outline for All-round Advancement of Law-based Administration.* Other government documents also contain relevant expressions, such as the government work reports delivered at the third Session of the tenth National People's Congress and the first session of the eleventh National People's Congress and the *Implementation Outlines for Building a Law-based Government (2015–2020)* jointly issued by the CPC Central Committee and the State Council. However, these documents are only central government policy papers instead of laws.
3. There are no legal provisions at the national level. In July 2004, the Chongqing municipal government began to implement the administrative accountability system and issued the *Interim Measures on the Administrative Accountability System of the Chongqing Municipal People's Government*. Subsequently, Hainan, Shenzhen, Tianjin and other localities have introduced accountability rules based on local conditions. This has put an end to the long existing embarrassment that there was no rule to abide by on cases of accountability. However, these local legislations still face many challenges. In particular, due to the involvement of local interests in such legislation and the limited rationality of the local judicial system, it is difficult to fully implement the administrative accountability system; therefore, a legal system at the national level is urgently needed.

II. Challenges at the micro level and the underlying causes

1. Incomplete coverage. According to the basic principle of administrative law, when administrative organs or their staff are authorized with power, they shall also bear corresponding administrative responsibility. The greater the power, the heavier the responsibility. However, the current laws and cases of accountability identification and punishment in China mainly target the heads of the administrative organs and seldom cover ordinary civil servants.
2. Weak cross-check between institutions. Currently, in China, administrative bodies hold their own staff accountable for wrongdoings mainly based on the documents of the Party and policies, regulations, rules and other normative documents of the administrative organs themselves. While accountability exercised by the administrative organs for their own staff is important, putting their staff under supervision by another administrative body is even more important. In a sense, it holds the key to the success of the accountability system. However, this is where China is lacking, which has, to some extent, undermined the effect of the system.
3. Ambiguous power and responsibilities. Clarity in responsibility is the precondition of administrative accountability. This requires a clear division of responsibilities between ranks, departments and posts, which must be written into the law. In China, however, the complexity of relations between the Party and the government and vaguely defined administrative responsibilities have resulted in quite a few sticking points for administrative accountability at the operational level.
4. Narrow scope of application. The scope of administrative accountability should include failure to perform statutory duties and incorrect performance of such duties. In practice, however, the scope of application is too narrow, mostly limited to the investigation of responsibilities concerning major safety incidents, while ignoring accountability issues in other aspects. This has limited the reach of the administrative accountability system.
5. Inadequate forms of punishment. In general, the punishment stipulated by Chinese laws for civil servants who have committed administrative malpractice includes notified criticism, administrative compensation, administrative punishment and criminal punishment. However, in practice, there is a tendency to call for resignation regardless of the weight of responsibility or evidence for the existence of any fault. This is not conducive to keeping to the true measurement of the responsibility one has to take.
6. Lack of judicial relief. Most of the provisions on relief for civil servants are embodied in the *Civil Servants Law*. Others are in the *Interim Measures on Complaints and Lawsuits of Civil Servants* and the *Rules on Handling Civil Servants' Complaints*. However, they are limited to internal remedies instead of judicial remedies.
7. Too much room for discretion. As administrative accountability has not been codified in China, it is easily influenced by the instructions of individual leaders

or public opinion. The room for discretion on punishment is too big and to some extent goes to extremes on both ends.

Improving the Theoretical Basis of China's Administrative Accountability System and Its Significance

I. Improving the analysis on the theoretical basis of china's administrative accountability system

Every system has a unique social background and a solid theoretical basis. The administrative accountability system is based on the following three theories.

1. The theory of social contract. This theory can be traced back to Aristotle, a philosopher in ancient Greece. It was later developed by Grotius, Spinoza, Hobbes, Locke, Rousseau and other followers of the classical natural law school. It advocates restraining the behavior of the state and government with contracts. Social contracts give citizens the right to supervise and restrict public power and the obligation to accept the administration of the public power. It also stresses that the government has the power of public administration, the obligation of social service and the responsibility to meet public needs, based on its commitment to protecting public interests.
2. The theory of entrustment. This theory is based on the thought of popular sovereignty. Popular sovereignty means that the people are the owners of sovereignty, and every citizen has equal rights to own state sovereignty and manage state affairs. However, it is impossible for sovereignty to be exercised jointly by all citizens. It can only be exercised by some of them through designated institutions. The theory proposes that citizens entrust their power to the government and hold it accountable. The government makes policies to meet the will and interests of the citizens and act in accordance with the laws made by the representatives elected by the citizens. If the government makes policies that go against the will of the citizens or harm the interests of the people or exercises power beyond its statutory limits, it must bear responsibility it owes to the people and be subject to punishment.
3. The theory of popular sovereignty. The theory holds that all state power belongs to the people. To make it a reality and a basic political principle, it is imperative to establish and enforce the right of the people to supervise state organs and their staff and hold them, especially government officials accountable in their exercise of state power, to ensure that the civil servants act within the constraints of the accountability system instead of going against the will of the people to enhance public interests .

II. The value and significance of improving China's administrative accountability system

1. It promotes national development. To better promote national development, government functions must be transformed. The government should clarify its role in economic and social development and respect market rules. It should strengthen macrocontrol of the market and effectively restrain the negatives of the market economy. Except for a small amount of public goods related to national security and important products critical to the national economy and people's livelihood, which should be controlled by the state, the government should no longer directly manage microeconomic affairs, such as allocating resources. Instead, it should give better play to its core functions. Therefore, vigorously promoting the administrative accountability system is of far-reaching practical significance.
2. This conforms to the global trend. Important changes have taken place in the functions of the modern government. The emphasis is shifting from economic growth first to all-round and balanced progress that includes social stability and the environment. In addition, the government has a bigger responsibility on its shoulder. The trend of economic globalization is gathering momentum day by day, and it has become increasingly important for the government to fulfill its social responsibilities. In addition, competition among sovereign states in the information age has become increasingly fierce. Market volatility and the rapid development of information technology are forcing changes in the traditional government operational system. While competing in economic strengths, national governments are spreading their new governance philosophies globally, which is different from the traditional sense of government responsibilities. Government reforms in the West in the past few years have triggered reexamination of the responsibility of modern governments. Further improving the administrative accountability system is required to adapt to evolving global dynamics.
3. It heightens the sense of responsibility of government staff. Enforcing the administrative accountability system will effectively address dereliction of duty by public servants and enhance their sense of responsibility. All government agencies must act in accordance with the law and effectively protect their citizens' rights. Government personnel shall develop a commitment to the public and uphold the supremacy of public interests and forge conviction and virtue around it in their daily work.
4. It strengthens the administration of government staff. The administrative accountability system calls for right holders to assume due responsibilities when exercising their powers. It helps government leaders improve their understanding of the links between power, position and responsibility and pushes for the establishment of a viable mechanism to disqualify staff of poor performance. The sense of accountability for government staff will be enhanced through institutional arrangement together with necessary safeguards to protect their rights and interests. At the same time, failure to act on part of the government will also be included in administrative accountability, and officials who have made solid

progress in enhancing public interests should have more chances for promotion. This will increase the enthusiasm and incentives of government staff.

5. It improves government accountability. The power of the government is entrusted by the people, and it comes with corresponding responsibilities. The government and the people constitute a contractual relationship of power and responsibility through election. The government shoulders responsibility that comes with the power entrusted by the people. To put it simply, the government power and responsibility both come from the people. A responsible government is the one where officials at all levels fulfill their duties. Enforcing the administrative accountability system helps improve the competence and performance of public management and minimize the chance of dereliction of duty. It will help reverse the malpractice of placing power before responsibility and build a government that exercises its power and fulfills its responsibility for public interests.
6. It enhances good citizenship. The influence of the thoughts from the feudal society and worship for officialdom and power lead to public indifference to political affairs. Some of the officials regard themselves as patrons and not servants of the people. As the political system provides limited access to political affairs for the public, the administrative accountability system will help close the gap. It enables the people to make comments and judgments on government acts, rids those leading officials who fail to perform their duties or demonstrate poor performance of popular support and institutional protection, and clears the way for the people to exercise their rights of supervision.

Policy Suggestions for Improving China's Administrative Accountability System

I. Establishing the right basic principles for the administrative accountability system

The basic principles of the administrative accountability system are its fundamental and core guidelines that play a pivotal role as the soul of the system. These principles are directly related to the legitimacy, precision and timeliness of administrative accountability activities. Specifically, the legislation and practice of administrative accountability shall abide by the following principles.

1. Calling to account in accordance with the law. The legal responsibility of administrative organs and public servants must be confirmed and investigated by designated state organs within their statutory limits of authority and in accordance with the conditions and procedures prescribed by the law. Under this principle, the principle of legality must be followed in determining whether administrative organs and public servants shall bear responsibility for their administrative acts, what kind of responsibility they must bear, who shall determine the responsibility and how to call them to account.
2. Matching rights with responsibilities. This reflects the dialectical unity of rights and obligations. A party in a legal relationship can be regarded as a holder of both

rights and obligations. Rights and obligations are generally equal in quantity. In the exercise of administrative powers, the match of rights with responsibilities fully reflects the balance of rights and obligations.

3. Due punishment. In the case of enforcing administrative accountability, the types of punishment should be determined according to the nature of the illegal acts, the severity of the fault and the effects of the harm to avoid a punishment that is too light or too heavy or even impunity. Imposing punishment according to fault is an important principle to measure and evaluate the appropriateness of the punishment. In practice, only when this principle is respected can we realize the purpose of administrative accountability and make those held accountable genuinely accept the punishment.
4. Combination of punishment and education. The establishment and investigation of legal responsibility of administrative organs and civil servants should not only determine the punishment of those responsible but also urge them to be lawful to realize the goal of both sanction and education. Punishment is imposed on organizations or individuals to commit illegal administrative acts. However, it is only the means and not the end. The purpose is to urge administrative departments and their staff to respect laws in performing administrative roles and minimize illegal acts and follow the right way to implement laws. Punishment and sanctions are in themselves a form of education, as they can educate those held responsible by imposing negative consequences on them and at the same time deter others from committing the same acts.
5. Combining accountability investigation with performance improvement. In exercising administrative accountability, those responsible shall be held accountable in accordance with the law and pay a price for their illegal administrative acts. Meanwhile, problems should be quickly addressed to improve governance. The system of administrative accountability, for the purpose of supervision and restraint, ties responsibility with power to ensure law-based governance by government agencies and civil servants at all levels. Accountable administration requires civil servants to assume the responsibility commensurate with the power of their posts. However, punishing those who are directly responsible is not enough. We must analyze the causes of the problems in government performance and take effective measures for improvement.
6. Holding accountable to both government organs and their staff. In establishing the responsibilities and calling organizations and people to account, we shall hold responsible both administrative organs and their staff who have committed the acts. The responsibility for law violations may be further divided into the responsibilities for administrative organs and those for their staff. The government enjoys extensive administrative powers and must undertake corresponding administrative responsibilities. In performing administrative duties, government agencies shall not only be held responsible for the illegal exercise of their powers or failure to perform their statutory duties but also assume corresponding responsibilities for illegal administrative acts carried out by their staff or organizations and individuals they have entrusted.

7. Efficiency and openness. Efficiency requires that accountability be determined in the shortest possible time with resource input as little as possible. The accountability process must be well designed to ensure efficient and coordinated operation of all the steps once the process starts and a quicker response to public concerns. As a basic principle of the administrative accountability system, openness is essential for a democratic and constitutional government. All acts that fall into the scope of accountability (except for state secrets) must be open. Public scrutiny shall cover supervision and restraint over administrative behaviors, the entire process of performing administrative power, and accountability procedures such as inquiry, dismissal, hearing and investigation. The media shall be allowed to disclose relevant information to the public promptly and accurately.

II. Establishing a unified national administrative accountability system

To date, there is no administrative accountability law at the national level, and administrative accountability in China is mainly based on a series of regulations over CPC members. It is highly necessary to set up a national administrative accountability system.

1. Designating a sound body to exercise administrative accountability. Such a body has the power to decide whether to call anyone to account, what kind of responsibility they shall bear, and how to punish them. Therefore, it must be set up in accordance with the law. The following issues should be addressed for its improvement. They include establishing a body for exercising administrative accountability, determining its scope of power, and shaping its relations with the public and government organizations.
2. Further identifying the target of administrative accountability. The forthcoming *Administrative Accountability Law of China* will first determine the target of administrative accountability or who should be subject to administrative accountability law. A clearly defined target is important for ensuring the legislative effect of the law. For example, the *Interim Measures on the Accountability of Chief Administrators of Government Departments of Chongqing Municipality* mainly targets the heads of the municipal government departments and only serves as a warning to the ordinary staff. It is stipulated in the Constitution that government staff work under the guidance of their department leaders, but it does not mean that they will not take any responsibility for government decisions and daily work. The law should define the responsibilities of the leading officials of government agencies and their staff by drawing reference from the principle of differentiated responsibilities in the *Civil Servants Law*. We suggest that there is enough flexibility for all kinds of circumstances while rigid principles are set. This will help construct an administrative accountability system with tiered responsibility and check the behavior of the staff working in the government bodies, ensure fairness and justice in law implementation, and provide concrete legal support for accountability investigation.
3. Setting unified standards for accountability. In administrative accountability practice, the following factors should be taken into consideration. First, whether

statutory duties are involved. Civil servants are required by law to perform their statutory duties. Second, failure to perform or correctly perform their statutory duties occurred. Performing statutory duties includes both action and inaction. Legal liabilities only apply to cases of failure to perform statutory duties or their incorrect performance. Third, whether the person responsible is at fault. This is an important basis for deciding the existence and severity of his liability. Fourth, there is a causal link between liability-inducing acts and the damage caused.

4. Building a complete accountability procedure. Administrative procedures are of crucial importance. Its transparency is closely related to the effect of administrative supervision. The higher the transparency is, the greater the public oversight. An open procedure must be followed. No one should violate it at will or make random changes, additions or omissions to the rules, which is likely to occur and in fact often happens when the procedure is not made open. A complete set of accountability procedures should mainly include case proposal, record filing, investigation, decisions and remedies. The *Administrative Accountability Law* should contain detailed information on each of these steps.
5. Strengthening the remedies for accountability Remedies are part of the administrative accountability procedure and not an independent process that comes after the accountability procedure. It is described in a separate paragraph because of its importance. China has not yet established a complete and sound administrative accountability mechanism. Remedies are weak and even nonexistent in China's current laws and regulations on relief measures for administrative personnel under punishment. The persons subjected to administrative accountability punishment are rarely covered by the current administrative relief laws and regulations. It calls for improvement.

III. Formulating laws, regulations and measures that are compatible with the *Administrative Accountability Law*

To put administrative accountability under the rule of law, the supporting systems must be improved. It is impossible for the *Administrative Accountability Law* to cover all cases. Its implementation needs support from other laws and regulations.

1. Establishing a system for disclosing government information. This means greater openness in government affairs, streamlining administration and ensuring that the public has the right to information on accountability. The premise of accountability is openness and the right to information. Citizens should be allowed access to information about what is going on in the country, the course of government actions and their possible consequences. To establish the government information disclosure system in China, existing laws and regulations must be revised. The secrecy law should be changed for a better definition of the relationship between openness and confidentiality. Moreover, laws and regulations should be formulated to provide for openness in procedure, supervision and relief measures, and the legal responsibilities of administrative organs to make disclosure of government information institutionalized and law-based.

2. Improving the system of civil participation in administrative accountability. Institutionalization and procedural development of public engagement should be stepped up to promote civil participation through legislative means and guarantee their rights in democratic decision-making through institutional arrangements. We should further improve the systems on election, hearing, civil participation in legislation, evaluation of government officials and collection of public criticisms and suggestions. While respecting the political rights and freedom of Chinese citizens as stipulated by the Constitution and laws, contents, methods and channels of civil participation must be clearly defined to make it law-based and rule-based. Civil participation in public power guided by administrative procedures will make public scrutiny of the government more effective.
3. Improve laws on people's congresses' supervision over administrative accountability in China. People's congresses at all levels should become the main executor of administrative accountability, but their role has not yet been fully played since the launch of the administrative accountability system. Their supervisory power over the government should be elaborated and strengthened, which means that the scope of supervision and ways of holding organizations or people accountable should be further clarified to make the system work effectively. For example, there must be clear rules for people's congresses on their way of exercising the power of supervision and holding governments accountable. The power the people's congresses to supervise and call for accountability must be strengthened as part of the efforts to raise their independence and authoritativeness in excising the powers. The resources needed to help perform their roles must be in place.
4. Ensuring the rights of the media to disclose accountability issues in accordance with the press law. The role of the press is so important that when there is a highly negative public perception of an official, it should be fully and freely reflected in the media. Under the public pressure thus created, the official will have to step forward and take the blame. As the main form of public scrutiny, the press has much to do with information disclosure. It is a tool of information disclosure and a means to call for accountability. The press is mandated to make quick, full, factual and accurate accounts of the fact. However, some local governments in China tend to intervene or dominate the theme and content of news reports with their administrative power and conceal or twist true information to protect their own images. In some localities, for example, when a public incident occurred, instead of telling the truth, the local government did nothing but trying to block access to information, hoping it would disappear in its own accord. In view of this, laws and regulations, especially the press law, should be formulated to protect the rights of the press to call for accountability and its independence in free and fair reporting.

Bibliography

Chen, D. (2007). Develop an effective administrative accountability legal system. *Hebei Law Science* (2).

Fang, S., & et al. (1998). *Principles and practice of the state compensation law*. Peking University press.

Hu, J. (2005). *A study on the administrative accountability of leaders*. Zhejiang University Press.

Larenz, K. (2003). *General theory of German civil law*. Law Press China.

Li, Y. (2013). *China's dual economic transition*. China Renmin University Press.

Mill, J. (1982). *Representative government*. The Commercial Press.

Rousseau, J.-J. (1980). *On the social contract*. The Commercial Press.

Wilson. (1985). *Congressional government: A study of American politics*. The Commercial Press.

Yang, J. (2003). *A study on administrative accountability*. Law Press China

Zhang, W. (1999). *Jurisprudence*. Higher Education Press, Peking University Press.

Practice

A Leaner Government and More Financing Functions of the New Third Board

Xiaoquan Zhou

Streamlining administration and delegating power is a continuous process of strengthening market rules. Its fundamental purpose is to release market vitality and stimulate creativity. The New Third Board is a product of streamlining administration and delegating power. Originating from the "equity stock transfer agent system" in 2001, it is created to address issues relating to STAQ and NET companies' share trading and the main board delisting. In January 2006, to support the development of small and medium-sized high-tech enterprises and improve the OTC market, the non-listed company share transfer system in Beijing Zhongguancun Science Park was established, which is now called the "New Third Board". In August 2012, the pilot scheme was expanded to include Shanghai Zhangjiang, Tianjin Binhai and Wuhan Donghu national high-tech zones. On January 16, 2013, the National Equity Exchange and Quotation System (NEEQ) was established to promote the growth of the OTC market. On December 14, 2013, the State Council issued the *Decisions on Issues Regarding NEEQ* to extend the coverage of companies from the previous four pilot zones to the whole country and drastically simplify the administrative licensing procedures. The CSRC then delegated the power for handling listing applications made by any joint-stock company with no more than 200 shareholders to NEEQ. Streamlining administration and delegating power has brought the OTC equity market into a period of explosive growth. To date, there are nearly 7500 companies on the New Third Board.[1] Compared with the end of 2014, the OTC market has become an important capital platform to support the development of small and medium-sized high-tech enterprises in China.

[1] Data source: Wind Information. Wind Information is an independent provider of financial and economic data covering stocks, funds, bonds, foreign exchange, insurance, futures, financial derivatives, spot trading, macro economy, financial news and other fields. Unless otherwise specified, the original data in this paper are from Wind Information.

X. Zhou (✉)
Zhongyuan Securities Co., Ltd., Beijing, China

Y. Li and Z. Cheng (eds.), *The Chinese Path Toward a Leaner Government*,
https://doi.org/10.1007/978-981-19-6718-4_15

The New Third Board in the Context of Building a Leaner Government: A Mechanism of Diversified Financing Channels

The efforts of building a leaner government have not only promoted rapid growth of the number of OTC market companies but also expanded financing channels, particularly additional stock offerings. The *Measures for Supervision and Administration of Unlisted Public Companies* (hereinafter referred to as the Measures), revised at the end of 2013, grants equity and debt financing and other financing rights to unlisted public companies represented by OTC market companies.

Compared with A-shares on the Shanghai and Shenzhen stock exchanges, the New Third Board private placement system is more flexible. It is based on post issuance record filing. There are no financial conditions or restrictions on issuance intervals. Article 45 of the Measures stipulates that for a company whose total number of shareholders does not exceed 200 after a private placement, the CSRC shall exempt it from review and approval and put it under self-regulation by NEEQ. This has cleared the way for the establishment of a flexible system for fast issuance of small amount of stocks and contributed to the blowout of stock issuance and financing of listed companies on the New Third Board since 2015. In 2015, there were 2571 secondary issuance events in NEEQ that involved 1884 enterprises, raising a total of RMB 123.3 billion, an increase of 8.68 times compared with 2014.

In addition to additional stock offerings, equity pledge financing has also taken its initial shape. Unlike private placement financing, equity pledge financing does not dilute the company's equity, and the financing approval process is shorter. NEEQ has cooperated with a number of state-owned commercial banks and joint-stock banks to provide stock pledge loan services for listed enterprises. To date, there have been nearly 1850 cases of equity pledge, totaling 18 billion shares. Since 2014 in particular, the expanding size of companies listed on the New Third Board and the introduction of the market-maker system have resulted in more equity liquidity and a rising scale of equity pledge business. The equity pledge shares rose to 2.3 billion in 2014, an increase of 4.61 times over 2013. It grew to 8.7 billion in 2015, an increase of 2.77 times over 2014, and continued to increase in 2016. By the middle of May 2016, the number of pledged shares reached 5.8 billion, equivalent to 67% of the amount in 2015.

Bond financing supplements equity financing on the New Third Board. Since 2012, a total of 17 NEEQ listed companies have issued 25 bonds with a total financing scale of RMB 6.138 billion, most of which are private equity bonds listed on the Shanghai and Shenzhen stock exchanges. This is mainly because the Shenzhen and Shanghai stock exchanges were issued in May and October 2012, respectively, the *Guidelines on Private Equity Bond Pilot Programs for Small and Medium-sized Enterprises*, which stipulated that small and medium-sized enterprises should raise and transfer private placement bonds in a nonpublic way with no administrative licensing or requirement on their net assets and profit-making ability, as these bonds are completely market-based and credit-based products. At present, the coupon rate of bonds issued by NEEQ enterprises ranges from 5 to 11%, and the amount of each issuance varies significantly. The largest single financing is a corporate bond issued by the CCIC at the end of 2015. Its total amount reached RMB 1.3 billion.

Main Challenges and Cause Analysis

Generally, the cancellation of administrative licensing and power delegation has boosted the financing efficiency of the OTC market. The small-amount, fast and flexible financing mechanism is basically up and running, and a diversified financing structure has been formed. However, compared with the huge financing needs of small and medium-sized enterprises, the existing system design and financing mode are faced with a number of prominent challenges.

I. The ability to undertake additional issuance has weakened, and the financing needs of businesses have not been fully met.

Despite the absolute size of the private placement of stocks in the New Third Board market, the growth rate began to fall in 2016. The proposed amount reached RMB 53.4 billion last December but has fallen to about RMB 14 billion since March. This is partly due to the decision of NEEQ to suspend the launch of informal financial institutions such as PE, microloan, guarantee, pawn and P2P companies and their secondary financing to mitigate financial risks. As a result, the financing scale in the financial sector has fallen sharply. It dropped to less than 5% of the total financing in the OTC market compared with over 30% in the previous year. In addition, the slowdown of growth in private placement also shows the weakening of its ability to undertake additional issuance and the capital supply capacity. In 2015, a general oversubscription of privately issued shares on the OTC market helped meet the financing needs of companies. However, since the beginning of this year, only 78% of the financing needs have been met. The average length of financing from issuance announcement to issuance completion has been extended from about 90 days at the end of last year to 115 days in April this year, which is a natural result of the imbalances in financing supply and demand. The threshold for individual investors in the OTC market is as high as RMB 5 million, but the speed of attracting institutional investors cannot catch up with growing financing needs in the market. PE, capital managers of securities companies, insurance, QFII and other institutional investors are not broadly represented in the market. While the introduction of the market maker system once eased the liquidity problem, their growing number has led to inadequacies in market making funds and further reduction of liquidity. The financing function of the OTC market has been affected as a result.

II. The scale of equity pledge financing and the number of participating securities firms are both small.

Despite its speed of growth, the equity pledge financing business on NEEQ is small in scale. Less than 800 of the 7000 companies listed have conducted financing through equity pledge, accounting for about 10% in number and even 5% in the ratio of pledged shares. The value of pledge financing is also small. In 2015, at an average of 40% discount rate of net value per share, the equity pledge financing scale for the whole year was less than RMB 7 billion or less than 6% of the total additional financing, while the equity pledge market value in the Shanghai and Shenzhen stock exchanges reached RMB 3.41 trillion or nearly RMB 1.4 trillion of the financing scale at a 40% discount rate, equivalent to the combined size of the equity financing from IPO, additional issuance and rights offering. Lack of liquidity is the main reason for the small scale of equity pledge business on the New Third Board. Low liquidity has made it hard to have a fair trading price on NEEQ, as pricing of equity pledge is mainly based on net assets per share, and this directly affects the size of pledge. The lack of liquidity also increases the difficulty of asset disposal and potential business risks, which adds to the anxiety of the financing institutions and directly affects the trading volume.

In addition, banks have dominated the equity pledge business on NEEQ. Since 2010, they have taken up 45% of the pledge parties and nearly 50% of the pledged shares. Guarantee companies take second place, accounting for approximately 15% of the pledge parties and 10% of the pledged shares. Brokerage, which should have been an important player, has lost its visibility in equity pledge in the NEEQ in recent years, leaving only Sealand Securities, Shanxi Securities and Pacific Securities in this market. This is in stark contrast with their dominating position in floor trade, having completed 4366 of the total 6815 equity pledge transactions or 64.06% of the trading in the Shanghai and Shenzhen stock exchanges in 2015. Compared with banks, guarantee companies and other financial institutions, securities firms stand out for their strong pricing power, flexible mechanism and easy process in conducing equity pledge and should have dominated NEEQ as they do on stock exchanges in Shanghai and Shenzhen. The current situation is mainly caused by regulatory restrictions. In July 2015, the Securities Association of China issued the *Measures for the Pilot Program concerning the Pledge-Style Repo of Over-the-Counter Equities by Securities Companies.*[2] However, the Measures did not say that securities firms can carry out equity pledge business in NEEQ.

III. Bond financing develops slowly, and corporate bonds have not been launched on the New Third Board.

At present, the total scale of bond financing on NEEQ is relatively small, and the cumulative scale of financing since 2012 is less than 3% of the additional financing. This is mainly because most of the NEEQ companies are micro and small businesses, with weak debt service ability and in want of effective means of credit enhancing such as mortgage and pledge. Their external rating is low or even nonexistent. Of

[2] In the Measures the "underlying equities for pledge-style repo mark equity" refers to (1) stocks of joint-stock companies and equities of limited liability companies, which are registered and quoted at China Securities Internet System Co., Ltd., (2) stocks of joint-stock companies and equities of limited liability companies transferred by quotation on qualified regional equity trading markets, (3) other equities prescribed by the CSRC and the SAC.

the 25 bonds issued, only 11 have external ratings, and most of them are lower than AA+. This has hampered the bond issuance capacity of NEEQ registered companies. In addition, NEEQ itself lacks innovative bond financing tools. All 25 bonds issued by NEEQ companies are in the Shanghai and Shenzhen stock exchanges or interbank markets (23 for the former and 2 for the latter). They are not traded in NEEQ and cannot be taken as NEEQ corporate bonds in real sense. In August 2014, the CSRC issued the *Ten Measures in Support of Micro and Small Business Development* (hereinafter referred to as the Ten Measures), which says that "NEEQ-listed companies are allowed to issue SME private equity bonds". The NEEQ also said that rules were ready for the business.[3] However, due to the frequent occurrence of credit default in bond markets recently as well as the lack of category-based regulation and information disclosure mechanisms for NEEQ, the rules for the issuance of nonpublic bonds on the New Third Board have not yet been issued due to policy constraints.

IV. New financing tools have yet to be found.

In September 2015, NEEQ issued the *Guidelines on the NEEQ Preferred Stock Business (for Trial Implementation)*, breaking the ground for this business on the New Third Board. As a hybrid capital instrument, preferred shares have the dual characteristics of equity and debt instruments and enjoy high expectations of the market. Since the release of the Guidelines, 11 NEEQ listed companies have disclosed their plans for issuing preferred stocks. However, regulators have treated preferred stock, a novelty, with caution from the very start, resulting in lengthy review and approval. Progress made in this field is behind market expectations, with only one approval, which is granted to Zose Culture. Moreover, due to poor technology support, the transfer and trading mechanism of preferred stock has not been established, which may affect their liquidity after listing. NEEQ has been advocating the development of convertible bonds, asset securitization, and other financing tools carrying the characteristics of derivatives. The *Guidelines on Further Promoting the Development of the National Equities Exchange and Quotations* issued by the CSRC in 2015 made it clear that the government will "develop bonds suited to micro and small businesses, and speed up the launch of preferred stock and asset-backed securities". However, due to the absence of the category-based regulatory system of stratified administration, such innovative financing tools are only in the demonstration and exploration stage.

[3] At the end of 2015, Sui Qiang, deputy general manager of NEEQ said that at present the *Rules for Nonpublic Corporate Bonds Issuance (for Trial Implementation)* had been drafted to facilitate nonpublic corporate bonds issuance by NEEQ registered companies and their trading on NEEQ. Further studies would be carried out to expand the range of issuers of nonpublic corporate bonds and launch the pilot program of publicly traded corporate bonds issuance by NEEQ companies based on market specification.

Strengthening NEEQ's Financing Function by Streamlining Administration, Delegating Power and Making Institutional Innovation

The performance of the NEEQ financing function is not self-generated, and the problems in NEEQ's financing process are essentially caused by institutional barriers. Therefore, to improve its financing function, it is imperative to further streamline administration and delegate power, accelerate institutional innovation, and improve market transaction rules, the microstructure, the regulatory system and other supporting facilities.

I. Taking the stratification of the New Third Board as an opportunity to clear the way for streamlining administration and delegating power.

The experience of NASDAQ shows that stratification is an important institutional arrangement to realize the leapfrog development of the OTC market. On June 27, 2016, NEEQ officially implemented the *Measures for Stratification of Companies Listed on the National Equities Exchange and Quotations System (for Trial Implementation)*, which preliminarily divided NEEQ into innovation level and basic level and regularly adjusted the market levels of listed companies. The introduction of the stratification system has cleared the way for further streamlining administration and delegating power in NEEQ. With the rapid growth of the number of NEEQ listed companies, differences of listed companies in business performance, development stage, equity size, number of shareholders, market value, business scale, financing needs and other aspects have become increasingly apparent. In this case, if a one-size-fits-all system is adopted and institutional innovation is carried out rashly, systemic risk may be triggered. The stratification system encourages power delegation and institutional innovation through pilot programs with differentiated policies. It can put risk under control, improve the NEEQ service ability, reduce the cost of investors' information collection, and strengthen the functions of NEEQ in trading, financing, investment and resource allocation.

Going forward, we need to take the stratification system as an opportunity and adopt category-based regulatory policies to strengthen the information disclosure obligations of companies at the innovation level. These companies will be required to improve corporate governance and systems on external investment, external guarantees, related-party transactions, investor relations, and profit distribution and set up a board secretary post. On the basis of better information disclosure, NEEQ can further consider streamlining administration and delegating power and improve the overall system design of competitive trading, stock issuance and bond issuance for companies at the innovation level to fully stimulate the vitality of the New Third Board.

II. Improving the market trading system and using the trading function to expand the financing function.

The financing function of the OTC market depends on its liquidity, which requires further improvement of the market trading system. The introduction of the market-maker system has significantly raised the liquidity of the New Third Board. Since June last year, the trading value through market making has exceeded the trading value through contractual agreements, but it is still far from meeting the urgent liquidity needs of NEEQ. By the end of May 2016, a total of 87 securities companies on NEEQ had launched market maker businesses. There are on average only 3.97 market makers for each of the over 1500 market making stocks. In contrast, on NASQUE, there are over 600 market players and on average 20 for each stock issued.[4] As the OTC market makers are now mainly comprised of securities companies, the liquidity needs cannot be fully met, and the profit-making model of market makers is not what was designed to be, as profit mainly comes from speculative inventory stock gains instead of bid-ask spread in the process of liquidity offerings. In the long run, this will weaken NEEQ's pricing and financing functions. Therefore, it is imperative to reform the market-maker system. One goal is to increase the number of market-makers as soon as possible and break the monopoly by securities firms. As early as December 2014, the CSRC issued the *Notice on Securities Broker-Dealer Firms' Participation in Relevant Business on the National Equities Exchange and Quotations,* which supports subsidiaries of fund management companies and futures companies and securities investment consulting institutions and private equity institutions in carrying out market making business on NEEQ after proper registration with the CSRC. However, to date, no specific policies or administrative measures have been announced. The reason might be that unlike securities firms whose risks can be easily brought under control with a full-fledged regulatory system, investment consultancy institutions and private equity funds are under loose regulation. Therefore, financial institutions that are under strict and all-round regulation can be considered the first group to launch market-making business to increase the number of market-makers.

In addition, the incentives and disciplines for market makers must be improved to enhance their functions as transaction organizers and liquidity providers on NEEQ. To increase incentives, a short selling mechanism of market makers can be in place to add to the risk hedging methods of market makers and provide institutional guarantees for the steady growth of market making earnings. To tighten restraint, the obligations of market makers should be further strengthened. For example, they should emphasize in the quotation update not only the time but also the rationality of making two-way quotations to improve the performance of the pricing function. In addition, the *Measures of NEEQ of Quality Evaluation for the Sponsoring Broker-Dealer Practice (for Trial Implementation)* issued at the beginning of 2016 shall be strictly implemented, and the evaluation system and reward and punishment mechanism for

[4] Data source. "With 70% profit margin per month for market-makers, how long will NEEQ catch up with NASDAQ", sina.com.cn, March 8, 2016.

market making business shall be continuously improved to enhance the diligence and dedication of market makers.

However, the market maker system has its own problems, such as high transaction cost, low transparency and lack of supervision, while call auction trading has advantages such as low operating cost, high transparency and fast market information transmission, which can make up for the deficiency of market making trading to some extent. In overseas markets, it has been a common practice to introduce call auction trading on top of the market maker system to build a mixed trading model. For example, NASDAQ issued the new Order Handling Rules in 1997 and established the mixed system of "price bidding + competitive market making". In November 2003, the London Stock Exchange launched a new hybrid trading system SETSmm, combining the strengths of SETS and the market maker system.[5] Borrowing overseas experience and introducing call auction trading to NEEQ, which is under stratification management, will be an institutional innovation that complements the market-maker system. However, facing challenges such as poor equity distribution for listed companies, inadequate information disclosure, and weak R&D capacity of institutional intermediaries, auction trading should be introduced step by step. In the initial period, trials can be carried out on the NEEQ market composition index.

III. Lowering the threshold for investors and optimizing the mix of investors on the New Third Board.

Better liquidity also depends on the expansion of the NEEQ investor size and the optimization of the investor mix. The lack of continuous capital inflow will make it impossible to fundamentally improve liquidity through either the market maker system or the call market system. A pilot program can be launched to expand the size of NEEQ investors for companies at the innovation level. First, institutional investors should ultimately be the main players on the New Third Board. Efforts should therefore be made to simplify procedures, introduce supporting policies, and attract public offering funds, self-run brokerage firms, and asset management schemes to invest in NEEQ. Institutional arrangements for QFII and RQFII to participate in NEEQ shall be put in place, and NEEQ should be included in the long-term capital investment packages for insurance funds, social security funds and enterprise annuities. Second, on the premise of good investor eligibility management and education, the threshold for individual investors should be appropriately lowered to attract high net-worth clients and complement institutional investors.

IV. Promoting regulatory transformation for healthy market development.

Building a leaner government does not mean that the government will simply do nothing and let the market do as it likes. Rather, it aims to combine power delegation with better service and promote regulatory transformation to let the market and the rule of law play a decisive role. Regulatory problems have been exposed since 2014 with the rapid development of the OTC market. For example, funds raised by some

[5] A Study on the Introduction of Market-maker System in China's Securities Market No. 0110 [Z]. Shenzhen Stock Exchange, 2005-3-31.

listed companies have not been used for their main businesses but for real estate investment and stock speculation, financial product purchases, and the purchase of controlling shareholders' personal property at a high price.[6] It is therefore necessary to constantly strengthen the regulatory requirements for NEEQ listed companies, crack down on all kinds of fractions and law-breaking acts, keep alert against all abnormalities and punish all law and rule breaking acts. NEEQ should heighten its sense of self-discipline, clarify the responsibilities of the regulatory system, give full play to the roles of regulation, market supervision, corporate autonomy, and information disclosure, and build an NEEQ regulatory system featuring well-defined responsibilities, a clear division of functions, information sharing and sound coordination to maintain an open and fair market. In addition, the protection of investors' rights and interests must be strengthened, and the investor eligibility management system should be enforced to hold brokerages fully accountable. Steps should be taken to further regulate account opening and product sales and improve the norms of risk warning and the dispute settlement mechanism.

Providing Diversified Financing Channels and Expanding the Financing Functions of NEEQ

The reform of the NEEQ supporting system will accelerate administrative streamlining and institutional innovation in financing. Diversified financing channels will be in place to raise its capacity to serve the real economy.

I. Improving the NEEQ shelf offering system.

Shelf offering means single approval for multiple issuances. Compared with the traditional issuance system, shelf offering simplifies the issuance process, reduces the cost of issuance regulatory approval and can better meet market financing needs. In addition, it provides long-term benefits of continuous refinancing for issuers, encourages issuers to promptly disclose relevant information and forestalls irrational behaviors of seeking short-term profits. It also helps investors make investment decisions by examining the use of funds raised in the previous round of offering. It can better protect small and medium-sized investors who are able to make more informed investment decisions. Because of a better institutional design, shelf offerings have been adopted by the United States, Britain, Japan, Malaysia and other countries. China has also used it in bond issuance. In August 2007, the CSRC issued the *Pilot Measures for Corporate Bond Issuance*, which stipulates that "issuers may apply for corporate bonds issuance approval once and issue bonds at different periods".[7] In

[6] Column Article "Raising Money for Speculation Will Kill NEEQ", March 24, 2016.

[7] To be specific, from the date of issuance approved by the CSRC, the company shall make the initial offering within six months, and complete the remaining issuance within 24 months. The *Measures for the Administration of Corporate Bond Issuance and Trading*, which came into effect in January

September 2007, the CYPC became the first issuer of shelf offering bonds, and the business later extended to enterprise bonds.

There is no legal barrier to shelf offerings on NEEQ. The *Measures for the Supervision and Administration of Non-Listed Public Companies*, which came into effect in 2013, stipulates that "when a company applies for private share issuance, it may apply for serial issuance with one approval. From the date of approval by the CSRC, the company shall make initial issuance within three months and complete the issuance of the remaining shares within 12 months." However, there are still enormous obstacles in practice. Rongxin Leasing, a NEEQ listed company, tried but ultimately failed to launch a shelf offering in March 2015. The regulators were cautious, perhaps because of their concern over the possibility of shelf offerings being taken as a tool for issuers to raise money for speculative purposes, which may undermine investors' interests when the NEEQ information disclosure mechanism is not yet fully developed. However, with the implementation of the stratification system of NEEQ and category-based regulation and information disclosure, the conditions for shelf offerings will continue to improve. Pilot programs on shelf offerings may start from high-quality companies that have continuously fulfilled information disclosure obligations and have no violation record to further improve NEEQ's fast and flexible microcredit financing mechanism.

II. Encouraging NEEQ securities brokerages to do equity pledge.

To accelerate the development of equity pledge on NEEQ, it is necessary to expand the size of market players in addition to improving liquidity, actively encourage securities firms to engage in trading, and give full play to their strengths in the capital market. First, it is important to release administrative measures on equity pledge business as soon as possible for securities brokerages. A membership rights management system as practiced in the Shanghai and Shenzhen stock exchanges can be used where NEEQ focuses on rights management of securities firms and conducts front-end control on the scale of business, leaving such things as pledge target, conversion rate and risk control mechanisms to intermediaries. Second, steps should be taken to gradually relax restrictions on the sources of funds for securities brokerages. During the pilot period, the source may be limited to securities firms' own capital, and the firms' business scale can be capped against their net capital. Under the guidance of the *Notice of the Securities Association of China on Issuing the Measures for the Pilot Program Concerning the Pledge-Style Repo of Over-the-Counter Equities by Securities Companies* released in July 2015, the balances of the money loan shall be limited within 50% of the brokerage's net capital, and the accumulative financing balances of the single money collector shall not exceed 5% of the net capital to guard against the potential spread of business risks. After the pilot is successfully completed, restrictions on the financing scale of securities firms' own funds can be gradually relaxed, and the firms' asset management programs will

---

2015, extended the time period for the initial offering to within 12 months, further expanding the financing flexibility.

be allowed to participate in equity pledge business to better meet the investment and financing needs of the equity pledge business.

III. Improving NEEQ bond financing tools to complement equity financing.

In view of the relatively small size of issuers and the high risk of default on NEEQ, corporate bonds should be issued mainly through private placement in the future. However, private bond issuance and trading in the Shanghai and Shenzhen stock exchanges are below expectations. The size of issuance is moderate and continues to shrink. At present, private bonds issued by SMEs in the Shanghai and Shenzhen stock exchanges account for only 0.6% of the total bonds in custody, which is in sharp contrast to the weight of the SME-60% share in China's national economy today. A new institutional design is needed to expand NEEQ's private bond market.

First, we must increase the information disclosure of issuers of private placement bonds. The Shanghai and Shenzhen stock exchanges only require bond issuers to fulfill their obligations of information disclosure for initial offerings and major events. There are no official requirements on regular disclosure. To help investors regularly evaluate and promptly deal with the risk of default, requirements can be made for issuers to perform regular disclosure obligations to improve the information disclosure mechanism and raise the attractiveness of private placement bonds.

Second, a sound credit rating system for private placement bonds needs to be established. Credit rating conveys to investors the signal that bonds carry low credit risks, which can enhance investors' recognition of bonds and reduce financing costs. The US high yield bond market has set strict rules on credit ratings, requiring issuers to provide credit ratings from at least one well-established rating agency, but there is no such rule in China. To promote the sound development of private placement bonds on NEEQ, it is suggested that NEEQ in its policies makes it mandatory for bond issuers to provide third-party credit ratings and regularly track the ratings. Credit rating agencies should also establish a special rating system and method for private placement bonds of SMEs based on their specific circumstances.

Third, the guarantee system must be improved. Guarantee is a means of credit enhancement that is commonly used to increase the protection of creditors' interests and facilitate the smooth issuance of bonds. However, SMEs are mostly companies with moderate assets and generally lack collateral and other means of property-based guarantees. New guarantee models need to be developed. Based on the experience of high-yield bonds in the United States, group credit can be introduced as a means of credit enhancement to allow relevant enterprises of a region or an industrial chain to form a collective bond issuer featuring intra-guarantee and supervision among themselves to fundamentally lower the default risk of bond issuers. In fact, China's SME collective bond adopts this model. However, it is difficult to organize and coordinate the issuance of collective bonds, and the cost of issuance preparation is relatively high. Therefore, it is necessary to give full play to the intermediary role of NEEQ to build a pool of bonds, coordinate and organize their issuance, and cut the issuance cost.

IV. Encouraging securities firms to increase direct investment in NEEQ and expanding financing channels for venture capital.

It has been an irresistible trend for securities companies to transform from their asset-light business to asset-heavy business, such as capital intermediary service and capital investment, and direct investment has become their core business. The vigorous development of the New Third Board, especially the introduction of call auction trading in the future, will facilitate the liquidation of direct investment funds, which not only helps to improve the profitability of securities firms but also helps expand the venture capital investment channels of NEEQ listed companies to drive the growth of NEEQ. The advantage of direct investment by securities brokerages is that it can borrow the experience of their parent companies in the capital market, identify high-quality NEEQ projects with high growth potential by means of project hosting and continuous supervision, and generate a strong demonstration effect to attract private capital. To encourage more direct investment by securities companies on NEEQ, it is essential to give securities companies strong incentives through preferential treatment and policy facilitation. First, securities companies with direct investment in NEEQ should be given priority and subsidies for such businesses at the back end as listing, market-making and refinancing to increase their engagement in the whole industrial chain. Second, the NEEQ direct investment fund should be launched to apply the asset management model to direct investment, attract more private capital owned by securities firms, and chart the course for private investment. Third, subsidiaries of securities brokerages on direct investment are encouraged to transform into subsidiaries of private equity firms. They will be required to establish a sound self-regulatory system to ensure proper control by their parent companies and self-discipline by themselves.

V. Innovating financing instruments and improving such new financing models as preferred shares and convertible bonds.

Progress in launching preferred stock is slower than market expectations. It is necessary to accelerate the approval process and complete the upgrading of the technical system as soon as possible so that preferred stock can be listed and traded to increase market liquidity. Furthermore, the role of the preferred stock should be given full play in the M&A and business reorganization for NEEQ listed companies. Currently, the purposes stated in the disclosed preferred stock issuance plans are all about replenishing the working capital, and none of them is related to supporting M&A or business reorganization. Overseas experience shows that using preferred stock as a payment instrument for acquiring assets or exchanging shares is conducive to the smooth progress of business mergers and reorganization. It is suggested that NEEQ should improve its rules of business merger and reorganization as soon as possible and introduce special provisions on equity calculation, tender offer and information disclosure requirements to make way for the innovation of preferred shares.

Convertible bonds are another focus of NEEQ financing innovation. Convertible bonds have the dual characteristics of stocks and bonds. Since their financing cost is low and there is possible secondary financing, they are more suitable for emerging industries with more financing needs and higher volatility in business growth. In Europe, convertible bonds are mainly issued by emerging industries such as medicine, biology and information technology. However, the threshold of profitability is high for convertible bond issuers in the Shanghai and Shenzhen stock exchanges; therefore, the majority of convertible bond issuers are from traditional manufacturing and banking industries, as small and medium-sized high-tech enterprises are unable to meet the criteria. This has dampened the role of convertible bonds. Given the unique characteristics of convertible bonds, considerations can be made to increase the diversity of issuers on NEEQ to support the growth of strategic emerging industries. Quota limits can be lowered, while the pre-issuance review focuses more on the invested projects instead of the qualifications of the issuers to help boost the high-tech industry. Convertible bonds in the Shanghai and Shenzhen stock exchanges are issued through public offerings. This does not apply to NEEQ, where they should be issued mainly through private placement with simplified procedures and shorter preparation periods. In addition, we can borrow overseas experience and create new types of convertible bonds with different characteristics and various terms, such as zero-coupon convertible bonds, ordinary convertible bonds and presale convertible bonds, to increase its financing instruments.

Bibliography

A Study on the Introduction of Market-maker System in China's Securities Market. *Shenzhen Stock Exchange* (2005).

Bai, B., & Lu, Y. (2012). Research on the development of China's OTC market. *Inquiry into Economic Issues* (4).

Chen, Y. (2011). Research on equity trading of nonpublic companies. *Securities Market Herald* (8).

Hui, J. (2015). Research on the interactive effect of China's OTC market and the development of micro and small businesses. *Research on Financial and Economic Issues* (10).

Li, J., & Yao, C. (2009). Information disclosure system of non-listed public companies and its improvement. *Securities Market Herald* (12).

Li, M., & Qin, F. (2015). Guarantee mechanism, credit rating and financing cost of private placement bonds for SMEs. *Securities Market Herald* (9).

Wang, X., & Du, K. (2016). Capital marketization and information disclosure system improvement. *Finance and Economics* (5).

Yang, X., Fan, C., & Guo, L. (2014). International comparison and reference of OTC market trading system. *South China Finance* (11).

Policy Adjustments for Addressing Financing Difficulties of Small and Medium-Sized Government—A Survey of Commercial Banks

Haibei Liu

Introduction

On March 14, 2013, the *Plan for Institutional Reform and Functional Transformation of the State Council* (hereinafter referred to as the Plan) was released, unveiling the seventh government institutional reform in China since the start of the reform and opening-up in 1978. The Plan put forward the concept of streamlining administration and delegating power and emphasized the need to properly handle the relationship between the government and the market and between the government and society. The government must delegate power that should be delegated and regulate the matters that fall into its responsibility.

In June 2016, Premier Li Keqiang of the State Council stressed when visiting the People's Bank of China, China Construction Bank and other financial institutions that more efforts should be made to provide easy and affordable financing to enterprises, especially micro and small businesses and the private sector, and reduce and regulate the fees of guarantee and evaluation in the process of providing financing to enterprises. Commercial banks should be encouraged to take more measures to meet the "short-term, moderate, frequent and urgent" financing needs of micro and small businesses and the private sector, boost private investment, and prevent credit crunches on businesses that enjoy good reputations and market sales.

The State Council has placed great importance on the financing of micro and small businesses because of their unique features. Micro and small businesses are important to people's livelihood and generate a large number of jobs. In recent years, the fast growth of the private sector has made micro and small businesses an important part of the national economy. However, they are naturally a disadvantaged group when applying for loans or seeking financing because of their business size, inadequate guarantees and unstable operation. Improving their financing services requires government policy guidance. This paper will analyze the causes of the financing

H. Liu (✉)
Guanghua School of Management, Peking University, Beijing, China

Y. Li and Z. Cheng (eds.), *The Chinese Path Toward a Leaner Government*,
https://doi.org/10.1007/978-981-19-6718-4_16

difficulties facing micro and small businesses, evaluate current policies, and suggest ways of addressing these difficulties through policy adjustments, particularly the financing services offered by commercial banks.

At present, in the CBRC's performance evaluation of commercial banks in offering financing services for micro and small businesses, there is no typical mentioning of the nature of borrowers, which may include both companies in need of working capital and individuals who apply for loans to keep their businesses going. This paper focuses solely on financing for companies.

Where Does the Financing Difficulty Lie for Micro and Small Businesses, and What Are Its Causes?

The financing difficulty of micro and small businesses includes a high lending threshold and sticky process. A high lending threshold means that commercial banks require micro and small businesses to provide collaterals as the second repayment source when applying for loans, which makes it difficult for micro and small businesses in the early stage of development to be qualified borrowers. A sticky process means that financing for micro and small businesses is characterized by high risks and low returns and thus involves high costs for banks. Therefore, it generally takes more than one week or, under extreme circumstances, several months to complete the registration process of housing as collateral.

I. High lending threshold for micro and small businesses and its causes

The current bank credit regulatory measures require micro and small businesses to provide double guarantees for loan repayment sources. The first source is determined according to the companies' performance, and the second source is based on the assessed value of the collateral. Both factors determine the availability and size of loans. The judgment of a company's performance is generally made by the staff of the bank through field investigation and account checking. The income recognized by the bank is calculated according to the financial data and transactions registered on the account, which, in combination with the industry to which the company belongs and the overall cost factors, determines a reasonable loan size. The second source of repayment refers to the assessed value of the collateral, which usually refers to the property of the owner or the actual controller of the company, or the property of their immediate family members. Collateral commitment made by the property owner is also needed. The value of the property multiplied by the collateral lending rate is the credit size determined by the second repayment source. The funding available for the borrower is the smaller one of the credit sizes calculated from the two repayment sources.

Many micro and small businesses at their early stage of growth find it impossible to obtain bank loans because of the sole requirement that they need to be profitable and at the same time have valid property as the collateral. Many internet financial companies have introduced account statement-based lending, financing for receivables and other financial products for micro and small businesses, where the amount of loans is determined by the receivables on the companies' bank account or financial statement, and there is no need for property as a second source of repayment. These collateral-free products, which have seemingly opened a new way for micro and small businesses to obtain financing, involve high risk premiums, as reflected in loan interest rates.

The author interviewed several business owners in Fengtai District of Beijing who have loan balance in banks and obtained almost the same answer. First, the Internet platform is faster than traditional commercial banks in terms of loan application approval. Generally, it takes 1–2 months for micro and small businesses to obtain bank approval for the working capital loan but only two days for the fastest collateral-free Internet platforms to deliver loans. Second, the financing costs through Internet platforms are significantly higher than traditional banks. The interest rates of account statement-based loans on Internet platforms are approximately 2–3 times that of bank credit for micro and small businesses. It is easy to understand the difference in financing costs. The cost for banks to take in deposit is relatively low, and the Internet platform provides wealth management for funds aiming at high yield. Therefore, credit provided through the two channels is bound to be significantly different in pricing. Third, traditional banks are more flexible in means of loan payment than Internet platforms, which generally require the start of payment of the principle soon after the loan is delivered. Banks do not ask for advanced payment of principal. Instead, borrowers only have to repay the interests specified in the loan contract. Repayment of all the principal can be as late as the expiration date of credit extension. This means that credits from banks to micro and small businesses can maximize the efficacy of capital use by companies.

Based on the above three findings, micro and small business owners believe that the financing efficiency of Internet platforms is high, but the financing cost and capital utilization ratio are obviously undesirable. The threshold for bank credit is high, and the approval period is long, but banks have absolute advantages in the cost and size of financing. For businesses that can raise funds from both banks and Internet platforms, bank loans are the preferred choice for long-term business operations, and high-cost Internet platforms will be considered only if there is short-term liquidity risk.

According to the results of market research, the main financing channels for micro and small businesses are still concentrated in traditional commercial banks because their profits are limited and unable to cover the high financing cost. Commercial banks have many physical outlets where lenders and borrowers can interact and cooperate. Therefore, the sound growth of bank credit for micro and small businesses is the key to solving their financing difficulties.

II. Sticky financing process for micro and small enterprises and its causes

The financing process adds to the difficulties facing micro and small businesses. Analysis is made into the difficulties they face in the financing process and its causes with a key player—banks—as an example.

1. Weak profitability. The financing scale of micro and small businesses is relatively small, mainly due to the company's size and the value of the property as collateral. Take the Fengtai branch of a state-owned bank as an example. By the first quarter of 2016, 35% of all its lending projects saw a financing scale of less than RMB1 million. Since the process remains the same regardless of the size of the loan, the profits the bank can make are negligible compared with the costs of processing the loan application.
2. High risk. Compared with relatively large companies, micro and small businesses do not have a well-established corporate governance structure. Corporate governance is relatively poor. Without audits by certified accounting firms, their financial data are unable to reflect the true performance of the companies. Because of information asymmetry, bank staff need to pay regular visits to the companies to see how they fair by checking accounts and inventories, but it is still not enough for the banks to have a true picture. In addition, even if banks execute the entrusted payment in the process of loan issuance, no one can prevent micro and small businesses from related-party transactions or misappropriation of the loans originally intended for supporting business operations. Moreover, the legal procedures of collateral transactions and the relevant litigation are quite lengthy. Most collaterals are the private property of individuals. Although a commitment letter is signed before loans are granted, it is now difficult for banks to make enforcement in the short term. Although the property is legally owned by the lender, it only serves as a moral constraint in reality and is rarely used to make up for nonperforming loans.
3. Complicated process. Financing for micro and small businesses is characterized as "short-term, moderate, frequent and urgent". However, property collaterals are mandatory in securing banks' approval for loans. At the loan application stage, both the borrower and the lender are required to sign many standard instruments and legal documents, and the owner of the property must work with bank staff to register the collateral at the government housing department where a collateral registration certificate is added to the property ownership certificate. Loans will not be granted until collateral registration is completed. In Beijing, for example, it takes at least five working days to complete the collateral registration from the date of appointment, and it may take as long as several months for registration. As it is the precondition for banks to issue loans, many micro and small enterprises in urgent need of capital have to give up the application in the collateral registration process.

Evaluation of Current Policies

The State Council attaches great importance to the financing of micro and small businesses. The financial regulatory authorities have also issued a series of policies and measures and made specific requirements to commercial banks and other financial institutions on improving service to micro and small businesses. These policies and measures can be classified into three groups. The first group is about the diversification of service providers; the second group is about the evaluation of the financing scale and additional financing needs of borrowers. The third group is about improving the efficiency of processing loan applications of micro and small businesses.

I. Diversifying service providers

The financial service scope for micro and small businesses is expanded mainly through the establishment of new financial institutions or the relaxation of restrictions on the business scope of the existing ones. Microcredit companies, guarantee companies, Internet P2P companies, private banks and other financial institutions have been established to offer micro and small businesses more financing channels. The policy has been successful in terms of lender diversification. However, there are structural problems in product coverage. As mentioned above, most of the micro and small businesses want to apply for short-term working capital loans from banks, and the product choice is limited. The bank's credit product structure varies. However, due to the uniqueness of financing risks and returns for micro and small businesses, bank executives, loan program initiators and customer managers all have concerns about product promotion. Therefore, expanding the scope of financial services for micro and small businesses is more important than lender diversification in improving the product mix, digging into borrowers' needs, and providing targeted financial services accordingly.

II. Raising financing size and the number of new clients for micro and small businesses

Financial institutions are evaluated by regulators on the amount of credit issued to micro and small businesses and the number of new customers of this category based on the regions they serve and the type of institutions they belong to. For a state-owned bank, generally, the quota is set at the beginning of the fiscal year for regional headquarters in light of their business features and then is further divided among local branches, where customer service departments are responsible for loan issuance to micro and small businesses. Progress on task fulfillment is an important item in the overall performance appraisal system for local branches. In other words, task assignment is top down, and evaluation is bottom up. The quota system, which acts like an executive order, has indeed boosted the enthusiasm of local branches to extend credit to micro and small businesses. Taking the Fengtai branch of a state-owned bank as an example, from 2013 to 2016, it issued RMB498 million of loans to private companies and micro and small businesses, at an average annual growth rate of over 60%. A total of 344 batches of loans were delivered, with the size of single issuance ranging between RMB 100,000 and RMB 30 million and the interest rates ranging between 10 and 20% above the benchmark interest rate of the central bank or 15% above the central bank benchmark rate on average. This shows that the financing cost of micro and small businesses through banks is relatively low. A total of 144 micro and small businesses had loan balance in the bank of that period, among which 87 were wholesale and retail businesses, accounting for 60%; 46 were in the manufacturing industry, accounting for 32%; and the remaining 11 businesses were in other sectors, accounting for 8%.

Data show that since the policy was implemented, the total financing size and coverage for micro and small businesses have increased, but the results are still lower than expected. First, it is impossible to set a precise quota based on the reality of each company at the beginning of the plan making because there may be information asymmetry between those who make the plans and those who implement them, but the latter must obey the former unconditionally as is required by the bank governance structure.

For example, if there is a gap between the size of financing and the number of existing customers in the evaluation indicators, and as the amount of financing for a single micro and small business ranges from several hundred thousand to several million yuan, it will be obvious that the bank has overfulfilled the target on the number of new customers, but the financing scale will remain small. Banks tend to list subsidiaries of some large companies with large financing needs as micro and small businesses so long as they meet the category standards issued by the MIIT on the number of staff and others to meet the required quota for the amount of credit extended to micro and small businesses.

Second, evaluation is made on the total amount of credit and the number of customers, but there are no specific requirements concerning financing products. What micro and small businesses need most is working capital from banks that can support their long-term business operations. Although bill discounting, the pledge of deposit certificates and other low-risk collateral-free financing products could be counted as new accounts of micro and small businesses in the evaluation, they in fact are unable to provide effective support to micro and small businesses in their business operations.

III. Improving the loan application efficiency for micro and small businesses

The CBRC issued the *Guidelines on Financial Service for Micro and Small Businesses* in March 2015, where the goals of banks in providing financial services to micro and small businesses in 2015 were shifted from "two no lower than" to "three no lower than", meaning the focus was transformed from the amount and speed of loan growth to the loan growth rate, number of customers and application success rate. This can help better examine the growth of loans for micro and small businesses. In the previous paragraphs, analysis was made on the target for the amount and speed of loan growth. Next, a policy evaluation is made on the new evaluation indicator of the loan application success rate in 2015.

The loan application success rate is the ratio between the actual number of loan recipients and the number of loan applicants. Its main goal is to improve the success rate of micro and small business loan applications. The regulatory authorities conduct monthly examinations of financial institutions on the success rate of micro and small business loan applications and make data comparisons at the end of each quarter. It is required that the rate must not be lower than that in the previous period.

The policy aims to improve the success rate of the loan application for micro and small businesses, but there are two challenges in data monitoring. First, the data monitoring only covers companies that are accepted by banks as applicants for loans as divisors of the success rate. Therefore, banks are more cautious when reviewing applications and tend to reject those that may not receive approvals. This has in fact raised the loan application threshold for micro and small businesses. The practice for banks to start processing loan applications after calculations and inquiry also prolongs the period before loan issuance. Second, the quarterly assessment links bank service efficiency with whether loan application and issuance are made in the same month. Banks therefore tend to accept application only when they are sure that loans can be granted in the same month. Otherwise, borrowers need to apply again the next month.

If, for example, a micro and small business makes a loan application on June 15th, the application will not be processed until early July when the deadline of the quarterly evaluation expires because it takes over ten days on average to produce a collateral certificate for the property according to the process described in the previous paragraph and no one can guarantee that the loan will be issued by the end of the month. The policy results in lower financing efficiency for micro and small businesses in a specific period. The focus of policymaking should therefore be specifying evaluation indicators. The timeline between loan application and approval can replace the old practice of date-based calculation, which may help banks continuously carry out the business within a fiscal year and better meet the urgent, frequent and moderate short-term financing needs of micro and small businesses.

Conclusions and Policy Suggestions

This research focuses on the credit products of commercial banks in the service of micro and small businesses in Fengtai District of Beijing. The geographic area is limited, yet credit policies of commercial banks are more or less the same in other places, so the conclusion of the research is true in a wider range of areas. It takes joint efforts of businesses, financial service providers and competent government departments to solve the financing problem of micro and small businesses once and for all.

Taking Beijing Fengtai District as an example, the majority of micro and small businesses in the area are in the initial stage of growth, with an average operating period of 5 years. Their shareholders are generally relatives or friends of the companies' legal persons. Larger enterprises have independent financial departments, while smaller ones entrust financial work to third-party bookkeeping companies. It is true that there is room for improvement in rule compliance and management of micro and small businesses that cannot even produce valid documents for business transactions. Their financial statements have not been audited by accounting firms, and their corporate income can only be estimated by comparing the tax returns provided by the tax authorities with entries on the companies' accounts.

Banks pursue maximum profit. There is serious information asymmetry in financing for micro and small businesses, which is small in scale, low in returns, but high in default risks. It is difficult to liquidate the collateral but easy for bad debts to occur. Commercial banks provide such service mainly for the purpose of completing the performance evaluation as required by financial regulatory authorities. In product design, more consideration is given to securing guarantees and risk mitigation instead of whether the design is proper, efficient or demand-driven. New approaches need to be found in addressing the inconsistency between policy goals and business targets in the following two aspects. First, financial service products that can generate intermediate business income should be nested in the credit financing products for micro and small businesses through public–private partnerships to increase profit-generating sources. However, prior consent of the legal persons of the businesses must be obtained; otherwise, it may result in higher financing costs for micro and small businesses in a disguised way. Property is currently widely used as collateral guarantee. However, the registration procedure is complex, and the enforcement efficiency is low, so it is mainly used as a reminder for debt service instead of a source of auction-based repayment. Bank staff who are usually local branch account managers responsible for micro and small businesses have to take the blame if there is a default or be punished if a bad loan occur. Improving the efficiency of collateral liquidation may, to some extent, ease the imbalance between little incentive and heavy punishment for bank staff. At the same time, it can also raise the awareness of borrowers with regard to the importance of good faith and the potential consequence of default.

Micro and small businesses are a unique group of borrowers. Precise policy support is required in addition to improving the financial service system and management of these companies to address the underlying financing difficulties. The government must combine power delegation with better regulation and service and tighten administration in some areas while streamlining governance in others. It should offer policy guidance and encourage financial institutions to increase support for micro and small businesses, refine regulatory policies regarding the evaluation of loan issuance, and eliminate unnecessary constraints on financial institutions. Other relevant government departments should also introduce policies conducive to financing micro and small businesses. The paper will discuss the addition and subtraction of financial regulatory policies and supporting policies from other government departments.

I. Cutting down financial regulatory policies

A cutdown of financial regulatory policies should be made in the following four aspects:

1. The fixed target for an increased number of micro and small businesses getting loans should be replaced by an interval one. This will help local bank branches set their targets that can be completed within a certain timeframe and more or less remove the information asymmetry between the decision maker and plan executors. It will also leave policy space for addressing uncertainties in areas where local branches operate.

2. The performance evaluation should include the ratio of the number of new accounts to existing accounts of micro and small businesses. In the past, evaluation focused on the number of new accounts. However, the number of new accounts in any given region is limited, and offering continuous service to existing accounts is also important for banks. New and existing accounts should receive equal attention in the evaluation of the account number of micro and small businesses to prevent banks from financing nonbusiness-related activities of the clients just for the purpose of adding new accounts.
3. A separate evaluation criteria should be established for credit extended to micro and small businesses in checking the bank's balance and ratio of nonperforming loans. The account manager in a local branch of a state-owned bank has to bear main responsibilities for bad loans, be it a nonperforming loan of RMB 500,000 issued to a micro and small business or a nonperforming loan of several hundred million yuan for a state-owned enterprise. The punishment is severe, but incentives are limited. As mentioned above, loans for micro and small businesses involve high risks and low profits. To increase incentives for banks on such loans, special risk assessment should be designed for special business types, in addition to assigning quotas top down.
4. The evaluation of banks on financing efficiency for micro and small businesses should take into account reality. Proper and effective methods should be adopted to avoid inconsistencies between policy objectives and real results. Assessment of the loan application success rate of micro and small businesses should be based on reasonable financing cycles in accordance with business procedures. Data should be obtained for each loan service to avoid simplistic evaluation methods such as setting deadlines at the end of each quarter or year.

II. Addition of financial regulatory policies

The addition of financial regulation mainly includes the following three aspects:

1. Financial institutions should be encouraged to conduct product and service innovation. The study shows that micro and small businesses that focus on their main businesses with sound performance are more inclined to obtain long-term loans rather than short-term funds as working capital. All industries have a relatively fixed annual cycle of capital use to meet business demand; therefore, businesses prefer a pay-as-you-go credit line. Most of the current working capital loan products for micro and small businesses offered by commercial banks are one-year nonrevolving credit lines. Reissuance of credit requires another round of loan application process involving pledge and repledge of collaterals. Regulators should help commercial banks design, on the premise of credit risk control, innovative products such as medium- and long-term revolving credit lines based on the needs of micro and small businesses to improve the financing efficiency for these businesses and minimize repetitive work for bank staff.
2. The evaluation should emphasize both quality and quantity. When calculating the number of new accounts and credit balance, evaluators should distinguish pledged loans from low-risk business, increase the weight of pledged loans and cut the

weight of low-risk business such as bank acceptance bill and deposit pledge financing in the evaluation. This will truly help meet the targets of financing quotas and new accounts of micro and small businesses and facilitate their long-term business operations.

3. A new micro and small business guarantee system should be in place. At present, the guarantee method of financing for micro and small businesses is relatively monotonous. The pledging process of private property of the legal person or the actual controller of the business is complicated, and there are obstacles in enforcement. A new guarantee system with the guarantor of final resort and mutual guarantee of companies should be established. Similar business coinsurance products have been tried in commercial banks. However, flaws in institutional design often lead to the scenario of "bad money drives out good money" where companies with good credit ratings withdraw from the mutual guarantee mechanism. The problems can be effectively addressed by bringing in the right guarantor of last resort and tightening the criteria for companies that provide guarantees.

III. Policy recommendations for relevant government departments

The supporting policies of relevant government departments should mainly include the following two aspects:

1. Tax authorities should improve the supervision and law enforcement of micro and small businesses. For example, they should verify their corporate income to ensure that their tax statements match their actual annual income to improve the authenticity of their financial data.
2. The housing registration center of the land and natural resources authorities should open a green channel for real estate pledge financing, simplify the approval process and improve processing efficiency. Now, most of the products of commercial banks serving micro and small businesses are pledged loans, with housing as the second repayment source. The most uncertain part of it is registering housing as collaterals, and the registration efficiency directly affects the waiting period for borrowers to obtain money.

Bibliography

China Banking Regulatory Commission. (2015). *Guidance on financial services for micro and small enterprises*.

Compilation of credit policies of a commercial bank (2015).

General Office of the State Council. (2014). *Guidance on alleviating the high financing cost of enterprises with multiple measures*.

Handbook of corporate products of a commercial bank (2014).

Li, Y. (2015). Streamlining administration, delegating power and cultivating independent market entities. *Administration Reform, 9*.

Plan for Institutional Reform and Functional Transformation of the State Council (2013).

Implementing the Negative List in the Xiamen Area of China (Fujian) Pilot Free Trade Zone

Ximing Dou, Feichi Han, and Huiling Liao

As Professor Li Yining suggests, a leaner government in the new era should start from the institutional building of the negative list, the power list and the responsibility list.[1] Among them, the negative list is at the center of the endeavor. Premier Li Keqiang stressed that the significance of the negative list for China's free trade zones is promoting reform through opening up and pushing the government to streamline administration and delegate power. The negative list of market access identifies industries, fields and businesses where investment and business operation are prohibited or restricted. Areas outside the list are open to all types of market players on an equal footing in accordance with the law, which reflects the philosophy that anything is allowed unless prohibited by the law.

The 18th CPC National Congress and the second, third and fourth Plenary Sessions of the 18th CPC Central Committee made plans and new requirements for all-round advancement of the reform and faster transformation of government functions. Streamlining administration and delegating power, as its first step, is key to easing the current downward pressure on the economy, creating an environment conducive to the healthy growth of businesses, and injecting fresh vitality into economic and social development. In the face of the current economic complexities, rolling back the government's power and implementing the negative list will open up new dimensions and opportunities for economic growth, social progress and the improvement of people's livelihood. In this context, the China (Fujian) Pilot Free Trade Zone, as an important step to upgrade China's economic structure, has become a pioneer in

[1] Preface by Prof. Li Yining.

X. Dou (✉)
Xiamen Municipal Government, Xiamen, China

F. Han
National Development and Reform Commission, Beijing, China

H. Liao
School of Economics and Management, Wuhan University, Wuhan, China

Y. Li and Z. Cheng (eds.), *The Chinese Path Toward a Leaner Government*,
https://doi.org/10.1007/978-981-19-6718-4_17

the new era of China's economic development and contributes to the lofty mission of national reunification.

In December 2014, with the approval of the Standing Committee of the National People's Congress, the State Council issued the *Decision of the Standing Committee of the National People's Congress on Authorizing the State Council to Temporarily Adjust Administrative Review and Approval of Relevant Laws and Regulations in China (Guangdong) Pilot Free Trade Zone, China (Tianjin) Pilot Free Trade Zone, China (Fujian) Pilot Free Trade Zone and the Extended Area of China (Shanghai) Pilot Free Trade Zone*. In 2015, the State Council released the *General Plan of China (Fujian) Pilot Free Trade Zone*. On April 1, 2016, Fujian Province adopted the *Regulations on China (Fujian) Pilot Free Trade Zone*, which adds an exception clause to highlight cooperation between Fujian and Taiwan. The Pilot Free Trade Zone adopts the management model of "pre-establishment national treatment+negative list" and grants equal treatment to both domestic and foreign investment in all areas outside the negative list.

This paper examines the practice of enforcing the Negative List in the Xiamen Area of China (Fujian) Pilot Free Trade Zone (hereinafter referred to as the Xiamen Area), provisions of the *Special Administrative Measures (Negative List) for the Access of Foreign Investment in Pilot Free Trade Zones*, the *General Plan of China (Fujian) Pilot Free Trade Zone* and the *Regulations on China (Fujian) Pilot Free Trade Zone* as well as measures fitting into the Negative List, including the mechanism on market access, review and approval, the regulatory mechanism, the systems of social credit and information disclosure and sharing, and relevant laws and regulations. Explorations are also carried out on the management system of foreign investment in the Negative List of the Xiamen Area to meet market rules and streamline government administration.

The Negative List Holds the Key to the Economic Development of the Xiamen Area

According to the circular of the State Council, the 118.04-km^2 China (Fujian) Pilot Free Trade Zone covers three areas: the Xiamen Area of 43.78 km^2 (including Xiangyu Bonded Area of 0.6 km^2, Xiangyu Bonded Area Logistics Park of 0.7 km^2, and Xiamen Haicang Bonded Port Area of 9.51 km^2), the Pingtan Area of 43 km^2, and the Fuzhou Area of 31.26 km^2 (including a bonded area of 0.6 km^2, an export processing area of 1.14 km^2 and a bonded port area of 9.26 km^2).[2]

The Xiamen Area is an important part of the Pilot Free Trade Zone. Its growth is closely linked to the implementation of the Negative List in the context of the global situation, China's national strategy and development for the region.

---

[2] The Notice of the State Council on Issuing the Overall Plan of China (Fujian) Pilot Free Trade Zone [Z]. *The Gazette of the State Council of the People's Republic of China*, 2015(13).

I. Global trends

As the world's economy grows, economic globalization and the international division of labor have become increasingly obvious. The free flow of production factors and the integration of resources are vital to regional economic development. Closer relations between countries and regions call for greater industrial collaboration between Fujian and Taiwan and more in-depth cooperation in the region. The establishment of pilot FTZs follows the trend of world economic and trade development. It will give full play to the strengths of all parties, promote mutual complementarity and enhance the vitality of the economy.

As a window that connects the region and the overseas market, the Xiamen Area bears the responsibility of bringing home high standards from abroad and fully integrating the region with the international market through reform and innovation. Another major strategic task for it and the wider provincial pilot free trade zone is to create a free and open market environment that conforms to national rules and encourages innovation and to attract advanced production factors from abroad through both "bringing in" and "going out". The ultimate goal is to facilitate the transformation and upgrading of Chinese companies.

History shows that the model of "pre-establishment national treatment + negative list" first appeared in the *North American Free Trade Agreement* (NAFTA). According to the statistics of China's Ministry of Commerce, the model is adopted by 77 countries for market access. The negative list model for foreign investment administration has been widely used globally.

II. National strategy

Developing the Xiamen Area is not only a key project in the 13th Five-Year Plan of Fujian Province but also a national strategy. The *Proposal of the CPC Fujian Provincial Committee on Formulating the 13th Five-year Plan for the National Economic and Social Development of Fujian Province* called for greater efforts in building the China (Fujian) Pilot Free Trade Zone and collaborating with neighboring regions to boost regional economic development that brings benefits to a wider region. In addition, the proposal also calls for building a transparent, efficient and service-oriented government. The government will continue to streamline administration, delegate powers, and strengthen regulation. It will foster an international, market-oriented, and law-based business environment and establish a sound system for the list of powers, the list of responsibilities, and the negative list. Based on the principle of streamlining administration and delegating power, the Xiamen Area is leveraging its unique strengths in its relations with Taiwan and its role in the twenty-first Century Maritime Silk Road to further expand the area, fields and industries of opening up and promotes the transformation of government functions through institutional reforms.

The strategic importance of building the Xiamen Area is as follows. As a pilot program and a pacesetter for reform, it will gather the reform experience of coastal free trade zones and apply it in other areas. In addition, it will look into the practice at home and abroad and conduct experiments to make comparisons and keep what fits local conditions. Speaking at the video conference on building a leaner and service-oriented government, Premier Li Keqiang said that the pilot scheme on the negative list for market access should be launched in some regions, and the list should be further narrowed. The government will step up efforts to set a negative list for industry access and remove unreasonable restrictions and invisible barriers that block private investment from entering the power, telecommunications, transportation, oil and gas, municipal utilities, elderly care, education and other sectors. Additional conditions and discriminatory clauses targeting exclusively private investment must be removed to ensure equal rights for equal stock shares and protect the lawful rights and interests of private capital.

III. Regional needs

Unlike Guangdong and Tianjin, Fujian issued the *Regulations on China (Fujian) Pilot Free Trade Zone,* which served as the "basic law" of the pilot free trade zone shortly before its first anniversary. The Regulations define the positioning of the province's pilot free trade zone, namely, promoting exchanges and cooperation between Fujian and Taiwan and providing a legislative basis for building the core area of the twenty-first Maritime Silk Road. More specifically, the Xiamen Area will create a model of cross-straits cooperation in emerging industries and modern service sectors and grow into a center for cross-straits financial services and trade. Its strengths in this area will be further leveraged to promote cross-straits cooperation with innovative reforms. Implementing the negative list of the Xiamen Area is essential to the creation of a new cross-straits cooperation mechanism, facilitation for trade and investment liberalization with Taiwan, and free flow of goods, services, capital, people and other production resources.

Implementation of the Negative List in the Xiamen Area

Since its establishment on April 21, 2015, the Xiamen Area has followed the management model of "pre-establishment national treatment+negative list". The management and implementation of the negative list is shown in Chart 1.

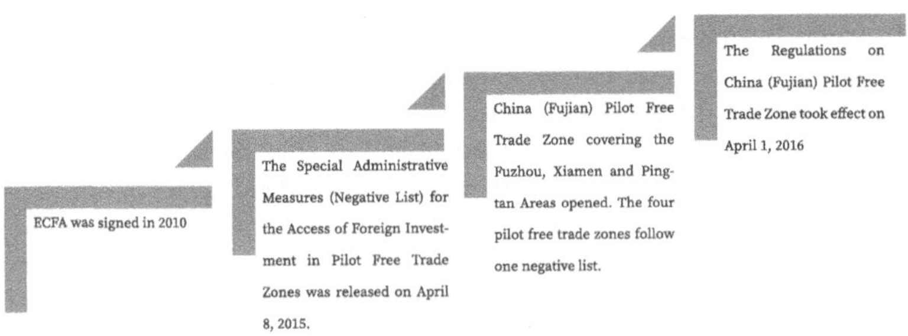

Chart 1: Implementation of the negative list in the Xiamen Area

ECFA was signed in 2010	The *Special Administrative Measures (Negative List) for the Access of Foreign Investment in Pilot Free Trade Zones* was released on April 8, 2015	China (Fujian) Pilot Free Trade Zone covering the Fuzhou, Xiamen and Pingtan Areas opened. The four pilot free trade zones follow one negative list	The *Regulations on China (Fujian) Pilot Free Trade Zone* took effect on April 1, 2016

On the whole, the negative list of the Xiamen Area has achieved noticeable results, stimulating great enthusiasm of private start-ups and foreign investors. Implementing rules and measures have been rolling out and improved soon after the start of policy implementation.

The negative list is more than an industry list. It also involves various supporting measures, the market environment and other issues for consideration. The negative list practice in Xiamen will be approached from the perspectives of the mechanisms and systems concerning access, review and approval, industrial regulation, social credit, information publicity, information sharing, and laws and regulations.

I. Access—interpretation of the negative list

On April 8, 2015, the State Council approved the *Special Administrative Measures (Negative List) for Foreign Investment Access in the Pilot Free Trade Zones*, which includes 15 categories, 50 items and 122 special administrative measures according to the *Classification of National Economy Industries* (GB/T 4754 – 2011). It is applicable to the four pilot FTZs in Fujian, Shanghai, Guangdong and Tianjin.

This document is not much different from the *Catalog for the Guidance of Industries for Foreign Investment* (2015 edition) issued by the National Development and Reform Commission and the Ministry of Commerce on April 24, 2015, in which foreign investment is encouraged in 12 sectors with 349 entries, restricted in 14 sectors with 38 entries, and prohibited in 12 sectors with 36 entries.

In April 2016, the State Council issued the *Draft Negative List for Market Access* (for trial) to be applied to Tianjin, Shanghai, Fujian and Guangdong. It includes 96 prohibited areas and 232 restricted areas (Table 1).

One of the biggest changes in the text of Catalog 2016 in comparison with Catalog 2015 is the easing of access for investment from Taiwan. Taiwanese investment in

Table 1 Number of sectors of prohibition or restriction for foreign investment in the documents of the negative list

Name of document	Prohibition	Restriction	Total
Special Administrative Measures (negative list) for the Access of Foreign Investment in Pilot Free Trade Zones (2015 edition)	43	21	122
Catalog for the Guidance of Industries for Foreign Investment (2015 edition)	36	38	432
Draft Negative List for Market Access (trial version)	96	232	328

pilot FTZs shall be regulated with reference to the *Special Administrative Measures (Negative List) for the Access of Foreign Investment in Pilot Free Trade Zones*. Investors who have met certain conditions will enjoy more preferential policies as provided for in the *Economic Cooperation Framework Agreement*. Restrictions on foreign investment have been eased considerably, especially in the financial, shipping, commercial and trade, cultural, social and professional services as well as advanced manufacturing industries. Thresholds for foreign investment companies are lowered. The mechanism for protecting investors' rights and interests is improved by allowing eligible overseas investors to transfer their lawful investment gains as they wish.

According to the negative list, maritime transport between the mainland and Taiwan requires approval, and the only prohibited item is banning people who have broken laws and regulations from engaging in specific tourism services, as written in the *Draft Negative List of Market Access* (for trial 2016). In terms of professional services, studies have been conducted on the registration and approval of new telecom businesses and the registration of nonprofit Internet information services. The management system for foreign investment has been better defined.

II. Approval and regulatory mechanisms—a new management model

Xiamen took the lead in promoting the reform and innovation of the management model concerning the approval and regulatory mechanisms specified in the negative list.

Record filing. Approval of the establishment and change of foreign-invested enterprises and company regulations concerning contract workers in the Xiamen Area shall enter the record filing process before going through other procedures in accordance with relevant regulations. Foreign investment is put under full-cycle regulation. Prior approval will be increasingly replaced by enhanced supervision during and after an investment project. Greater efforts will be made to promote integrated online approval by seizing the opportunities created by the "Internet plus".

Three-in-one license. There are three forms of such license in the Xiamen Area. The first form is simultaneous issuance through a designated window of the three certificates, namely, the business license, the organizational code certificate and the tax registration certificate. The second form marks the codes of the three certificates on one license. The third is the "one license one code" reform of the registration system, which is also one of the first steps taken by the taxation bureau of Xiamen. A license with a unique code that carries the functions of the three certificates will be given to the applicant. The above three forms simplify the procedures of business license application. Integration of business, taxation and organizational codes has drastically shortened the waiting period for business registration and further reduced the business cost of start-ups.

Single window. In the past, an applicant had to submit 5 sets of 35 documents to 5 different departments. It required at least 10 visits and 10 days to have the application processed. With a single designated window, an applicant only has to submit one document pack, and the processing time is reduced to one day. The practice has significantly facilitated international trade by accelerating the application process.

Companies can make application at a single window and have it processed on a single platform all in one go for 87 service items. Thus, a large number of application processes at the port of entry can be handled at a faster pace to save time and labor.

The Xiamen Area has launched a distinctive onshore "agency bank" to promote cross-strait financial industry cooperation and exchanges. This cross-straits RMB settlement mechanism has served as a supervisory and regulatory platform, met market demand and boosted cooperation and exchanges.

III. Information publicity and sharing—promoting institutional innovation

The official website of the Xiamen Area makes public national and municipal laws, regulations, policies, working procedures, and organizational and personnel information about the free trade zone.

According to the *Regulation of the People's Republic of China on Government Information Disclosure*, the Administrative Committee of the Xiamen Area of China (Fujian) Pilot Free Trade Zone shall publicize at least the following information:

- government information at its own initiative (341 entries in 2015, and 431 in total);
- information on government work upon request (25 entries of normative documents, 12 entries on fiscal affairs, 10 entries on business service, 11 entries on project bidding invitation, and 283 entries on other matters);
- administrative appeals and litigation due to government information disclosure (no such cases in 2015).

In general, the Xiamen Area has a sound information disclosure and sharing system, which indicates that its market environment is moving toward greater fairness and openness.

IV. Laws and regulations

1. Issuing the power list

The Xiamen Area has drawn the list of power for its administrative committee and all resident agencies in the area and their operational processes. According to the latest power list released by the administrative committee on March 11, 2016, 18 items for provincial administrative approval were removed, and 252 items for provincial administrative approval undertaken by the administrative committee were cut to 234. This means that the administrative committee now has approval power over 234 items, punishment power over 224 items, enforcement power over 3 items, and administrative power over 2 other items, adding up to 463 items.

2. Soliciting views from the public

When laws, regulations, rules and normative documents on the development of the Xiamen Area are formulated, the drafts are made public, and opinions are solicited on a wide scale. For example, comments were invited for the *Regulations on China*

(Fujian) Pilot Free Trade Zone (revised draft) from February 25, 2016, to March 10, 2016, leaving a reasonable amount of time for collecting public opinion.

The laws and regulations of the Xiamen Area are also being gradually improved to build a law-based market environment.

V. Strengthening cross-straits cooperation and attracting investment from Taiwan

The China (Fujian) Pilot Free Trade Zone differentiates itself from other FTZs in strategic positioning. It aims to promote communication and cooperation between Fujian and Taiwan and build the core area of the twenty-first Century Maritime Silk Road. It focuses more on industrial and financial cooperation between Fujian and Taiwan and creates new models of cross-straits cooperation in the service sector for joint economic growth.

The features of the Xiamen Area include cross-border financing and trade facilitation.

1. Build an all-around business services platform through innovative financial services

"Streamline administration, delegate power, strengthen regulation and improve services." Xiamen simplified the procedure of cross-border RMB business under the current account and specified the process of RMB settlement under the current account for all enterprises except those on the negative list. It streamlined the management process for the pilot program of cross-border RMB loans to Taiwan and cut the time limit for record filing receipt to no more than one working day. It also clarifies the record filing matters of the cross-border RMB business in the Xiamen Area, including materials, procedures, statements and accounting books, to make record filing simple, well-regulated and efficient.

The cross-straits cooperation platform has made fast progress with expanding cross-border currency settlement. By the end of April 2016, the cross-border RMB business volume in Xiamen had reached RMB 628.337 billion, among which the settlement volume from January to April reached RMB 79.043 billion, up 33.51% year-on-year. It accounted for 30.8% of the international balance of payments, up 4.73 percentage points year-on-year. Since the establishment of the Xiamen Area, 834 companies in the area have completed a cross-border settlement of RMB 37.752 billion, including RMB 16.606 billion for trade in goods and RMB 7.77 billion for cross-border financing. In July 2015, Xiamen received approval to launch the pilot cross-border RMB loan business. By the end of April 2016, 13 companies in Xiamen had made a total of RMB 319 million cross-border loans to Taiwan. Four of them accounted for 40.44% of the currency withdrawals.

Reform and innovation in foreign exchange management and progress in trade and investment facilitation. The "three principles" for handling the foreign exchange business of companies in the Xiamen Area have effectively reduced the burden on them and the banks. Since the pilot launch of the implementation rules, $5.85 billion in foreign exchange has been processed, accounting for 19.8% of the city's total. Foreign exchange settlement has reached $2.8 billion, or 18.6% of the city's total. In addition, Category A businesses in the area do not need to open a special account to be checked for foreign exchange income from trade in goods to ensure faster receipt of payment. Under the implementing rules, a total of $370 million inbound foreign exchange was processed without going through the special account, accounting for 45% of the inbound foreign exchange in the same period.

Supporting financial institutions in making innovation and improving services. Adhering to the principle of "encouraging financial institutions to serve the real economy, launching pilot programs of reform and innovation, and making steady progress by keeping risks under control", the Xiamen Area has put in place step-by-step financial policies to promote free trade and gathered experience from nearly 30 financial innovation projects that can be replicated elsewhere.

2. Trade in services

In terms of trade in goods with Taiwan, the China (Fujian) Pilot Free Trade Zone took the lead in streamlining procedures of submitting ECFA certificates on place of origin for unilateral recognition of the certification and test results issued by Taiwan inspection and testing institutions. According to the Fujian provincial inspection and quarantine bureau, the free trade zone implements a fast-track policy of "source management, certification recognition and spot checks" on 120 kinds of goods from Taiwan. The duration of check and release is now cut from 5–7 days to 1–2 days. In addition, on the basis of CFPA and ECFA, the requirements for the submission of certificates on place of origin are simplified, and the criteria for goods shipped by sea are also relaxed. This practice, which has been applied by the General Administration of Customs to the four pilot free trade zones in China, has produced good results.

In 2015, the trade volume between Fujian and Taiwan reached RMB 69.5 billion, with investment from Taiwan disbursed standing at $1.31 billion, up 10.3%. Exports to countries and regions along the maritime Silk Road increased by 5%, and new outbound investment increased by 2.7 times.

3. Professional services and talent management

According to the *Overall Plan of China (Fujian) Pilot Free Trade Zone*, professional service providers from Taiwan who open offices or businesses in the mainland are subject to restrictions concerning the scale of investment, a one-year limit of their stay in the mainland and the ratio of Taiwanese employees. However, the *Regulations of the Pingtan Comprehensive Experimental Zone* and the *Regulations on China (Fujian) Pilot Free Trade Zone* adopted on April 1, 2016, have provided much preferential treatment and convenience, such as mutual recognition of professional qualifications and having internships or taking professional qualification examinations in mainland institutions, to encourage institutions and individuals from Taiwan to provide business services in the mainland. Professional qualification recognition is highly important pursuant to China's laws and regulations and relevant industrial rules.

6. The effect of implementing the negative list in the Xiamen Area

Since the launch of the negative list, the Xiamen Area has undergone positive changes in at least the following three aspects.

First, the foreign investment management system is basically in line with international practice, which benefits China in its bilateral trade protection negotiations and local businesses in going global. Second, the negative list covers a wide range of areas and has a high level of transparency, which helps form a more transparent foreign business management system. Third, as required by the negative list management system, the review and approval system is now replaced by the record filing system. This has streamlined procedures, strengthened supervision during and after the investment, and saved labor costs. Domestic and foreign capital are subject to the same administrative management system to raise efficiency.

Since its inception, the Xiamen Area has launched a series of reform measures that have produced good results. The number of companies in the area increased by 12,185, with registered capital of RMB 171.1 billion one year into the area's establishment. A total of 194 reform measures have been introduced, 30 of which are the first of their kinds in China. In 2015, foreign investment committed in Xiamen amounted to $4.16 billion, of which $2.09 billion were disbursed. A total of $2.31 billion foreign investment was committed in the Xiamen Area in the first four months of 2016, accounting for 94% of the investment in Xiamen.

In addition, the Xiamen Area is pushing forward various key experimental projects. Thirty-five of them were completed by June 2016, involving intellectual property support and legal services. The 105 key projects for 2016 mainly include industrial transformation and upgrading, financial innovation and cross-straits exchanges and cooperation.

In the context of peace and development across the Taiwan Straits, the Xiamen Area has made great efforts to promote cross-straits economic cooperation by tapping into its unique strengths. At present, 336 Taiwan-funded enterprises have been set up in Xiamen, including Quaker, which has invested RMB 4.07 billion. The cross-border RMB loan project to Taiwan was launched, and the Xiamen Area now accounts for 85% of the total project investment in the mainland pilot zones. The Xiamen Area has also set up a cross-straits young entrepreneurship center. For the first time, young entrepreneurs from Taiwan are allowed to set up businesses in the center as self-employed business owners without the need for foreign investment registration. It also provides all kinds of professional consultancy services for them to accelerate integration between the two sides of the Taiwan Straits.

Problems in the Implementation of the Negative List in the Xiamen Area

In the past year, the Xiamen Area has accomplished a lot, but problems that have occurred in the implementation of the negative list need to be solved to further replicate the practice of the foreign investment management system in the pilot FTZ.

I. Increased regulatory challenges in commercial registration

The Xiamen Area adopts a record filing system. The commercial registration system that supports the negative list management system may face the following challenges. First, a lower threshold for entry will make regulation enforcement more difficult, and the risk of fraud and money laundering may come to the fore and become more difficult to avoid. Second, tighter regulation has replaced a high threshold for access. This requires regulators to spend more time collecting information about the businesses to gain a full picture of their performance. Regulators also have to meet higher expectations regarding their capabilities. Therefore, more detailed requirements should be made for the specific number and competence of the staff in the relevant departments. Third, there is a "time lag" in the implementation of the commercial registration system. As the process requires cross-departmental information sharing and coordination, information asymmetry and delays may appear after the merging of government platforms.

II. Low level of integration of the new information platform

The management model and practice of the negative list requires transparency and prompt release of information, as well as close cooperation on information exchange between departments. However, since the negative list is an institutional model designed at the top level, the practice of departments at the lower level may not serve policy goals due to differences in policy interpretation. Problems such as unclear procedures and delayed information release may discourage foreign investment.

III. Slow progress and weak legislative support for building the credit system

China has yet to have a full-fledged credit system. This has given rise to problems such as fake products and commercial fraud. Despite the effort that the Xiamen Area has made in creating a favorable business environment to attract more foreign investment, a weak credit system remains a major challenge.

Streamlining Administration and Delegating Power as a Solution

According to Qian and Hu (2015), the pilot FTZ is in essence an economic system supported by the government and developed under market rules. Therefore, to address issues that may arise in the zone, one has to detect problems in areas where the government, the administrative committee or companies in the zone all have a part to play. Their roles must be put into full play to ensure continuous innovation and maintain competitive advantages for pilot FTZs. The negative list is more than a list. It also includes the mechanisms of approval and regulation, the systems of social credit and information disclosure and sharing, and relevant laws and regulations.

The Xiamen Area regulates market players mainly through laws and market rules, taking into full consideration their business interests. It needs a stable policy environment. Ultimately, however, it is the market that decides whether it can be upgraded into an industrial cluster. To make it successful, business behaviors must be studied and properly guided.

I. Improving laws and regulations

The negative list management system is not an isolated system of market access. Its establishment and improvement depend on the improvement of other legal systems of the whole country. Therefore, the existing laws and regulations need to be sorted out, and outdated provisions that do not serve the needs of the pilot FTZ should be abolished or adjusted. The gaps in law should be filled by corresponding legislations. The enactment of laws should help create a fair and just business environment and ensure economic security in the region. Since the government plays an important role in market access, there should be laws and regulations to supervise their functions in this regard. This makes the power list very important.

II. Building a credit system

In view of the weak planning of China's credit system, there is an urgent need to improve the public information network platform and establish a centralized and unified market supervision and law enforcement system for efficient supervision and higher transparency.

It is also necessary to establish a system of random checks on companies' annual reports to strengthen oversight, standardize procedures and raise information transparency. Businesses are required to provide annual reports to the administrative committee through a designated system in accordance with the relevant provisions before receiving qualification certificates. The industrial and commercial administrative departments conduct random checks on 5% of the annual reports according to rules. Those who fail to pass the checks will be put on the list of companies with abnormalities by the commercial registration authorities, and their names will be made public through the business credit information disclosure system. A company that is on the list for less than five years and has made necessary corrections can apply to the commercial registration authorities for removal of its name from the list. However, if it is on the list for more than five years, the name cannot be removed.

III. Cutting access restrictions and matching responsibilities with power in project review and approval

First, further narrow the negative list on market regulation. Although the scope and depth of opening up as required by the negative list are much larger than in the commitments China made when it joined the WTO, there are still issues in practice, such as poor implementation effects, high entry thresholds and incomplete supporting laws and regulations. The negative list shall write down industries closed to foreign investment and list measures outside the commitment made on the most-favored-nation treatment, national treatment and market access. Sectors other than this shall be fully open. This will enhance transparency, encourage all commercial sectors to truly open up, and promote reform of the commercial registration system, government function transformation and institutional innovation.

Second, clearly define rights and responsibilities for each government department. Every government department shall make a "positive list" of its review and approval authority and undertake to supervise the projects and contents approved. This will help match responsibilities with power and raise the efficiency of supervision and law enforcement.

Third, implement one-stop approval. This will cut down and improve approval procedures by making them more standardized and simplified. To address complicated review and approval procedures, there is a need to integrate desks of document acceptance and review and clarify procedures so that only one application is needed for the review of multiple items. There is also a need to improve the efficiency of approvals by removing repetitive and unnecessary procedures, particularly those involving multiple departments. Procedures with the same effect should be merged or minimized, and results should be recognized between departments.

Conclusion

The reform of pilot FTZs in China is unfolding, and the negative list will be used in more places. The Xiamen Area has played an exemplary role in building a new open economic system. More successful experience of such models at home and abroad is needed as a reference for the Xiamen Area in implementing its own negative list in a way that fits into its realities. Keeping in mind the effect of TPP, China-ROK FTA and other free trade areas, it will gradually develop a negative list of market access based on solid experience that can be replicated elsewhere and further leverage its role and strategic location in cooperation with Taiwan.

In addition, the Xiamen Area should act as a hub in developing Xiamen into the core zone of the Belt and Road Initiative by supporting local businesses going global, advancing the negative list, streamlining administration and delegating power, reforming the regulatory system, and narrowing the items requiring administrative approval. Larger steps of opening up will drive the efforts of building a leaner government with the negative list at its core. As Premier Li Keqiang said, "streamlining administration, delegating government's power and strengthening regulation will leave more maneuvering space to the market, create a fairer environment, and unleash the creativity, potential and competitiveness of market players. This is in itself the most effective stimulus package."

Bibliography

Catalog for Industrial Guidance for Foreign Investment. (2015). *The Gazette of the State Council of the People's Republic of China, 14.*

Chen, E., Qi, Z., & Han, J. (2015). *Upgrade China's economy: A documentary of the central government's reform of streamlining administration and delegating power*. China Yan Shi Press.

Decision of the Standing Committee of the National People's Congress on Authorizing the State Council to Temporarily Adjust Review and Approval of Relevant Laws in China (Guangdong) Pilot Free Trade Zone, China (Tianjin) Pilot Free Trade Zone, China (Fujian) Pilot Free Trade Zone and China (Shanghai) Pilot Free Trade Zone. (2015). *The Gazette of the Standing Committee of the National People's Congress of the People's Republic of China, 1.*

Feng, L. Draft negative list of market access (for trial). *Guangming Daily*, April 13, 2016.

Li, B. Regulations on China (Fujian) pilot free trade zone takes effect this month. *Fuzhou Daily*, April 4, 2016.

Lin, F., & Wu, F. (2015). Taiwanese investment and improvement of the negative list system in Fujian pilot free trade zones. *Economic and Social Development, 6.*

Notice of the General Office of the State Council on Special Administrative Measures for Foreign Investment Access in Pilot Free Trade Zones (Negative List). (2015). *The Gazette of the State Council of the People's Republic of China, 13.*

Notice of the State Council on Issuing the Overall Plan of China (Fujian) Pilot Free Trade Zone. (2015). *The Gazette of the State Council of the People's Republic of China, 13.*

Opinions of the CPC Fujian Provincial Committee on Formulating the 13th Five-year Plan of Fujian's Economic and Social Development. *Fujian Daily*, November 18, 2015.

Overall Plan of Fujian Pilot Free Trade Zone. (2015). *Fujian Quality Management, Z2.*

Qian, Z., & Hu, Y. (2015). *Operation mechanism and legal norms of free trade zones in a comparative perspective*. Tsinghua University Press.

Regulations of Pingtan Comprehensive Experimental Area. *Fujian Daily*, April 22, 2016.

Wu, Y. (2016). Regulations on China (Fujian) pilot free trade zone come into force. *The Light & Textile Industries of Fujian, 4.*

Zhang, G. (2014). *Liberalization of trade in services between Guangdong, Hong Kong and Macao: A negative list management model*. China Social Sciences Press.

Zheng, J., & Wang, Z. et al. (2015). *China's market access environment and new policies on trade and investment—Empirical research based on several industries*. University of International Business and Economics Press.

Streamlining Administration and High School Education

Cheng Jiang and Haidi Qin

Senior high school education plays an important role in China's educational system. As the Ministry of Education pointed out in the *Senior High School Curriculum Program (for trial)* issued in 2003, "senior high school education is basic education for the public for further improving their educational levels on the basis of nine-year compulsory education." The *Outline of the National Plan for Medium and Long-term Education Reform and Development (2010–2020)* (hereinafter referred to as the *Outline*) calls for "quickening the steps in making senior high school education universally available" and provides guidance for the development of senior high schools over the next ten years. In March 2016, the *Outline of the 13th Five-year Plan for National Economic and Social Development of the People's Republic of China* made it clear that China would popularize senior high school education by 2020 to fully meet the needs of junior high school graduates to receive senior high school education. China has placed more importance on senior high school education because of its essential role in promoting national education and the all-rounded development of citizens. This has generated new opportunities for development. Researchers and practitioners have been discussing ways to promote the development of senior high school education in the new historical circumstances. This paper will present its views in the context of the government efforts of streamlining administration and delegating power.

C. Jiang (✉)
School of Education, Peking University, Beijing, China

H. Qin
Hebei Hengshui Second Middle School, Hengshui, China

Y. Li and Z. Cheng (eds.), *The Chinese Path Toward a Leaner Government*,
https://doi.org/10.1007/978-981-19-6718-4_18

New Circumstances for Streamlining Administration and the Development of Senior High School Education

I. Senior high school education encounters challenges as the reform deepens

1. The main goal for senior high school education is cultivating students' core abilities instead of simply helping them go into institutes of higher learning. New indicators, such as social responsibility, civility, and abilities of independent development and social communication, have gradually become the main evaluators for senior high school students. However, the current system of elite school education and policy of selecting a few top-grade students and ensuring further education for them at the cost of the great majority of students is contrary to the goal of modern senior high school education, which focuses on nurturing students' core competencies.
2. The reform of the examination and enrollment system makes it difficult to enforce the unified senior high school curriculum as required by the education authorities.

Senior high schools will face large complexities in student composition, class type and curriculum arrangement in Zhejiang, where students can choose three out of seven exam subjects in a pilot program, and in Shanghai, where they can choose three out of six. The traditional means of teacher performance evaluation thus become useless. Moreover, education authorities are unable to make unified requirements and instructions on class size and management, teachers' structure and curriculum setting as they did before.

3. The dual management models and types of senior high school have been broken.

Ordinary senior high schools and vocational senior high schools that were run separately in the past are now merged into integrated senior high schools or senior high schools of special features. The change has created various management models. Greater involvement of private capital has diversified school ownership and goals. This poses a challenge to traditional educational policies, laws and regulations.

In the face of these new challenges, bold exploration and innovative practice are needed in the educational system and school management philosophies and systems. It requires the earnest implementation of the reform aimed at transforming government functions in the field of education.

II. Streamlining administration and delegating power aimed at transforming government functions becomes a strong driving force behind the development of senior high school education

On May 23, 2015, Premier Li Keqiang emphasized at the national video conference on streamlining administration, delegating power, strengthening regulation and improving services that this reform is the government's self-initiated revolution to cut its own power and narrow its own interests. Less government power and regulatory reform will generate more market vitality and people's creativity. It was decided at the conference that relations between the government at one end and the market and the society at the other must be properly handled, and equal emphasis must be placed on both power delegation and market regulation. In summary, the coverage of streamlining administration and delegating power has extended from the economic sphere to the entire society. As the power is delegated to the government at the lower level, the public and the market, the reform becomes more comprehensive. It has paved the way for removing the resistance to reform policies on senior high school education.

For streamlining administration and delegating power in the field of education, the *Outline* also states that effort should be made to "advance the reform of the educational management system, focusing on streamlining administration and delegating power and transforming government functions to improve the performance of public education services. More power should be delegated from the central government to local governments and from the government to schools. The responsibilities of governments at all levels should be clearly defined. The government should regulate the conduct of schools, further separate oversight, management and evaluation of schools, and form a well-regulated and orderly educational system. It should roll back involvement in school management and specify its powers and responsibilities, so that education is provided in a coordinated and orderly manner."

There are examples of how streamlining administration and delegating power promote senior high school education. In September 2015, an education company released a ranking of the top 100 senior high schools in China. Among them, five are from Hebei Province, namely, Hengshui Middle School, Shijiazhuang No. 2 Middle School, Hengshui No. 2 Middle School, Zhengding Middle School and Wuyi Middle School. Hengshui has three places on the list, ahead of Shijiazhuang, the provincial capital. In addition, among the top 10 middle schools in Hebei Province, Shijiazhuang and Hengshui each have four seats, while Tangshan and Handan each have one, and schools in Hengshui rank above those in Shijiazhuang. According to the economic statistics released by Hebei Province, Hengshui's GDP was RMB 113.9 billion in 2014, accounting for only approximately one-sixth of Tangshan's RMB 622.5 billion and one-fifth of Shijiazhuang's RMB 510 billion, ranking last in the province. However, its senior high school education is as good as that of Shijiazhuang, the provincial capital. There are many reasons behind its success, and the overarching reason is the effect of streamlining administration and delegating power on education. A survey shows that schools in Hengshui have more autonomy than schools in other places in curriculum setting, program competitiveness, education philosophy and resource allocation. Even the power of teachers' recruitment is delegated to local senior high schools. The efforts have paid off.

Analysis of the Policy Barriers Facing Senior High School Education

It is true that the current educational and relevant administrative systems have significantly promoted the development of senior high school education. However, we have found that "over the years, the educational authorities have been struggling with such issues as overstepping authorities, mismanagement and inaction in dealing with school education." Although laws and regulations on school autonomy have existed for years, it is still quite common for educational authorities to intervene in, restrict and take back the lawful management rights of schools. To promote senior high school education, it is imperative for the government to roll back more regulatory powers and facilitate the establishment and improvement of the modern school system in wider areas. It has been found that policy barriers for senior high school education may exist in the following aspects.

I. Administrative system

In the current educational system, the government runs the schools. It plays the roles of the investor, regulator and manager of the schools at the same time. The schools are, to a great extent, affiliated with the government and take orders from it, although they have some autonomy in teaching and research. They have to work hard to improve the quality of education and promote all-round development of students and at the same time divert much of their attention to a large number of government checks, inspections and evaluations on rule compliance, campus safety, financial management, the rule of law and disease prevention. "The checks, inspections and evaluations have pushed up the administrative cost and dampened the initiative and creativity of the school leadership and teachers."

Schools have little autonomy in the allocation of educational resources. First, the setting of key middle schools means that the educational authorities need to give preferential treatment to key middle schools in resource allocation, which has added to the educational imbalances. Second, laws and regulations on education, which are based on a tiered management system, require local authorities to be responsible for basic education. Due to economic disparities in China, there is a big difference in the capacity of investment in basic education by the government, especially those at the primary level, and in the resulting educational quality between regions. Third, the government and the competent departments allow little flexibility in the use of educational resources and funds, resulting in the idling and waste of resources.

To some extent, the way of selecting school principals and the role they are given also hinder the development of senior high schools. Most of the principals of public senior high schools in China are still appointed by the regulatory authorities, and school management and teachers have little say on this matter. Despite efforts by the government and the educational authorities to select people with both integrity and competence to run schools, there are many examples of "laymen" serving this post. In addition, many principals have several concurrent positions outside the schools.

They spend too much time on social engagement or even money-making activities and are unable to devote themselves to their administrative roles and school reforms.

II. Personnel system

Teachers are the core element of the school's educational work and the main component of the school's human resources system. They are crucial to the school's survival and development. The success of a school depends to a large extent on whether it can manage its teachers well, promote capacity-building, and nurture an outstanding team of educators. In the current system, the government's supervision of the personnel affairs of public senior high schools covers almost every aspect, which has put on hold the reform on the school personnel system. The following are mainly what it entails.

1. School personnel autonomy has been constrained across the board.

A school can only manage the teachers by submitting plans to the authorities in charge of education and personnel management and accept whoever they recruit and allocate to it. It is difficult or even impossible for any school to send teachers back once they are in. The role of the school recruitment office has very limited roles to play in promoting merit-based recruitment, strengthening the competence of teachers or encouraging competition. They are still large administrative bodies.

2. The personnel system focuses too much on the identity management of teachers because of restrictions on staffing.

In practice, staff teachers can easily develop a feeling of superiority, which may lead to inertia and a sense of fatigue. Some of them have lost their sense of responsibility, mission and crisis in their work. The school-contract teachers, in contrast, have no way to gain the "teachers' identity" and find themselves unable to enjoy the same treatment as enjoyed by staff teachers in pension and medical insurance. This has hurt their initiatives.

3. The personnel system restricts mobility and feeds inertia among teachers.

Many teachers, especially elderly teachers, lack career drive or passion as they should have. A teacher's salary is less linked to his quality of teaching than his seniority and professional title. Therefore, the principle of higher pay for better performance is hard to implement in schools.

III. Obstacles in evaluation mechanisms

The *Decision of the CPC Central Committee and the State Council on Deepening the Educational Reform and Promoting All-rounded Development of Students* requires that the government "establish an evaluation mechanism for schools, teachers and students that promote all-rounded development of students". However, problems related to the judges, criteria, mechanism and feedback of evaluation have yet to be solved, which affect the authenticity of the evaluation and the development of the schools.

1. School evaluation is carried out solely by the educational administrative authorities.

Schools have no other choice but to hide their weakness and even resort to deceptive means to satisfy the government on the indicators of evaluations set for them. There is hardly any room left for them to think about building an independent school mechanism that is tailored to their own circumstances and can help analyze and resolve problems.

2. The criteria are too simple and mostly dominated by "rates" and "scores".

It is like measuring all schools with "one ruler" regardless of their levels and categories. Under such a one-size-fits-all type of evaluation arrangement, it is difficult for schools to develop their unique features. In many places, the college admission ratio and examination scores have become the sole criteria for assessing the quality of senior high school education and the only basis for reward and punishment, salary adjustment and decisions on professional titles for teachers. In this context, deviations from good practice and general guidelines easily occur in teaching and school management, which has hindered breakthroughs in transforming school education for years.

3. The evaluation mechanism focuses too much on the result instead of the process, which has taken the initiatives off the schools.

The current evaluation focuses on its distinguishing, screening and selecting functions. It pays more attention to the results of school management (such as the quality of educational conditions and the improvement of college admission rate, etc., and rarely considers the efforts and progress of schools in the course of development. As a result, schools can easily slide into the track of unbalanced development featuring single-headed pursuance of the college entrance rate and fierce fighting for good students in exchange for more resources from the government.

IV. Student admission

Unlike universities, the government is the sole decision maker on student enrollment for each senior high school in most provinces. The tight administrative control has hindered school development.

The size of senior high school enrollment is set by the government, which is also responsible for preparing exam papers, arranging exams, scoring, setting admission scores and approving student admission. The deepening of the educational reform has laid bare the loopholes of the current enrollment system.

1. The current unified student enrollment and admission system places too much power in the hands of the government.

The schools are responsible for enrollment, and the government decides on admission. The system fails, to some extent, to help schools of different types, levels and educational goals in student selection and therefore dampens the enthusiasm of schools and examinees.

2. Too much attention is focused on scores.

Schools should take in students with all-round development in areas such as morality, intelligence and physique specified in the educational goals. However, under the system where the government determines student admission mainly based on scores from high to low, students with special abilities whose total exam scores are not high may not be admitted.

3. The enrollment model lacks vitality.

Senior high school enrollment is made in accordance with government plans. The exam is held, and enrollment is made only once a year. There is no other chance of recruitment for schools or exam application for students. The practice can neither give full play to the unique characteristics of individual schools nor allow students to choose which school they like to study at.

V. School education requirements and curriculum setting

The *Outline* called for the diversified development of ordinary senior high schools. On this basis, Tao Xiping analyzed and defined the nature, function and education model of ordinary senior high schools in China, providing theoretical support for the inevitability and the need for their diversified development.

However, there is a long way to go for ordinary senior high schools to develop unique features. The competent administrative department for education "has absolute power in school management, students training, curriculum setting, teaching content and appointment of principals" in ordinary senior high schools. As a result, "the schools have little leeway in resource allocation, curriculum setting and educational goals and thus are unable to develop their own features." Their enthusiasm to explore a management model that fits their own conditions has also been dampened.

In addition, educational authorities seldom pay attention to the effect of the curriculum, which makes the courses relatively monotonous and utilitarian. The content and class hour of the optional courses are highly related to the nine main subjects and fail to play the roles they are meant to play. To ensure the quality of teaching or for regulatory convenience, some local governments require schools to open a number of designated courses and use designated teaching materials. This has resulted in widespread administrative-based course settings in schools.

Feasibility Design of Streamlining Administration and Delegating Power in Senior High School Management

The *Outline* states that "Government administration shall be kept away from school management. A modern school system featuring law-based and independent schools running under democratic supervision with public participation shall be established. This benefits China's national conditions in the current development stage and supports efforts to build a new type of relationship between the government, schools and society. As required by the reform of the state administration system, the power and functions of the government and the rights and responsibilities of schools at all levels and of various types must be clarified to form different school models and avoid monotony." This sets the direction for further streamlining administration and delegating power, removing institutional and managerial obstacles, and promoting the development of senior high school education. The measures may include the following.

I. Expanding the power of independent management for schools

1. There should be less administrative intervention, such as inspection, rating and evaluation of schools.

Educational authorities can set standards for schools to help them improve management and conduct evaluation by themselves. A third party may be invited to participate in relevant supervision. The pilot program in Zhenjiang, Jiangsu Province on independent school management can be replicated in other regions. It requires that schools manage their own affairs except for campus security and finance affairs, which is regulated by the local educational bureau. However, the relevant offices of the educational bureau will not, in principle, conduct uninvited school inspections.

2. Educational funding should be guaranteed through a proper investment system.

The government needs to increase overall funding for education. More financial resources should be allocated to basic education and schools with weak foundations. Both the national and the provincial governments should increase the ratio of funding to education. Regional gaps in funding must be narrowed. There should be more financing channels for senior high schools to promote equity in basic education. Trials should be launched for schools to conduct budget management in line with government rules, in which they are entitled to use special funds for infrastructure repair, equipment and book purchases and other purposes. Capital construction and campus maintenance projects with investments under certain amounts should be managed and examined by the schools themselves.

3. The professionalism of school principals should be enhanced.

Government regulators should select candidates from teachers with qualified educational backgrounds, in-depth knowledge of education and teaching, experience in educational management and respect for the law of education, among whom the principal should be publicly elected by the faculty of the school to ensure that the school is run by experts. Faster steps should be taken to build a modern school system, empower principals with enough autonomy in school management at the policy and institutional level, and push for the transformation of school principals from administrators to service providers. There should be less administrative intervention in school management so that schools will have more say on matters concerning their own development.

II. Expand the autonomy of schools in recruitment and personnel affairs

Article 39 of the *Outline* says that "the government will expand the autonomy of ordinary senior high schools and secondary vocational schools in their educational models and ways of students training, resource allocation, personnel management, collaboration with other schools and community services." Breakthroughs can be made in the following areas accordingly.

1. The mechanism of setting an overall limit and conducting dynamic adjustments for teaching posts of senior high schools inside a region should be established.

Schools should have more participating rights, greater say and more decision-making power in teachers' recruitment and can decide on recruitment matters. Recruitment practices for first-time teachers should be improved. Features of different schooling phases, subjects and posts should be considered in teachers' recruitment. The labor contract-based management of primary and high school teachers should be fully implemented. Teachers' behaviors must be strictly regulated during the contract terms. Competitive contract-based recruitment should cover all school faculties.

2. Personnel management should be post-based instead of identity-based.

The government must decide the number of posts instead of teachers for each school in accordance with the size of student enrollment and staffing requirements. A dynamic management model of overall control, demand-driven post and flexible use should be put in place for personnel management. Contract positions will not be linked with teachers' professional titles, and no one can rest on his professional titles for ever.

3. Contract-based management should be fully implemented to encourage the proper movement of teachers.

Contracts offer school management and teachers an equal chance of making choices. On this basis, the school can form a new personnel system featuring fair competition, merit-based selection and free movement and establish an evaluation system for teachers focusing on virtue, ability, performance and contribution with the participation of teachers, students, parents and the public. It can also improve the personnel management system with larger gaps between remuneration levels that reward teachers for their diligence, good virtue and high-quality teaching to encourage teachers to conscientiously fulfill their job responsibility and maintain strong enthusiasm in the work.

III. Further improve the evaluation mechanism

The evaluation should be carried out by more parties. It must include not only the educational authorities but also schools, society and even teachers, students and their parents. The introduction of a third party can make the evaluation result fairer and more objective to help the school improve more on the basis of the feedback.

As the first step, schools, instead of the government, should take the main responsibility for the evaluation. They should be encouraged to conduct self-evaluation by setting their own development plans, evaluation criteria, procedures and methods and implementing processes and result evaluations by themselves to bring out more initiatives for self-development. Their main focus should include areas of both strengths and weaknesses for promoting long-term and feature-oriented development while reaching the national evaluation standards.

In addition, the voices of parents and society should also be heard during school evaluation, and various information channels should be kept open so that school evaluation can truly become an interactive activity for regulators, school leadership, teachers, parents and professionals.

IV. Explore a new approach of "senior high school autonomy in student admission"

1. Schools should have the right to select students with outstanding all-round abilities.

The all-round abilities test represents a school's autonomy in its management and student admission practices. Schools should place great importance on the methods of the test and carefully design it to fulfill their key expectations for talent selection. Regarding the unified examination, educational and enrollment authorities should allow schools to select students within a certain range of scores or of the same grade.

2. Trials can be launched on setting up the "school principal recommendation system".

Independence in student enrollment is an important measure taken by the government to delegate power, expand the autonomy of schools and deepen the reform of the enrollment and admission system. It is also a new way to select outstanding and creative students. For schools, the test score should not be the only criterion. It must be part of a more comprehensive evaluation by which schools can make their own selections. In 2009, Peking University pioneered the trial, which, to some extent, reflects the effort to diversify college entrance examination-based selection methods and ensure fairness in this process. Senior high schools can borrow this practice and put in place a rigorous supervision system through campus notification, online release and other ways.

3. A sound academic level exam system for junior high school students should be in place.

With the gradual realization of full coverage of high school education in China, the function of high school entrance examination as the means of selection and diversion of senior high school students should be gradually replaced by the function of promoting all-round development of students. To facilitate senior high schools in carrying out independent student selection, a sound junior high school academic level examination must be in place, and specific rules on the weights of exam scores and all-round abilities tests must be included in the selection process.

V. Diversifying the school management models and curriculum design of senior high schools

1. Ordinary senior high schools should be diversified.

They may branch out into schools that teach comprehensive knowledge and those focusing on technology, science, humanities, foreign language, arts, music sports and academic research and international schools. These schools with distinct characteristics should enjoy the same status as ordinary and vocational senior high schools.

2. Featured courses should be developed for each school.

The schools, in doing so, should take into consideration the need for students' development, the number of teachers and other resources available. "Schools must do localization or redevelopment of national courses while creating local courses unique to them, including practical courses and students' association activities", to promote individualized development, provide more options to students and cultivate their academic interest.

3. More institutional breakthroughs should be made.

Policies should be less restrictive in the efforts to nurture integrated senior high schools. For example, students of integrated senior high schools can have dual identities in both ordinary and vocational senior high schools. Efforts will be made to offer them "dual certificates" of academic credentials and vocational qualifications.

Vision of Senior High School Development in a Better Institutional Context

A leaner government will push senior high school education in the direction of creating a modern school system featuring "law-based educational practice, independent management, democratic supervision and social participation". Step by step, a new development model for senior high schools driven by schools themselves and supported by society with the government playing a facilitating role will be set up.

I. A better management system and greater autonomy will bring more vitality to schools and reduce imbalances in senior high school development.

As educational authorities minimize their administrative intervention and reduce their roles, the leadership and management of schools can focus more on "how to manage and develop schools according to laws and educational planning." The government, on their part, can exert its influence on schools by formulating and implementing laws and regulations, allocating funds, and supervising and evaluating schools through professional institutions and intermediary agencies. Efforts should be made to put in place mechanisms on reviewing school development plans as well as self-evaluation, supervision and assessment of their implementation. In this way, the government and its competent departments will truly become "the ones who build the system, create conditions, make rules, ensure fairness, set standards and monitor the quality of education".

Empowered schools will have greater autonomy in the allocation of educational resources. Better allocation of resources will result in more effective use of designated funds and minimize waste. An improved financing mechanism will better regulate the flow of private funds into senior high schools and help diversify the channels of educational investment, narrow the funding gap between regions and schools, and check the imbalance in the development of senior high schools.

II. Reform of the personnel system will expand the school's autonomy in personnel affairs and add new impetus to senior high school development.

The reform of the personnel system includes expanding the school's personnel autonomy, exercising contract-based management of teachers, creating a new faculty management mechanism, gradually establishing an effective human resource management and professional competition mechanism, and improving the efficiency of government expenditure in education. The steady progress of the reform will help address issues such as freeloading, go-slow and retirement-like behaviors, and tensions resulting from too many nonteaching staff and insufficient teachers. The reform will raise the incentives of teachers and schools and inject more vitality into senior high school development.

State laws, regulations and policies should be released to provide for flexibility in the school's personnel management system and continuity and consistency of regional policies. This will protect the lawful rights and interests of teachers and ensure that their abilities are fully tapped. Wuhou District of Chengdu has launched a pilot program to expand the autonomy of school personnel with valuable experience. In 2014, to minimize restrictions on schools concerning personnel, projects and financial matters through streamlining administration, the local government decided to allow schools to hire teachers, manage schools and allocate funding independently in the west branch of the high school affiliated with Sichuan University. The reform aimed to solve the problem in staffing and increase the motivation of teachers. It has made significant progress in the past two years.

III. An independent third party can become a stakeholder in the school's development as part of the efforts to create a diversified evaluation mechanism to reflect public expectations on senior high school education.

The practice will set the right direction for senior high school education and further improve the quality of teaching. With the participation of teachers, parents, education experts, universities and the public in the evaluation of the educational quality of senior high schools, the role of public oversight will increase. Thus, a diversified, multidimensional and effective evaluation system is created. The evaluation result will reflect public expectations on the core abilities of high school graduates, unlike those in the past, which put screening and selection functions before encouraging improvement and offering incentives and valued scores over abilities. Only by putting the development of senior high schools under public scrutiny can schools think hard about rectifications on issues listed in feedback and carry out targeted reforms to follow the trend of development and further improve educational performance.

IV. To create more types of senior high schools with unique features and promote the development of students' personality and specialty, there is a need to break away from the government practice of drawing an admission line for schools in the order of the exam scores and gradually expand the autonomy of schools in enrollment.

Schools need to have greater independence in setting teaching plans based on the general requirements of educational authorities and at the same time display their unique features. The government should exercise macro management in promoting educational development. Democratic processes need to be set up both inside and outside the schools to further "delegate the power" to teachers, students, parents and social organizations and encourage multiple players to join school management in an effort to avoid power concentration on school principals or blocking voices from outside the schools.

Authorized by the government, senior high schools can enroll students upon recommendation or for their special qualifications. A diverse model of student admission will offer more chances to students, promote the growth of junior high schools, schools with weak foundations in particular, and facilitate balanced development of education across the region. Moreover, tests on all-round abilities and academic levels of students will be carried out to tap into their potentials and promote individualized development as required by the policy for all-round development of students.

V. Diversified school models and curricula of senior high schools are necessary to meet the interests of students and their desire to grow their specialties and cultivate innovative graduates as the nation shifts the economic growth drive from traditional resources to innovation.

The diversified development of ordinary senior high schools and an increased number of comprehensive senior high schools should be our strategy now and going forward. It will help remove the old model of monotonous and homogeneous school development and serve the students' need for diversified development. In addition, diverse educational models for senior high schools can provide learners with more options and train more people with all-round capabilities for China's economic and social development.

For example, as part of the curriculum reform, schools can have more autonomy in course selection and design. They will be able to work out flexible, open, individualized curriculum systems based on their own circumstances. Efforts will also be made to break the barriers between disciplines, further connect campus life with off-campus programs to open up students' minds, and cultivate their initiatives. Moreover, a diversified curriculum system can further promote a series of reforms in academic counseling, featured education, and college entrance examination and enrollment. This will put senior high school education in China in a virtuous cycle of fast, sustainable and balanced development.

Bibliography

Ape Question Bank Evaluation Research Center. (2015). *2015 Chinese high school ranking list*. Publishing House of Electronics Industry.

Dai, L. Out of power Dilemma for public schools—Pilot program in Wuhou, Chengdu city. Sichuan News Network. Retrieved March 15, 2016.

Liu, Z. (2003). School evaluation reform based on the new curriculum. *Elementary and Secondary School Management, 10*.

Outline of the national medium—And Long-term Plan for Education Reform and Development (2010–2020).

Tao, X. (2011). The trend of diversified development of ordinary high schools. *Elementary and Secondary School Management, 9*.

Ye, Z. (2009). Transformation of the relationship between schools and government: From state administration to public governance. *Educational Science Research, 8*.

Zhang, J. (2006). Evaluation of developmental schools. *Journal of Liaoning Educational Administration Institute, 1*.

Zhao, J. (2014). Streamlining administration and delegating power: Building a new pattern of independent development of primary-level schools. *Elementary and Secondary School Management, 1*.

University Administrative Management System Reform

Shuaixiong Fu

The reform of the university administrative management system aims to streamline administration and delegate power, expand the autonomy of universities, promote separation of the administrative functions of the government from the educational functions of universities, and improve the university's internal Party, administrative and academic management system. The *Outline of the National Medium and Long-term Plan for Educational Reform and Development (2010–2020)* calls for "speeding up the construction of a modern school system, promoting the separation of government administration from school management, and implementing and expanding the autonomy of schools in education." The document has, to a certain extent, expanded and ensured the autonomy of universities and advanced higher education and economic and social development in China. The *Overall Plan for Developing World-class Universities and Disciplines in a Coordinated Way* issued by the State Council encourages and supports differentiated development of different types of premium universities and disciplines.

That said, universities are still in want of autonomy. They have yet to build a proper relationship with the government, and their academic activities are not closely related to China's economic and social development. Thus, the reform should sort out the relationship between universities and the government and the one between the administrative and academic branches of universities and improve their way of governance. The aim is to unleash teachers' potential through a science-based evaluation system and ensure university autonomy through a flexible human resource management structure. "Streamlining administration and delegating power" in the administrative management system of universities will become the general trend of the comprehensive reform of higher education and the basic requirement for promoting the development of world-class universities and disciplines.

S. Fu (✉)
Guanghua School of Management, Peking University, Beijing, China

Y. Li and Z. Cheng (eds.), *The Chinese Path Toward a Leaner Government*,
https://doi.org/10.1007/978-981-19-6718-4_19

Importance of Streamlining Administration and Delegating Power in the University Administrative Management System

I. Streamlining administration and delegating power in the university administrative management system helps expand university autonomy in educational affairs.

The core of the university governance reform is to expand its autonomy in educational matters, which means that a university can make its own charter and decisions suited to its circumstances in accordance with the law. The *Higher Education Law of the People's Republic of China* promulgated in 1998 stipulates that nongovernment players are allowed to set up institutions of higher learning in accordance with the law, and institutions of higher learning run their own affairs independently in pursuant to laws and market rules. The efforts made by the state through various measures, such as issuing laws on rights confirmation and rolling back the government's power to grant and expand the university's autonomy in educational affairs, have significantly promoted the development of higher education in China.

However, inaction and power abuse still exist in the government's regulation of universities due to blurred boundaries of authorities.[1] The government is used to dominating universities' development through administrative, legislative and fiscal means, making universities unable to make their own choice on disciplines and in academic system design. The role of the university is to train people to meet the needs of society, carry out basic research with its resources, and promote economic and social development with its think tanks and knowledge expertise. To ensure proper functioning of these roles, it is important to provide universities with educational autonomy and promptly adjust the goals of university education with the right means to meet the diversified needs of society. In addition, the government should change the administration of universities by reducing direct intervention and encouraging differentiated development of universities and disciplines. The most crucial part of the efforts to expand university autonomy is to streamline the administrative management system of universities, accelerate the shift of government functions and build a sound relationship between universities and the government.

II. Streamlining administration and delegating power in the university administrative management system helps build a sound university governance system.

Streamlining administration and delegating power in the administrative system of modern universities is required by the modernization of the governance system and capacity of universities. It is also a major part of the efforts of the CPC and the Chinese government to comprehensively promote the modernization of the national governance system and governance capacity. To modernize its governance system, universities need to be able to formulate rules and regulations that meet the requirements of a modern governance system, and all stakeholders can exercise their rights and fulfill their responsibilities in the governance framework under the rule of law. Currently, universities follow a unified governance model. With the government

[1] Peng (2013).

playing a dominating role and an incomplete governance system, few of them can put in place an effective governance model that suits their own conditions. They must bear the old governance model, which is unable to catch up with the general trend of a modern governance system. To improve the modernization of the administrative system and governance capacity, universities need to establish a science-based, well-regulated and effective system in accordance with the law of higher education and the basic requirements of economic and social development in conjunction with China's all-out efforts to modernize its governance system and governance capacity. Establishing well-defined and regulated powers and responsibilities of the government and universities is at the center of a sound university governance structure. In this process, the system whereby the president takes overall responsibility under the leadership of the CPC university committee should be followed, and at the same time, the government, universities and society should jointly take part in the university administrative management system. The system, which is more of an administrative nature, should gradually be taken over by a law-based governance system. There should be more decision-making power for universities and clear-cut powers and responsibilities among the CPC, administrative and academic branches of universities to raise their efficiency in organization, management and development.

III. Streamlining administration and delegating power in the university administrative management system helps coordinate progress in building world-class universities and disciplines.

A main goal of China's higher education in the new era is to build world-class universities and disciplines, and specifically, put China among the top in the world in terms of the number and strengths of its world-class universities and disciplines by the middle of the twenty-first century and turn China into a nation strong in higher education.[2] To meet the world-class standard, universities and disciplines should be encouraged to pursue differentiated growth. Unlike the once-for-all titles of "985 Project" and "211 Project", evaluation will be held on a rolling basis to stimulate universities' passion for competition. Disciplines with distinctive features, strong competitiveness and growth potential shall be given priority in their development as universities see fit, which will drive further growth of the universities. Ultimately, each university will follow its own development path. The government will give more support to small universities with competitive strengths instead of those expanding into all disciplines. It will no longer set an overall development plan but encourage the industrial sectors to partner with universities in academic improvement so that universities and their disciplines can better meet the needs of economic and social progress.

[2] The State Council (2015).

IV. Streamlining administration and delegating power in the university administrative management system promotes building of a modern university system with Chinese characteristics

Building a modern university system with Chinese characteristics is an important foundation for the well-regulated, healthy and dynamic development of higher education in the new era. It is also an urgent task in the all-around reform of education. The essence is to encourage universities to meet the needs of society, assume more decision-making power and exercise democratic governance under the overall regulation of the government.[3] A Chinese-style modern university system integrates the country's unique governance, operation and discipline systems into the modern university system to place universities at the service of the socialist system with Chinese characteristics. In this process, streamlining administration and delegating power can further enable universities to set up structures that meet their own needs and display Chinese characteristics. A leaner university administrative management architecture is the foundation of a Chinese-style modern university system. It will, in combination with the development of laws and regulations, promote power devolution and better regulation on the part of the government while separating government administration from school management and improving the university's governance structure. Universities will have greater autonomy and pursue orderly growth. On this basis, the unique role of academics in university governance and system building should be enhanced. The authority of the academic committee and other relevant organizations should be fully respected in discipline improvement and academic evaluation and development.

Problems in the University Administrative Management System

I. Bureaucratism in administrative management has withheld the delegation of decision-making power to universities.

1. Bureaucratism in government regulation of universities

The government regulates universities as it does to itself and extends the unique dual Party and government leadership structure right from the State Council and government agencies to schools, departments and sub-departments of universities. It has put the personnel power of universities under its control through the appointment, removal and selection of university leaders. Universities are unable to make all decisions in their own will, and higher education is managed by the government

[3] Yuan (2000), 23–26.

through administrative control and top-down leadership in a hierarchical system.[4] A government-sponsored administrative management model has pushed for the development of higher education through budgetary support and, to some extent, ensures that universities can readily produce different kinds of talent that the country needs for economic and social development. However, the autonomy enjoyed by universities specified in the *Higher Education Law of the People's Republic of China* has not been fully granted in practice, and little change has been made to the administrative relationship between universities and the government. Due to inadequacies in laws and regulations, the government can still interfere with the overall management and specific affairs of universities by means of issuing notices and guidelines. Meanwhile, it puts undue constraints on their efforts to meet genuine development needs and their initiatives of growth. Resources are allocated to universities mainly through evaluation, review and appraisal instead of long-term norms. This has stifled the ability and vitality of universities and made their internal structures and operational mechanisms less flexible, making it hard for university resources to be fairly distributed according to market rules. Such a bureaucratic way of management fails to define rights and responsibilities of the government and universities as it takes away the decision-making power of universities through administrative control.

2. Bureaucratism in the internal management of universities

The internal administrative management of universities somewhat resembles the way the government regulates universities. With organizational setups similar to those of government agencies, university administrative establishments are also wrangling with issues such as bureaucratism, overstaffing and overlapping responsibilities. The hierarchical setup of the governance structure makes it easy for university administrative authorities to dominate school affairs. The practice has had its success, but it has also given rise to issues such as worship of official ranks and weak voice of the academic community on key issues. The root cause of universities having little say is the bureaucratization of universities as part of the government.[5] Some universities have increased layers of administrative hierarchies or set up new institutions more than they need. The move has exacerbated the gender disproportion in the university management teams at all levels and narrowed the size of staff directly related to teaching, research, faculties and students. This has resulted in too many tiers of administration and little contact between departments of the same level, or simply put out the administrative distance between university authorities and primary-level organizations.

II. Poorly defined rights and responsibilities between the Party, administrative departments and academic institutions have placed academic decisions more under the purview of the university administrators.

1. Overlap of powers and responsibilities in a system where the university president takes overall responsibility under the leadership of the Party committee

[4] Qi (2013), 26–31.

[5] Qi (2011), 49–53.

In 1985, the CPC Central Committee adopted the *Decision on the Reform of the Educational System.* As an important decision in the reform of the educational system, it required university presidents to assume overall responsibility. The *Higher Education Law of the People's Republic of China* defines the responsibilities of the Party committee and president of the university. The university president responsibility system under the leadership of the Party committee meets the needs of China's economic and social development. It enables universities to nurture human resources that China needs based on China's national conditions and keep the growth of universities in line with the overall planning on disciplines and state policies under a modern university system with Chinese characteristics. As power is divided between the Party leadership and university president, there is no way to avoid overlapping of responsibilities between their teams at the management level. In particular, the dual identities of the president and the Party secretary in the Party committee and the university executive team and intervention of the Party leadership and administrative officials in the academic committees have blurred the lines between the Party, administrative departments and academic institutions as well as the roles of universities, making them less capable of meeting the needs of economic and social development.

2. University administrative branch assuming greater power over academic affairs

Most of the university resources are in the hands of its administrative departments, which also have a greater share of power. The academic authorities exercise their power under the guidance of the administrative authorities, and academic groups find it hard to play their due roles in the daily affairs of the universities. The rights of academics in democratic participation in and supervision of university affairs are taken away. Administrative personnel were involved in the teachers' recruitment, professional title appraisal, research project application, teaching and research, academic committee member selection and other academic affairs. University academic organizations are unable to make their own decisions when performing their duties. Instead, they rely too much on the administrative authorities, as their staff play more important roles in these organizations and have greater influence. The trend of rising administrative power in universities has marginalized academic authority and hindered the development of universities.[6]

III. Inefficient organization and management and increasing internal transaction costs

Ballooning management bodies have raised the cost of internal transactions. The transaction costs of universities are mainly costs involving internal management and information communication. Affiliated with government institutions, universities lack autonomy, and their internal institutions are set up as required by the government instead of legal provisions, often out of an impulse to fulfill certain tasks without any due process. For example, a designated office is set up to deal with the evaluation of undergraduate teaching performance, and a disciplinary affairs office

[6] Zhong (2010), 4–7.

is set up for application for bachelor's, master's, and doctoral degree disciplines. The increase in administrative organs that are designated to complete certain tasks easily causes overlapping functions among departments and low work efficiency. Consequently, university leadership will have less control over individual departments, and administrative costs will increase.

Routine administrative functions are extended to lower-level schools and institutions, and the workload on teachers has increased. As university enrollment increases together with campus size and the number of academic disciplines and programs, universities are facing more complex tasks and a greater workload in terms of government appraisal and project application. They have in turn put in place a two-tiered management structure by delegating power, especially routine campus administrative functions, to schools and departments. The university offices are responsible for guidance, monitoring, inspection and evaluation. However, schools and departments are teaching bodies with relatively few administrative staff. The conflict between administrative work pressure and lack of hands and due processes has exerted a heavy toll on work efficiency. The reform has also extended the bureaucratic organization of universities down to the subdivision level, increasing the administrative levels and cost of information communication, which in turn leads to undemocratic decision-making and low efficiency. Moreover, compared with the teaching faculty, administrative staff are at a disadvantage in terms of welfare benefits and professional title evaluation, which hurts their morale and hinders any improvements in administrative efficiency.

IV. Poorly designed teachers' assessment system and lack of drive among teachers

A sound university teachers' assessment system plays an important role in stimulating teachers' creativity, enthusiasm and initiative. As universities' administrative, academic and appraisal systems are still mixed, teachers rarely participate in their evaluation, as the system is designed by government departments and administrative institutions of universities. In such an evaluation system, the basic principles, evaluation index, methods and targets are based on organizational and management goals, whereby teachers are assessed by how many established educational goals they have completed without taking into account their own values. As a result, teachers are not happy with the system, which fails to deliver any sense of achievement. The evaluation method pays more attention to the quantitative data that can be obtained easily and the quantity of teachers' work instead of its quality. In particular, research is taken as an important aspect of the evaluation, which compels teachers to focus on publishing papers and research project applications instead of teaching. Those who earnestly fulfill teaching tasks and earn respect from students may not obtain professional titles due to insufficient research work. This has significantly harmed the enthusiasm of teachers who have devoted themselves to teaching.

V. Rigid personnel management system restricting the forms of university education

Personnel reforms in universities go hand in hand with the overall development of China's educational reform. It is necessary to deepen personnel reform in universities to improve the quality of higher education. At present, the main problems in the personnel system of universities are rigid staffing management, unreasonable post settings and inflexible employment mechanisms. The personnel system of universities is similar to that of the government, with strict procedures for recruitment, evaluation, appointment and dismissal. As a result, it is hardly possible for the university to dismiss or demote anyone. This has seriously dampened the enthusiasm and creativity of the faculty. Universities are unable to choose the educational model and corresponding personnel management system suited to themselves. It is very difficult to make changes to staffing and the personnel management model once they are determined by the government. Human resource distribution in universities has become more rigid and unable to meet the need for social progress. In 2013, the Personnel Department of the Ministry of Education conducted a questionnaire survey on the leaders of more than 200 universities directly under the Ministry of Education, affiliated with other ministries and run by local governments. Inflexible employment mechanisms and strict control by government authorities topped the list of concern.[7] The actual number of employees in most universities has far exceeded the size of staffing approved by the educational authorities. This rigid and restrictive personnel management system has alienated higher education from society and affected the vitality of universities.

Suggestions on Streamlining the University Administration System

I. Transforming government functions and delegating more autonomy to universities

First, straightening out relations between the government and universities. The relationship between the government and universities should be changed from the traditional one-way administration whereby universities only take orders from the government to two-way interaction. Checks and balances should replace the existing management model based on administrative level, which means shifting the current model where the government plays a dominating role to the one featuring law-based autonomy of universities and participation of multiple stakeholders. To build a modern university system with Chinese characteristics, it is necessary to clarify the boundary of power, responsibility and interests between the government and universities and slow down the tendency of adding more administrative and bureaucratic elements to the government-university relationship. Separation of the administrative, academic and evaluation system should be carried out in universities to transform government functions, grant universities more autonomy, give full play to the role of public stakeholders and regulate the educational performance of universities to form a higher education management model involving the government, universities and

[7] Questionnaire Survey Team (2014).

society, each playing its own roles with clear-cut rights and responsibilities. Evaluations and inspections that have little to do with the quality of education should be removed to let universities decide on their own affairs. The government should improve top-level design and overall planning, chart the right course for universities, and improve oversight. It should also establish and maintain a good market order, provide universities with an external environment of fair competition, and speed up the transformation of its own roles from managing to supervising university affairs.

Second, laws and regulations for better exercising of university autonomy should be improved. The government should harmonize the interests between the government and universities by constantly improving laws and regulations. The scope of university autonomy needs to be made clearer. Universities should be put under stricter oversight while enjoying more administrative power as part of an effort to build a co-governance model involving the government, universities and society. A sound third-party evaluation mechanism should be adopted to build a better and a more credible university management system. New ways should be found to ensure the government's financial support to universities through a performance-based restraint and incentive mechanism that favors distinctive and high-level disciplines and universities so that universities can play their due role in running for the "world-class" titles and displaying their own characteristics and dynamism.

Third, developing a robust three-party cooperation mechanism among the government, society and universities. The reform of the administrative management system in universities should aim to weaken the say of the government in university affairs, strengthen the participation of social actors, and diversify funding and support. In particular, relevant institutions and industries should be encouraged to participate in discipline improvement. The three-party cooperation should be strengthened to address the bottleneck issues on human capital and technologies that are in urgent need and give full play to the capability of universities to serve economic and social development.

II. Improving internal governance and strengthening supervision and restriction of power

While ensuring and expanding universities' autonomy, we should rely on macro-control and legal provisions, properly balance the government's authority with the autonomy of universities, improve the university internal governance structure and promote interaction and balance between academic and administrative interests to establish supervision and self-restraint mechanisms for university autonomy.[8] A sound relationship between the Party, the administrative branch and the academic communities is essential for improving the internal governance structure.

First, the responsibility system of the university president should be improved under the leadership of the Party Committee. This system featuring a Chinese-style Party-government relationship can guide the internal governance of universities and promote the construction of a modern university system with Chinese characteristics. As the foundation and core of improving the internal governance mechanism of

[8] Sun (2014), 9–15.

universities, it helps avoid the loss of direction, guidance and target in the university administrative and academic development under the leadership of the president. It calls for a clear definition of the boundary of responsibilities and powers between the Party and the government, draws a power list that makes responsibilities and powers more specific, better regulated and law-based, and ensures their proper functioning with improved procedures.

Second, properly handle the relationship between administrative and academic powers. Respecting academic authority is a dominating feature of the modern university system, with Chinese characteristics that distinguish universities from the government and enterprises.[9] It is important for universities to improve administrative management, but it is also important to keep administrative influence away from academic affairs and highlight the academic nature of universities. Efforts should be made to strengthen the role of academics in university governance and restrict administrative power with academic power. Academic and administrative departments should operate within their clear scopes of rights and responsibilities to promote the law-based exercise of administrative power. The administrative branch should serve university academic development mainly by improving its management efficiency, while academic organizations take an absolutely dominant position in disciplinary and academic affairs. The academic committee should be composed entirely of experts without involvement of the administrative leadership and give more say to experts and scholars on academic issues.

Third, exercise governance in accordance with the university charter. As the government delegates more power to universities, the university charter shall serve as the main guiding principle for running university affairs. A modern university system with Chinese characteristics calls on universities to manage according to their charters.[10] To promote the sustainable development of universities and the rule of law for the modern university system, the charter should be jointly developed by all faculty and students. It should be carefully designed to suit the reality and development plans of each university and specify how power is exercised within the university. It should be strictly implemented and respected as a legally binding document. Supervisory bodies should be set up to regularly monitor its implementation, with a view to forming a governance system on the basis of the university charter.

III. Restructuring institutions to realize streamlined and effective management

In the face of complex administrative tasks, universities need to carry out necessary internal institutional reform to meet multiple management goals. First, they have to streamline administrative bodies to flatten out their organizational structures and make them matrix-based and flexible. Ordinary staff should be given more decision-making power and fully mobilized to provide better serve to teaching and research. The administrative system reform should aim at making university institutions streamlined, unified and effective, consolidating departments with similar functions and placing the institutional setup, staffing and operational mechanism

[9] Shi (2009).

[10] Zhang and Zhou (2006), 7–10.

under the supervision of such institutions as the teachers' congress. Administrative bodies inside universities should be streamlined in terms of both number and staffing. E-school technologies should be used to advance the reform of administrative institutions. Structural adjustment and well-designed institutional setups help clarify the responsibilities among the university headquarters, logistics and teaching auxiliary units. The administrative staff should place serving teaching and research needs before moving up their own administrative ranks, streamlined offices and service procedures. Second, the relationship between the university and its schools and departments should be properly handled. When administrative affairs are placed more under the responsibility of the latter, there should be a clearer division of their responsibilities versus those of the university, and a pragmatic working mechanism needs to be established among them. Responsibilities such as developing major strategies and policies shall be left to the university. Schools should strengthen their dominant position in teaching and research, while departments should focus on academic management and see to it that the goals of teaching and research are fulfilled. Schools and departments shall break away from the original management model based on administrative ranks by finding new ways of improving institutional settings and work flow to better serve teachers and students and raise management efficiency. The university should coordinate powers across levels and departments and refrain from imposing its own management model on schools and departments or increasing administrative review and approval steps to generate the vitality and special features of the schools and departments based on the characteristics and law of various disciplines.

IV. Improving the evaluation mechanism to give full play to teachers' initiative

A robust teachers' evaluation system is fundamental to raising the quality of higher education and improving the governance system of universities. As an important part of university education, teachers have diverse roles, and their evaluation system should be able to score the performance of different kinds of teachers. It should focus more on the quality and not the quantity of their work so that they can have greater initiative in teaching, academic research and social service. It is necessary to establish a category-based evaluation mechanism for teachers of different professional interests, in which indexes are set according to their contribution in various aspects to make teachers assured that everyone can advance in professional titles according to their own contribution. There should be more evaluators in this mechanism, and teachers' participation and voice should also be raised, with a view of building a joint evaluation system involving the university, students and third parties. Unlike the current model, the new evaluation system can help teachers play a key role in self-assessment and encourage them to contribute more to teaching, academic research and social service based on their interests and abilities.

V. Reforming the personnel system to ensure autonomy in personnel management

Advancing the university personnel system reform is essential to the modern university system and greater vitality of universities, as it can fundamentally deliver autonomy to universities in its educational affairs. It strengthens the category-based management of university employees and the role of faculty and staff in the development of universities through contracts and appointments. The personnel management autonomy of universities should be fully implemented to enable universities to select human resources according to their own development needs and strategic positioning and formulate and adjust policies and systems concerning internal organizations and positions as well as the appointment and evaluation of personnel as they see fit. This will help form a dynamic and flexible mechanism of talent flow and personnel adjustment. Reform should also be carried out on the establishment and staffing of university institutions and human resource allocation, classified management of teachers and building a position-specified contract system for faculty and staff. Efforts should be made to explore career development channels for different types of employees and strengthen their professionalism.

Bibliography

Peng, H. (2013). *Research on the history, problems and measures of university autonomy in China.* Unpublished master's dissertation, Nanjing University of Aeronautics and Astronautics.

Qi, W. (2011). Analysis of the causes of growing administrative attributes for universities and suggestions for solution: From the perspective of organizational sociology. *Education Research Monthly, 2.*

Qi, Z. (2013). Three dimensions of the university autonomy—Remodeling the relationship between universities, government and society and improving the internal governance structure. *Journal of Higher Education, 5.*

Questionnaire Survey Team. (2014). Streamlining administration and delegating power: What universities expect. *China Education Daily*, 14 Apr 2014.

Shi, N. (2009). Professors make academic decisions: Basic philosophies of sound development of universities. *China Education Daily, 9.*

Sun, X. (2014). Development and operation of China's higher education autonomy. *China Higher Education Research, 9.*

The State Council. (2015). Overall plan for developing world-class universities and disciplines. *People's Daily*, 6 Nov 2015.

Yuan, G. (2000). Establish a modern university system and promote higher education reform and development. *Journal of National Academy of Education Administration, 2.*

Zhang, W., & Zhou, Q. (2006). University constitution: Carrier of modern university system. *China Higher Education, 20.*

Zhong, B. (2010). Analysis of important issues concerning getting universities out of administrative control. *Educator (Higher Education Forum), 9.*

The Role of Collective Economic Organizations in the Trading of Collective Land for Construction Purposes in the Context of Streamlining Administration

Liwen Liu and Qi Chen

The changes in China's rural land policy can be considered a microcosm of the country's economic and political policies since its founding in 1949. After the launch of the reform and opening-up in 1978 in particular, the implementation of the household contract responsibility system opened the way for combination of unified and separated rural land management. Under the policy, land ownership belongs to the village collective, while contract rights belong to farmers and can be transferred. In reality, however, the trading of rural land, especially the collectively owned construction land in China, is subject to many restrictions and regulatory constraints. To further improve the property rights of farmers and rural collectives in China, trading of collectively owned construction land should be allowed in the process of streamlining administration and delegating power.

Streamlining administration and delegating power is, after all, a measure of the reform of the administrative system, which runs parallel to and coordinates with the reform of the economic system. Streamlining administration and delegating power is not an expediency, nor is it an emergency response measure that only treats symptoms instead of the root cause. China is carrying out the land ownership reform to ensure that farmers have the right to manage contracted land, use their homesteads and own the property built on their homesteads, which is specified in separate certificates. This reform needs support from a leaner government, but it is mainly about transforming the rural property rights system.[1]

The author holds that in the context of building a leaner government, supporting measures are needed to confirm land ownership and allow collectively owned construction land to be tradable. In particular, collective economic organizations should play a key role in this process. To better serve the trading of collectively owned construction land and protect farmers' interests, these organizations must

[1] The paragraph is quoted from the preface of the book by Professor Li Yining.

L. Liu (✉) · Q. Chen
Guanghua School of Management, Peking University, Beijing, China

Y. Li and Z. Cheng (eds.), *The Chinese Path Toward a Leaner Government*,
https://doi.org/10.1007/978-981-19-6718-4_20

quickly improve their own procedures while the government streamlines the approval process.

Market Trading of Collectively Owned Construction Land

Rural collectively owned construction land refers to the land used for nonagricultural construction purposes by township and village collective economic organizations and rural individuals through investment or fund raising. It includes homesteads as well as nonprofit and for-profit construction land. Since the 1990s, township enterprises whose growth was initially supported by local governments have been battling with falling returns and widespread losses. Village collective economic organizations then began to lease or transfer the land originally used by township enterprises for rents. At the same time, to attract investment for faster economic growth, local governments have pushed for the transfer of collectively owned construction land to build industrial parks, and the leasing and transfer of rural collectively owned for-profit construction land have further increased.

At the end of 1999, the Ministry of Land and Resources officially approved Wuhu, Anhui Province, as the first pilot for the transfer of the right of use for collectively owned construction land. The *Land Management Law* amended in 2004 and the *Property Law* taking effect on October 1, 2007 both stipulate that the right to use the construction land of township and village enterprises cannot be regarded as a separate collateral. Rather, it has to be combined with the enterprises' plants and other buildings. The *National Plan for a New Type of Urbanization (2014–2020)* allows for transfer, leasing and share investment of rural collectively owned for-profit construction land so long as they conform to planning and use control. The land shall be treated the same as the state-owned land in market access, rights and price. On February 27, 2015, the 12th Standing Committee of the National People's Congress adopted the *Decision on Authorizing the State Council to Temporarily Adjust the Implementation of Relevant Laws and Regulations in Beijing's Daxing District and 32 Other Administrative Areas at the County Level* at its 13th session. In these areas, regulations on rural land requisition, trading of collectively owned for-profit land and homestead management should be adjusted.

Despite the national pilot programs, the trading of collectively owned construction land, in general, is still subject to policy constraints. It is still unable to obtain equal rights and prices or the same way of trading compared with urban construction land. Streamlining administration and delegating power become an urgent task in lifting the restrictions on the trading of collectively owned construction land to meet market demand and the interests of rural collectives.

In nonpilot areas, there are more restrictions on the trading of collectively owned construction land. Commercial development of the land must come after state expropriation, with the urban government acting as the intermediary and the owner of the additional profit generated by the land. As a result, collective economic organizations tend to develop such land by themselves or simply lease it, which suppresses the creation of new trading models for collectively owned construction land. Streamlining administration will be essential for lifting these procedural restrictions and creating new trading models for this type of land. At present, rural collectively owned construction land is in the hands of many small businesses and individuals. The land is not used efficiently, and the development intensity is low with ill-advised expansion of the industrial development scale. Generally, the development and utilization of rural collectively owned construction land has encountered a bottleneck for the following reasons:

(1) The land development capacity of collective economic organizations is limited, and leasing has become the main method of use for collectively owned land. Due to the weak development capacity and financial strength of rural collectives, their self-built property mostly includes low-standard factory and office buildings, and the rental income has been low for years.
(2) The planning of collectively owned construction land is under more restrictions than that of state-owned land. It takes a long time to obtain approval for industrial project planning, and some land planning is difficult to implement after approval. The lack of overall industrial guidance has failed to generate economies of scale or promote the growth of other relevant industries.
(3) Infrastructure construction, public services and urban management in rural areas are undertaken by collective economic organizations. The limited investment scale and lack of effective financing channels have made it difficult for them to attract external investment.
(4) There are many restrictions on the property rights of the existing rural collectively owned construction land, and the rights and interests of land users cannot be guaranteed. The law has many restrictions on the utilization, the right to use and validity of the mortgage of the collectively owned construction land, which hinders its market trading.

Urbanization has brought about changes in the transfer and allocation of rural land, which has a far-reaching impact on the distribution of land rights and interests, agricultural production and farmers' income, and these changes in turn have a long-standing effect on the promotion of urbanization. The change in the use of rural collectively owned construction land, the migration of population between urban and rural areas and the change in allocation of labor resources in agricultural and nonagricultural industries may raise new questions on the existing collectively owned construction land system. According to existing laws and regulations, rural land is owned by collectives, which means that collectives will represent farmers to make decisions on matters related to land expropriation in urbanization and coordinate the use and distribution of land expropriation compensation. In general, this process can obtain the consent of most villagers, thus effectively reducing transaction costs, which is of great significance to the smooth progress of urbanization. However, in practice, due to various reasons, it easily causes differences in compensation payments, calculation periods and sizes of homesteads and contracted land, which will again open the door to inequality. At the same time, the weak villagers' self-governance system in China and the lack of corresponding supervision and restraint mechanisms have resulted in frequent occurrence of corruption, misappropriation of compensation, unfair distribution and other problems that can seriously affect social stability.

The compensation standard of land expropriation is another problem that easily causes problems. According to relevant regulations, the compensation for rural land expropriation compensation must be determined in accordance with land use. For example, for public land such as urban roads and parks, the compensation standard shall not exceed 30 times the agricultural output value of the land expropriated. However, there is no set compensation standard for commercial land, which is open for negotiation between developers and farmers. Compensation for the same land may differ, which may seriously hinder land expropriation work, especially land for public use.

The Role of Collective Economic Organizations and Their Problems

After the third Plenary Session of the 18th CPC Central Committee, farmers' land in some regions was allowed to be traded on the market, including agricultural land, collectively owned construction land, farmers' homesteads and rural collectives' business assets. These all belong to rural collective assets and can be put into three categories. The first category involves land expropriated by the state, including rural collective land used for industrialization and urbanization. The second category is rural collectively owned construction land, including homesteads and land used for township enterprises and public facilities. The third category is land used for agricultural production. The resolution of the third Plenary Session of the 18th CPC Central Committee opened the way for the first and second categories to enter the construction land market for trading with the same rights as state-owned land. However, if farmers mortgage, guarantee or transfer their houses, it will breach the original nature of farmers' homesteads as something belonging to members of the collective organization and may involve fundamental changes in the rural homestead system. Therefore, allowing collective economic organizations to play a greater role in the process of bringing rural collectively owned construction land into the market should be the focus of China's rural economic reform in the future.

The reform to streamline administration, delegate power and reshape collective property rights is crucial in promoting the smooth entry of collectively owned construction land into the market. The No. 1 Document of 2015 focused on promoting the reform of the rural collective property rights system, including the land policy reform. Reforming the rural collective property system, clarifying the ownership of collective property rights, and streamlining administration and delegating power to improve the definition of collective property rights are the basis for promoting the free transfer and better combination of rural collective property rights.

In 1999, the *Constitution* defined collective economic organizations as "rural collective economic organizations that implement a dual management system based on the household contract responsibility system and feature both unified and individual management". Although this definition clarifies the status of the collective economy in rural China, there are no corresponding laws and regulations on how to manage and dispose of collective assets.

Over the years, among rural collective resources, the right to use agricultural land belongs to farmers, most of the means of production have flown to townships, and the ownership of land belongs to collective economic organizations. However, collective organizations are poorly defined, with blurred property rights and a lack of corresponding disposition procedures. This has given rise to complex and chaotic management, interference by government agencies and frequent occurrence of corruption. Therefore, it is imperative to streamline administration and delegate power, clarify areas of responsibilities, and minimize the procedures and hidden rules for the market entry of collective assets, collectively owned construction land in particular.

At present, China's rural collective economic organizations are facing many challenges, which hampers their role in promoting market trading of rural collectively owned construction land.

First, the overall scale is relatively small. At present, China's rural collective economic organizations are small in their overall scale compared with those abroad, and they fail to form a sufficient economy of scale. Thanks to years of development, China's rural collective economic organizations have taken initial shape, but they are still lagging far behind those in other countries, especially in the number of members and size of land. There is still a long way to go for the development of China's rural collective economic organizations. In addition, China's rural collective economic organizations lack financial resources. In China, their funding is only higher than that of self-employed people and much lower than that of the Japan Association of Farmers and other such organizations in advanced economies. Limits in scale have hampered their growth and performance.

Second, leadership positions of rural collective economic organizations are usually held by village officials. This is a common phenomenon in China that easily leads to actions that cause low efficiency. The heads of many primary-level rural collective economy organizations are village officials, who tend to engage in rent-seeking behavior. Village officials have too much power. They can determine how profit is distributed in village collectives and interfere in the operation of rural cooperatives. This has led to rent-seeking acts and affected the performance of economic organizations. Moreover, placing village officials in the leadership positions of rural collective economic organizations will likely affect the market decisions of economic organizations. Village officials with various titles will have to do more calculations when making decisions, which may directly affect the efficiency of decision-making and market response to the detriment of the interests of economic organizations. This will also cause an uneven distribution of benefits. In village collectives with multiple economic organizations, those with village officials holding concurrent positions are more likely to obtain preferential policies, resulting in an uneven allocation of benefits or resources. It goes against the policy that the market plays a decisive role in resource allocation and seriously affects overall productivity.

Third, the governance structure is in disarray. Due to various factors, the internal governance structure of rural collective economic organizations in China is poorly structured without proper internal or external supervision. Village officials holding positions in rural collective economic organizations put decision-making power in their own hands. Even though they may not hold leading positions, they can easily sideline those who are at the top. Too much concentration of capital leaves the board of governors and the board of supervisors of economic organizations in the hands of a few people, resulting in dis-functioning of the board of supervisors. In addition, some farmers are less willing to participate in democratic decision-making. This easily makes the internal supervision mechanism of rural collective economic organizations a symbolic setting. Inadequacies in laws and regulations and some institutional factors result in the absence of external supervision of rural collective economic organizations. The poor governance structure of rural collective economic organizations and the lack of internal and external supervision mechanisms have increased the vulnerabilities of farmers in upholding their rights and interests. The development space of rural collective economic organizations will be limited if the current situation remains unchanged.

Fourth, the economic performance is poor. China's rural collective economic organizations are poor in both economic performance and growth potential. At present, most rural collective economic organizations in China are running with no profit or at loss, which is directly caused by their low management capabilities. Because of poorly structured governance, they are unduly controlled by a few individuals. In addition, the low educational level of farmers and their hesitation to embrace novelty makes it difficult for such organizations to improve performance through continuous learning. The outdated business model is unable to fit into market rules as rural reform deepens. It is therefore easy to understand why these organizations have been running at perpetual loss or unable to make any profit for all these years.

Trials of Collective Economic Organizations in Foshan in the Context of Building a Leaner Government

Dali Township is located in the east of Nanhai District, Foshan City, Guangdong Province. The town covers an area of 95.9 km^2 and has 28 communities (villages) with a permanent resident population of 610,000.

After the reform of the rural property rights system in Dali was completed, in accordance with the *Regulations of Guangdong Province on the Administration of Rural Collective Economic Organizations* (Order No. 189 of Guangdong Province), each community (village) has set up an economic association, and each villager group (natural village) has set up an economic organization (currently, there are more than

360 such organizations). In 2015, the per capita dividend of farmer shareholders reached RMB 8000 (RMB 5000 in Nanhai District).

Since 2010, the government of Nanhai District has established a public resource trading center, a financial regulatory center and a stock exchange management center and developed corresponding systems under the authority of the district's science and technology bureau. The systems have covered all people, property and funds of collective economic organizations at the district, township and village (community) levels.

I. The establishment of the financial regulatory center

Established in 2012, the financial regulatory center of Dali is responsible for the overall management of the capital inflow and outflow and processing of more than 400 accounts of 28 economic associations and over 360 economic cooperatives in Dali. The details are as follows:

1. Organizational structure and staffing

Based on the Foshan Rural Administration Information System, the center has established a three-tiered online regulatory system at the district, township and community (village) levels, with functional modules of capital, bill, contract, leadership and accounting regulation.

Professional financial companies serve as the intermediary. Cashiers work in villages, and accountants work in townships to ensure centralized accounting and separate-account management of designated funding. More specifically, there is an accountant for each community (village) in the capacity of an intermediary staff member who works in the centralized office of the township regulatory center. Each community (village) has two full-time cashiers working in the community (village) as intermediary staff. Each economic cooperative selects a staff member to work as its fund custodian.

At present, a total of 28 accountants and 56 cashiers are working for communities (villages) of Dali. They are staff of the intermediary company entrusted by the financial regulatory center of Dali. The labor cost is borne by the township government. Over 300 custodians are staff of economic cooperatives, and their labor costs are borne by economic cooperatives.

The office and equipment of the abovementioned staff are provided by township or village authorities where they work according to the rules.

2. Operational process and access to funds

The financial bills of each community (village) are signed by the relevant operator and person in charge in accordance with the prescribed authority and sent by the village cashier to the township regulatory center in the form of fax, E-mail or picture to be processed after being approved by the accountant (and the accounting supervisor of the center) in charge of the business of the village. At the end of the month, each village sends the original financial documents to the regulatory center, and the accountant prepares the monthly financial statement (and returns the materials of the previous month to be kept by respective villages). The financial statements of each community (village) are published regularly on the village bulletin board.

The approval authority for the use of funds in each village is as follows: the daily single bill of less than RMB 100,000 is reviewed and approved by the community (bills of RMB 80,000–100,000 are reviewed jointly by the head of the regulatory center). Bills of over RMB 100,000 are checked by the relevant leaders of the township government. Funds designated for special purposes must be reviewed and approved at the township level no matter the amount.

If certain capital expenditures reach the set amount without going through the required review and approval procedure, the regulatory platform system will give an early warning to the township regulatory center to help promptly identify problems and ensure the financial security of collective economic organizations.

At present, a major problem in the fund management of collective economic organizations is that according to rules, the funds of collective economic organizations cannot be directly lent to enterprises and individuals, nor are they allowed to buy nonbreak-even financial products. At the same time, the current income of collective economic organizations mainly comes from land and property lease and trading instead of investment in physical projects. Therefore, the stock of funds in economic cooperatives is relatively large and is not used efficiently. In Nanhai District, the total amount of funds on the accounts of economic cooperatives and economic associations has topped RMB 12 billion.[2]

II. Asset trading platform

The collective assets of Dali are traded at the township public resources trading center. The center was established by the Nanhai District government in 2010 and has covered the entire district, including all its townships and villages (communities). It mainly deals with government procurement, government asset disposal and collective asset trading. More than 50,000 collective asset trading projects have been completed in Nanhai District, with a total transaction value of more than RMB 40 billion since 2010. In Dali, the transaction volume was over RMB 2.9 billion in 2015 (over RMB 2.7 billion at the township level and over RMB 100 million at the village (community) level). The collective asset database of the whole township has been basically completed based on the government's regular property and capital verification and transaction records over the years. At present, the asset trading platform and the financial regulatory platform are being integrated to gradually realize data correlation so that effective supervision of collective assets can be realized through comparison of capital flows and asset changes.

[2] As there is no physical project for collective economic organizations in Nanhai District, most of the income from such sources as land expropriation is distributed to shareholders according to their shares. This is different from the practice in Beijing which in principle requires such funds to be used for developing collective industries and strengthen the collective economic organizations instead of being divided among shareholders. Such difference is caused by the fact that suburban areas like Nanhai District are growing into towns while Beijing wants to urbanize its rural part into the city proper and provides greater impetus for industrial upgrading.

1. Trading process and authority

The main process of collective asset trading is as follows:

(1) The project is filed for record by the Urban and Rural Affairs and Manpower Bureau after application by economic cooperatives and economic associations;
(2) The transaction plan is formulated and adopted through voting by shareholders of the economic cooperatives or economic associations. It is then reported to the township public resources trading center;
(3) The plan is reviewed and approved by the township public resources trading office, the township commission for discipline inspection and other departments that authorize the public resources trading center on information release;
(4) The public resource trading center releases the project information;
(5) The public resources trading center organizes transactions and bidding and notifies the results through the Internet, TV, newspapers and other means.

The rules on trading authority are as follows. If the term of usage exceeds five years or the target value exceeds RMB 1 million, the transaction must take place at the township level public resource trading center. Other small and short-term transfer projects can be carried out in the community (village) branch of the public resource trading platform, and the township authorities can control and supervise the transaction process online or through video cameras.

The public opinion in Nanhai District, including Dali, has been fostered in favor of collective asset transactions through the trading center. The management of collective economic organizations is under the scrutiny of shareholders to conduct trading through the trading platform.

2. Trading and overall planning of collective commercial construction land

Guangdong is a pioneer of reform. From the 1980s to the 1990s, a large amount of agricultural land was converted to collectively owned construction land. Although most of them were approved by the Ministry of Land Resources and other relevant government departments, they did not carry certificates for ownership and use, which is the case in Nanhai District. The trading of collectively owned commercial construction land in Nanhai District is led by the land department of the government but conducted on the collective asset trading platform and follows the relevant trading process.[3]

The *Implementation Measures for The Transfer of Collectively owned Construction Land Use Right in Nanhai District, Foshan City* was issued in September 2014. To date, 21 projects in Nanhai are on the market, and 10 projects are in the pipeline.[4]

[3] This practice aims to recognize the converted nature of the land and complete all procedures and certification needed for land privately transferred in the past, and therefore is not generally applicable.

[4] Most of them are reform projects typically carried out in Guangdong to turn collectively owned land to state-owned land, and convert land for industrial use to land for residential use. The value-added part is equally shared by the government and the collective (not including the cost and profit for the primary developer).

According to the Measures, 30% of the transaction value shall be reserved for future use. However, because of strong resentment from farmers in all communities (villages) and the resulting land price hike and corresponding fall in the number of projects in the market, in practice, the value equivalent to only 5–15% of the transaction price is reserved. Even so, trading volumes have decreased by 50%.

In practice, a few villages are not willing to contribute to the reserved fund. An alternative means is that after project transaction, part of the land will be converted to land for public facilities, and the right of use belongs to the government. The land will be used for the construction of hospitals, highways and other public facilities to offset the contribution to the reserve fund.

One of the problems concerning the collectively owned commercial construction land transaction is that the renewal policies and procedures after the expiration of land use rights are not clearly stipulated, resulting in the uncertainty of the subsequent value of the land. As the land approaches the end of the term for use, the value of the land will go down in contrast to the state-owned land, which goes up in value with the improvement of surrounding facilities.

For projects that involve the coordination of collectively owned construction land between villages or collective economic organizations, as exist in Dali and other parts of Nanhai District, there is no government mechanism of negotiation and profit distribution. The villages concerned have to negotiate by themselves.[5]

Dali also wants to establish a management center for the intensive use of collectively owned construction land across all collective economic organizations, but the work needs guidance from the land authorities. Thus far, it remains only an intention of the township coordination office.

III. The collective share trading platform

1. Shareholding reform of collective economic organizations

Guangdong Province launched the household contract responsibility system in the 1980s. By the 1990s, the household-based model could no longer meet the needs of economic development there. Meanwhile, as a pioneer of reform, Guangdong began to transform the property rights system of collective economic organizations earlier than other regions. Therefore, at the end of the 1990s, instead of the household model, most of the collectively owned land was managed by the collectives. Reform on the property rights system was carried out at the same time that converted land and other collective business assets to shares owned by the collectives after a comprehensive asset review. Meanwhile, the shareholder status of farmers was confirmed in collective economic organizations, and their shares were determined according to the number of farmers in the organization.

The reform turned individual farmers into shareholders who earn profit from the collective land and other assets based on their share volumes. At present, 780,000

---

[5] The *Notice of Nanhai District People's Government on the Setting and Implementation of the Benchmark Land Price for Collectively owned Construction Land in Nanhai District* issued in 2013 sets a benchmark land price which can be used as the basis for negotiation.

out of 790,000 odd farmers in Nanhai have become collective economic organization shareholders and receive dividends. After the reform of the property rights system, some problems in the operation of collective economic organizations still need to be addressed. They are mainly as follows:

First, the legal status of collective economic organizations remains unclear. This leads to problems concerning taxation and number of shareholders when they register with the industrial and commercial departments. Their inability to become independent market players causes confusion in categorizing rural collective economic entities. The "economic organization certificate" issued by the coordination office of the Nanhai District is unable to ensure the certainties of their legal person status.[6]

Second, collective economic organizations have unbalanced rights and obligations as they need to perform both government and business functions. After the reform, these organizations were still governed by administrative models. The elections of villagers' committees and collective economic organizations are merged into one, and their management positions overlap each other. Collective economic organizations still need to perform such government functions as covering the community public expenditure cost and providing social service.[7]

For this reason, Nanhai District launched the reform to separate government functions from business management in 2012. The election of community residents' (villager's) committee is separated from the election of the management of collective economic organizations. Only villagers with shareholder status can participate in the election of the management of collective economic organizations. The main leaders of the villagers' committee and the Party committee are not allowed to hold leadership positions in collective economic organizations to protect the interests of shareholders. As a supporting measure, the salaries of the heads and members of the community residents' (villagers') committees are borne by the government of Nanhai District. It cuts the villagers' committee's economic connection with the collective economic organization and ensures smooth functioning of the community (village) public service agencies.

[6] Beijing is faced with the same problem. After the reform of the property rights system, some villages have registered the rural collective economic organizations as joint-stock enterprises. This requires such organizations to pay business, corporate income and shareholders' dividend taxes. Most of the collective economic organizations are not registered with the business and taxation authorities. Instead, they are registered as shareholding cooperatives with the economic administrative authorities and their legal person status is in question. Guo Guanglei, head of the Beijing municipal economic administrative department, stressed the need to "formulate the *Regulations on Beijing Rural Collective Economic Organizations* to determine the legal person status of collective economic organizations and provide them with legal power in signing contracts in economic activities".

[7] For example, in some villages, the resident population is 12,000, and shareholders of the collective economic organizations are only 4000. Theoretically, the profits of the collective economic organization are distributed to the shareholders. However, in fact, as the leaders of the village committees are also in charge of the collective economic organizations, the resources of the economic organizations are often used for construction of village public facilities in order to win votes from the remaining 8000 villagers. This has hurt the rights and interests of shareholders and put heavy burden on the collective economic organizations. The serious asymmetry between rights and obligations also leads to fierce competition and even illegal practices in the election of the villagers' committee.

2. Practice of share transfer of collective economic organizations

The issue of share transfer was not included in the early days of the reform of the property rights system of collective economic organizations. The need for collective share transfer gradually emerges with the development of society.[8]

The government of Nanhai, Foshan released at the end of 2013 the *Measures for the Management and Trading of the Equity (Shares) of Members of Nanhai District Villagers' (Residents') Collective Economic Organizations (Exposure Draft)*, which regulates the transfer, inheritance, donation and pledge of collective equity within collective economic organizations. It mainly includes institutions that collective economic organizations need to set up for managing equity transfer and their responsibilities, as well as transfer procedures and restrictions.

Nanhai District is one of the 33 rural land reform pilot areas in China. One of the reform priorities is to "confirm ownership of shares for each household". The shares that were originally determined for individuals by the collective economic organization are redistributed to households based on family size. At the same time, the head of each household is determined. Henceforth, collective shares and dividends are distributed to households, and it is up to each household to determine the distribution of shares and dividends among family members.[9]

To date, most places in Nanhai District have carried out this reform, and Dali is ready to launch this reform this year.

3. Share trading platform

In 2013, Nanhai District established the share management and trading center and developed the share management system, which now keeps records for 780,000 shareholders of collective economic organizations, including the data of their share volume and dividends, in an effort to protect shareholders' lawful right to obtain dividends. In practice, no share transfer has been conducted on the platform.[10]

[8] Zhang Hongyu, Director-general of the Economic Management Department, Ministry of Agriculture pointed out that the collective assets share reform "explores terms, scopes, procedures and forms of farmers' paid withdraw of collective asset shares, specific means to liquidate the collective asset shares as collateral when borrowers are unable to repay the loan, and ways to inherit the shares for qualified heirs who are not members of the collective economic organizations."

[9] Such practice conforms to the regulations on household contract of collective land by matching equity with management rights. However, in fact it does not serve the purpose of share transfer. First, equity is determined by the number of people in the household and involves redistribution of shares for individuals by the collective, which in itself is a violation of private property rights (some villages in Beijing have similar policies). Second, distribution of headcount-based equity to households in essence shifts problems to family members. With population migration and changes in household members, blood ties become loose, causing conflict of interest. In particular, those shareholders who have moved out may find it difficult to have their rights and interests secured, which may not help with efficient movement of human resource. Third, household share transfer will not be possible unless all the shareholders of the household reach consensus. With the change of the household population, the relationship between shareholders will be more detached, each going for their own interests. It will be increasingly difficult to seek consensus on matters relating to share transfer.

[10] As the share transfer method is developed on the basis of headcount-based share allocation, it is unable to provide any guidance after the shift of share distribution to households and cannot be

Trials made in Dali Township of Foshan City on the collective economic organization management structure are an important supplement to the government efforts on administrative streamlining, relaxing control on land and allowing for trading of collectively owned construction land. The financial regulatory system, asset trading platform and collective share trading platform established thus far are sound measures to address the problems facing collective economic organizations and can be replicated nationwide.

Bibliography

Gao, Y. (2014). *Service function of farmers' professional cooperatives: Theoretical and empirical research.* Unpublished doctor's dissertation, Zhejiang University.

Liang, H. (2014). Research on risk management of rural collective economic organizations. *Policy Research & Exploration, 18.*

Liang, Q., & Huang, Z. (2011). Theoretical and analytical framework for cooperatives research: A comprehensive review. *Economist, 12.*

Wang, Y. (2012). An analysis of the new dynamics faced by rural collective economic organizations. *China Rural Survey, 5.*

Zheng, D., & Wang, W. (2011). Development status, problems and policy suggestions of rural collective economic organizations. *Forum on Science and Technology in China, 2.*

implemented unless going through drastic revision. However, the regulation requiring shareholders to retain some shares during share transfer is worthy of reference for other regions, and the establishment of its shareholder database also lays a good foundation for the transfer of shares in collective economic organizations.

Streamlining Administration and Delegating Power for Better Use of Agricultural Reclamation Land Resources

Jiangtao Liu and Xuhong Li

Background of the Study

China's agricultural reclamation system has rich state-owned land resources and plays an important role in agricultural modernization driven by its unique advantages of massive land, big industries, large enterprises and market-oriented, specialized and organized operations. At the beginning of 2015, the No. 1 Document of the CPC Central Committee entitled *Opinions on Strengthening Reform and Innovation and Accelerating Agricultural Modernization* called for "accelerating agricultural reclamation reform and development". On November 27, 2015, the CPC Central Committee and the State Council adopted the *Decision on Further Promoting the Reform and Development of Agricultural Reclamation.* This shows that as the economy moves into the new normal, the central leadership places high importance on the reform of the agricultural reclamation system, an important state-owned economic entity in agriculture. Reform has thus picked up pace.

China's agricultural reclamation system covers 366,000 km^2 of land. It manages 93.16 million *mu* of cultivated land, 228 million *mu* of grassland and 59.55 million *mu* of forestland and other state-owned resource assets. In China, land is owned either by the state or by the collectives. "Urban land belongs to the state. Land in rural and suburban areas is owned by collectives except for those that belong to the state as provided for by the law. Homestead sites, private plots of land and private hills are also owned by collectives."[1] Accordingly, China's land system includes the

[1] See Article 10, Chapter I, *Constitution of the People's Republic of China.*

J. Liu (✉)
Guanghua School of Management, Peking University, Beijing, China

X. Li
Tax Administration Division, Ministry of Finance, New Delhi, India

Executive Finance Division, Liaison Office of the Central People's Government in the Hong Kong Special Administrative Region, Sai Ying Pun, Hong Kong

Y. Li and Z. Cheng (eds.), *The Chinese Path Toward a Leaner Government*,
https://doi.org/10.1007/978-981-19-6718-4_21

urban land system and rural land system. Urban land is owned by the state, while rural land is owned either by the state or by the collectives. The particularity of land for agricultural reclamation lies in the fact that these land plots are generally located in rural areas and urban suburbs. However, they are owned by the state and not collectives and represent the state ownership of rural land. Therefore, the reform of the agricultural reclamation land system plays an important role in the reform of both the agricultural reclamation system and the rural land system.

The *Decision on Further Promoting the Reform and Development of Agricultural Reclamation* points out that China's agricultural reclamation system was established to undertake the mission entrusted by the state under specific historical conditions. The reform should adhere to the path of the socialist market economy and separate business management from government functions and social responsibilities to ensure national food security and an effective supply of major agricultural products. Enterprise groups should be set up in reclamation areas, and corporate reform should be carried out on state farms. Their growth model should be shifted at a faster pace through innovation-driven development. Resources and assets will be integrated to promote industrial upgrading. Major modern agricultural production centers and large enterprises should be established to foster a stronger industry featuring greater vitality, driving force and overall strength, with modern agriculture playing a leading role. Efforts should be made to strengthen the Party's organization and leadership over agricultural reclamation work and asset management to prevent the loss of state-owned assets. Steady progress should be made in accordance with the principle of taking all factors into consideration, addressing both symptoms and root causes, coordinating steps across different levels of government and combining spread-out reform with pilots in key areas. Paragraph 13 of Article 3 specifically calls for "innovating the land management mode".[2]

On November 16, 2015, Vice Premier Wang Yang of the State Council published a signed article titled "Vigorously Promote Agricultural Modernization with A New Development Philosophy" on the People's Daily. The article proposed strengthening the leading role of the agricultural reclamation system in agricultural modernization. Professor Li Yining, a renowned economist, described the general goal of the agricultural reclamation reform as generating better returns by revitalizing state-owned resources or assets, including land, capital and manpower.

The land of the agricultural reclamation system is an important state-owned resource in agricultural reclamation reform. In the new economic circumstances, reform and innovation in this field will accelerate to improve land utilization and the capability of sustainable development for the entire agricultural reclamation system and make new contribution to agricultural modernization and rural land system reform in China. At the same time, the improvement of government policies and regulations and the review and approval processes play a very important role in better utilization of land resources in the agricultural reclamation system. This paper

---

[2] See Paragraph 13, Article 3 of the *Decision on Further Promoting the Reform and Development of Agricultural Reclamation* issued by the CPC Central Committee and the State Council on November 27, 2015.

will focus on the importance of administrative streamlining for better utilization of land resources in the agricultural reclamation system in China and issues that need to be addressed and put forward a general approach and policy suggestions for the reform.

Analysis of the concept of better utilization of agricultural reclamation land resources and administrative streamlining

I. Better utilization of agricultural reclamation land resources

Better utilization of land resources means using technical means and sound management methods to improve the structure and distribution of land resources, maximize the economic, social and ecological benefits of land resource utilization, and ensure a proper balance and sustainable development between the human population and land resources in light of certain social economic and technological conditions, the current situation of land resource utilization and land properties and the law for the land use system. It can be achieved by improving the utilization mode, quantity structure, spatial layout and overall returns. As a systematic endeavor, it contains multiple subsystems with complex logical relations and involves many factors, such as economic development, ecological protection and resource development. The goals are multifaceted and sometimes mutually restrictive, and proper coordination is therefore needed.

The goal can be achieved with the following measures: maintaining an overall balance between supply and demand of agricultural reclamation land resources; improving the quantity and structure of agricultural reclamation land resources under the current situation; improving the spatial layout of agricultural reclamation land resources, which means designing the special layout within a region based on the analysis of the development trend of various types of land and the zoning of land resources; maximizing the productivity and utilization rate of the land resources on the basis of the land quantity and spatial structure; and improving the institutional arrangement to make the role of land resources more important in people's work and life and achieve economic, social and ecological progress at the same time.

II. The concept of streamlining administration and delegating power

In his reply to 30 entrepreneurs of Fujian Province on July 8, 2014, General Secretary Xi Jinping said, "Governments at all levels in China are transforming functions at a faster speed to streamline administration and delegate power. One of the goals is to strengthen the market force and make companies more innovation-driven. The delegation of authorities further frees up businesses and offers a new opportunity for entrepreneurs to give full play to their wisdom and resources."

By its definition, streamlining administration and delegating power aims to curtail government functions and cut undue power and straighten out the relationship between the government, society, market and individual citizens. The government's responsibilities are clearly defined so that the government can channel its limited resources to areas that require government administration, service and supervision. Such fields include economic regulation, market supervision, social governance, public service, city management and environmental protection. It can reduce the cost of production, business and living, deliver reform benefits, strengthen social governance, stimulate social vitality and promote economic growth.

The importance of administrative streamlining in improving land use of the agricultural reclamation system

I. The importance of reform and development for the agricultural reclamation system

China's agricultural reclamation system originated from the efforts of Brigade 359 to turn barren land in north Shaanxi into farmland in the 1940s. It was later formally established by the PRC government to engage in agricultural production on behalf of the national government and has made important contribution to China's economic and social development, including agricultural modernization, food security, new types of urbanization, ecological sustainability, rural development, border stability and national defense. The importance of agricultural reclamation system reform and development is mainly reflected in the following aspects:

First, the reform and development of the agricultural reclamation system will increase the proportion of the state-owned agricultural sector and enhance the controlling power of the state in the strategic agricultural industry. Unlike the land under collective ownership in rural areas, the land of the agricultural reclamation system belongs to the state and is regarded as state-owned assets. Likewise, the staff of the land reclamation farms are SOE employees. The farms and the employees form an employment relationship based on the labor contract, which is different from the land contract between farmers and rural collectives. As the main form of the state-owned agricultural sector, the agricultural reclamation system represents advanced agricultural production relations and productive forces. Sustainable development will help shape a land reclamation system that is mainly state owned and family farm-based with various ownerships developing side by side. This helps raise their productivity, industrial intensity and international competitiveness and ensure the implementation of the national agricultural development strategy.

Second, the reform and development of agricultural reclamation systems will accelerate the process of agricultural modernization. China has entered a new period of faster transformation and upgrading from traditional agriculture to modern agriculture. The sustainable development of agricultural reclamation systems will advance this process. In terms of the scale of agricultural production, per capita land for employees in the planting business of the agricultural reclamation system nationwide is estimated to be roughly 2 ha, significantly higher than the average level in the countryside. The reform will reverse the current small scale and scattered distribution of farming entities, ensure unified organization and management of agricultural production and trading, foster new types of farming entities and appropriately expand the scale of farming to create an economy of scale for agricultural production. In terms of agricultural industrialization, the system enjoys competitive strengths in industries such as grain, cotton, natural rubber, sugar, dairy products and seed, and the reform will further extend and improve their production chains and promote industrial integration featuring synergy and complementarity between internal and external stakeholders from production all the way to marketing. Meanwhile, building enterprise groups can help improve their operational scale, management expertise, business performance, market competitiveness and industrial reputation and ultimately advance the process of agricultural modernization.

Third, the reform and development of the agricultural reclamation system will accelerate the new type of urbanization. The *Report on the Work of the Government 2014* set the goal for "a new type of people-centered urbanization" by "helping 100 million rural migrant workers register as urban households, renovating shanty towns inhabited by 100 million people and encourage 100 million rural citizens in the central and western regions to live in nearby towns." On March 16, 2014, the CPC Central Committee and the State Council issued the *National Plan for a New Type of Urbanization (2014–2020)*, which charts the course for urbanization, spells out its main goals, strategic tasks and institutional and policy changes in relevant fields. There are over 1000 small towns in China, especially in the central and western regions and the border areas that belong to the agricultural reclamation system. In recent years, dilapidated houses have been renovated for more than 1.6 million households, and farm towns have taken on a new look. They have basically grown into small towns of considerable size and contributed to advancing a new type of urbanization in China. The reform and development of the agricultural reclamation system will further promote efforts in this field.

Fourth, the reform and development of the agricultural reclamation system will ensure China's food security. General Secretary Xi said that the Chinese people must "keep the rice bowl firmly in their own hands at all times". This means that China must have full control of its own food security. As the agricultural industry becomes more globalized, China is facing greater challenges in food security. Food security calls for enhancing the overall food production capacity of China. As an important player in implementing the strategy of national food security, the agricultural reclamation system has a large-scale farming base with stable production capacity and supply channels. It has advantages in terms of agricultural science and technology, economy of scale and industrialization. The sustained development of the agricultural reclamation system will help improve its organization, scale, mechanization, land and labor productivity and commodity supply and create first-class food production centers and world-class food dealers, thus ensuring our national food security.

II. Importance of streamlining administration and delegating power in improving the utilization of agricultural reclamation land resources

Due to the special nature of land resources, better land utilization is inseparable from the improvement of government functions. The importance of streamlining administration and delegating power in improving land use in the agricultural reclamation system is mainly reflected in the following aspects:

First, streamlining administration and delegating power will maximize the use of land resources for agricultural reclamation and facilitate the reform in this sector.

Land is an important resource of the agricultural reclamation system, and it is state-owned property. Streamlining administration and delegating power will promote the full use of farmland and agricultural productivity and advance China's food security. It will also push for full use of the construction land in the agricultural reclamation system and a new type of urbanization in China. Turning land into capital and assets will increase the capital income of China's agricultural reclamation company groups and promote their development.

Second, streamlining administration and delegating power will advance the process of rural land system reform. Agricultural reclamation land resources are state-owned land in rural areas. It is an important part of rural land in addition to land owned by rural collectives. Its utilization hinges on the reform of the rural land system. Streamlining administration and delegating power will improve the utilization of agricultural reclamation land resources and facilitate rural land system reform and can be advanced by drawing on good practices in improving the use of land owned by rural collectives, and vice versa.

Third, streamlining administration and delegating power will contribute to supply-side structural reform. General Secretary Xi proposed for the first time at the 11th meeting of the Financial and Economic Leading Group of the CPC Central Committee on January 10, 2015 that "While moderately expanding the overall demand, we should intensify the supply-side structural reform, improve the quality and efficiency of the supply system, and strengthen the driving force for sustained economic growth." The goal of the supply-side structural reform is to let the market better play a decisive role in allocating resources and let the government play a key role in promoting economic growth through reform and innovation to ensure proper allocation of resources, expand effective supply, improve the structure of the supply side and increase its flexibility and adaptability to changing needs. As total factor productivity and long-term potential growth increase, economic and industrial restructuring will continue to ensure the long-term sustainable economic growth of the country. At present, supply-side structural reform mainly involves the allocation of the labor force, capital, land, technology, management expertise and other factors. Streamlining administration and delegating power in improving the utilization of agricultural land resources focuses on land in the supply-side structural reform. The productivity of the land will be improved to provide sufficient, safe and much-needed farm products and raise total factor productivity and the long-term potential economic growth rate. This will add more impetus to the supply-side structural reform.

III. The current state of agricultural reclamation land resources

China's agricultural reclamation system covers 36.6 km^2 of land (about 3.8% of China's territory) in 31 provinces, managing 93.16 million mu of arable land (about 4.6% of the national arable land), 228 million mu of grassland (about 6% of the national grassland), 59.55 million mu of forestland (about 1.8% of the national forestland) and other state-owned resources. It has a population of 14.13 million, including 3.19 million employees, 1779 state-owned farms and more than 3200 state-owned and state holding enterprises, with 1.039 trillion yuan of state-owned assets (excluding land and other resource assets). It has developed its own economic

Table 1 The agricultural reclamation system's share of land in China

Type	Size for agricultural reclamation areas	National size	Share (%)
Land	366,000 km^2	9.6 million square kilometres	3.8
Arable land	93.16 million mu	2.027 billion mu	4.6
Grass land	228 million mu	3.798 billion mu	6.0
Forest land	59.55 million mu	3.292 billion mu	1.8

Source Official websites of the Ministry of Land Resources and the Bureau of Agricultural Reclamation, Ministry of Agriculture

and social systems with integrated agricultural, industrial and commercial establishments that enjoy all-round growth of the primary, secondary and tertiary industries and relatively complete technological, educational, cultural and health facilities. It has made vigorous efforts in implementing the "go global" strategy by launching 113 overseas businesses and development projects in 42 countries and regions (Table 1).

From 2010 to 2014, the GDP of the agricultural reclamation system increased from 338.2 billion yuan to 642 billion yuan. Calculated at comparable prices, the annual growth rates in 2011 through 2014 were 13.5%, 13.8% 12.8% and 9.5%, respectively, higher than the GDP growth rates. Xinjiang Production and Construction Corps and Heilongjiang Province Farms and Land Reclamation are the two largest reclamation areas in terms of gross production. The steady growth in the overall production of the agricultural reclamation system year-on-year provides strong economic support for the reform and the improved utilization of land resources of the agricultural reclamation system.

Total output of the agricultural reclamation system (100 million yuan).

Growth rate (% at comparable price).

Chart 1 Total agricultural reclamation output and growth rate 2010–2014.

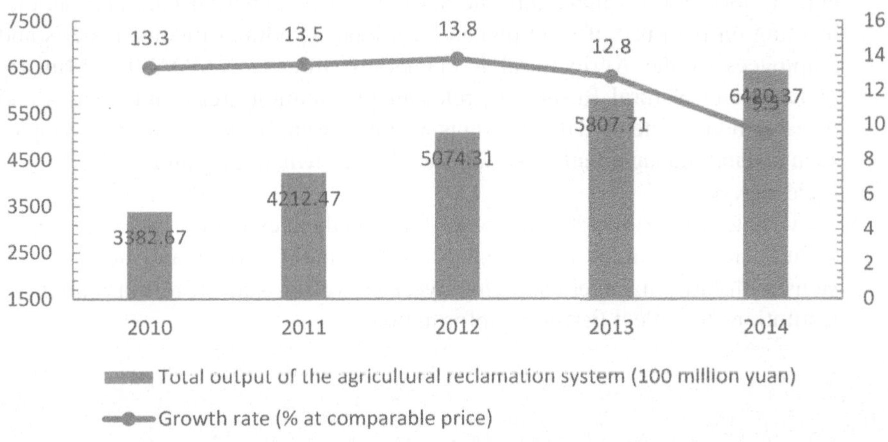

Source: Bureau of Agricultural Reclamation, Ministry of Agriculture

It can be seen that the agricultural reclamation system, with its rich state-owned land resources, plays an important role in agricultural modernization driven by its unique advantages of extensive farmland, big industries, large enterprises and market-oriented, specialized and organized management.

Issues concerning streamlining administration and delegating power in the process of improving the agricultural reclamation land resources

I. Survey briefing
1. General information

The author participated in the research carried out by the Ministry of Agriculture entitled *Key Issues in the Reform and Development of China's Agricultural Reclamation Sector*. To obtain a full picture of the issues concerning streamlining administration and delegation power in the process of improving agricultural reclamation land use, the author conducted research and in-depth analysis of the highly representative reclamation areas and state-owned farms in these areas.

2. Key respondents

Key respondents of the survey mainly included managers, staff workers, employees of relevant financial institutions and others in the reclamation areas of Anhui, Jiangxi, Shanghai, Ningxia, Guangxi, etc.

3. Research methods
(1) Questionnaires
A research outline on improving agricultural reclamation land use was drawn that included basic information on land resources, management mechanisms, contract management systems, scale expansion, land ownership, capitalization and planned use. A survey was carried out in the targeted reclamation areas.
(2) Workshops
In July 2015 and March 2016, the Agricultural Reclamation Bureau of MOA held a workshop on managing the agricultural reclamation land and another meeting on paid use of state-owned farm land. Leading officials, experts and employees of the Agricultural Reclamation Bureau of MOA, the Ministry of Land and Natural Resources, relevant reclamation areas, universities and research bodies attended the meetings where they analyzed and discussed topics such as land management and paid use of state-owned farmland.
(3) Field survey
We went to primary-level state-owned farms in the reclamation areas of Jiangxi, Anhui, Heilongjiang, Chongqing, Shanghai and Guangxi and held discussions with farm managers and employees as well as staff of relevant financial institutions to collect first-hand information.

II. Challenges in streamlining administration and delegating power for better utilization of the agricultural reclamation land resources

The survey summarized the challenges as follows:

1. Agricultural reclamation management systems vary in kind and need targeted reform plans that suit the circumstances of different areas

In China, there are various types of agricultural reclamation management systems that can be divided into three categories: Xinjiang Production and Construction Corps, reclamation areas directly under the Administration of Agricultural Reclamation, and reclamation areas under local government. The Xinjiang Production and Construction Corps are under the direct administration of the central government, where the functions of the Party, government, military and businesses are well integrated. Reclamation areas in Heilongjiang Province and Guangdong Province are directly under the Administration of Agricultural Reclamation. They are under the dual administration of the provincial government and MOA, with the provincial government as the main authority. The MOA is responsible for in-budget capital construction investment and state-owned asset supervision, and the provincial Party Committee is responsible for their personnel management. Reclamation areas under local government are divided into two categories. One is provincial-level reclamation groups, such as those in Anhui, Shanghai and Guangxi Provinces. The other is municipal (county)-level farms, with provincial authorities performing the industry guidance function, such as those in Jilin and Jiangxi Provinces.

Agricultural reclamation management system			
Reclamation areas directly under the central government	Reclamation areas directly under the administration of agricultural rcclamation	Reclamation areas under local government	
Xinjiang production and construction corps	Heiongjiang, Guangdong		
		Provincial-level reclamation groups	Municipal (county)-level farms

Chart 2 Agricultural reclamation management system.

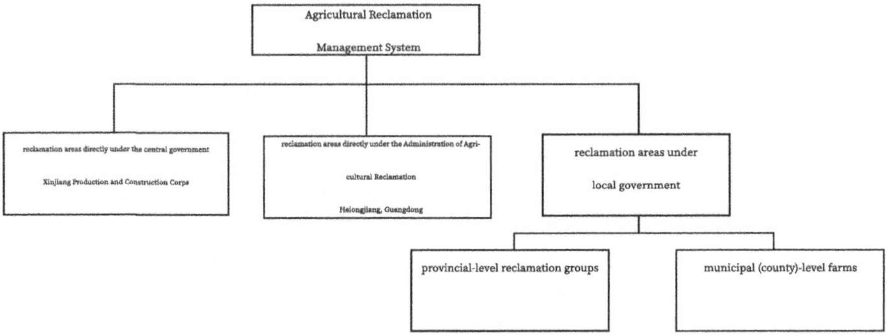

There are 17 provincial-level reclamation groups. Their competent provincial authorities are transformed into parent companies while keeping the traditional way of administration, or in other words "wearing two hats". The farms and secondary and tertiary industry enterprises within the group are reorganized into group subsidiaries or branch companies according to their development needs and have capital links with their parent companies. However, it is difficult for municipal (county)-level reclamation areas to be transformed into provincial-level group companies.

A variety of management systems are at play in China's agricultural reclamation sector due to historical reasons, each with its own particularity. Therefore, when formulating the policies of the streamlining administration and delegating power in the process of improving land use, targeted schemes should be formulated according to the characteristics of different reclamation areas.

2. Laws and regulations on the utilization of land resources for agricultural reclamation need to be revised and improved

(1) Laws and regulations on the utilization of land resources for agricultural reclamation.

The laws and regulations related to the utilization of land resources for agricultural reclamation are listed in chronological order in Table 2.

(2) Areas to be improved in laws and regulations.

The release and enforcement of the above laws and regulations provide necessary guidance for the utilization of land resources for agricultural reclamation. However, there are many types of land resources for agricultural reclamation. Based on our findings, the following aspects still need to be improved and clarified in practice to make administrative streamlining more targeted.

Table 2 Laws and regulations related to the utilization of land resources for agricultural reclamation

No	Name	Issuer	Time
1	*Land Administration Law*	National People's Congress	Adopted in June 1986, revised in December 1988 and August 2004
2	*Interim Regulations on Urban State-owned Land Use Right Transfer*	State Council	May 1990
3	*Law on Guarantee*	National People's Congress	June 1995
4	*Interim Regulations on Management of the Right to Use Allocated State-owned Land in SOE Reforms*	Former State Land Administration	February 1998
5	*Regulations on Basic Farmland Protection*	State Council	Issued in December 1998, revised in January 2011
6	*Notice on Further Promoting the Bidding, Auction and Transfer of State-owned Land Use Right*	Ministry of Land and Natural Resources	January 1999
7	*Notice on Strengthening the Administration of State-owned Land Assets*	State Council	April 2001
8	*Law on Rural Land Contract*	National People's Congress	August 2002
9	*Measures on Rural Land Contracting Certificate Management*	Ministry of Agriculture	November 2003
10	*Notice on Matters Concerning Use of Some Land Transfer Fees in Rural Land Development*	State Council	March 2004
11	*Law on Property*	National People's Congress	March 2007
12	*Measures on Pilot Programs Connecting Urban and Rural Land Supply for Construction Purposes*	Ministry of Land and Natural Resources	June 2008
13	*Opinions on Strengthening Land Use Administration of State-owned Farms*	Ministry of Land and Natural Resources, Ministry of Agriculture	October 2008
14	*Measures on Review of General Planning of Land Use*	Ministry of Land and Natural Resources	January 2009
15	*Regulations on Land Reclamation*	State Council	February 2011

(continued)

Table 2 (continued)

No	Name	Issuer	Time
16	*Measures on Investigation and Handling of Land Right Disputes*	Ministry of Land and Natural Resources	December 2002
17	*Implementing Rules on the Land Reclamation Regulations*	Ministry of Land and Natural Resources	December 2012
18	*Opinions on Encouraging Orderly Transfer of Rural Land Management Right and Agricultural Development of Appropriate Scale*	General Office, CPCCC	August 2014
19	*Regulations on Raising Land Use Performance*	Ministry of Land and Natural Resources	September 2014
20	*Guidelines on Pilot Programs of Transforming Farmers' Contracted Land Use Right and Housing Property Right into Mortgages*	State Council	August 2015
21	*Opinions on Further Promoting Reform and Development of the Agricultural Reclamation Sector*	CPCCC, State Council	November 2015

First, land for agricultural reclamation is allocated for use by the state free of charge. However, there is a lack of clear legal provisions on the acquisition and exercise of the right to use state-owned farmland, leading to many deviations in practice. Therefore, it is necessary to study and further clarify the user's rights to state-owned farmland. As there is no clear provision on the right to use state-owned farmland, which is needed in land protection and utilization, a legal definition of the right to use state-owned farmland should be developed. In addition, the provisions on the structure and composition of rights for state-owned farmland and the acquisition and exercise of such rights need to be improved to fully reflect the will of the state and owners' rights and interests.

Second, some provisions of laws and regulations need to be clarified. For example, the *Land Law of the People's Republic of China* emphasizes that only "public welfare projects" can be a proper reason for "taking back the land from state-owned farms", but there is no clear explanation for what "public welfare projects" means. Some policies mentioned the need to set aside "resettlement funds and land" without specifying how to quantify and regulate such arrangements or whether "an agreement on compensation and resettlement" shall be signed with farms for land requisition. The absence of local implementing rules has made it difficult for state farms to seek proper compensation for the loss of land.

3. It is somewhat difficult to determine the rights for agricultural reclamation land
(1) Company groups have no direct power to manage the land

Few reclamation company groups host land administrative offices dispatched by provincial land authorities. The agricultural reclamation administration has become sidelined and has no say once problems occur. Anhui is an exception. The provincial authorities have set up an administrative office in the company group. Important issues such as land planning adjustment and the revision of the annual plan, commissioned land transfer and sharing of the transfer fees, joint development and utilization of land, land rights certification and registration and law enforcement supervision have been properly dealt with thanks to this arrangement.

(2) Except for a few developed areas, most of the reclamation areas face difficulties in determining land use rights

Due to problems left over from history, the reclamation area and the local government still have disputes over many aspects of land ownership even if the rights have been confirmed. It may be more difficult to reconfirm the rights due to human factors. The main causes for the difficulties in issuing land rights certifications are as follows:

First, fees for land rights investigation and measurement are high, and there is no fiscal support from the government. Taking the Guangxi agricultural reclamation area as an example, the investigation fee remains RMB166 per mu, which was set in the 1994 document of the provincial price bureau. The measurement fees for agricultural land and construction land are both RMB13 to RMB130 per mu and have to be paid separately at the same time. There are 1.21 million mu of uncertified state farmland in Guangxi, which means RMB200 million (RMB166 per mu × 1.21 million mu) of investigation fees plus RMB120 million for measurement (average RMB100 per mu × 1.21 million mu). This is beyond the financial capacity of Guangxi state farms.

Second, neighboring land owners do not cooperate in the demarcation and signing of boundary lines.

Third, a small number of local governments fail to promptly intervene in or deliver a fair judgment on acts of encroachment on state-owned land.

Fourth, there is an imbalance between the number of people and the size of farmland. The number of farm workers is smaller than that of villagers. A small number of people working on state farms have a weak sense of responsibility in protecting state-owned land.

4. Land planning and management for agricultural reclamation needs to be strengthened

Due to various factors in the past and at present, there are many challenges in the planning and management of state-owned land for agricultural reclamation. The planning is developed and approved by the local government, which seldom consults the agricultural reclamation organization in the plan formulation and revision period. The latter lacks the initiative to communicate with the local government, local land authorities or farms. As a result, the need for land to ensure the economic and social development of agricultural reclamation areas is not fully reflected in the *General Plan of Land Use* adopted by local governments.

5. The Land Contract Management System for Agricultural Reclamation Needs to Be Improved

The following areas need to be improved in the land contracting management system for agricultural reclamation: Some management fails to fully understand the policies or conduct proper communication and explanation of the policies. Land contracting and contract management are not well regulated. The contracting fees change frequently and too drastically. Business service charge is not transparent.

General thinking and policy suggestions for streamlining administration and delegating power in improving the utilization of agricultural reclamation land resources

I. General thinking

In the framework of overall agricultural reclamation development planning, more efforts should be made to delegate authorities. New ways should be found to improve land use, and laws and regulations in this field should be improved. Efforts should be strengthened in land rights confirmation and land contracting management to expand the scale of land reclamation business at an appropriate level. A sound pricing mechanism should be in place with effective measures to protect agricultural land of the reclamation areas, farmland in particular, from being encroached upon. Land planning and management should be strengthened through institutional improvement. Greater efforts should be made to turn land into capital and assets with more financial support. More attention should be given to risk mitigation and relevant mechanism building in improving the use of agricultural reclamation land to contribute to the reform and development of the agricultural reclamation system.

II. Policy suggestions

1. Improve relevant laws and regulations on the utilization of agricultural reclamation land resources to provide institutional support for administrative streamlining
   The government needs to sort out existing laws on land rights in China, clarify the relationship between state-owned agricultural land rights and other rights, and analyze the main issues involved. It should also spell out the structure of state-owned agricultural land rights and put forward opinions on their acquisition and disposal.
2. Improve the review and approval process and delegate approval powers for higher efficiency
   The competent authorities are advised to give full consideration to the characteristics of state-owned land in agricultural reclamation areas when formulating policies and regulations, clarifying rights and obligations and improving the institutional framework to support the efforts of streamlining administration and delegating power.

The government should revisit the scope and process of administrative review related to reclamation land use and make improvements where necessary, consolidate steps, authorities and content of the review, and delegate approval powers while controlling risks for higher efficiency.
The scope of administrative review and approval concerning the utilization of agricultural reclamation land resources includes land use rights, land contracts and management rights, auction, transfer, development and expropriation of land, general planning and mortgage of land, etc.

3. Push for confirmation of agricultural reclamation land rights
Confirmation, registration and certification of agricultural reclamation land rights should be accelerated. Land is the fundamental means of production for agricultural reclamation. We suggest that on the basis of land survey data, new ways should be explored to increase the proportion and efficiency of land certification in the form of public notification. The fees for state-owned land certification in agricultural reclamation areas should be lowered with reference to rural collective land rights service fees standards. Both the central and local governments should provide financial support to basically complete land rights confirmation and certification within three years. To be more specific, we suggest that the change in the land owner's name for state-owned organizations should be processed free of charge to ensure consistency between the name on the land certificate and the name of the organization's official seal.
4. Improve the communication and management mechanism of overall land planning for agricultural reclamation
The communication and management mechanism of overall land planning for agricultural reclamation needs to be improved. A faster communication channel should be built between the state-owned farms and the land authorities at the municipal (county) level for prompt reporting of the urgent need and planning for land use to support economic and social programs of the agricultural reclamation system. We suggest that the Ministry of Land Resources and the Ministry of Agriculture issue a document that expresses understanding and support for the development of agricultural reclamation organizations while asking them to cooperate with the delineation of basic farmland. When formulating relevant plans, the government should listen more to the views of agricultural reclamation organizations and step up two-way communication to improve the quality of their overall land planning.
5. Improve the land contract management system
The management model of the agricultural reclamation areas is a combination of state-owned farms and employees' family farms (in the form of contract management). In the process of streamlining administration and delegating power, it is important to give such areas more autonomy in terms of land contract management and large-scale operation so that the state-owned farms will be able to adapt to reality, take care of their own gains and losses in accordance with the law and improve their own market competitiveness.

Bibliography

Bureau of Agricultural Reclamation of the Ministry of Agriculture. (2015). Statistical Bulletin of Economic and Social Development of National Agricultural Reclamation in 2014. *China State Farm* (7).

Li, Y. (2013). *Dual transition of China's economy*. China Renmin University press.

Li, Y. (2015). *Growth of the blue-collar middle class: The Chinese path*. The Commercial Press.

Liu, J. & Li, X. (2015). Research on sustainable development strategy of the agricultural reclamation system under the new normal. *China State Farm* (10).

Qian, M., Pu, L., et al. (2010). A review of studies on land use structure optimization. *Resources and Environment in the Yangtze Basin* (12).

Wan, R. (2013). Analysis on policy direction of agricultural reclamation land development. *Agriculture and Technology* (4).

Beijing's Practice of Strengthening Its Strategic Position as the Capital City and Deepening the Institutional Reform

Zhilong Yu and Zhenhua Han

On 26th Feb, 2014, General Secretary Xi Jinping made remarks during his inspection of Beijing, emphasizing Beijing's status as a national center for political, cultural activities, international exchanges and technological innovation. He set the goal of building Beijing into a harmonious and livable city of international standards and gave instructions on advancing and better managing Beijing's development and coordinating development among Beijing, Tianjin and Hebei Province. His remarks chartered the course for Beijing. The city has entered a new phase with new tasks of strengthening its position as the capital city, relieving itself of functions nonessential to its role and further coordinating its own development with that of Tianjin and Hebei. Completing these three tasks requires both the government and the market to better play their roles. Institutional reforms need to be further deepened, and the planning and management of Beijing need to be improved.

Theoretical Basis and Goals of the Institutional Reform

Unlike the legislative and judicial systems, the administrative system encompasses the arrangements of government bodies responsible for administrative affairs and the division and exertion of their functions and powers. As a kind of superstructure, it is an integral part of China's political systems and institutions. To put it simply, it is about the establishment of administrative departments and the exercise of their powers. Administrative systems have long been the topic of discussion among economists of classical schools, especially with regard to relations between the government and the market and the government and society.

I. Relations between the government and the market/society are at the center of institutional reform.

Z. Yu (✉) · Z. Han
Research Office of the Beijing Municipal Government, Beijing, China

Y. Li and Z. Cheng (eds.), *The Chinese Path Toward a Leaner Government*,
https://doi.org/10.1007/978-981-19-6718-4_22

According to Adam Smith of the classical economy, humanity is born to be selfish; thus, the pursuit of personal gains is anything but immoral. If competition is given full rein, people will seek maximum personal interest based on their own judgment. At the same time, there is an "invisible hand", namely, the market, to ensure the best allocation of resources in society. He expounded on how the government behaves as a night watcher in three ways: protecting the nation from violence or invasion by any other separate society; protecting the people so that none of them will be subject to injustice or oppression from others, or in other words, establishing an equitable judicial and administrative system; and building and maintaining certain public institutions and public works. He also encouraged the government to take over postal services, control interest rates in accordance with the law, provide universal access to compulsory education and give license tests to all freelance and credit businesses. According to his views, public regulations should be used to guarantee a nation's tangible security. For instance, public health measures are needed to prevent the spread of infectious diseases. Overall, although known as the father of laissez-faire economics, Adam Smith also recognized the due role of the government in promoting the efficient functioning of the market economy.

In the context of the economic and social development of Europe in the nineteenth century, Karl Marx revealed the development law of human society based on the theories of dialectical and historical materialism. When analyzing the capitalist mode of production, he put forward the labor theory of value, the theory of alienation and the theory of surplus value. He stated that social changes occur as a sequel to class struggle, the state is a machine of violence for one class to rule the other, and human society will gradually evolve toward the abolition of classes, exploitation and oppression. Therefore, economically, labor should be united to control the means of production and carry out production together; politically, nations will disappear, and the working people should go for cooperative self-governance and establish a community of free persons.

The advent of the Great Depression in the 1930s in the western world and the booming economy of the Soviet Union paved the way for Keynesian economics, named after the economist John Maynard Keynes, who argued that the government plays an important role in expanding effective demand and balancing overall supply and demand. According to him, the government should appropriately intervene in and regulate the economy at the macro level to stabilize employment and promote economic growth.

The Austrian school of economics represented primarily by Eugen Böhm-Bawerk, Ludwig von Mises and Friedrich von Hayek harshly criticized Marxism and socialist thoughts, as well as their theoretical bases, such as the labor theory of value. It also opposed Keynesian economics, which stands for putting the economy under state regulation. Instead, it advocated laissez-faire and spontaneous dynamics of the market as against the socialist planned economy and government intervention, any of which, it argued, would distort the market, lead to disorder or create new monopolies. This argument was further developed as capitalist countries entered a period of stagflation in the 1970s.

A general revisit of these economic schools shows that all of them argued about the relations between the government and the market from their own perspectives and played important roles at different times. The conclusion can be drawn that both the government and the market are important in the economy of countries with various social systems. In our globalized world, the market economy is treated by most countries as a basic economic system, and governments are playing an increasingly important role in macro-regulation, public services, social security, market supervision and other fields.

China is a socialist country transiting from a planned economy to a market economy, where the government is shifting from an omnipotent steward for economic development to a service provider with limited powers. By transforming its own functions and advancing the institutional reform, the government aims to improve its performance in macro-regulation while letting the market play a decisive role in resource allocation. It is important to uphold the positions, views and methodologies of Marxism and reject the neo-liberal thoughts, maintain the dominant role of the public sector and promote the common development of economic entities under diverse forms of ownership instead of pushing for economic privatization single-mindedly. It is also important to uphold the leadership of the CPC, pursue the system whereby the people are the masters of the country and respect the rule of law, and develop socialist democracy with distinctive Chinese features.

II. The goal of the institutional reform is to build a service-oriented government.

The second Plenary Session of the 17th CPC Central Committee set the goal of establishing a relatively full-fledged administrative system with Chinese characteristics by 2020. This means that China will build a service-oriented government in terms of its relations with the market.

First, government functions should be transformed. As institutional reform deepens, government administration should be further separated from business affairs, capital investment and the running of public institutions. The government should scale back the direct management of and interference in specific business activities and ensure that the market plays a more decisive role in resource allocation while the government improves its regulation on the economy. The market should be further regulated and play a greater role in the allocation of public resources. In particular, a more mature system should be set up for the transfer of the land use rights of state-owned land and the mining rights of state-owned mines to prevent the intervention of administrative powers in violation of relevant rules. Crackdown will be tightened against malpractices threatening market order or public interests, including manufacturing and selling fake products and cheating and swindling, to maintain fair competition and good market order. New ways will be developed to improve social management with greater emphasis on delivering public services by providing more public resources and building a service-oriented government.

Second, government structure and organization should be optimized. The reform of consolidating government institutions will continue, under which administrative institutions with more comprehensive roles and greater authoritativeness will be established in the principle of building a leaner and more integrated and efficient government. It will provide the basis for the gradual setup of a system of administrative institutions with well-designed functions and greater efficacy. Reforms on administrative strata should also be advanced steadily to gradually compress the administrative tiers. Relations between the central and local governments should be straightened out for better definition of their powers, functions and responsibilities. The powers and responsibilities of local governments at different tiers under the provincial level should be determined to give full play to their initiatives and creativity,

Third, law-based governance should be implemented. Relevant legal systems, especially the administrative legal system, should be improved so that laws and regulations will better govern the relations between the government and the market, businesses and society, and the government will perform its functions, such as managing economic and social affairs in accordance with laws, regulations, and due systems and procedures. Laws and systems must be in place to supervise government powers, responsibilities and personnel.

Major Tasks in Strengthening Beijing's Strategic Position as a Capital City

The *Outlines for Coordinated Development of the Beijing-Tianjin-Hebei Region* (the *Outline*) states that to strengthen Beijing's strategic position as a capital city means to relive Beijing of functions nonessential to its role as China's capital, create an economic structure centering on high-end, precision and sophisticated industries, build the Beijing Municipal Administrative Center (BMC) and turn the city into a national innovation center.

I. Reliving Beijing of functions nonessential to its role as China's capital

To relieve Beijing's functions nonessential to its role as China's capital is a core step and the top priority in implementing the national strategy of coordinated development of Beijing, Tianjin and Hebei region. The strategy is aimed at tackling issues associated with megacities[1] by relieving Beijing from those unnecessary functions it is burdened with. Recent years have witnessed heavy pressure on local resources and the environment caused by rapid urbanization and increasing population, which has largely constrained Beijing's sustainable development. According to the *Outline*, the following four areas will be the priority in function reallocation: production and processing in general and high-end manufacturing sectors with low comparative advantages; regional logistic centers and wholesale markets; some educational and public health services; and some administrative and public service agencies.

Urban function reallocation is a sophisticated project for Beijing that requires long-term planning. The *Outline* divides this task into three phases, namely, capping the number of functions and starting the transfer of existing nonessential functions

[1] *problems arising from urbanization.

by 2015; breakthroughs in relieving existing functions by 2017; and considerable progress in relieving Beijing of functions nonessential to its role as China's capital by 2020. To ensure that the targets are met on schedule, Beijing will formulate annual plans and push for their implementation in all relevant fields.

II. Create an economic structure centering on high-end, precision and sophisticated industries

To encourage industries to embark on a new way of development, including the upgrading and transformation of the manufacturing sector and establishing a high-end, precision and sophisticated industrial layout in line with Beijing's functions as the capital city, efforts should be made to change the drivers of industrial development and economic growth and build an economic structure featuring high-end, precision and sophisticated industries. Innovation chains will be knitted with industrial chains to improve the industrial innovation system, with enterprises as the main players in an effort to promote innovation-driven development. Such an industrial layout is necessary in the context of the new normal when industries are transforming the growth model to move up the value chain. It should be supported by new policies on industries, service models and management mechanisms.

III. Building the Beijing Municipal Center (BMC)

Building the BMC is important because it seeks to optimize the spatial structure, tackle the challenges associated with megacities and expand development spaces for Beijing and at the same time promotes coordinated development for Beijing, Tianjin and Hebei and explores new ways of developing economically and demographically dense areas. At the meeting on May 27th, 2016, the Political Bureau of the CPC Central Committee discussed the planning and construction of the BMC and efforts to bolster the coordinated development of Beijing, Tianjin and Hebei. Decisions were made to press ahead with the work in accordance with the law on urban development to realize new, coordinated, green and open development for all. International standards should be upheld while Chinese features are embodied in carrying out the work. The BMC should be designed and built with high quality, bringing with it historic significance and aesthetic senses. A clean and green eco-city with a network of waters, woods and close-knit urban neighborhoods, the BMC will showcase a world-class harmonious and livable city and a new type of urbanization as well as the coordinated development of Beijing, Tianjin and Hebei. A people-centered approach should be adopted to meet public expectations. World-class energy conservation technologies, materials, processes and standards should be used to build Beijing into a smart city, a sponge city and an eco-city with sizable forests. Overall planning is needed in arranging production, living and green spaces, offering people more convenience for their work, life, leisure, commuting, education and health care. The BMC should characterize Chinese culture and embrace elements of other cultures. The meeting also emphasized the importance of proper planning before construction on the basis of the city's positioning. An overall spatial structure should be in place at first, and urban development should be strictly controlled. Boundaries for urban development and the red line for ecological protection must converge. To improve urban morphology, more open spaces are needed to make the city greener and smarter and more livable and accordable. New policies, institutions and mechanisms in support of this work must be in place.

IV. Fostering a national innovation center

Beijing is also strategically positioned as a national innovation center. It will implement major plans on innovation at multiple levels and in various areas to turn itself into an innovation center of global influence by 2020 and lead the efforts of transforming China into an innovative country. Efforts will be made in the following fields. First, we implement the plan of building a knowledge innovation center and a source of original innovation. Efforts should be made to develop scientific infrastructure, launch applied and basic research and frontier technology development ahead of others and build three science cities, namely, Zhongguancun Science City, Huairou Science City and Future Science City. Greater support should be given to "big science" projects, including research on brain sciences, quantum communication and nanosciences. Beijing will invest in its capability for original innovation on its way to become a world-renowned science center. Second, we advance the project of leapfrog development in innovation and build the national innovation pilot zone. The project covers eight areas, including the new generation of information technology, biomedicine, energy resources, new energy vehicles, energy conservation, strategic and competitive materials, digital manufacturing and rail transit, and aims to support the growth of high-end, precision and sophisticated industries in Beijing. Third, supporting the strategy of regional coordinated development and opening a new dimension in coordinated, innovative and open development for shared benefits. Beijing, Tianjin and Hebei will witness the establishment of a cooperative system with high efficiency and connectivity as well as a regional center for coordinated innovation. Opportunities presented by the Belt and Road Initiative for greater connection with the rest of the world will be fully utilized for attracting global innovation resources. Fourth, gathering high-end innovative resources from the world and nurturing a global pacesetter for openness and innovation. To attract more external resources, Beijing will encourage local generation of cutting-edge technologies on its way to become a world center of technology transfer. To extend the city's global reach, local enterprises will be encouraged to set up overseas R&D centers, file more applications of proprietary IPR abroad and take part in international standard setting to remain competitive in the global industrial chains. Fifth, deepening the reform for the creation of a better environment for innovation and entrepreneurship. Further reform will be carried out to give greater incentives to innovation. A large number of high-caliber innovators of various professions will be nurtured. The pilot zone for all-round innovation and reform will be constructed at a faster pace. This will help create a more enabling ecosystem and greater motivation for innovation and entrepreneurship in society as a whole.

V. Tackling the problem associated with megacities

On his inspection tour in Beijing, General Secretary Xi Jinping pointed out that Beijing was, to some extent, wrestling with challenges commonly seen in megacities, which is mainly reflected by the increasing conflict between available resources and the environment and a rising population.

Beijing's population is growing too fast. By 2015, the number of permanent residents in Beijing reached 21.71 million, higher than the expected limit of approximately 18 million set for 2020. Beijing has become the second largest city in China (only after Shanghai with a population of 24.256 million). Since 2011, an average of 500,000 residents have been added to the population in Beijing each year, almost the size of a large city abroad. This has imposed a formidable burden on Beijing.

The number of motor vehicles in Beijing stood at 5.61 million in 2014. A total of 44.54 million trips are made each day in the downtown area. The average speed on the road network during morning and evening rushing hours is 25.8 km/h, with nearly 2 h of continuous congestion on workdays. Beijing tops the country in terms of community time per person. The functions are too concentrated in central areas, which account for 71% of industrial activities and 71.8% of the workforce in Beijing. If the trend continues, the central areas will only see a worsening of traffic congestion.

As a city that lacks water and energy resources, Beijing is unable to afford too many functions and industries. In 2015, the total amount of water resources in Beijing dropped to 2.16 billion cubic meters, with only 100 cubic meters of water resources per capita, less than 1/20 of the national average. 70% of electricity, 40% of refined oil, 98% of coal and 100% of natural gas supply in Beijing are not locally generated. If Beijing continues to develop big and all-inclusive industries, the normal functioning and even the security and stability of the city will be affected.

Air pollution remains severe. The air quality in Beijing is lagging far behind the new national standards. PM 2.5 tops the list in air pollution control. Garbage disposal and water environment improvement still require huge efforts. Further innovation and technological advances are needed to reduce emissions and energy waste. A proper order is needed in environmental management.

Measures in the Institutional Reform of Beijing in the New Circumstances

To fulfill such tasks as relieving Beijing of functions nonessential to its role as China's capital, tackling megacity challenges and fostering high-end, precision and sophisticated industries, the government and the market must each play their due roles and strengthen coordination. The market should play a more decisive role in industrial coordination, corporate innovation, flow of production factors, resource allocation and other economic activities. The government is expected to better plan, coordinate and promote the development of infrastructure, public services, ecological progress, etc. Following General Secretary Xi's guidance and instructions on Beijing's development, the municipal government has endeavored to reform the administrative system in accordance with the capital's strategic positioning to provide a sound institutional framework for both the government and the market to perform their roles well and make progress on priority tasks.

I. Transforming government functions through deeper institutional reform
1. A better institutional setup

Aiming at transforming government functions, all-round efforts have been made to further reform the municipal government agencies and guide the reform in government bodies at district/county levels. Beijing has taken the lead in building regulatory systems on food and drug safety at the municipal, district/county and township/subdistrict levels. It has completed the consolidation and establishment of a number of municipal-level government agencies, including the health and family planning commission, the press, publication, radio and television administration, and the government service center. Reform has been completed for the municipal administration of reeducation and correction. Real-estate registration bodies and their responsibilities have been reshaped. The municipal commission of tourism development, the state-owned cultural assets supervision and management office and the municipal hospitals administration have been set up. Agriculture-related agencies at the county/district level and their responsibilities have also been readjusted. The township-level institutional reform has been largely completed. Municipal institutions for deliberation and coordination have been streamlined. The reform has further improved the organizational structures and functions of all government bodies in Beijing.

2. Major breakthroughs in the reform of administrative approval systems

Since 2013, Beijing has achieved marked results in streamlining items for administrative approval and optimizing relevant procedures in response to public concerns. Government authorities at the municipal level have canceled or delegated 438 administrative approval items or 45% of the total number, meeting the target set by the central government of cutting such items by 1/3 within the current government's term. Approval procedures have been improved citywide. The time frame for approvals of investment projects was narrowed by a large margin. Government services have become more convenient. Over 740 approval and service items under 40 municipal-level departments were transferred to the Municipal Government Service Center. Initial outcomes have been produced in releasing the government's power list. The powers of the municipal government bodies have been basically defined. Under the new category-based model, the list of general responsibilities and the list of specific responsibilities on key and thorny issues that require efforts across departments and administrative levels were published, thus forming a sound power and responsibility system for the municipal government and all its departments. Significant improvements have been made in such key reform areas as clearing non-administrative approval items, regulating intermediary agencies, and building on-line platforms for approval and regulation of investment projects. Initiatives were made, and pilot programs were launched on administrative streamlining, mass entrepreneurship and innovation in Zhongguancun. A sound system of prompt disclosure of the list of powers and responsibilities is in place for the government at the municipal and district/county levels. Cancellations and readjustments of non-administrative approval items designated by the central government and enforced at the municipal level have been strictly implemented, and a similar approach is taken for a municipal list of administrative approvals enforced at the district/county level. All-round rectification and regulation on licenses and certificates has been carried out.

II. Supporting sound development of the capital city through institutional renovation

1. Strengthening institutional buildup to tackle megacity challenges

To help Beijing better play its role as China's capital and deliver the "four services" well, the new Dongcheng District, which covers the old Dongcheng and Chongwen Districts, and the new Xicheng District, which covers the old Xicheng and Xuanwu Districts, were established, and 177 division-level authorities and 1357 administrative positions were streamlined. Adjustments were made to the areas of jurisdiction and the administrative system of Dongxiaokou, Changping District. Mechanisms were established to promote the coordinated development of Beijing, Tianjin and Hebei as well as emergency responses to heavy air pollution. Overall planning for improving urban management at the municipal, district/county and subdistrict/township levels was produced, and pilot reforms were carried out in Shijingshan District. The law enforcement system on urban management was further improved, and explorations were made in building an "all-inclusive" urban management system. Stronger institutions and mechanisms were in place for air pollution control and prevention, illegal building demolition, rectification of overloaded vehicles, traffic congestion mitigation and removal of unlicensed taxis. More resources have been allocated to rail transport safety, the South-North Water Diversion Project, energy conservation, emission reduction and the handling of the aftermath of the "7·21" natural disaster, thus providing sound institutional support for better performance of urban functions. Efforts have been made to deepen the reform of the regulatory and law enforcement system with pilot programs launched in areas such as water supply and transport, as well as in Shijingshan, Mentougou and Pinggu Districts. The government has sent more law enforcement officers to work at the primary level, which has had an impact. Law enforcement agencies of emergency response, environmental protection and land and resources have been strengthened.

2. Reinforcing institutions and mechanisms to uphold security and stability

Actions have been taken to improve and strengthen the safety and security regulation responsibilities of municipal authorities. A municipal security regulation mechanism of full coverage has been set up. Further steps have been taken to promote institutional building on social services and management and give full play to the role of leading social organizations. The government has improved the system for maintaining law and order and social stability, adjusted the responsibilities of relevant agencies, provided more resources to law enforcement and judicial bodies and strengthened regulation over migrants and house rental. The municipal police system has been readjusted to improve staffing and human resource allocation. The headquarters were streamlined, and more policemen were sent to the primary-level posts in key areas and places requiring special attention. A full-fledged Internet administration and external communication mechanism was put in place with the establishment of the municipal cyberspace administration office. Institutional improvements have also been made to combat terrorism and ensure social stability. More resources have been poured into emergency response, complaint handling and social relief to strengthen support for maintaining stability and security in Beijing.

3. Reinforcing institutions and mechanisms for innovation-driven development

Improvements have been made in the institutions and mechanisms for managing the Zhongguancun National Innovation Demonstration Zone, the Future Science City and county/district-level industrial functions zones. A coordination mechanism was set up for the planning of the capital economic circle. Better coordination is in place for such work as afforestation projects, IPR protection, Capital Steel high-end comprehensive industrial services and quality standardization. Departments in charge of economic planning and layout and SME administration with similar functions have been merged, and the system for rural economic management has been adjusted. Quality service was put in place for work concerning overall economic and financial affairs, business services, financial risk prevention, integrated development of radio and television networks, telecommunication networks and the Internet, the China International Fair for Trade in Services (CIFTIS) and the World Tourism Cities Confederation. Governing bodies in functional zones have been set up to promote the economic growth of various districts and counties. Support has been provided for the construction of key municipal projects, such as the Beijing Garden Expo Park, the Museum of Chinese Garden and Landscape Architecture and Beijing Daxing International Airport.

To help deepen the reform across the board, Beijing has set up the Office of the Leading Group for Comprehensively Deepening Reforms under the Municipal CPC Central Committee. Corresponding mechanisms have been established in governments at the county/district level to strengthen the leadership of the reform. As part of the reform on the institutions of disciplinary inspection, the leadership and working mechanisms and the structure of disciplinary inspection and supervision at municipal and district/county levels have been improved. The capacity of the inspection institutions and the manpower of the municipal disciplinary commission have been strengthened. All government authorities are under the scrutiny of inspection bodies dispatched by the commission, and seven more inspection bodies have been set up. The Beijing Intellectual Property Court and courts and procuratorates working across administrative jurisdictions have been established as part of the efforts to reform the judicial system.

III. Enhancing public services and achieving initial success in the reform and management of public institutions

1. Completing the classification of public institutions

More efforts have been made in clearing and regulating public institutions. A total of 655 public institutions were canceled, and 6714 positions were retrieved under government subsidies. A total of 96.9% of public institutions have been classified, making Beijing a national forerunner in such work. The reform of profit-making public institutions has deepened. More than 30 publishing houses engaging in business other than political news coverage, art troupes and public institutions under SASAC have been transformed into enterprises. Acting upon the instructions of the central disciplinary inspection groups, 144 government training centers operating as public institutions in Beijing have been canceled or merged. The establishment of public institutions at all levels is under stricter regulation, and their staffing and structures have become more balanced.

2. Exploring new ways of managing public institutions

Beijing was among the first in China to release the Opinion on Innovative Management of Public Institutions and Acceleration of Reform of Public Institutions of Different Categories, which proposes tasks and concrete measures concerning public institution management, such as adopting new approaches to general staffing management, services delivery for public good and personnel management in nonprofit public institutions. These measures, together with steps taken to improve their corporate governance structures, have been piloted in over ten public institutions.

3. Improving registration and regulation of public institutions

New registration methods have been developed, such as online registration and application processing. Work is underway toward simplifying registration requirements and procedures and significantly narrowing the time frame for license registration and modification. The requirements for registered capital and forms of public notification have changed. Public notification is now free of charge. Annual business inspections have been canceled in favor of annual reports. The Beijing Enterprise Credit Information website was opened together with the systems for handling complaints and tip-offs and for reviewing, regulating and evaluating the annual reports. This has improved the *interim* and *ex post* regulatory system for registration of public institutions.

IV. Keeping staffing size under strict control and making it more appropriate, law-based and better regulated

1. Putting the size of staffing under strict control

By making sure that the number of people on the government payroll will go down and putting a limit on staffing in public institutions, Beijing is working hard to control staffing while fulfilling the goals for various undertakings. The government has followed the principle of capping the current size of staffing and putting it to better use. It has made dynamic readjustment to administrative staffing at all levels and the staffing for public security agencies, procuratorates, courts and judicature in combination with the changes in areas of administrative jurisdictions and reforms in township and public institutions. Checks and inspections have been carried out on government staffing through regular joint meetings and supervision mechanisms. Violations of disciplines and regulations were seriously dealt with to ensure that the size of institutions and staffing were kept within the limit during the "12th Five-year Plan" period (2011–2015).

2. Finding new ways for staffing management

New approaches have been implemented in function-based structural management of staffing. The municipal organizational structure of "six horizontals" and "eight verticals" for the Party, government and mass organizations were applied to staffing management. New models of staffing and personnel management have been tried to meet the needs for manpower in public security, education and public health institutions. The staffing of public security agencies, procuratorates, courts and judicatures is under dynamic management. The public security agencies have been equipped with more auxiliary police with administrative duties who are under proper regulation. Five municipal hospitals are piloting the quota control of staffing for public institutions. Similar programs have been in place in Beijing Tsinghua Changgeng Hospital, the Capital Library of China and other nonprofit public institutions. Government hospitals are looking into ways to abolish administrative rankings, recruit non-staff employees and outsource services to make better use of human resources.

Bibliography

Compilation and Translation Bureau of the Central Committee of the Communist Party of China. *Collected works of Karl Marx and Friedrich Engels* (Vol. 10). Beijing: People's Publishing House (2009).

David, H. (2016). *A brief history of neoliberalism*, 16th ed. Shanghai: Shanghai Translation Publishing House.

Decision of the Beijing municipal government on advancing the reform of administrative approvals for local investment projects. August 26th, 2013.

Decision of the Beijing municipal government on deepening the institutional reform. April 23th, 2015.

Decision of the general office of the Beijing municipal government on creating new models of management for public institutions and advancing reforms of public institutions based on their categories. May 14th, 2015.

Decision of the general offices of the Beijing municipal government on standardizing government administration and service with more transparency. June 25th, 2015.

Guidebook on the decision of the CPC central committee on several important issues of comprehensively deepening reform. Beijing: People's Publishing House (2013).

Notice of the Beijing municipal government on establishing the power list and the responsibility list for municipal departments. December 6th, 2015.

Notice of the Beijing municipal government on canceling, adjusting and undertaking some administrative approval items. December 9th, 2015.

Notice of the general office of the Beijing municipal government on releasing the responsibility lists on air pollution control and prevention and other specific tasks. March 3th, 2016.

Notification on formulating the 13th five-year plan for the national economic and social development of the People's Republic of China. Beijing: People's Publishing House (2009).

Plan on simplifying and improving public service procedures and providing convenience for businesses and individuals in Beijing. March 8th, 2016.

Wang, H. (2016). Effectively relieving Beijing of functions nonessential to its role as China's capital. *China Economic & Trade Herald, 07*, 55–56.

Yao, L. (2014). Performance evaluation of government's public services-taking Beijing as an example. *Sci-Tech Information Development & Economy, 24*(12), 142–144.

Streamlining Government Administration and Advancing Reform in the Power Sector

Guangyi Tong, Junli Wang, and Haichao Ma

Achievements and Challenges of China's Power Industry

Electric power is a basic industry bearing the national economy and people's well-being. Power supply and security are critical to the national security strategy and the overall economic and social development. During the 12th Five-Year-Plan period (2011–2015), the power industry registered fast growth and scored remarkable achievements as China topped the world in installed power generation capacity, hydropower, wind power and solar power generation, coal power generation and the size of the power grid. China significantly enhanced its capability of power supply to better meet the demands of the national economy and social development.

The world energy landscape is undergoing profound adjustment, and China's economy has entered the phase of a "new normal". The rising environmental and resource constraints have presented new opportunities and challenges for the power industry. For China, the 13th Five-Year Plan period is a decisive period to complete the building of a moderately prosperous society in all respects, a crucial period for deepening the reform and a period of important opportunity for accelerating the transformation and development of the power industry. In the new development stage, the CPC Central Committee and the State Council put forward the five-point development philosophy of innovation-driven, coordinated, green, open and shared development, the strategy of energy development of "four revolutions and one cooperation" and the energy development policy that highlights conservation, cleanness and safety, which provide overall guidance for the sustainable and healthy development of the power industry.

G. Tong (✉)
Electricity Affairs Department, National Energy Administration, Beijing, China

J. Wang
School of Mathematical Science, Capital Normal University, Beijing, China

H. Ma
Guanghua School of Management, Peking University, Beijing, China

Y. Li and Z. Cheng (eds.), *The Chinese Path Toward a Leaner Government*,
https://doi.org/10.1007/978-981-19-6718-4_23

I. Achievements

The power industry has reached a new level of development. During the 12th Five-Year Plan period, its growth rate accelerated, and a number of indicators ranked first in the world. By the end of 2015, the total power consumption reached 5.55 trillion kwh, the installed power generation capacity was 1.51 billion kw, of which hydropower stood at 320 million kw (including 230 million kw of pumped storage), wind power registered 129 million kw, solar power reached 430 million kw, nuclear power was 280 million kw, and thermal power was 990 million kw (including 884 million kw of coal-fired power and 660 million kw of gas-fired power). The transfer of power across provinces and regions reached 200 million kw nationwide, including 140 million kw of power transmitted from west to east. China's 220 kV and above AC lines totaled 610,000 km, with a substation capacity of 3.1 billion kva. Electricity accounts for 25.8% of the total terminal energy consumption. China's per capita installed capacity was approximately 1.1 kw, and its per capita electricity consumption was 4080 kw, both exceeding the world average.

During the 12th Five-Year Plan period, improvements were made in the key framework of the six regional power grids in North, Central, East, Northeast, Northwest and South China and provincial grids, together with urban distribution networks and rural power supply conditions, to basically ensure people's access to electricity use. The quality of the power supply was improved significantly. The reliability rates of the power supply in urban and rural areas were 99.967% and 99.878%, respectively, and the qualification rates of integrated voltage were 99.982% and 98.808%, respectively.

New achievements were made in structural adjustment. During the 12th Five-Year Plan period, the development of non-fossil power sources in China accelerated significantly. China's hydropower capacity steadily increased, with a total of 110 million kw put into operation, accounting for 21.2% of the country's installed power generation capacity. Wind power is growing rapidly, rising to 8.5% from 3.1% in 2010, making it the third largest power source in China. Photovoltaic power generation achieved leapfrog development, with a cumulative increase of 41 million kw. China's installed and operational capacity of nuclear power ranked fourth in the world, with 26.96 million kw under construction, more than any other country.

The structure of coal power generating units was steadily improved with a higher proportion of supercritical and ultra-supercritical units. A total of 78.6% of them were units each with a capacity of 300,000 kw or above, and 41% were units each with a capacity of 600,000 kw or above.

Energy conservation and emission reduction reached a new level. China continued to phase out outdated coal-fired power plants and pushed for their upgrading and transformation for energy conservation. It closed down a total of 28 million kw of small thermal power plants, upgraded some 400 million kw for energy conservation, and upgraded some 170 million kw of plants for ultralow emissions. The average coal consumption of the country's coal-fired power generating units was reduced to 315 g of standard coal per kwh, reaching the world's advanced level. The carbon dioxide emission intensity of coal-fired power generating units was reduced to approximately

780 g per kwh. Over the past five years, the reduction reached 18 g of standard coal per kwh, saving over 70 million tons of standard coal annually and a total of over 170 million tons of carbon dioxide emissions accumulatively.

Strict standards for the discharge of air pollutants were implemented for coal-fired units. The coal-fired units were equipped with desulfurization devices. The proportion of denitrified units reached 92%. In 2015, the total emissions of major air pollutants such as sulfur dioxide and nitrogen oxide in the power industry were reduced by 4.25 million tons and 5.01 million tons, respectively, over 2010, exceeding the targets set in the 12th Five-Year Plan.

II. Challenges

While registering fast growth, the power industry also faced challenges. During the 12th Five-Year Plan period, power supply gradually shifted from a state of overall balance and tight supply in some regions to a state of relatively abundant supply and even surplus in some regions. While non-fossil power grew quickly, some areas are closing the door on wind power, solar power and hydropower development. It was difficult to encourage wind power consumption in northeast, north and northwest China, and Yunnan and Sichuan Provinces are giving up on hydropower. In some areas, the capacity for power grids of peak-time adjustment is quite weak, especially for those in northern China during the winter heating period, which further aggravates the imbalance of non-fossil energy supply and demand. The power equipment and transmission system utilization rate is not high, and thermal power utilization hours continue to decline. The structure of the regional power grid needs to be optimized, and the transmission network is operating under heavy pressure and rising safety risks. The power supply reliability of the urban power distribution network needs to be improved, while the power supply capacity of the rural power network is insufficient. The system and mechanism for the power market to play a decisive role in the allocation of resources have not yet been established, and the regulation policies for the optimization and transformation of the power structure need to be further strengthened.

The 13th Five-Year Plan period is crucial for China to complete the building of a moderately prosperous society in all respects, in which the government needs to take on hard issues in deepening the reform while seizing the opportunity for accelerating the transformation and development of the power industry. In the context of the profound adjustment of the world energy landscape, relatively abundant supply and demand in China, and increasing environmental and resource constraints, the electric power industry is facing new developments and challenges.

Easing of electricity supply. During the 13th Five-Year Plan period (2016–2020), as the economy entered a new normal, with shifts in the speed and structure of the economy as well as in the growth drivers, the growth rate of electricity consumption slowed down significantly. The power generation equipment built in the 12th Five-Year Plan period has been put into operation, resulting in the oversupply of electricity in some regions and low overall cost efficiency of the power system and utilization hours of equipment. China has moved into a new phase of steady and abundant power supply.

Cleaner energy mix. Preventing and controlling air pollution and responding to climate change remain daunting tasks. Eco-environmental constraints are getting tighter. China has made the commitment to the international community that the proportion of non-fossil energy consumption will account for approximately 15% by 2020. It is imperative to accelerate the development and utilization of clean energy and the clean utilization of fossil energy, and it is extremely urgent to build a clean, low-carbon, safe and efficient modern power system.

Intelligent power system. To promote the supply-side reform of the electric power industry, it is necessary to improve the supply model to enhance power supply efficiency and the flexibility and intelligence of the system operation. The consumption of large-scale grid-connected wind and photovoltaic power and the need for safe operation of nuclear power call for greater flexibility and adaptability of the power system. The construction of an efficient and intelligent power system is urgently required to comprehensively enhance the interaction between power suppliers and users, improve the collaborative ability of power grids, realize the parallel development of centralized and distributed power supply and collaboration between conventional and new energy power generation, enhance peak regulation capacity, and improve the response level on the load side.

Market-based mechanisms. A new round of power system reform will transform the function setup and profit model of power grid enterprises and promote rational investment, construction and operation of power grids. A market-based electricity pricing mechanism has gradually taken shape. New forms of business models are emerging. The market has begun to play a decisive role in resource allocation, and market demand represents a new direction for the development of the power industry.

Review of the Theory of the Government-Market Relationship

The aim of streamlining administration and delegating power is to reduce administrative intervention and let the market play a more important role in the allocation of resources. Its theoretical basis is, in essence, how to handle the relationship between the government and the market and strike a balance between the "visible hand" and the "invisible hand". To better understand the theory, there is a need to systematically review the theoretical evolution of the government-market relationship and the lessons it brings.

I. Theoretical evolution of the government-market relationship

In general, the economic theories on government-market relationships evolve through four stages.

1. Laissez-faire

Adam Smith, founder of classical economics, and other early researchers of economics advocated for a laissez-faire economy where the market is responsible for resource allocation. They held that the government should not interfere too much in the economy. During the industrial revolution in particular, the western bourgeoisie believed that the "invisible hand" in the market could make reasonable allocation and proper use of resources, and the government should play the role of a "night watchman", whose roles could be limited to maintaining market order and providing public welfare.

2. Government interventionism

From 1929 to 1933, the capitalist society experienced the unprecedented Great Depression, the limitations of laissez-faire were exposed, and economists recognized the need for government intervention in the market. In 1936, Maynard Keynes, the father of modern macroeconomics, published his magnum opus *The General Theory of Employment, Interest, and Money*. Keynes believed that laissez-faire could not eliminate the economic crisis and advocated that the government should intervene in the economy, which was later known as Keynesianism. The theory effectively solved the economic crisis in the capitalist society at that time but also resulted in the rapid expansion of government functions and budgets in many countries.

3. Neoliberalism

After the end of the 1970s, a new economic phenomenon called stagflation appeared in capitalist society. In the face of the new challenges brought about by the stagflation, government intervention failed expectations, and the "Keynesian" economists were unable to find a solution. A large number of economists called for the return of the free market, and this was named "neoliberalism". Neoliberalism opposes the government's all-around economic intervention and seeks to strike a balance between the government and the market, which provides a theoretical basis for the roles of the government and the market.

4. New Keynesianism

In the early 1990s, low inflation and high unemployment occurred in many countries, which was unable to be addressed by neoliberalist theory. This triggered the emergence and development of the "New Keynesianism". The "New Keynesianism" economists inherited the core idea of traditional "Keynesianism" and absorbed some of the theories of neoclassical economics. On the basis of summarizing the practical experience of the macroeconomy since the 1980s, they put forward a series of new propositions on state intervention in the economy.

II. Sorting out the relationship between the Chinese government and the market

1. The era of an omnipotent government

For a long period of time after the founding of the People's Republic, China implemented a highly centralized planned economy system that helped restore economic activities and national development. At that time, the government had great power, and there was no place for the role of the market. All economic activities of production and distribution and even the market were under the control of the government, which had unprecedented power. As a result, there was no vitality in the economy to speak of.

2. Transitional period

China has been exploring the market economy for more than 20 years since the start of the reform and opening up. The government functions have been adjusted as required by the economic reform. In transitioning from serving the planned economy to serving the market economy, the government's functions have changed from all-around intervention to limited intervention. Some power has been gradually delegated to the market. However, in the early stage of the development of China's socialist market economy, as a full-fledged market economic system was not in place, the government still carried out conditional intervention in many areas. Under a general framework of "big government, small market", the role of the market and government intervention often bumped into each other, creating a number of issues.

3. Exploration period

China is still in the primary stage of the socialist market economy, and the market economic system needs to be further developed and improved. The *Decision of the CPC Central Committee on Some Major Issues Concerning Comprehensively Deepening the Reform* adopted at the third Plenary Session of the 18th CPC Central Committee set forth the guiding ideology, objectives, tasks and major principles for comprehensively deepening the reform and pointed out that the market should play a decisive role in resource allocation and that the government should better play its role. In the era when China's economy is in a new normal and supply-side structural reform deepens in all aspects, there is a need to continue to explore how to better handle the relationship between the government and the market.

III. Inspiration from the development of theories on government-market relationships

1. Identifying areas for government intervention

The areas for government intervention form the boundary of government power. A clear delineation of the boundary for government intervention is conducive to playing a better role of the government while avoiding excessive intervention in the market. In the field where the market is mature, the government should step aside and let the market play a decisive role in resource allocation. In areas where the market is unable to function well, the government should intervene in time to fill the gap. The relationship between the government and the market is dynamic. The scope, content and method of government intervention should vary in light of different stages of the market economy.

2. Establishing the concept of a government of limited responsibilities

A government with limited responsibilities means that the level and scope of government power should be somewhat checked. It is the prerequisite for a functioning and effective government. Only when the government knows where its limits are can it effectively perform its duties within the boundary of responsibility. The market economy calls for the establishment of a government of limited responsibilities as well as appropriate restrictions to government power and administrative intervention to reduce undue intervention in the market. An effective market and a functioning government are the two fundamental guarantees for the healthy development of the socialist market economy.

Historical Review of China's Electric Power System Reform

China's electric power system reform has been carried out for more than 30 years. It can be roughly divided into four stages, namely, easing market access for multiple market players, separating government administration from enterprise management to break administrative monopoly, separating power plants from grid companies and core business from noncore business according to market rules, and promoting market-oriented reform in an all-round manner. The basic direction of the reform in these four stages is to give more play to the role of the market, but the effect thus far has not been satisfactory, and issues and challenges have propped up one after another. Now, with the launch of a new round of power system reform, the reform that has been stalled for nearly a decade is back on the agenda. To provide a better understanding of the philosophy behind China's electric power system reform, there is a need to present a comprehensive review of the course of China's electric power system reform by stages.

I. Easing market access for multiple market players (1985–1994)

The first stage of China's electric power system reform covers the period from 1985 to 1994. The main objectives of this stage of reform were to solve the power shortage, encourage private capital to invest in electric power and promote diversification of power investment. The main feature of the reform in this stage was the relaxation of market access and the license granting to several power companies.

In 1985, China began to reform its electric power investment administrative system to generate funding for the electricity sector. In accordance with the State Council's *Interim Provisions on Encouraging Fundraising for the Electricity Industry and the Diversifying Electricity Pricing* (Guo Fa [1985] No. 72, or in short, Document No. 72), local governments, departments and enterprises were encouraged to raise funds for developing electric power. Investment in electric power would be gradually shifted from government budget expropriations to bank loans, and pricing could vary for some electric power. This round of reform broke the monopoly of power generation and laid the foundation for the subsequent separation of power plants from power grids.

However, the reforms also produced some negative effects. First, although the "cost premium" pricing model helped recover the investment cost of new power plants, it also fueled the expansion of inefficient enterprises, and as a result, the electricity price could not reflect market competition on the power generation side. Second, the electricity price system was a chaotic mixture of mandatory and reference prices. The reference price followed the grandfathering clauses, which resulted in nine different prices. The price formation mechanism featuring "one plant, one price", "one machine, one price", cost-based calculation and case-by-case approval caused chaos in the electricity pricing system and hindered the reform of the electricity pricing system to some extent.

II. Separating government functions from enterprise management and breaking the administrative monopoly (1994–2002)

The second stage of the reform ran from 1994 to 2002. The excessive supply of electricity to some extent made it necessary to introduce the market mechanism in the formation of the trading model for electricity. The main feature of the reform in this stage is the separation of government administration from enterprise management to break administrative monopoly and build a market-based electricity power trading mechanism.

In 1996, the State Council approved the *Reform Plan of the Ministry of Electricity* and decided to set up the State Electric Power Company while keeping the Ministry of Electricity during the transitional period. In 1997, the National Electric Power Company was established. In March 1998, the Ministry of Electricity was abolished. To put in place a market-based mechanism, the separation of power plants from power grids and competitive on-grid bidding began in 1998 to solve the problem of unfair access to the power grids for standalone power plants, guide power plants to reduce costs and improve power generation efficiency.

There were also some problems in this round of reform, such as issues between power plants and grids and barriers between provinces. First, the pilot program of plant grid separation did not achieve the expected results, as it only separated power plants directly affiliated with power companies from the power grids in accounting instead of the asset link. It is still difficult for standalone power plants to have fair access to power grids. Second, local protectionism spread wide. The reform dismantled the wider regional power grid layout in favor of the provincial grids, which led to segmentation of the power market and erection of barriers between provinces.

III. Separating power plants from grids and core business from noncore business according to market rules (2002–2015)

The third stage of China's electric power system reform aimed to push forward market-oriented reform in an all-around manner. The main focus was the separation of power plants from power grids and core business from noncore business of electric power companies, establishment of standalone power transmission and power distribution companies, and price bidding for putting electricity on grid.

In 2002, the State Council issued the *Notice on the Reform Plan of the Electric Power System* (Guo Fa [2002] No. 5, referred to as Document No. 5). The goal was clear: separating grids from power plants, core business from noncore business and power transmission from distribution, and price bidding for on-grid electricity. The reform successfully separated grids from plants and divested the noncore business of power companies. The State Power Company split into two power grid companies, five power generation groups and four power business groups providing supporting services (which were later consolidated into two corporate groups). This marked the beginning of the market-oriented reform for the electric power sector.

However, the electric power system reform was more complex and difficult than expected, and the progress in building a market-based system was slow. Document No. 5 required that during the tenth Five-Year Plan period, power distribution should go with separate accounting by the financial department of power companies. However, the policy met with severe resistance. Separating the power distribution from power transmission and launching price bidding for on-grid electricity were basically stalled.

IV. Foster market players and advance the market-based reform in the electricity sector (2015 onward)

China's electric power system reform entered the fourth stage in 2015. The goal is to foster diversified market entities and further deepen the reform of the electricity market.

There are three main factors that hinder the process of power market reform. First, monopoly blocks competitive market transactions and makes it impossible for sellers and buyers to meet each other. Second, there is a lack of price-sensitive players in the market. Third, supporting mechanisms have yet to take shape. China is fighting an uphill in building a competitive power market, as relevant systems and mechanisms are not yet in place and challenges keep cropping up, which call for intensified reform efforts. Based on the comprehensive analysis of the history, experience and progress of power market reform, there is no other way but to pursue China-style market reform in the electric power sector.

On March 15, 2015, the CPC Central Committee and the State Council issued the *Opinions on Further Deepening the Reform of the Electric Power System* (Zhong Fa [2015] No. 9, or Document No. 9). As a general strategic guideline for advancing the reform of the electric power system, it places emphasis on market competition for power companies and better regulation of power transmission and distribution, thus opening a new chapter of the reform.

The new power market reform plan should follow the direction set in Document No. 5. Efforts should be made to straighten out the power grid system, reform the electricity price formation mechanism, foster market competition in transactions, cultivate diversified market players, and launch pilot reform programs. Breakthroughs of the new round of electric power reform should be made by changing the monopoly status and profit model of power grid enterprises and turning them into power transmission and distribution service providers. Under such settings, the government is responsible for planning and allocating power resources nationwide, promoting the development of power grids, and delivering public goods. Power grid enterprises at all levels should undertake specific power grid projects in accordance with the planning issued by the government with the goal of maximizing investment returns.

Path of Power Delegation in the Electricity Sector

I. Goal of the reform

On March 14, 2013, the *Plan of the Institutional Reform and Function Transformation of the State Council* was issued, marking the launch of the seventh government institutional reform in 1978. The reform focuses on government power delegation and faster transformation of government functions to promote sound regulation by the government in accordance with rules and laws.

The essence of power delegation is to decentralize the power, administrative control, approvals and orders of the planned economy; improve the efficiency and performance of government operations; remove restrictions on businesses for greater vitality; and stimulate enthusiasm of primary-level organizations and investors. The ultimate goal is to implement the decision adopted at the third Plenary Session of the 18th CPC Central Committee that the market shall play a decisive role in resource allocation and complete the transition to a market economy where market rules prevail, companies become true market players and the role of the market in economic regulation and resource allocation are brought into full play.

When the reform on power delegation was launched, governments at all levels began to review the existing administrative approval and management systems one by one and made cancellations, revisions and new arrangements where necessary to minimize government restrictions on the market. The measures taken come in three forms: a negative list, a list of powers and a list of responsibilities. The negative list of market access, the list of powers of the government and the list of responsibilities of the government and its departments highlight the main tasks of power delegation now and in the future. It is also an important part of improving China's market economy.

II. Characteristics of power delegation in the electricity sector

In the new circumstances, further decentralizing steps will provide a new impetus for China's electric power system reform and sustained social and economic development. With the deepening of China's socialist economic system reform and the reform of the electric power system, China needs to take a power market reform path with its own characteristics. The general philosophy is in line with that of the overall reform set by the central government, but it also has its unique features.

The scale of China's electricity sector and the size of the market are so big that it is difficult to find reference models in other parts of the world. The electric power industry in China is faced with a number of complex challenges, such as a weak long-term development mechanism, a rigid management system, flaws in review and approval, inefficient planning, unstable pace of growth and investment, supply and demand imbalances, market monopoly and ill-advised investment. A market-based approach is required to remove these issues once and for all.

To push for power delegation in the electricity sector, the government should follow the fundamental call of shifting the power to the market instead of the lower-level administrative bodies. The ultimate goal is to replace administrative intervention and executive orders with the market mechanism and price signals, cultivate diversified market players and a market-based trading mechanism, and let the market play a decisive role in the allocation of electric power resources.

Power delegation is an important part of deepening the reform of the electric power system. More effective measures will be taken to streamline administration, delegate power, strengthen regulation and improve services. This will help put the development of the electric power industry under market rules and remove institutional barriers that restrict the growth of electric power enterprises as well as unreasonable and hidden restrictions for private investment. It will help ensure sound, effective and targeted power project distribution and investment, cut production, operational and institutional costs, improve the business environment, stimulate the vitality of market players, and promote fast and healthy development of China's electric power industry. The authorities in the power sector have also introduced a number of measures to delegate power to lower levels regarding the approval of electric power projects, further promoting administrative reform on delegating power, strengthening regulation and improving services.

III. Measures and progress of power delegation in the electricity sector

Since the State Council decided on power decentralization, the power regulatory authorities at all levels have followed through with a series of measures covering the following four aspects.

Streamline items and delegate the power of review and approval. After the power supply project approval authority is delegated by the central government, the regulatory authorities shall, in accordance with the requirements of streamlining the approval items and China's laws and regulations, define items and procedures for preliminary review of power supply projects and review all supporting documents needed. No prior approval shall be made unless the project is specified in the law, and prior approval conditions shall not include decisions that can be made by businesses themselves. In accordance with the principle that review and approval should be conducted by authorities at the same level of the project, provincial authorities shall be responsible for the work. Relevant organizations shall further improve the approval process for higher efficiency.

Thermal power projects: In 2013, the approval authority of distributed gas power generation projects was delegated to provincial governments in the *Catalog of Government-Approved Investment Projects (2013 Edition)*. In 2014, in the *Catalog of Government-Approved Investment Projects (2014 Edition)*, the power for approval of all thermal power projects was delegated to provincial governments. It was made clear that coal-fired thermal power projects should be approved according to the plan formulated by the central government based on total volume control.

Thermal power projects: In 2013, in the *Catalog of Government-Approved Investment Projects (2013 Edition)*, the approval authority of coal-fired back-pressure thermal power projects was delegated to provincial governments. In 2014, in the *Catalog of Government-Approved Investment Projects (2014 Edition)*, the power for approval of coal-fired thermal power projects was delegated to provincial governments, and it was specified that pumped coal thermal power projects should be approved by provincial governments according to the plan formulated by the central government based on total volume control.

Power grid projects: *The Catalog of Government-Approved Investment Projects (2014 Edition)* delegated approval power to local governments for non-cross border or interprovincial (autonomous region or municipality under direct administration of the central government) ±500 kV and below DC power grid projects and the non-cross border or interprovincial ±500 kV, 750 kV, 1000 kV AC power grid projects, of which ±800 kV DC and 1000 kV and above AC projects should be reviewed and approved according to the national planning.

Formulate supporting policies on power delegation. In 2013, the National Development and Reform Commission issued the *Notice on Standardizing the Project Management of Non-Cross Border or Interprovincial 500 kV AC Power Grid* (GNDL [2013] No. 430) to guide local governments in carrying out relevant project administration. After the power for approval of thermal power projects was delegated to lower levels in 2014, "construction plans shall be formulated in accordance with overall volume control," and no more preliminary permit will be granted for such projects. In 2015, the National Development and Reform Commission issued the *Notice on Improving Planning and Construction of Electric Power Projects after the Delegation of Power Approval Authority* (FGNY [2015] No. 2236), which set the requirements for electric power project planning and supervision after the decentralization of power.

Draw a flow chart for the preliminary stage of power project planning. The chart should define the roles of various departments in the preliminary joint review and approval, specify procedures, time frames for processing applications and responsible departments at provincial, municipal and county levels for handling the supporting documents.

Fulfill the responsibility of joint review and approval of the preliminary work of power projects. Provincial departments shall be responsible for the review and approval of relevant documents. They should seize the opportunity for the reform of the administrative review and approval system to integrate different steps, raise efficiency and promote early project approval and launch. Project applicants shall take the primary responsibility for the preliminary stage of the work. They should abide by the work responsibility system, make plans and arrangements according to the flow chart and ensure that personnel with clearly defined responsibilities and funding are in place for the smooth progress of the joint review and approval of the early stage of the project. The local development and reform commission (energy administration) is responsible for the preliminary stage project coordination. This includes setting up a leading group, delivering better services for key projects, urging applicants to complete the work on personnel, funding, environmental protection, land, water resources and others related to the preliminary project approval, and assisting in project application to provincial authorities.

IV. Progress and challenges of power delegation in the electricity sector

Since the CPC Central Committee and the State Council launched the reform program to streamline administration and delegate power, electricity regulatory departments at all levels have come a long way in delegating power, strengthening regulation and improving services. However, compared with the requirements of the central government, there is still some distance to cover, especially in terms of meeting the power industry reform goals.

1. Progress

Canceling or delegating administrative review and approval powers to lower-level governments plays a leading role in promoting all-round reform, invigorating the market, strengthening the development momentum, and transforming government functions. Since the start of the reform, the National Energy Administration has cancelled or delegated the power for approval on 17 items, sorted out regulatory documents, established a law-compliance review system, and promulgated or revised a large number of laws, regulations, industrial policies and standards on electric power.

Power delegation has further unleashed the vitality of the market and society and facilitated the implementation of policies and measures to ensure steady growth, promote reform, make structural adjustments, and benefit the people. Take Henan Province as an example. In 2016, eight coal power projects with a total size of 9.82 million kw, including Longda in Zhoukou and Longfeng in Puyang, were approved with an average time frame of six months, 12 months faster than that before the reform. It attracted 8 billion yuan of investment by 2016 and significantly promoted investment and growth. To promote the healthy development of cogeneration, the Henan provincial government has further devolved the approval authority for back pressure-type thermal power units to energy regulatory bodies at the prefecture level. The provincial authorities will only be responsible for checking policy compliance in project planning. The approval power for agriculture and forestry biomass thermopower cogeneration is also delegated to the prefecture-level authorities. This has significantly raised the efficiency of review and approval.

Streamlining the approval process has lessened the burden on enterprises, raised their productivity and improved their performance. Take Guangdong Province as an example. The decision of the South China Energy Regulatory Administration in May 2014 to cancel power generation license approval for projects of capacity under 1000 kw benefited more than 3000 power generation companies. According to the survey conducted by Guangdong Electric Power Engineering Enterprises Association, since the simplification of the application materials for the construction license of the power projects, 460 member companies of the Association have found that the time needed for license approval has been drastically shortened, and their business efficiency has been further improved.

2. Challenges

The purpose of power delegation in the electricity sector is to shift from the planned allocation of power resources to letting the market play a decisive role in this process. However, in practice, power was decentralized first from the central to provincial or even lower level governments. Then, due to the inconsistent steps in power delegation, power projects are now under the regulation of both the central and provincial governments. This has made the work more complex, and the role of the market in resource allocation less prominent. The main challenges that the electricity sector faces are as follows.

First, powers are not sufficiently delegated. Instead of canceling or delegating all necessary items subject to administrative review and approval, some items still need to be approved by the central government, which dampens the role of local governments in the market-based allocation of power resources. Some approval powers are merely delegated to lower-level administrative departments or exercised in the later stage instead of being abolished. The government has only lowered the level of authority rather than simplifying the procedures. Take the adjustment of preliminary approval for investment projects as an example. Those items have been reduced from more than 30 in 2014 to less than 3, making it easier for projects to obtain approval. However, the post-approval reporting requirement has not been consolidated, and the procedure remains long, complex and inefficient.

Second, decentralization is less coordinated. Some approval items need to go through several departments. However, because of different policy goals and insufficient coordination among them, it is difficult for them to think in the same direction. Some approval powers are delegated to lower authorities, while others remain in the central authorities. Rather than raising administrative efficiency, this has made things more complicated. For example, the approval of new power generation projects involves the use of land, coal and water, as well as railway and power grid connections. However, the departments responsible for land and resources, environmental protection, transportation and water use are delegating power at their own pace. This has affected the efficiency of project approval.

Third, some local governments are not ready to take over the power. The evolution of a large number of approval items requires local governments to take over the power and perform their duties in accordance with laws and regulations. However, at present, some local governments are not capable of taking over the authorities delegated from the central government and need to further strengthen capacity building in this regard. Two issues must be resolved. First, the workload at the grassroots level has increased sharply with government streamlining. Due to insufficient staffing and lack of guidance and professional training, officials at the primary level are burdened with heavy tasks and are unable to work with high efficiency. In addition, some local authorities have failed to take into account the overall interests or collect enough information about the projects, so they are more likely to make mistakes and prolong the approval process than the central authorities. For example, after the reform of the administrative review and approval system, the approval authority for thermal power projects was taken over by the local authorities. However, many of them, out of local interests and development inertia, are keen to expand investment in building power plants. Instead of slowing down the construction, they have even quickened the approval process, which runs counter to the goal of the reform.

Fourth, regulation remains weak in some areas. When delegating the power of review and approval, the government also needs to strengthen regulatory efforts. Otherwise, regulatory deficiencies will become more prominent as more powers are delegated. Lack of laws and regulations, insufficient law enforcement personnel and poor coordination between the regulatory authorities and local governments have resulted in weak regulatory capacities or even a regulatory vacuum when government powers are canceled or delegated. Cases of illegal selling of preliminary photovoltaic project permits and illegal project approval and construction, as we have seen in the past, are the result of such regulatory failures.

Fifth, nongovernment resources need to be strengthened. The professional evaluation market of the electric power industry is not well regulated, and the evaluation conducted by third-party institutions has brought great pressure and cost to enterprises. At the same time, because of the small number of qualified professional institutions and huge business demand, some intermediaries have turned speculative. They have disrupted the market order and affected government efficiency.

V. Proposals and prospects for power delegation in the electricity sector

Power delegation in the electricity sector is an industrial reform carried out in accordance with the guidelines set by the central government. As part of China's overall reform on administrative streamlining, it is of great importance to push through the reform of the electricity and energy systems and advance the overall reform. Going forward, we must take a multipronged approach and chart a clear course for the reform in the electricity sector based on the following principles.

1. Power should mainly be delegated to the market.

The goal of power delegation is to fully implement the guiding principles of the third plenary session of the 18th CPC Central Committee, give full play to the decisive role of the market in resource allocation, and focus on addressing flaws in the market mechanism, excessive government intervention and inadequate supervision in the power sector. The reform in the electricity sector should include breaking monopoly, improving the market role, opening up competitive business, strengthening supervision of monopoly, building an effective market platform, advancing price reform, leveraging the market force in allocation of electric power resources, and actively creating institutional conditions for delivering reform benefits.

In short, the reform should be carried forward in the principle of market competition for power companies and better regulation of power transmission and distribution businesses. The market plays a decisive role in the allocation of resources, and the government regulates pricing on the market and exercises control over the pricing of noncompetitive goods and services. More specifically, the following two aspects deserve our attention.

First, good planning is needed to inform the market. When power is delegated, it is important to put projects under the guidance of the planning. The overall project capacity should be consistent with the planning after the approval power is delegated for electricity projects. A regulatory mechanism should be in place to promote sound industrial development and avoid excessive installation capacity and waste of investment. In fact, owners of projects that have been included in power planning who have completed the approval process will decide whether and when to begin project construction according to the market conditions. It is necessary for China to follow the international practice of distinguishing monopolistic business areas from competitive ones with separate planning. Areas of natural monopoly, such as power grids, require sound planning with a stronger binding effect. For competitive areas such as power generation, planning should mainly offer guidance, and market players should have the right to decide on their own investment, operation models and timelines according to market conditions.

Second, the market mechanism should be set to replace administrative review and approval. Planned and competitive electricity prices for power generation and consumption should be more flexible. The scope of involvement for market players in direct trading and the amount of electricity supply should be expanded. A market-based interprovincial and transregional electricity trading mechanism should be gradually established. These steps will help form a nationwide market system featuring full competition, orderly openness and sound development. If relevant enterprises do not make timely investments in the construction of projects specified in the plans, a third party may be introduced for making the investment through bidding or other competitive means together with identifying project owners and streamlining administrative procedures.

2. Administrative streamlining in the electricity sector should aim at greater efficiency.

It is important to identify which areas must be streamlined, which areas can be streamlined, and which areas are easy to streamline in the electricity sector. Greater efforts should target areas of low efficiency and efficacy of government administration. Evaluations must be made on the results of the reform with full participation of local governments and businesses. They should aim at reaching a sound definition of approval authorities of governments at all levels by identifying items that can be canceled or retained and areas where improvements can be made and where supervision should be strengthened. It has been proven that it is not the fewer the better for approval items or the lower the better for the level of authorities. Cancellation is better than delegation for some projects that do not need government coordination. The focus of streamlining administration in the electricity sector should be reviewing and revising the normative documents that have restricted private investment. Sound supporting policies should be in place with bold and steady steps to remove obstacles blocking private capital's participation in electric power projects and creating conditions for private enterprises to enter this sector. The following two aspects require specific attention in practice.

First, a collaborative mechanism involving multiple departments with different roles should be established. Interdepartmental coordination should be further strengthened to enhance the weak links. A regulatory mechanism featuring coordination along authority lines and between departments and the institutional setting for *interim and ex post* supervision must be in place. We must give full play to the supervisory role of power users and public organizations and improve the effect of supervision. Revision of laws and regulations and adjustment of ministerial rules should catch up with the pace of the reform. The reform of the administrative review and approval system should be carried out in a law-based manner.

Second, the capacity of intermediary agencies should be regulated and strengthened. The government should remove intermediary services for administrative review and approval that run counter to regulations. No existing or canceled items of administrative review and approval shall be converted into intermediary service items. Separating an intermediary service item into multiple steps should be prohibited to avoid increasing the burden on applicants. Agency qualifications, service charges and procedures, market access and business supervision must be put under stringent oversight. A sound data bank of intermediary agencies should be established, and their service list should be publicized to raise their capacity to deliver fair, well-regulated, trustworthy and efficient services.

3. Power should be delegated with steady steps in a well-coordinated manner in the electricity sector at this stage.

At the current stage, it is important to keep a steady and coordinated reform pace in the electricity sector to better implement the decision of the State Council to transform government functions, streamline administration and delegate power, and build a new power project planning, construction and management mechanism that integrates and coordinates the work of planning, policies, rules and supervision. Specifically, the following two aspects deserve special attention in practice.

First, the devolution of power and responsibility must go hand in hand. The government should keep a proper pace in carrying out power delegation in the electricity sector based on the capacity and readiness of the lower-level departments and strengthen guidance over their capacity building. At the same time, lower-level departments should take over the responsibilities in accordance with laws and regulations, follow the new requirement in the principle of "openness, transparency and efficiency", simplify the preconditions for the approval of power projects, improve the review process, publicize the progress and results for public scrutiny, and promptly report relevant information to higher authorities.

Second, regulation and supervision should be strengthened simultaneously. A sound planning system for the electricity sector with a clear definition of power and responsibilities should be in place at an earlier date. Measures for electricity power planning should be formulated for overall volume control. The whole-process supervision of power project selection with full participation of local energy agencies at all levels should be implemented. *Interim and ex post* supervision should be strengthened to cut project capacity exceeding the total quantity control target and adjust those inconsistent with the planning to form a closed-loop supervision of power projects. A hearing system for energy project review and approval, a mechanism for post-decision project evaluation, an abnormal project list and an enterprise blacklist should be in place to address all kinds of illegal acts in accordance with the law.

Bibliography

An, H. (2013). Theoretical evolution and enlightenment of the relationship between government and market. *Northern Economy and Trade* (7).

Bai, M. (2014). The goal, difficulty and path choice of the new round of electric power system reform. *Price: Theory & Practice* (7).

Li, Y. (2013). *China's economy in dual transition*. China Renmin University Press.

Liu, J. (2015). *The U-turn of a big ship—Reflection and prospect of eighteen years of electricity sector reform*. The Oriental Press.

Shi, D. (2014). The target selection of china's electric power system reform. *Energy of China* (36).

Tang, Y., Xie, Y. (2012). Difficulties and breakthroughs in China's electric power system reform. *Prices Monthly*, (2).

Tong, G. (2015). Taking the road of a market-oriented electric power system reform with Chinese characteristics. *Peking University Business Review*, (5).

Wu, M., Xu, J., Huang, Z. (2014). Energy system reform: An efficient market and a capable government. *International Economic Review*, (4).

Xu, W., Cheng, Z., Zhang, W. (2011). Analysis and countermeasures of China's persistent power shortage. *China Business and Market*, (9).

Yan, D. (2012). Research on deepening the reform of China's electric power system. Unpublished mater's dissertation, Southwestern University of Finance and Economics.

Ye, Z., Zhang, X. (2013). *Research on system and policy of promoting electric power market reform*. Economic Science Press.

Zhang, Z. (2015). New breakthroughs in the reform of streamlining administration and delegating power in the new normal. *Administration Reform*, (1).

Zhu C. Staying alert against relapses in streamlining administration and delegating power in the power sector. *China Energy News*, 2015-6-29.

Fostering Strategic Emerging Industries in the Context of Building a Leaner Government—A Case Study of Yongchuan District of Chongqing Municipality

Zhijie Wang and Rui Wang

Advancing the institutional reform and further streamlining government administration and delegating its power are vital to the all-round progress of reforms, improvement of the socialist market economy, steady enhancement of market vitality, and greater social creativity and domestic demand. China is still undergoing a dual transition of the economy, which means it is shifting from the planned economy to the socialist market economy (Yining, 2015a, 2015b). The prolonged weakness in global economic growth and the "new normal" of the Chinese economy have brought significant changes to economic landscapes at home and abroad. The economy is now driven by innovation rather than resources as in the past. For government institutional reform, more efforts are needed to transform the government functions and make it more efficient to reduce transaction costs, improve resource allocation, and stimulate the vitality of businesses (Guangqing, 2016). That is, effective institutions and systems are essential in maintaining stable growth, making structural adjustments, advancing reform and improving people's livelihood. Power delegation is an integral part of institutional building. It aims to reform the method of administration that restricts the growth of the market economy and fair market competition to mobilize market entities and encourage them to make further investments. As the pace toward the market economy quickens, the market will play a more decisive role in resource allocation (Yining, 2015a, 2015b). A more efficient institutional setting is the key to the fast growth of strategic emerging industries and the upgrading of the industrial structure at the regional level. The transition and adjustment of economic engines are also pivotal to the creation and development of strategic emerging industries. The

Supported by China Postdoctoral Science Foundation (Project No. 2012M520087).

Z. Wang (✉)
Guanghua School of Management of Peking University, People's Government of Tongnan District of Chongqing Municipality, Beijing, China

R. Wang
Institute of Sustainable Development of Chongqing University, Chongqing, China

Y. Li and Z. Cheng (eds.), *The Chinese Path Toward a Leaner Government*,
https://doi.org/10.1007/978-981-19-6718-4_24

"invisible hand" of the market and the "visible hand" of the government can have a direct or indirect impact on the efficacy and potential of industrial development by changing the way resources are allocated for improved efficiency. Therefore, it is important to coordinate and balance the market and the government and enable the former to play a decisive role and the latter to play its role better. In this context, the government should, through rebalancing the power, improve the process and delegate its authority, raise its efficiency and introduce sound policies on industrial development to create a favorable institutional environment.

Delegating Government Authority and Developing Strategic Emerging Industries

Strategic emerging industries bear on the improvement and upgrading of a nation's industrial structure and its overall and long-term economic and social development. They also evolve with the times (Siwei, 1999). The *Decision of the State Council on Accelerating the Fostering and Development of Strategic Emerging Industries (2010)* defines them as knowledge and technology-intensive industries that employ less materials, promise huge potential and generate good returns. They promote comprehensive and long-term development of the economy and society based on major technological breakthroughs and demand for growth. Since the financial crisis in 2008, China's industrial policies have focused more on phasing out backward and excessive production capacity, eliminating zombie companies and fostering strategic emerging industries and modern services. A series of guidelines, plans and policies were rolled out by the central and local governments with a view to boosting those industries, including the *Decision on Accelerating the Fostering and Development of Strategic Emerging Industries,* the *2014 Catalog for Guidance on Standard Complexes of Strategic Emerging Industries* and the *Plan on Strategic New Industries During the 13th Five-Year Plan Period (2016–20).* According to the *Outline of the 13th Five-Year Plan for the National Economic and Social Development of the People's Republic of China,* 15% of China's GDP will come from strategic emerging industries by 2020. A survey conducted by the State Information Center indicates that the revenues and profits of major industries in the strategic emerging sectors grew by over 15% in the first half of 2015, of which the industrial revenue growth rate was 5 times that of all industrial sectors and industrial profits grew by 15% year-on-year. Fixed asset investment in nine major strategic emerging industries grew 1.5 times faster than fixed asset investment growth in urban areas across China. All of the above demonstrates the good momentum of growth in strategic emerging industries. However, if the industries or technologies encouraged by the government fail to match China's comparative advantage, they will find it hard to grow on their own and will need continuous and massive policy support and subsidies from the government (Yifu, 2008). Strategic emerging industries are weak in self-driven growth capabilities at the early stage and are not ready for large-scale growth in the short term. As they are different from traditional industries in administrative approvals, investment, financing, land management, technological R&D and IPR protection, the government should play an active role in maintaining market order, designing policies and mechanisms and creating a sound institutional environment to minimize systematic risks in the development of strategic emerging industries and facilitate their faster growth. Delegating government authority and finding new administrative methods are also needed to further reduce transaction costs, raise policy efficacy, stimulate business vitality, promote industrial upgrading at the regional level and sustain progress in innovation capability. The government is facing new challenges in terms of transforming its functions, improving services, better dividing the roles between itself and the market and building a new type of relationship with the market.

In 1988, the government for the first time stated that "transforming government functions is the key to institutional reforms". Since then, "transforming government functions" have been high on the agenda of institutional reforms. Since the 18th CPC National Congress, the CPC Central Committee with Comrade Xi Jinping at its core has made clear instructions on deepening the institutional reform. The second plenary session of the 18th CPC Central Committee concluded that the transformation of government functions is at the center of the institutional reform. The third plenary session of the 18th CPC Central Committee stressed that to advance the economic restructuring, the government should transform its functions and sort out the relationship between it and the market, which means the market needs to play a decisive role in resource allocation and the government should play its role better (Keqiang, 2016). The development of strategic emerging industries is not possible without transforming government functions. Streamlining administration and delegating authority is not only about the reform of the government. It is a systematic project connecting all fronts and the whole process of the reform. It should not be seen simply as a "power cut" because unduly cutting administrative approvals and devolving authority before clarifying the roles of the government and the market would cause misfunctioning and low efficiency of government services and mismatch between policies and industry needs. When the relationship between the government and the market becomes clear, efforts should be made to continue to streamline administration, delegate power, strengthen regulation and improve services. A well-regulated system of administrative approvals should be established to cut the government's unnecessary approvals and direct interference in the projects and business activities of enterprises. The government should create a sound and favorable policy environment for market competition and work out a negative list for market access, a power list of the government, and a responsibility list of its departments, with a view to rendering stronger support to the healthy development of strategic emerging industries.

Delegating the Government Authority in Yongchuan District of Chongqing

Located in western Chongqing Municipality, Yongchuan District is of strategic importance for the Yangtze River Economic Zone, Sichuan-Chongqing Economic Zone and the city clusters around Chengdu and Chongqing. As the main driver of industrialization and urbanization, it is classified as a new urban development area among the five key functional areas of Chongqing. It is also home to new industries and migrants, a major manufacturing center and a demonstration zone of parallel progress in industrialization, information technology, urbanization and agricultural modernization.

In recent years, Yongchuan District has been adapting itself to the "new normal" of economic growth in implementing the strategy of developing Chongqing's five key functional areas, strengthening institutional building and innovation in supply-side structural reform to address the most urgent issues in economic and social development. Delegating government authority has been progressing while the government has strengthened regulation and improved services to boost industrial development. Items for administrative approval have been delegated or cancelled in a phased manner, while the focus of the reform has shifted from increasing the number of delegated items to better efficiency in government service. More importance has been placed on general administration, such as power delegation, tighter regulation and better services, instead of simply cutting approval items. Institutional setups have been improved to address overlapping authorities on item approval among multiple departments, thus clarifying their respective responsibilities. To further streamline administration, improve regulation and services and transform government functions, the work on delegating government authority has been included in the local outline of the 13th five-year plan for economic and social development, which states that the powers and responsibilities of the government and the market should be further clarified. Government administration should be separated from business affairs, asset investment, public institutions and social affairs. The decisive role of the market in resource allocation should be given full play, and the government should drastically reduce the direct allocation of resources. Instead, it shall advance the reform of the administrative approval system, fully undertake powers devolved from the higher authorities, and establish its power and responsibility lists and negative lists. The plan provides guidance for the reform in the next five years.

To reduce application materials, simplify administrative approvals, and compress administration procedures in building an efficient market and a capable government, Yongchuan District has rectified all the administration approval items in 36 departments by canceling approvals of 51 service projects, 952 application materials and 790 approval procedures that are not required by law or prereview conclusions or have already been collected by the same department. All items in the category of "review" were moved to that of "immediate review", and the processing time was narrowed to 4020 working days. Eighty-two approvals are delegated to the township and subdistrict levels. Twenty-nine items can also be dealt with at the village and community levels. Eighteen items of business decisions will not require government review for project approval.

Parallel approval is replacing serial approval in which an applicant only needs to fill out one form to be processed through one window. Online and self-services, appointment-making, "no-form" processing, visiting service, administrative guidance and other services are also offered on demand. One stamp approval is implemented in this process, under which the government of Yongchuan District will issue a joint opinion of approval and acceptance together with the stamp of the joint administrative review and approval of the people's government of Yongchuan, Chongqing and the stamp of joint acceptance of the people's government of Yongchuan, Chongqing. Then, within one working day, competent authorities at the district level shall issue relevant certificates and approval documents. The administrative approval for construction projects is divided into six phases, namely, project initiation, land provision, approval of plan, approval of initial design, issuance of construction permit, completion and acceptance. The Reform and Development Commission, the Administration of Land Resources and Housing, the Urban Planning Bureau and the Commission of Urban–rural Development of Yongchuan are responsible for administrative approval. Joint administrative guidance, field investigation, approval and acceptance are carried out, and fees and charges are listed in a single form. Administrative approval is separated from technical review and shall be issued on the day of approval. Efforts will be made to apply information technology to administrative approvals through online service centers where download, self-service, declaration, prereview, processing and approval can be made. To better regulate intermediary services, administrative approvals from land supply to project acceptance should be completed within 26 working days for industrial projects and 30 working days for nonindustrial projects.

The power list of administrative approval is made public. It has ten parts, including the project title, department in charge, application conditions, application materials, procedures, timeframe, supervision, and ways and reasons for charging. The power list of 620 items of approval services and the list of 328 items processed at the government service center have been made public. Smooth progress has been made in power delegation at both ends. Items that can be decided by companies themselves no longer require approvals. Reforms are carried out on business registration services. The threshold for application has been lowered. Services have been made more accessible. Business license and other required certificates have been integrated into one single certificate called Three-in-one License. Preferential policies for mass entrepreneurship and innovation have been implemented to energize the market. In 2015, 10,657 new businesses were created with a registered capital of RMB11.99 billion. More efforts have been made to promote integrated taxation services, face-to-face service, single window processing and self-service. The state and local taxation bureaus now process applications with one standard in a "one-stop service" for taxpayers, and service resources are integrated inside the government.

The reform of business registration is underway. Companies can obtain business licenses before completing procedures to obtain other required certificates. Pre-approval is replaced by post-approval. In 2014, 126 pre-approval items were transformed into post-approval items, leaving only 47 items for pre-approval. The figures in 2015 were 103 and 34, respectively. Simplified deregistration for self-employed businesses has been piloted, which offers great convenience to applicants, as they are not required to fill out forms at registration centers. The threshold has been lowered to make registration easier. The paid-in-capital registration requirements have been replaced by the requirements for committed capital, and the minimum registered capital requirement is canceled. Online platforms for Chinese-funded enterprises' name approval are launched, offering more flexible conditions on names and business premises. Registration for companies moving in from other regions is simplified. Business registration is available across jurisdictions. It now only involves two steps: review and confirmation. They may merge into one step in some cases. Local industry and commerce agencies are authorized to handle registration matters to narrow approval procedures and cut administrative costs.

Practice of Fostering Strategic Emerging Industries and Delegating Government Authority in Yongchuan

Efforts have been made to build Yongchuan into a modern manufacturing center of Chongqing. Acting on initiatives such as "Made in China 2025", "Internet Plus" and the plan to develop ten major strategic emerging industries in Chongqing, Yongchuan is trying to make the most of its livable and accordable urban environment, abundant skilled workers and broad market to better match industries with the functions of the new urban development area and enable industrialization and information technology to complement each other. Industries have been upgraded through innovation, and their structures have adjusted along with the growth of size. The government has decided to foster the strategic information industry led by robots and smart equipment to keep abreast of the growth trend of the strategic emerging industries. A number of leading, backbone and supporting businesses will be nurtured to form an industrial system that accommodates a complete industrial chain, including R&D, production, integration, testing and service.

Industrial development is guided by the model of "3 + 3 + 6 + 7". The first "3" refers to three platforms for collaborative innovation and R&D of public services, business incubation and commercialization, and financial and capital services. The second "3" means three types of businesses, which provide assembled machine and whole production chains, key components and system integration. "6" represents the integrated development mechanism involving the efforts of the local governments, industries, universities and colleges, research institutes, investors and users. The last "7" means success in leading companies, industrial clusters, industrial chains, technology application, new ways of financing, coordinated growth among industries and human resource training. Financial support and talent pools have been built to attract and foster leading companies. The development of complete-plant manufacturing helps localize the R&D and manufacturing of key components. Efforts are made to coordinate the development of industrial robots, service robots, robots for special purposes and 3D printing to create industrial clusters of robots and smart equipment with a market value of over RMB10 billion and a full-fledged industrial ecosystem. A total of 106 robot and smart equipment manufacturers have committed to investing in Yongchuan, of which 35 have started production. Yongchuan, now rated as "the best and largest industrial basis for robot and smart equipment production" by the Ministry of Industry and Information Technology, has become the first national demonstration center for a new type of industrialization and saw the creation of the National High-tech Industrial Development Zone of Chongqing.

Effective institutional building provides major support for the development of strategic emerging industries. Further delegating government authority is key to stimulating market and business vitality. In the early days of the robot and smart equipment industries, by transforming government services and delegating government authority in particular, Yongchuan sorted out the relationship between the government and market, reduced government interference in market activities, and established effective institutions with clear responsibilities and powers. Streamlining administration and delegating government authority have underpinned the growth of the robot and smart equipment industries there.

I. Deepening the reform of administrative approval

The Bureau for Comprehensive Administrative Approval was established in the industrial park to perform delegated approval functions for projects that will at the same time be registered with corresponding government departments. The bureau is composed of officials at the rank of office clerk selected from Yongchuan District's Administration of Land, Resources and Housing, Urban Planning Bureau, Commission of Urban–rural Development and other departments, where they keep their personnel records. The bureau takes over administrative approval powers delegated to it on planning, land use, construction of industrial projects, environmental protection and other items. The park's management commissions are responsible for regular supervision of their work. Staff of the municipal departments of fire, industry and commerce and power supply who are dispatched to the district departments should work in the industrial park on a regular basis. These measures aim to ensure that all applications submitted by enterprises in the industrial park are handled by the industrial park authorities. Matters falling into the business management authority are no longer taken as the prerequisites for project approval. Eighteen prerequisite items, including loan commitments, letters of intent on financing, and the review of feasibility study reports, have been canceled.

II. Greater role of planning in administrative approval

Efforts have been made to determine the locations, preconditions and requirements of development plans and projects for each industry to attract businesses, boost industrial restructuring and open more areas for investment. The government provides administrative guidance based on these plans before the launch of construction projects and strictly follows the plans in project review and approval to improve efficiency.

III. Mechanism of departmental coordination and information sharing in place

Synergy has been formed through smoother communication and cooperation between administrative approval authorities and other departments, clear division of their responsibilities and prompt collection of information on matters such as project progress. Construction projects are approved in a timely manner to ensure early project launch. A mechanism for sharing data and information is established jointly with relevant departments, covering fields of environmental impact assessment, geological disaster assessment, planning of water and soil conservation and monitoring and mapping. The mechanism provides data and information for registered companies to produce documents needed for construction projects and reduces the time for intermediary services.

IV. Unified Standard of Administrative Approvals

Delegated authority is fully enforced. In accordance with legal provisions and mandates, the requirement of streamlining administration and specific circumstances of various departments, the responsibilities of government departments have been sorted out, and a "one-stop" service platform has been established. To unify the standards of administrative approvals in the industrial park with those of corresponding government authorities, standardized procedures of administrative approval have been developed as required by the Administration of State Land, Resources and Housing, the Urban Planning Bureau, the Commission of Urban–rural Development and other departments to make administrative approvals efficient and well-regulated. The delegated authority is strictly enforced in making approvals in the industrial park and filing the projects with relevant government departments to ensure that approvals are made within mandate and officials dispatched there can complete all approval procedures smoothly and efficiently without resorting to higher authorities.

V. Higher Service Quality and Efficiency in Approvals

"Green channels" have been opened to improve the approval process. A service center for project implementation was set up to provide counseling, policy guidance and agent service for administrative approvals. Applicants can hand in materials at designated windows and get notification on one visit only. One-stop service is offered, and feedback is given in one form. "Green channels" have been opened for key projects, where 48 prerequisites have been removed. During negotiations on project investment, staff responsible for administrative approval in the industrial park will get in touch with enterprises in advance, inform them of the procedures and prerequisites of administrative approval and provide technical guidance to improve the efficiency of administrative approvals. Efforts have also been made to reduce the processing time and raise efficacy. By pooling resources, adjusting approaches and clarifying responsibilities, the time needed for administrative approvals has been further narrowed.

It now only takes 26 working days for industrial projects to be approved. Information needed for approvals such as identity materials of applicants, organization code certificates of enterprises are now needed only for the first step and will be shared with the Administration of Land, Resources and Housing, the Urban Planning Bureau, the Commission of Urban–rural Development and other departments inside the government as necessary. Progress in review and approval will be tracked to improve service. The industrial park authorities pair up with project companies and conduct regular visits to collect information on certificate issuance and opinions from businesses so that they will know which phase of administrative approval these companies are in, make sure good services are provided while applications are reviewed and a sound environment of administrative approvals are in place.

Despite progress made in fostering the development of robot and smart equipment industries, Yongchuan still faces challenges in the following areas. First, the integration of administrative approval functions has not been completed, and the "one window" and "one-stop" services are not yet available. Second, service capabilities need to be improved. The Administration of State Land, Resources and Housing, the Urban Planning Bureau, and the Commission of Urban–rural Development, as key agencies that grant administrative approval, are dealing with loads of applications that require high professional expertise. Their staff need to have an overall picture of the projects, acquire professional knowledge and be familiar with every step of administrative approvals. Third, the platform for information flow is not well developed. Therefore, projects cannot be approved online, and resources cannot be shared across platforms. Only the Commission of Urban–rural Development offers online services and access to Chongqing's Online Platform for Government Services. Sharing of data and information is not available for the Administration of State Land, Resources and Housing and the Urban Planning Bureau. Fourth, some projects are approved without handing in required materials or are approved too quickly. In such cases, it is difficult to achieve both efficiency and due procedure at the same time.

Policy Recommendations

I. Power delegation under the model of "Internet + Government Services"

Based on "Internet + Government Services", an O_2O model of "Internet + Power Delegating" can be established with the help of big data and cloud computing. Efforts can be made to set up government service and data sharing platforms connecting the government, public servants, businesses and individuals. Thus, single pieces of information in all departments can be integrated and coordinated with high efficiency. Traditional administrative approvals can be digitized through the project approval tracking system and a database using information technologies to follow approval procedures. Online platforms and apps can be utilized to provide government services or combine it with offline services and improve the procedures for e-government approvals, including online processing, approval transfer and back office monitoring.

It can also help track the real-time progress of government approval, identify causes for delays and give early warnings to raise process efficiency. Standards of all steps of administrative approvals should be gradually defined, such as the guidelines, application materials, conditions and standards for approval, charging standards, timeframes, approval procedures and operational methods (Yanjie et al., 2015). Hiccups between project approval and regulation need to be addressed for better connection. Public data resources should play a larger role in facilitating government decision making.

II. Strengthening the rule of law over government power delegation

Laws provide predictability and a binding effect in regulating behaviors over a long period of time. As such, the government must have relevant systems in place and ensure strict enforcement and severe punishment for any violations in power delegation. The reform must follow the rule of law, and government power should be specified, cut, devolved, regulated, published and exercised in strict accordance with the law (Shuhong, 2015). The rule of law should continue to guide the reform of delegating government authority. Awareness should be raised of the importance of advancing the reform under the rule of law and relevant systems and establishing law-based government institutions, functions, powers and responsibilities to ensure that progress made will be solidified. The "power list" of the government, the "responsibility list" of the government and its departments and the "negative list" of market access should be released as part of the institutional building. The process of power exercise should be improved. Powers should be delegated under the *Administrative License Law of the People's Republic of China*, adjusted or canceled according to statuary mandates and procedures, to put power delegation on a sound and legal footing. Government departments would bear legal liability for retrieving, expanding or increasing their powers without legal mandates. Government officials must take responsibility when exercising power, and their conduct is scrutinized. Law-breaking acts will be held accountable, and compensation must be made to violate others' rights. In other words, the government's responsibilities should grow with its power. The greater the power is, the greater the responsibility (Lixia, 2014).

III. Putting in place supporting mechanisms for delegating government authority

Bearing on every aspect of the institutional reform, delegating government authority indicates not only power cuts and delegation but also redefining the scope of governments' functions and institutional arrangement and readjusting powers, responsibilities, working procedures and staffing of government bodies. In doing so, efforts should be made to focus on reform priorities, avoid "fragmentation" in power delegation, and make reform measures more systematic, integrated and forward looking. Relations among government departments should be made clearer by formulating supporting mechanisms for greater coordination among them. Delegating government power should go hand in hand with reforms in other relevant areas so that resources are readily available and no "weak links" will occur in the reform. Establishing a third-party supervision and evaluation mechanism is a good way to study the feasibility of major reform measures and seek the broadest possible consensus on the reform.

IV. Strengthening the overall planning and coordination of the reform

The reform needs to be carried out in a holistic, coordinated and effective manner to forge synergy between government departments at the same level and promote smooth communication along reporting lines. Joint meetings for project approval should be established to address overlapping or blurred functions among government departments. Under this mechanism, major approval items will be discussed to ensure rule compliance and coordinated action in making prompt decisions on project approval. Departments at lower levels should take the initiative to follow the norms of the higher authorities for effective enforcement of delegated powers. They should formulate standards and procedures of exercising the powers based on their types, relevant policies, laws and regulations and put limits on discretionary power. Officials should be better trained to improve their professionalism, efficiency and awareness of rule compliance in exercising their administrative power. More efforts should be made to delegate powers to markets, society, and businesses and roll back governments' roles in business activities. Minimizing government interference will fundamentally solve the "last mile" issue in delegating government authority.

Bibliography

Cheng, S. (1999). Complex science and management. *Bulletin of Chinese Academy of Sciences, 03*, 3–5.

Feng, L. Administration should be streamlined under the rule of law. *Xinhua Daily*, 2014-6-25.

Lin, Y. (2008). *Development and transformation: Thoughts, strategies and viability*. Peking University Press.

Li, Y., Lv, Y., & Tian, H. (2015). Deepening the reform of administrative approval system: Effectiveness, issues and resolutions. *Chinese Cadres Tribune*, (01), 57–59.

Li, Y. (2015a). Chinese socialism is showing positive signs in the new era—Remarks on the effectiveness of reform on administrative streamlining. *China Economic &Trade Herald*, (31), 30–32.

Li, Y. (2015b). Delegating government authority and fostering independent market entities. *Administration Reform*, (09), 10–16.

Li, K. (2016, May). Deepening administrative streamlining and power delegation, strengthening regulation and improving services, advancing government reforms, transforming functions and boosting efficiency—Speech at a national teleconference.

Xiong, G. (2016). Transforming government functions under the "new normal" of china's economy. *Journal of Harbin Institute of Technology (social Sciences Edition), 18*(02), 2–6.

Yuan, S. (2015). A leaner government boosts China's innovation and entrepreneurship. *Administration Reform, 07*, 14–18.

Administrative Streamlining and Development of High-Tech Enterprises

Quansheng Zhang and Shujun Lin

Introduction

As the "first move" to comprehensively advance the reforms, administrative streamlining has changed not only the basic functions of the government but also the underlying culture and norms of the government's daily operations. According to data, as of the end of June 2014, the State Council had canceled and delegated a total of 468 administrative review and approval procedures, producing substantial effects in further stimulating the vitality of the market. Under the administrative contract responsibility system in which local authorities are the main drivers in economic development, administrative streamlining helps stimulate the vitality of the market and improve the operational efficiency of government agencies by focusing on the very source of local governance—the government. As China enters the middle-income stage in its economic development, the upgrading of the industrial structure requires more high-tech enterprises (HTEs) to provide technical support, and administrative streamlining as an effective market incentive will promote the institutional development of HTEs and play a guiding role in the market.

In this context, a number of measures represented by the *Measures on Administration of Certification of HTEs* have been adopted. At the State Council's briefing on administrative streamlining policies for HTE certification held at the beginning of 2016, certification measures were improved in several aspects. First, the threshold for small enterprises is lowered by cutting the minimum R&D expenditure ratio from 6% of the total avenue to 5% so that the policies can benefit market participants more. Second, the certification procedure is simplified by shortening the public notification period from 15 working days to 10 working days and further streamlining the filing process for change of names so that reporting to various functional offices

Q. Zhang (✉)
Fujian Institute of the Internet of Things in Haixi, Qinghai, China

S. Lin
Guanghua School of Management, Peking University, Beijing, China

Y. Li and Z. Cheng (eds.), *The Chinese Path Toward a Leaner Government*,
https://doi.org/10.1007/978-981-19-6718-4_25

is no longer necessary. Third, follow-up regulation is strengthened through random and targeted inspections conducted in various regions. A comprehensive regulatory system shall be established that covers the pre-certification, *interim* and *ex post* phases to penalize post-certification violations committed by market players and ensure business compliance. Fourth, technology will be upgraded in key high-tech sectors. Smart cities, modern sports and other news concepts of service industries will be blended into the economy. Efforts should be made to enhance industrial technology in emerging fields such as cultural creativity, e-commerce, and modern logistics and eliminate obsolete technologies in the course of industrial upgrading.

There are also several other highlights in the *Measures for the Administration of the Certification of HTEs*. First, high tech-driven growth as a direction is firmly maintained, creating broader development space for high technology in enterprises. Second, technology has been widely applied in emerging strategic industries, modern services and new business models. Third, the threshold for business scale has been lowered so that more small and medium-sized enterprises that are relatively young can pass the threshold as emerging innovative companies. Fourth, a combined method of power delegation and enhanced regulation is adopted for process supervision, and *ex post* review and verification is also strengthened to improve the overall quality of the certification process.

Development of Chinese HTEs

I. The overall development of HTEs

China's HTEs have traversed a relatively long journey of development. In terms of the total number, as of the end of 2011, there were altogether 40,954 certified HTEs in 31 provinces (autonomous regions and municipalities). In terms of geographical distribution, HTEs are widely distributed in the southeast coastal regions, and 65% of them are in Beijing, Guangdong, Jiangsu, Zhejiang, Shanghai and Shandong. The number of certified HTEs in western China is relatively small, representing 4447, or 11% of the total. The number for the 6 provinces of the central region is 5292, accounting for 13% of the total. The number for the 10 provinces in east China is 29,658, accounting for 72%, and there are 1557 HTEs in the three northeast provinces, accounting for 4%. Of all these enterprises, 39,343 or 96% of the total are under a unified administration system—the Torch Statistical System. As of the end of 2010, the income tax reduction and exemption for HTEs reached RMB139.3 billion.

The distribution of HTEs in terms of scale and type as provided by the Torch Statistical System are shown in the following charts:

Revenue above RMB 100 million

Revenue between RMB10 million and RMB100 million

Revenue between RMB5 million and RMB10 million

Revenue under RMB5 million.

Chart 1 Data structure of HTEs in 2011.

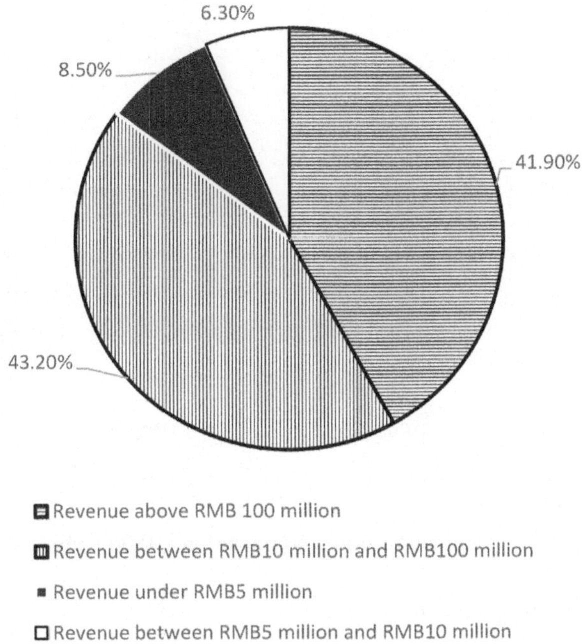

Data source: Torch Statistics System

The chart shows that 16,487 HTEs generate a revenue of more than RMB 100 million, accounting for a large proportion of the total. Approximately 17,004 HTEs have revenue between RMB10 million and RMB100 million, accounting for 43.2%, the largest proportion of the total. A total of 2495 HTEs, or only 6.3% of the total, have revenue between RMB5 million and 10 million. A total of 3357 HTEs, or only 8.5% of the total, generate revenue below RMB5 million.

In terms of their contribution to economic growth, HTEs maintained a relatively high growth rate in 2011, with their total actualized industrial added value accounting for approximately 15.2% of the nation-wide added value generated by the secondary industry. The total foreign exchange they earned from exports accounted for 23.8% of the national total in the same period. Their profit margin remained at a high 7.0%, and their return on net assets was 12.4%.

Regarding the reserve of human resources in HTEs, the total number of employees is 15.083 million, with approximately 7.153 million, or 47.4% of them, holding a college degree or above, which is a 1.5% increase over the same period of the previous year. The specific distribution of employees with a college degree and above is shown in the following chart:

Doctors; Masters; Returned overseas students; University graduates.

Human resource composition (10,000 persons).

Chart 2 Human capital of HTEs in 2011.

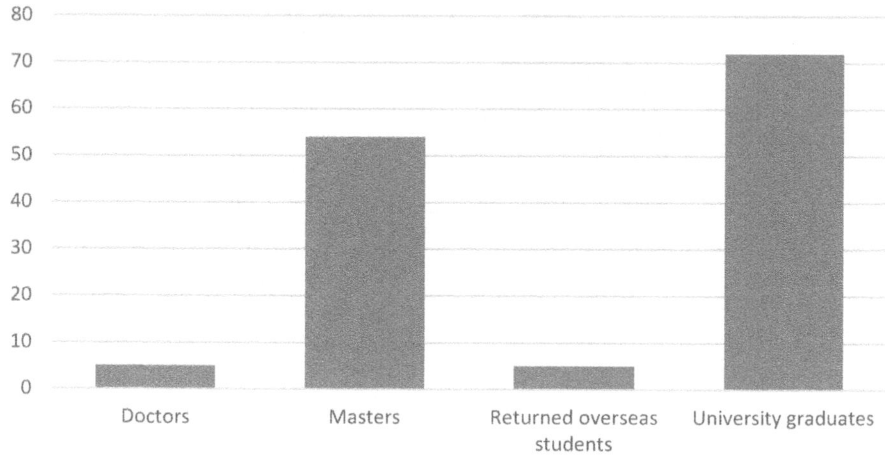

Human resource composition (10,000 persons)

Data source: Torch Statistics System

It can be drawn from the data above that the number of employees with doctoral degrees is 51,000, which is a relatively small proportion. Those who hold master's degrees, with a total number of 538,000, have taken up a significant share of the professional workforce. Returnees from overseas, similar to the doctoral group, account for a relatively small proportion, at 49,000 in number. College graduates are the main component of THE employees, with a total number of approximately 715,000. If we look at the distribution of technical titles among the abovementioned employees, approximately 1.69 million hold either an intermediate or a senior title, accounting for 11.2% of the total number of employees. A total of 3.821 million employees are engaged in general scientific and technological activities, accounting for 25.3% of the total number.

The data indicate that HTEs have made substantial progress and formed a sizable sector, both in business scale and in the number of employees. In regard to putting high technology to practice, these enterprises, with their signature information technology, have become the main driving force behind the structural upgrading of industries, injecting much-needed vitality into China's new growth areas. At the same time, high-tech companies have expanded into frontier industries such as new energy and aerospace. These companies rely on regional high-tech incubators to continuously build their strengths. Local governments also promote the transformation of the growth driver by building high-tech industrial parks. To date, there are 83 national high-tech industrial development zones, 93 national high-tech industrial bases, 127 national economic and technological development zones, and 58 national science and technology innovation bases. These government-sponsored innovation platforms continue to provide space for HTEs and have become important incubators for high-tech development.

For the regional expansion of industrial structure, it can be observed that high-tech industry has been established and developed in the eastern region of China for a relatively long time. The technology is being further upgraded and to a more advanced level. In comparison, the central and western regions still have large room for growth. In recent years, the layout of the industry in these regions has become more balanced, with innovation playing a more important role. Such development is closely related to the broader context of state-spearheaded investment-driven industrial growth. According to the data from the National Bureau of Statistics, the state's investment in high-tech R&D expenditure has increased by 25% annually since 2005. In particular, national-level laboratories have been established in frontier fields such as biology and new energy. Through the development units of these laboratories, a development path that combines production, teaching and research has been paved to strengthen the foundation for industrial innovation. At the same time, the main traditional industries, such as high-speed rail and computer manufacturing, have gained significant shares in civilian-use markets. With increasing international market share, preeminent enterprises such as Lenovo and Huawei are leading and driving the overall development of the high-tech industry in China. As economic globalization gathers pace, Chinese high-tech products have entered the global trading system. In recent years, the total export volume of HTEs in China has been increasing, and there has been a shift of focus from quantity-based exports to the exports of capital, high-tech and high added value products. HTEs are constantly enhancing their comparative advantages, strengthening themselves through market competition and the accumulation of both capital and technology.

II. Challenges for Chinese HTEs

While Chinese HTEs enjoy vigorous development, they are facing challenges in their industrial structures and general direction. China lags behind advanced industrial countries substantially in its total investment in R&D and application of science and technology. The proportion of its R&D investment in the total output value remains low. The global market share of our high-tech industry is also limited, and the overall industrial cluster effect is weak. In general, Chinese high-tech industries are still in the stage of technological assimilation. The lack of core technology and relatively low investment in original scientific research are holding back the momentum for the sustained development of high-tech industries.

The high-tech funding is an important indicator used by the OECD in its report entitled *The Knowledge Economy* to indicate the level of knowledge intensity of industrial technology. The figure is lower in high-tech industries than in other industries in the case of China. Moreover, the development of Chinese HTEs is structurally unbalanced. Compared with other high-tech industries, China's electronics industry enjoys faster growth, but it has not created many jobs. Such mismatch between the distribution of employees and the industrial growth rate has brought about imbalances in a number of areas and serious fragmentation within the industry.

During the 13th Five-year Plan period, with further upgrading of the industrial structure and growing frictions in international trade, industrial upgrading of HTEs can generate greater impact. Against this backdrop, HTEs need to further increase technological investment and accumulate more technological capital.

In terms of policy orientation, state policymakers should have a broader vision amidst a new round of technological revolution. They should promote the sustained development of advanced technology through the accumulation of investment and strategic planning of national sci-tech development to accelerate the growth of emerging strategic industries. As the new era is ushered in, the division of labor under the old world order has begun to break up, and a new international industrial order and division of labor are taking shape. In this fluid situation, especially after the financial crisis that broke out in 2008, the slowdown of the world economy and shrinking of the global market have brought more uncertainties to such a division of labor. The competition for talent, markets and resources has become more intense, and industrial transfer and technological alliances between countries have become more coordinated as regional integration progresses. HTEs are facing a more complex global environment and have increased cross-border collaboration.

With continued economic development and the improvement of its core technology, China is earning comparative advantages in the world. More service industries and core technological planning have begun to emerge in the country, resulting in an industrial cluster effect, while industries with lower technological intensity have begun to shift to the interior regions of China as well as other developing countries. However, the development of the high-tech industry in China also faces various challenges from the outside world as developed countries, based on their technological advantages, restrict Chinese companies' access to the international market through requirements on proprietary intellectual property rights and technical standards.

To achieve industrial upgrading in China, HTEs must maintain strong vitality and a high degree of competitiveness. Only with the sustained development of HTEs can China's industrial structure be fundamentally cleansed of the obsolete and inefficient model of development, and stronger economic growth momentum be generated through sound industrial planning and upgrading.

III. Science and technology policies and economic policies regarding HTEs

The institutional support and development of China's HTEs began with the adoption of the reform and opening-up policy. The industry started from scratch and has gone through an industrial integration process. Gaohui (2011) traced the development of China's science and technology policy and divided this process into five main stages. 1984 was an important year for it witnessed the release of the *Decision of the Central Committee of the Communist Party of China on the Reform of the Science and Technology System*. The Decision specified the basic programs and purpose of the reform of China's sci-tech system. During this period, China's technological development went through a transformation from sporadic to systemic development.

Then, in 1998, the State Council issued the *Decision on Strengthening Technological Innovation, Developing High Technology and Accomplishing Industrialization*, indicating that China's technological innovation by that time had started to accumulate some momentum and grew from an inchoate stage into a more mature stage. In 2006, the State Council issued the *Outline of the Medium and Long-term Science and Technology Development Plan (2006–2020)*, which was more specific in content and allowed innovation policies to be more practical and operational. Zhou (2011) also selected 533 newly formulated policies that are related to technological innovation by the central government agencies ever since the beginning of the reform and opening-up, and through descriptive and other statistical analysis, demonstrated that these policies have experienced shifts from merely focusing on science and technology to promoting coordination between technology and economic policies, from the old government-led model to the new model highlighting market regulation, and from single policy formulation to the promulgation of a package of policies.

Jisheng et al. (2008) conducted a quantitative study of China's science and technology policies and developed a regression model. From a candidate pool of technology policies promulgated by the state between 1978 and 2006, they selected 423 sample policies related to technological innovation and discovered the trend of evolution of such policies during that time period. They also introduced the Cobb–Douglas production function into the study and thereby measured the output effects of innovation policies on technology through the impact of exogenous policy variables.

What can be inferred from this brief literature review is that technological innovation can be achieved only through a complex system of cooperation and coordination that requires the participation of a variety of social institutions and actors such as universities, enterprises, and the government. These institutions and actors constitute a technological research and development cluster that in turn plays an indispensable role in the promotion of economic growth and social development. During the course of R&D and the application of technology, policy is supposed to play an essential guiding role for the market by constantly refining the concept of innovation policy through continuous research. Initially, conducted in developed countries, such research on the management of technological innovation is built on the foundation of basic innovation and plays a more important role in guiding the general direction of social progress. While it seems that there is not a unified and clear definition of the concept in the academic community, many believe that the research on innovation policy is mainly carried out in the following three aspects. The first is to conduct general theoretical research on technological innovation policy. For instance, Chunfa and Xelin (2004) carried out a comprehensive study on the research that addresses a combined topic of policy theories and technological innovation. The second is to study policies specifically formulated for technological innovation. A good example is the detailed quantitative analysis made by Qingrui and Wei (2013) on the effects of the fiscal, financial and procurement policies of the state on the research and development of innovative technologies. Then, the third is to conduct a comparative study of technological innovation policies. For instance, Yanhua et al. (2007) conducted comparative research on means selection by state policy, key fields supported by state policy, and policy effects. Most of these studies, however, focus too narrowly on policies of technological innovation per se or the policy system. In the context of economic globalization, more international comparisons are needed. Comparative studies on differences in culture, country, and market mechanism are relatively small in number. In particular, studies on the impact on policymaking in China have not been systematically developed into a comparative theory.

Policy Reference from Other Countries on the Development of HTEs

From the point of view of Keynesian economics, the government needs to use visible hands to regulate the market. While government intervention can achieve desirable results in a range of market environments through administrative means and fiscal and monetary policies, it has several shortcomings. First, the government's fiscal and monetary policies depend on taxation and the overall economic development level of the society, so the resources that the government can tap into are only a limited part of the social resources. Second, businesses become more efficient as they are extensively engaged in market-driven operations. The market allocates resources in a more rational manner than the government. Therefore, what the government needs to do is to create a relatively ideal market environment, to give businesses more room for innovation, and to promote the industrial development of HTEs through appropriate policy guidance. In this way, the social resources held by the government can be expanded and increased exponentially, and existing resources can be put to more rational use, thereby increasing the utilization rate of resources in general. A common path adopted by many developed countries is to provide tax relief for HTEs and expand the scale of HTEs through burden reduction and effective capital guidance.

I. The case of the United States

The United States' tax incentives for high-tech companies are mainly embodied in the following aspects: reducing tax on new investments; reducing companies' income tax rate; implementing tax incentives for special scientific research projects; and allowing increased expenditure by scientific research to offset the amount of tax.

Tax relief is an important policy adopted by the U.S. government to promote the development of HTEs and encourage enterprises' technological innovation. In terms of more specific policy implementation, for instance, 25% of the net increase between a company expense on scientific research for the current year and that of the previous base period can directly offset its income tax for the current year, given that the amount does not exceed half of the total expense of the base period. This particular policy of the US government has greatly encouraged companies to invest in scientific research and development. Later, the U.S. government further turned this temporary "research and experiment" tax concession into a permanent tax reduction and exemption policy, which thereafter significantly benefited new businesses, especially small businesses that plan to purchase new equipment with a relatively long period of tax relief. In the 1990s, during the information technology revolution, the United States vigorously extended its policy to HTEs, which powered the growth of HTEs and facilitated the transformation and sustained growth of the US economy.

II. The case of Japan

The Japanese government also adopts preferential tax reduction and exemption policies for domestic HTEs, which are specifically reflected in the following aspects:

First, we ensure that key HTEs are able to acquire all the essential research equipment that they need and formulate a special depreciation mechanism together with further tax and fee policy support.

Second, building a system of tax deduction specifically for research expenses. The system was launched in 1966, according to which if the annual research and experiment expenses of a company are higher than the maximum amount in each past year, the part of the tax above 20% of the difference will be deducted. In addition, in the above two tax policies, regulations are made to provide a 6% tax exemption for SMEs' research and experimental expenses. The expenses on raw materials and experiments for the purpose of scientific and technological innovation can be used to offset up to 15% of the income tax of that year.

Third, preferential tax policies for imported technologies should be formulated. The government has formulated more tax policies for promoting basic technological research and strengthening the foundation of technological research among SMEs, with the purpose of increasing Japan's technology import and R&D capabilities. More preferential policies of the two main tax systems are as follows. A special depreciation system for fixed assets is implemented for SMEs, in which 30% of the depreciation fees can be accrued within the first year. For some enterprises, risk insurance premiums are exempted. The inheritance tax for SMEs is reduced, and commission interest in the late payment of taxes is also reduced under certain circumstances.

These tax incentives have drastically increased the funding for Japanese high-tech companies. With tax and fee concessions from the government, they are able to further expand the room for growth and play a leading role in industrial upgrading.

III. The case of Republic of Korea

In view of its relative dearth of resource endowment, the Republic of Korea needs more imports to maintain steady investment in R&D and the development of HTEs. The main method adopted by the Korean government to support HTEs and enhance their core competitiveness is to reduce or exempt import taxes levied on the scarce high-tech products imported from abroad. On this basis, the government also helps improve the ability of HTEs to transform technology into output and product policies on the reduction or exemption of consumption taxes on their products. The policies are mainly concentrated on innovative products, with a provisional preferential tax rate of 10% of the benchmark tax rate for the first four years, 40% for the fifth year, and 70% for the sixth year. The tax concessions will end at the beginning of the seventh year. Furthermore, for small, technology-intensive and venture capital enterprises, corporate income tax property tax and overall land tax will be halved in the first five years of the company's establishment.

At the same time, in support of foreign-funded enterprises, a 7-year tax exemption is granted to enterprises with cutting-edge technologies, and after the expiration of the tax exemption period, a half-cut of income tax reduction will continue to be granted. In the development of core technological fields, the company's research funds, personnel funds and education expenses can be deducted before income tax and can be carried over within 5 years (within 7 years for capital-intensive enterprises). In terms of equipment procurement, experimental equipment used for technological research and development can enjoy a tax relief of 5% of the equipment expense (10% for domestic equipment) or accelerated depreciation at half of the purchase price (70% for domestic equipment).

IV. The case of India

India has also adopted tax incentives and exemptions to foster the development of HTEs. In view of the weakness in the country's high-tech R&D, the Indian government encourages companies to establish R&D centers and use them as drivers for technological innovation. As long as a company's R&D center is certified, it can enjoy tax exemption on imported products. In addition, a certain amount of capital income obtained by the R&D team is exempted from income tax if it is reinvested in R&D and innovation activities. All research projects or products developed are also meticulously classified, and those that fit into the national special research plan can be exempted 125% of taxes and fees. Researchers undertaking these plans are eligible for extra reduction or exemption on their income tax. Companies engaged in high-tech research and development, if so designated, are eligible for tax reduction within 5 years of their certification. If the imported technology is a patent from developed regions such as the United States, Japan and the European Union, commodity tax is exempted for three years.

On the other hand, there is no tax on capital gains and dividend income of high-tech investors bearing long-term risks. To promote investment, for HTEs invested by foreign investors, all income tax can be reduced or exempted up to five of the first eight years of the business operation. To encourage cooperation between high-tech enterprises and research institutes, if an enterprise has its own research institute, all expenditures on R&D projects can enjoy full pretax deduction. In support of R&D and its commercialization in the domestic market, depreciation of equipment can be raised to a rate of 40%. The R&D tax for domestic enterprises that have introduced advanced foreign technologies is lowered to 5% of the introduction cost. These tax funds will become a new source of funding to support scientific research and technology applications. However, if a state-owned or private enterprise spends 2% of its revenue on R&D, its R&D tax can be reduced or exempted. The government uses tax relief to encourage R&D and presses enterprises to continue their R&D activities through tax collection.

The experience of these countries shows that, in terms of specific tax preferential policies, the United States mainly focuses on its own scientific research and development and technological innovation and maintains its core competitiveness in these fields. As a technology leader, it does not place much emphasis on importing technologies from abroad. Japan is strong in science and technology, but because of its relative shortage of resource endowments, it does not possess an absolute advantage in core technologies. Therefore, it adopts a parallel measure of both fostering domestic technology and importing advanced technology from abroad. At the same time, its government also maintains an active guiding role on high-tech research and development to create more opportunities for enterprises and increase their enthusiasm in R&D. The ROK government has provided significant institutional and legal support for HTEs and thereby created a relatively favorable environment for innovation. This is particularly reflected in its legislations, such as the *Tax Reduction and Exemption Control Law,* the *SME Entrepreneurship Support Law*, and the *Technology Development Promotion Law,* which have effectively stimulated the innovation and regulated the behavior of HTEs on law compliance. India, as a developing country that places much importance on HTEs, prioritizes the government's incentives on the information industry led by software technology. It encourages the introduction of foreign-funded HTEs and overseas capital for research and development and offers more support to venture capital. These policies have made tax relief for high-tech companies better targeted.

Promoting the Development of HTEs Through Administrative Streamlining

I. The key to the development of HTEs is the talent pool

To promote the development of HTEs, it is necessary to strengthen the training of human resources. Currently, the predominant problem China faces is the mismatch between human resources and market needs. A large number of people are looking for jobs in sectors where supply surpasses demand. Because of the poor integration between technology research and industrial development, many people working in the high-tech industry are unable to adapt what they have learned to what the market wants. The gap leads to a tremendous waste of human capital for a specific time period. Therefore, businesses should cooperate closely with educational and research institutes, and universities need a higher degree of autonomy in curriculum design and a joint training system with enterprises to generate a more potential workforce for the high-tech industry with stronger theoretical knowledge, professional skills and practical capabilities. Institutes of higher learning and technical education must not only focus on research and theoretical study but also pay attention to the practical needs of businesses so that their graduates are better trained with the skills that the industry needs. At the same time, companies can provide more internship opportunities for college students and offer more scholarships and research funding to further strengthen their cooperation with educational institutes and thereby expand the room for their development.

II. The government can delegate the accreditation power of product standards and business qualifications to HTEs

Administrative streamlining aims to endow more latitude to enterprises. Through the establishment of third-party accrediting and standard-setting institutes and more mechanisms of negotiation and communication with enterprises, the standard of products and the threshold for market entry can be improved continuously. In addition, whether it is a third-party organization or a government agency, one pivotal prerequisite for formulating standards is meticulous market research and analysis, which makes the formulation of more appropriate standards possible. Intermediary agencies can play the role of coordinators and communicate with enterprises more efficiently. As standards are set by businesses themselves, communication and comparison between businesses will help raise industrial standards and qualifications. The government should retain a limited supervisory role to increase incentives for market players and make good use of the efficiency created by the market. It should refrain from unnecessary intervention in the market to provide more space for the growth of high-tech businesses.

III. Publicity and supervision for more investment in HTEs and administrative streamlining should be strengthened to gain popular support

It is important to regularly analyze and summarize the experience and lessons obtained in work related to HTEs and enhance their awareness of innovation in the process of communication to encourage more R&D investment to strengthen their core technological competitiveness. This will promote overall industrial upgrading and support the acceleration of the shift of the growth model and economic transformation. Such publicity and communication can also stimulate innovation of the society at large and create a more favorable cultural and social environment for the growth of HTEs.

IV. Pilot programs should be launched for HTEs

It is important to expand the growth space for HTEs through tax relief and new policy initiatives in the course of administrative streamlining. High-tech zones with good prospects and infrastructure can be selected as key pilots. A mature high-tech incubation system can help integrate various political, economic and cultural resources and promote administrative streamlining. It will also help the public gain a clearer picture of the achievements made by HTEs and attract more technological expertise, human resources and capital for their development.

V. Technical support for HTEs must be maintained

The government should use its visible hand, namely, fiscal policy and monetary policy, to support the development of HTEs in the market in countering risks. HTEs have the ability to obtain high returns, but at the same time, due to problems such as insufficient capital accumulation and large initial capital investment, their ability to counter risks tends to be weak. The government needs to adopt preferential fiscal policies to provide more financial subsidies for HTEs to enhance their ability to develop and upgrade technologies at the initial stage. It should also grant more tax relief and business subsidies and support HTEs with low-interest loans in executing the monetary policy.

VI. A more comprehensive patent policy should be formulated to protect research results

The government needs to create a more favorable and suitable environment for HTEs, the key of which is to formulate a comprehensive patent system to ensure that the core research results of HTEs are not infringed on or pirated. According to the public product theory of economics, science and technology are noncompetitive, and technology sharing for some returns is widely practiced and justifiable. However, as science and technology are not completely exclusive, the government should conduct more stringent regulation in response to these externalities, ensure proper order of the development of the high-tech industry and provide institutional incentives and protection for technological innovation.

Summary

During the course of administrative streamlining and encouraging the development of HTEs, the government needs to selectively delegate powers. However, decentralization does not necessarily mean the adoption of a laissez-faire policy. Instead, it should lead to the strengthening of supervisory measures through which the government can play the role of a regulator and supervisor, rely on the market to make best use of resources, promote innovation and establish a code of conduct for HTEs through the formulation and enforcement of new systems and laws.

HTEs play a vital role in promoting China's scientific research, innovation, economic development and employment. During the course of administrative streamlining, the government should aim to enhance collaboration between businesses, universities and research bodies and encourage universities and industries to produce more cutting-edge technologies through academic research and business collaboration. At the same time, the government should also support HTEs by encouraging R&D through a variety of mechanisms, such as technical supervision, institutional support, fiscal and monetary policies, and tax reduction and exemption. The upgrading of technologies will spearhead China's economic restructuring and ensure sustained economic growth for the country.

Bibliography

Ba, S. (2000). Financial support in the development of China's high-tech industry. *Finance Forum*, (5).

Kuang, X. & Xiao, J. (2007). Integration of preferential tax policies for the cultivation of independent innovation ability of China—Analysis of preferential tax policies for high-tech enterprises. *Finance & Trade Economics*, (S1).

Lian, Y., Zheng, Y. & Yu, H. (2007). Exploration of technology innovation policy evaluation—Evaluation of fiscal and tax preferential policies to encourage business R&D investment. *Science and China Youth Technology*, (2).

Peng, J., Zhong, W. & Sun, W. (2008). Policy measurement, policy collaboration evolution and economic performance: An empirical study on innovative policies. *Management World*, (9).

Wang, C.& Liu, X. (2004). Strategy of science and technology development for building a society of moderate prosperity in all respects—Analysis of the national innovation system. *Science of Science and Management of S. & T.*, (25).

Xu, Q., & Luo, W. (2013). A brief analysis of the development environment and related policies of Chinese high-tech enterprises [OL]. Official website of Torch High Technology Industry Development Center, Ministry of Science and Technology.

Zhang, W. (2006). Roles of tax policy in promoting the development of high-tech industry and its mechanism analysis. *Journal of Renmin University of China*, (1).

Zhou, Y. (2002). Human capital, uncertainty and governance of high-tech enterprises. *China industrial Economics*, (10).

Zhou, G. (2011). Evolution of China's technology innovation policy since the reform and opening-up. *Economy Forum*, (11).

Zhu, W., & Lun, R. (2004). An empirical analysis of the correlation between R&D investment and performance of high-tech enterprises. *Science and Technology Management Research*, (24).

Practice and Reflections of Streamlining Administration and Delegating Power in the Context of Macrocontrol—A Case Study of Wuhai City, Inner Mongolia

Ye Bai and Fuhan Wang

Macrocontrol policies in different historical periods carry different characteristics. Under the "new normal" of economic development and the complex situation at home and abroad, the CPC Central Committee and the State Council have developed new thoughts and measures in applying macrocontrol. The state has deepened reform in an all-around way, streamlined administration and delegated power to lower-level governments while strengthening regulation and capacity building. These efforts have created a new source of strength for economic and social development.

Macrocontrol Policies Under the Planned Economy and Their Characteristics

In the early days of the PRC, the country's industrial foundation was very weak. By the standards of that time, modern industry accounted for only 10% of the total industrial output value, the share of the total output value of the manufacturing industry was only 30%, and the output value of heavy industry accounted for less than 8% of the total industrial and agricultural output value. To accelerate the process of industrialization, the central government decided to give priority to heavy industry to push forward the overall process of industrialization and realize the policy goal for economic and social development. At the same time, the government faced three challenges in the development of heavy industry: long construction period and high cost of capital; dependence on import of equipment and insufficient foreign exchange payment capacity in the early stage of development; big initial investment requirement and limited financing capacity.

During that period, capital supply was limited, making the cost of heavy industry development extremely high. It was difficult to mobilize resources from all quarters

Y. Bai (✉) · F. Wang
Guanghua School of Management, Peking University, Beijing, China

Y. Li and Z. Cheng (eds.), *The Chinese Path Toward a Leaner Government*,
https://doi.org/10.1007/978-981-19-6718-4_26

to implement the strategy of prioritizing heavy industry. Therefore, a set of macro policies different from those of the market economy was needed to artificially reduce the cost of heavy industry development to obtain a cheap supply of labor, capital, raw materials and imported equipment and technology. By excluding the role of the market, the policies that distorted the relative price of factors of production and products became the core element of macro control under those circumstances.

I. Low interest rate and exchange rate policies

Heavy industry is characterized by high capital intensity and a long construction period. If the capital price were determined by the market, a high interest rate would have held back industrial growth, which relied on a low capital price and low interest rate. For example, China's industrial credit monthly interest rate was 2% in July 1950 but was steadily lowered to 0.42% in August 1971. Technology and equipment underpin the development of heavy industry, and they were mainly imported in the early days of China's industrial development. Foreign exchange was also a scarce resource when capital was in short supply and there were few products available for export. To import key equipment at a lower price, the government intervened in the exchange rate. In 1950, the exchange rate of RMB against the US dollar was lowered 15 consecutive times, from 1:4.2 to 1:2.23. By 1978, the exchange rate had fallen to 1:1.72.

II. The policy of low wages and low prices of energy, raw materials and household products

In the early stage of China's economic development, the country had to mainly rely on its own efforts to secure a high accumulation rate required for the growth of heavy industry. The accumulation rate goes with profit margin, which depends on the spread between output value and investment. Lowering labor, energy and raw material costs is thus an important way to achieve high accumulation in heavy industry. From the 1950s to the end of the 1970s, wages were set by the central government, and local governments and enterprises had no right to adjust them. A low wage level limits people's ability to purchase daily necessities. If the price of daily necessities had been determined by the market, it would have affected social stability and the labor supply for the heavy industry. Therefore, the state maintained a low living cost policy.

III. Highly monopolistic financial and foreign exchange control

Due to the low interest rate policy, the bank's capital inflow was far less than the potential capital supply, and capital accumulated through channels outside the state control was not allowed to support the growth of the heavy industry. To keep the heavy industry growing, a financial monopoly must be implemented. What followed was the establishment of the financial system with the People's Bank of China at the center, the nationalization of the banking industry, and the creation of the credit fund management system of "unified collection and expenditure". A highly centralized financial system and a single financing channel achieved the purpose of prioritizing key industries in the national economic plan in the context of limited funds. At the same time, a low exchange rate dampened the willingness to export but made it cheaper to import foreign goods.

IV. A highly centralized system for the management of materials and the purchase and sale of agricultural products

In the context of material shortages, to support the development of heavy industry, policies of low wages and low material prices were implemented, which suppressed the enthusiasm of production on the supply side, while demand rose daily. A unified distribution system of important materials was implemented nationwide to support the policy of low prices of energy and raw materials and realize the direct allocation of materials by the state for economic development. Meanwhile, to ensure that farmers pooled resources into the production of agricultural products needed for industrialization, the state put agricultural production under direct control through administrative power and gradually realized the unified purchase, distribution and sales of important materials, non-staple food and raw materials for industrial use.

V. The state-owned economy took an absolutely dominant position.

Although the policies of low interest rate, low exchange rate and low material price reduced the production cost of industrial enterprises and improved the profit margin and accumulation rate of enterprises, private businesses were more inclined to invest resources in sectors that could maximize their profits, which was not in line with the national strategic goal of developing the heavy industry. Since 1954, the state began to gradually encourage big private enterprises to go for public–private partnerships, which were later made compulsory industry-wide across the country. Private enterprises by and large disappeared by 1956.

China's Macrocontrol Policies Under the Market Economic System and Their Characteristics

After the third Plenary Session of the 11th Central Committee of the Communist Party of China (CPC), two theoretical breakthroughs were made in the law of socialist commodity production and its value. The 12th National Congress of the CPC established the principle of regarding the planned economy as a mainstay with market regulation as a supplement, and the third Plenary Session of the 12th CPC put forward the theory of a planned commodity economy. The 14th National Congress of the CPC set the goal of establishing a socialist market economic system, ushering China's economic reform into a new historical stage. China took an incremental approach in the process of transitioning from the planned economy to the market economy by taking into account the national conditions at that time to realize a smooth transition to the new system through a top-down compulsory institutional arrangement. There are three reasons for choosing an incremental approach. First, the planned economy in China was not sophisticated enough. Compared with the Soviet Union and East Europe, China was running its planned economy in a strong idealistic style with low levels of productivity, technology, education and division of labor. However, this is precisely what a market economy needs for fast growth once the government relaxes its control and provides proper guidance. Second, many market factors came into play. The reform combined industrialization with market forces, which was an important condition for such incremental reform to succeed. At that time, due to the low level of industrialization, the collective agricultural sector accounted for a large share of the economy, but they were outside the state-owned economic system and could not enjoy the benefits of the planned economy. This made the transition to the market economy possible by starting from areas outside the state-owned system. Third, the macroeconomy was relatively stable. In countries with relatively stable macroeconomic performance and strong economic growth momentum, there is generally little desire for drastic reform. Instead, a more gradual reform approach is often adopted, as was the case in China. The roles of macrocontrol exercised by the state through economic, administrative, planning and legal means were as follows:

I. Maintain steady and balanced growth of the national economy

First, macrocontrol targets the market instead of businesses. Market changes lead to business readjustment. This is where the market can play a dominating role. Second, the goal of macrocontrol is to ease economic fluctuations instead of pursuing a high growth rate. Under the new circumstances, the goal of macrocontrol is to ease economic fluctuations, maintain the balance between aggregate supply and demand, and achieve slower yet sustainable economic growth. Instead of quantitative control, efforts are made to adjust the economic structure and give full play to the dominating role of the market. Macrocontrol thus plays a supporting role in maintaining the steady and sustained growth of the national economy.

II. Balance aggregate supply and demand

One of the key goals of macrocontrol is to balance the aggregate supply and demand. The main cause of economic fluctuations in China that have occurred since the start of the reform and opening-up is inflation or oversupply. At present, China needs to coordinate the four aspects of total supply: finance, credit, materials and foreign exchange. First, fiscal balance must be maintained with fiscal surplus or deficit minimized. Second, financial credit must be balanced. A prudent monetary policy should be pursued to avoid currency over-issuance and match credit growth with economic growth. Third, balance in the reserve of goods, especially balance between investment and consumption, should be maintained. Fourth, foreign exchange payments should be balanced. Overreliance on foreign exchange creates trade deficits. Given the grim prospects of the global economy, more attention should be given to bringing in talent, technology and investment from abroad.

III. Align industrial structure with market demand

The market plays a decisive role in the allocation of resources. The industrial structure must match the market demand to promote sustained growth of the economy. In optimizing the industrial structure, it is necessary to ensure sufficient growth of energy, agriculture and other industries critical to the national economy and people's livelihood before the growth of the secondary and tertiary industries. Only by abandoning the backward industrial structure can the economy continue to develop. Emerging technologies are the sole drivers of the transformation and development of enterprises and represent a new growth area for the economy.

IV. Coordinate economic interests of all sectors

As the proportion of state-owned enterprises gradually decreases and that of private enterprises moves in the opposite direction, an unfair distribution has appeared in various sectors. While diversifying enterprise ownership, efforts should be made to ease frictions in distribution, especially those between companies of different ownerships. Consideration should be given to balancing the overall and individual interests and the interests of the general public and market players.

Macro Control Policies Under the New Normal and Their Characteristics

Since the 18th National Congress of the CPC, profound changes have taken place in the domestic and international economic landscape, and China's reform and development have entered a critical period. Faced with complexities at home and abroad, the CPC Central Committee and the State Council assessed the situation and developed new thinking and features in macrocontrol.

I. Adhering to the "market-oriented" approach

Market and government are two basic means of resource allocation. The core issue of resource allocation is to deal with the relationship between the government and the market, or in other words, determine whether the market or the government plays the dominant role in resource allocation. In the context of the new normal, the 18th CPC Central Committee elevated the role of the market in resource allocation from "basic" to "decisive" at its third plenary session, reflecting a greater determination to pursue market-oriented reform. Efforts have been made to separate administrative management from macrocontrol. Steps have been taken to respect market laws in pushing forward the reform. The government is also working to suit macrocontrol policies to businesses and improve the policy transmission mechanism and relies more on the market to regulate the economy. What the market can do should be left to the market. The government's main task is to formulate rules, create a level playing field, refrain from overstepping its authority and fill in regulatory gaps. Thus, the market will play a decisive role, and the government will play a limited but better role.

II. Put forward the concept of "range-based and targeted regulation"

In the previous rounds of macrocontrol, China tended to select a definitive economic growth rate (such as "8%") as the policy target. After China's economy entered the "new normal", guided by the new development philosophy, the central government put forward a new thinking of "range-based regulation" in 2013, which was meant to secure stable growth and employment, prevent inflation, protect people's livelihood and defuse financial risks. The shift from "growth rate-based regulation" to "regulation within a reasonable growth range" allows more flexibility instead of taking frequent countermeasures against short-term fluctuations in macroeconomic indicators. As long as the economy runs within a reasonable range, macroeconomic policies will remain basically unchanged.

To address the outstanding structural imbalances among regions and industries and between urban and rural areas, "targeted regulation" was further proposed on the basis of "range-based regulation" in 2014. In terms of regulation intensity, moderate measures similar to "sprinkling" and "dripping" in farm irrigation were set to replace strong stimuli, focusing on strengthening weak links, the economic foundation and the momentum of economic growth. The targeted areas of regulation are closely linked to the transformation and development of the real economy. Support is offered to "mass entrepreneurship and innovation", "Internet+", green development, the Belt and Road initiative and other national development programs. A wider range of policies in the real economy, monetary, fiscal, social security and financial areas have been employed to make targeted regulation more effective.

III. Pay more attention to expectation management and guidance

First, priority is given to maintaining stable expectations with the government making repeated statements on its determination and confidence in maintaining steady economic growth and "not letting growth slip below the lower limit" to boost the confidence of the market. Second, to address information asymmetry, the government needs to improve the spokesperson system and increase the frequency of the release of key information on the macroeconomy, which is closely followed by the general public. The government should also interact with the public to explain economic and social development policies and reform measures and promote a better understanding of new policies and regulations. It should also respond to hot issues and take into consideration public expectations in decision-making. Third, government information and policies and their key points must be released promptly free of charge to boost the transparency and credibility of the government with timely and authoritative policy interpretation made through various means to ensure stability, transparency, predictability and smooth implementation of the rules, goals and orientation of government policies.

IV. Establish a global vision

Economic integration has created a closer bond among various economies. China is now the world's second largest economy, the world's largest trading nation and a major capital exporter. Its economy is deeply integrated with the world economy. Because of the faster integration of the global economy, the new round of macrocontrol in China has, to a large extent, gone beyond its borders and carried with it a global dimension. Policies in China increasingly have a "spillover" effect on the global economy. It is mainly reflected in three aspects. First, the robust export of goods, competitive industries and capital outflow provide a new impetus for China's economic growth and industrial structure upgrading and contribute to long-term global strategic planning for China's economic development. Second, China is no longer constrained to the platforms for international economic activities set up by developed countries. It has begun to establish or sponsor international economic institutions based on its own needs, put forward the China agenda on various international occasions, and actively join or lead in international economic rule settings to open an "international channel" for Chinese capital to go global. Third, China actively promotes economic liberalization by launching pilot free trade zones in Shanghai, Guangdong, Fujian and Tianjin and advancing the Belt and Road Initiative globally. It has expanded economic cooperation with developing countries, especially neighboring countries in the Asia–Pacific region, to build a "community of shared futures", which brings economic benefit to all and strengthens the momentum of economic integration.

V. Pay greater attention to supply-side management

Demand- and supply-side management are two commonly used tools of macrocontrol. Proper demand and supply side management in addressing factors that lead to macroeconomic imbalance plays an important role in meeting macrocontrol targets. However, in recent years, fiscal and monetary policy adjustments have focused more on demand-side management. China has achieved fast growth, but its economy has long been dominated by industries of high consumption, high emissions and low added value. This has resulted in massive resource consumption, worsening of the ecological environment, overcapacity, diminishing returns on investment, development imbalances, distortion in distribution and other economic and social problems.

In view of the problems in demand-side management and the slow-down of growth in key economic drivers such as investment, consumption and export in the context of the new normal, General Secretary Xi Jinping stressed at the meeting of the central leading group on fiscal and financial affairs on November 10, 2015 that China should focus on strengthening supply-side structural reforms while moderately expanding aggregate demand to improve the quality and performance of the supply system, sustain growth momentum and upgrade the overall production level. The central leading group held its 12th meeting on January 26, 2016, to review the supply side structural reform plan and adjust the approach of macrocontrol, namely, shifting macrocontrol focus from the demand side to the supply side, concentrating long-term macrocontrol on supply side management, promoting innovation through reform, giving play to the role of enterprises and entrepreneurs as market players, and securing medium- and long-term healthy and sustainable development through structural adjustment and institutional reform and improvement instead of addressing short-term economic fluctuations. While focusing on the supply side, the government should also pay more attention to innovation and upgrading of the demand side to achieve proper division of roles, coordination and cooperation between management on both the supply and demand sides for sustainable and healthy development of the economy.

Streamlining Administration and Delegating Power Under the Macrocontrol Policy

Since the reform and opening up, China's overall strength has been significantly enhanced. Greater national prosperity has boosted people's living standards. China's development achievements have attracted worldwide attention, but in the course of its development, some economic and social problems have gradually emerged. Facing a complex economic situation at home and abroad and downward pressure on the national economy, China has carried out reforms in all areas. Streamlining administration and delegating power is among the first group of concrete measures to advance the reform and macrocontrol and has created a better relationship between government and market. It aims to break all barriers that hold back economic growth and vitality to improve the quality and performance of economic development.

The institutional reform centering upon decentralization and function shifts aims to transform a monopolistic and omnipotent government, an attribute inherited from the era of the planned economy, to a law-based government with limited functions to create a level playing field for market players of all kinds of ownership, break industry monopolies, streamline approvals, and eliminate institutional obstacles against the reform. This is an important measure to unleash the benefits of the reform and upgrade the Chinese economy.

I. Streamlining administration and delegating power are of critical importance to advancing institutional reform and transforming government functions

For a long time, the government has intervened too much in and exercised too much control over market players. Review and approval assumed greater roles than regulation. This has dampened economic vitality, increased administrative costs and bred corruption. Streamlining administration, delegating power and strengthening regulation are the keys to solving these acute problems. Focusing on the core of administrative and economic restructuring holds the key to improving the socialist market economy and advancing development. The relationship between the government on one side and the market and society on the other should be straightened out. The government should know where the borders of its responsibilities are and act accordingly. It should cut its ownership, control, and the right of approval, decision-making and allocation over high-quality resources. The relevant powers and interests should be returned to businesses, the public and the market. The government should undertake more social management and macrocontrol responsibilities and minimize direct intervention in market activities. Streamlining administration and delegating power therefore is of critical importance to the overall reform agenda of China.

II. Streamlining administration and delegating power should focus on addressing red tapes and the low efficiency of the government

Some government departments have had overlapping functions and unclear responsibilities, and the inefficiency of some government agencies with approval powers has created sticky issues such as complicated and lengthy processes, high fees, low efficiency, rule bending, shifting responsibilities and inaction. Approval of some industrial projects takes too much time to complete and requires consent from dozens of departments and offices. It also involves over one hundred steps and seals and multiple payment procedures. The whole process sometimes takes one or two years or even longer. Given such a long approval period, many projects have been delayed. This has seriously affected the enthusiasm of enterprises and the market and has led to the loss of good projects and the practice of launching projects before obtaining approval. At the same time, excessive concentration of review and approval power and too much discretionary power have yet to be solved, which easily leads to willful approval, under-the-table maneuvering and rent-seeking. As a result of the reform, red tapes and low efficiency have been addressed by streamlining the government, removing and delegating some review items, adopting responsibility, power and negative lists and granting licenses before issuing certificates, which means moving from prior review to *interim and exp post* regulation for some items.

III. Innovating government management and improving the service environment are the core contents of streamlining administration and delegating power

Irregularities in China's market economy linger, and unfair competition is quite common. Delegating power to the market does not mean giving a free hand to it. Instead, the government should work harder on strengthening regulation. Better regulation leads to greater liberalization. To build a leaner government, it is important to advance the reform of the administrative system with new models and better tools and make *interim* and *ex post* supervision more targeted and effective. It will help nurture a vibrant and orderly market, promote fairness in rights, opportunities and rules, and create a dynamic and harmonious society where everyone can enjoy the benefit of reform and development. At the same time, the government should fill the gaps in performing its public service duties, shift its priority from administration to service to foster a sound environment for development, provide quality public services, and safeguard social equity and justice. Building a learning, service-oriented and law-based government will help further improve the government's service capacity and make people more satisfied with its work.

IV. The ultimate goal of streamlining administration and delegating power is to foster vitality of the market and promote sound development

The reform to streamline administration and delegate power will, in essence, invigorate the market and promote development. With the goal of building a leaner government, efforts are made to streamline institutions, decentralize authorities, return relevant power and interests to businesses, society and markets and straighten the government's relations with the market and society. The market should be allowed to do whatever it can do to fully leverage its due role, while the government should take care of what the market cannot do. The government must remove outdated practices, unreasonable constraints and bureaucracies that hamper entrepreneurship and innovation. It should stimulate the vitality of the market economy and the potential of domestic demand and create new momentum for development by offering abundant public goods and quality and efficient public services. It should also create an enabling environment for social progress, facilitate entrepreneurship and innovation, promote economic development, make people more satisfied, and make society more empathetic, harmonious, cohesive and dynamic.

The Practice of Streamlining Administration and Delegating Power in Wuhai City, Inner Mongolia

Wuhai is an emerging industrial city in the western part of the Inner Mongolia Autonomous Region. It is located on the upper reaches of the Yellow River, facing the Ordos Plateau in the east, Shizuishan city of Ningxia in the south across the river, the Alxa Grassland in the west, and the fertile Hetao Plain in the north. It borders North China and Northwest China and the "Ningxia, Mongolia, Shaanxi and Gansu economic zone" and sits in the middle of the Yellow River Basin Economic Belt. In 1958, with the implementation of key national projects such as the Baotou-Lanzhou Railway and the Baotou Iron and Steel Company, large-scale development and construction began in Wuhai. In 1976, with the approval of the State Council, the former two county-level cities of Wuda and Haibuwan were merged into Wuhai. Its jurisdiction now covers the three county-level administrative regions of Haibuwan, Wuda and Hainan, with a total area of 1754 square kilometers, a permanent population of 550,000 (household registered population of 445,000) and 40 ethnic groups, including Mongolian, Han, Hui and Manchu.

In recent years, Wuhai has taken steps to streamline administration and delegate power, strengthen regulation and improve services by rolling back administrative authorities and approval power, better regulating the decision-making power, and strengthening the power of supervision. These efforts have created a favorable environment for promoting economic and social development.

I. A new round of government reform has been carried out to streamline government institutions and promote innovation in government administration

Streamlining administration and delegating power is not only about canceling or delegating power but also about innovating and improving government administration. The government should strengthen regulation on affairs falling into its responsibility and coordinate regulation with power delegation instead of giving a free hand to the market. In accordance with the principle of "transforming functions, straightening out relationships, optimizing structure and improving efficiency", Wuhai carried out a new round of reform of government institutions in 2015. As a result, the government has become leaner, and its performance has improved significantly. For example, the role of industrial and commercial administration has been relocated from the central authorities to local governments, and the market regulatory commission was created with power covering business administration, quality supervision, and food and drug regulation. Thus, a unified market regulatory framework under a single government authority has been established to fill the regulatory gaps. The city management commission was established by integrating the urban management functions of different government agencies to create an integrated authority on city management featuring unified leadership and better coordination. The establishment of these new administrative institutions has effectively addressed issues such as overlapping authorities and buck-passing practices of the government and improved city management. In the 2015 evaluation of the civility level of Chinese cities, over 92% of the people in Wuhai expressed satisfaction with city management. Hainan District launched a comprehensive administrative law enforcement reform in September 2015 to integrate law enforcement functions and teams through joint and commissioned law enforcement. The functions of eight departments, including regulatory bodies on sanitation and funeral services and water and forestry administration, have been merged, and more law enforcement teams have been sent to industrial parks and subdistrict/township level government offices to ensure swift responses to public complaints by a single law enforcement team. City management efficiency has in this way been improved by a large margin.

II. Continuously advancing the reform of the administrative review and approval system has improved the service environment and government efficiency

Wuhai opened the new government service center in 2010 and moved all staff and items of the municipal review and approval to the general service hall and specific offices of the center. Multistep approval processes have been replaced by "one-stop" services with a maximum time frame of 20 working days. The processing period for most of the items has been cut from 30 to 5 days on average, and applicants can now finish the process on-site for some items that used to require a waiting period of 5 days. With "one-stop" service for all approval items and on-site completion of review processes once documents are fully submitted, applicants no longer have to visit multiple agencies and wait for 3–5 months to obtain approval for a single item. In September 2013, Wuhai carried out a new round of clean-up of non-administrative license review and approval items and administrative fees, keeping only 87 items and cutting 106 items, with a reduction rate of 55%. A total of 50 items of fee collection were canceled, and 48 items of administrative fees were kept, with a reduction rate of 51.02%. After several rounds of clean-up, the number of items subject to review and approval has been reduced, the relevant procedures have been simplified, and businesses and individuals have had easier access to public services with less cost. According to the public opinion survey, the satisfaction rate of the people with Wuhai's government services is as high as 99.7%.

In addition, the Wuhai Municipal Commission for Discipline Inspection has moved its supervisory office to the government service center. The organizing department of the municipal CPC committee has included information access to government work and government services in the performance assessment of government bodies of the three districts, municipal departments and their service offices in the center. People can raise suggestions and complaints through the online complaint platform. Thanks to these efforts, the government service center has reached "three 100%", namely, 100% processing of the review and approval items, 100% network connection with all commissions and bureaus, and 100% coverage of electronic supervision and monitoring.

III. The power list, responsibility list and negative list system has put government behavior under better regulation and promoted the moral integrity of civil servants

Government institutions, functions, powers, procedures and responsibilities are clarified in accordance with the law in the principle of building a leaner, law-based and open government. Efforts have been made in cutting administrative powers other than administrative licensing, implementing the administrative power and responsibility list and the negative list system, and making public the process of exercising government power in accordance with the law. Steps have been taken to develop an efficient administrative power system with sound and clearly defined responsibilities with a view to establishing a government that is open, fair, clean, efficient and law-abiding with robust functions, law-based responsibilities, stringent law enforcement capabilities and good faith. After self-review by administrative departments and confirmation and public notification by the legislative affairs office of the municipal government, the 38 municipal administrative departments have kept a total of only 4251 administrative items, including 152 administrative licensing items, 3146 administrative punishment items, 113 compulsory administrative measures, 49 administrative enforcement items, 39 administrative expropriation items, 103 administrative confirmation items, 35 administrative payment items, 87 administrative reward items, 309 administrative supervision and inspection items, 218 other administrative items and 77 items of delegated authority. All of them are published on the Wuhai government website. Administrative power is cut to ensure greater market vitality. The power, responsibility and negative lists are formulated to define the boundaries of powers and responsibilities of the government, the market, enterprises and society to better regulate the "visible" hand, better use the "invisible" hand and forestall any rent-seeking in accordance with the law. The list of powers is used to clarify what the government can do and ensure that "no action is permitted unless authorized by law". The list of responsibilities defines how the government should regulate the market and requires the government to fulfill its statutory duties. The negative list is used to spell out the restrictions on enterprises, which means "anything unless prohibited by law can be done". Since the launch of the three lists, government behaviors have been placed under effective oversight, as its exercise of power is open to the public and better regulated.

IV. Streamlining administration, delegating power, improving regulation and providing better services have unleashed market vitality and boosted regional development

The reform of streamlining administration, delegating power, strengthening regulation and providing better services has significantly improved Wuhai's business environment, eased restrictions on businesses, reduced burdens on the people, left more space to the market and enhanced the government's integrity. A lower institutional cost for market access and operation has stimulated market vitality and social creativity. First, it promotes fast growth of the tertiary industry and further improves the industrial structure. The ratio for the primary, secondary and tertiary industries evolved from 1:71.7:27.3 in 2010 to 0.8:60.3:38.9 in 2015, and the share of the tertiary industry in the GDP has increased by 11.6 percentage points. In particular, the growth of new drivers has accelerated, and enthusiasm for mass entrepreneurship and innovation is at an all-time high. Due to the low threshold for starting businesses, flexible operational models and the wide-ranging impact on social life, self-employed businesses, the preferred choice for business starters, are growing exponentially. In 2015, the number of self-employed businesses in Wuhai reached a record high of 37,100, an increase of 33.65% compared with 2012. They have created more than 87,000 jobs and attracted 2 billion yuan of investment. The number of jobs and the amount of investment increased by 41.08% and 52.17%, respectively, compared with 2012. Areas of investment cover e-commerce, wholesale and retail, accommodation and catering, residential services, repair and other service sectors. With the continuous expansion of investment fields, new industries such as information transmission, software and information technology services, scientific research and technology services, culture, sports and entertainment have also developed rapidly and gradually become new growth drivers, further promoting the transformation of the economic growth model and industrial upgrading in Wuhai.

In short, streamlining administration and delegating power is an important measure to deepen the reform of the administrative system, transform government functions and explore new administrative methods under the "new normal" of the economy. In the process of streamlining administration, delegating power and strengthening macrocontrol, the government needs to take integrated and proactive measures to improve regulation while decentralizing its powers, coordinate steps on the two tracks, and strengthen *interim* and *ex post* supervision while delegating powers to avoid the vicious cycle of "decentralizing–chaos–tighter control". Streamlining administration and delegating power should be carried out in combination with macrocontrol measures, as they are mutually complementary and reinforcing. Only by taking proper measures in these areas can we promote sound development of the socialist market economy featuring greater vitality of market entities.

Bibliography

Chen, E., Qi, Z., Han, J. et al. (2015). *Upgrading China's economy: A documentation of the new Chinese administration's reform of streamlining administration and delegating power*. China Yan Shi Press.

Gao, H., et al. (2000). *Western economics*. China Renmin University Press.

Liu, G. (1988). *Research on the model of China's economic reform*. China Social Sciences Press.

Li, K. (2015). Streamlining administration, delegating power, strengthening regulation, and improving services—Deepening the reform of the administrative system and effectively transforming government functions—Speech at the national teleconference on promoting the work of streamlining administration, delegating power and transforming government functions [OL].

Lin, Y., et al. (1999). *China's miracle: Development strategy and economic reform: 2nd Edition.* Shanghai Joint Publishing Company.

Sun, Z. (2009). *From planning to market: Analysis of China's economic transformation.* China Social Publishing House.

Wang, D., Xiang, Z. & Lin, Y. (2015). Advancing administration streamlining and power delegation to stimulate market vitality and social creativity. *Administration Reform*, (7).

Zhang, S. (2002). *The linkage of policy and system: Macroeconomic analysis in the market-oriented reform.* Shanghai University of Finance & Economics Press.

Building a Leaner Government to Stimulate Market Vitality and Serve the Supply-Side Structural Reform—A Case Study of Suqian City, Jiangsu Province

Jun Yin and Huanxing Liu

The History of Streamlining Administration and Delegating Power in China Since the Reform and Opening-Up

I. Evolution of the relationship between the government and the market

Properly handling the relationship between the government and the market is the core issue in China's economic restructuring. Since the reform and opening up, the definition of this relationship has changed four times.

It first changed from "relying on government planning and rejecting market roles" before 1978 to "government planning playing a dominant role and the market playing a supporting role" in the early days of the reform and opening-up. At that time, the market played a supporting role in expanding the autonomy of state-owned enterprises, especially in terms of decision-making power in personnel, finance, material and planning. The market also gradually helped develop special economic zones and private enterprises.

The second change came in 1984 at the third Plenary Session of the 12th CPC Central Committee, which decided to "develop the socialist commodity economy", stating that both the government and the market were effective tools for resource allocation. The concept of resource allocation by market was formally included in the state policy, which mainly aimed to reform the corporate ownership and the price system and promote the development of the socialist commodity economy and greater vitality of the market.

The relationship changed again at the 14th CPC National Congress in 1992, which set the reform goal of establishing a socialist market economic system, namely, to "let the market play a basic role in the allocation of resources under the state's

J. Yin (✉)
Planning Bureau, China Development Bank, Beijing, China

H. Liu
Guanghua School of Management, Peking University, Beijing, China

Y. Li and Z. Cheng (eds.), *The Chinese Path Toward a Leaner Government*,
https://doi.org/10.1007/978-981-19-6718-4_27

macrocontrol". It required the government to respect the market rules and leave to the market what the market can do as much as possible. An overall reform strategy with a clear focus was adopted. The 15th CPC National Congress reaffirmed the policy of "letting the market play a basic role in the allocation of resources under the state's macrocontrol". The 16th CPC National Congress decided to "further expand the basic role of the market in resource allocation". The 17th CPC National Congress asked for "giving better play to the basic role of the market in allocation of resources from the institutional perspective". The 18th CPC National Congress required "giving play to the basic role of the market in resource allocation in a wider scope and at a bigger scale". The role of the market in resource allocation has continued to increase. Over the two decades since 1992, the relationship between the government and the market has increasingly become better defined and delivered increasing benefits.

The fourth change came at the third Plenary Session of the 18th CPC Central Committee in 2013, which decided to "let the market play a decisive role in resource allocation". It is an essential law of the market economy that the market plays a decisive role because it has been proven that the market is the most efficient force in resource allocation. The decisive role of the market means that the government should let the market do what it can even if the government can do the same thing. Instead, the government shall do what the market cannot, such as providing public goods and conducting macrocontrol and social governance. However, this does not mean that the market will replace the government or we will go for "a small government and a big market". This means that an efficient government and a functioning market must work together.

II. The development path of streamlining administration and delegating power

Since the start of the reform and opening up, China has launched the reform on streamlining administration and delegating power six times in 1982, 1988, 1993, 1998, 2003 and 2008 in light of the changes in the relationship between the government and the market and gradually delegated the power of resource allocation from the government to the market. On March 14, 2013, the *Plan for Institutional Reform and Functional Transformation of the State Council* was released at the very beginning of this administration, which unveiled the seventh round of the reform on streamlining administration and delegating power since 1978.

Since the third plenary session of the 18th CPC Central Committee, the central leadership has attached great importance to this reform. General Secretary Xi Jinping has stressed on many occasions the need to take substantive reform measures. He said that one of the goals of the accelerated efforts made by government bodies at all levels to transform functions and delegate power is to give better play to the market and encourage businesses to be more innovative and creative. This is a further step taken by the government to ease restrictions on businesses and another historic opportunity for entrepreneurs to make best of their wisdom and resources.

Premier Li Keqiang of the State Council has convened several national video and telephone conferences on the reform to streamline administration, delegate power and improve regulation and services. He put forward three specific criteria to measure the reform success: first, how much time is shortened for enterprises to get approval for starting business; second, how faster it is for investment projects to be approved; and third, how easier it is for the people to receive government services.

Streamlining administration and delegating power means streamlining administrative procedures and returning or delegating some of the government's powers to the market, society and the primary-level authorities. It generally includes three dimensions. The first is the adjustment of the relationship between the government and enterprises; that is, the government will reduce its intervention in business activities such as their independent registration, operation and management. The second is the adjustment of the relationship between the government and society; that is, the government transfers some highly professional public service functions to such social organizations as industry associations, chambers of commerce, science and technology groups, charity organizations, and urban and rural community-level cultural, sports and service organizations. The third is the adjustment of the relationship between the central government and the primary-level governments, which means that the central government delegates some financial, administrative and resource allocation powers to the primary-level governments.

China's economy is in the new normal, facing both new opportunities and new challenges. Advancing supply-side structural reform is both a natural requirement for adapting to and guiding economic development in the new normal and the fundamental solution to the problems emerging in this period. In short, the reform aims to cut production capacity, inventory and cost, deleverage, and strengthen the weak links. Each of them relies on the macrocontrol of the government, the vitality of market players in investment, consumption and innovation, and the service capacity of social entities. The reform adjusts the relations and builds synergy among the government, market players and social entities. It is critical to create a law-based, facilitating, service-oriented and international business environment to stimulate economic growth and market vitality, enhance the international competitiveness of the Chinese economy and enterprises, cut production capacity, inventory and cost, deleverage, strengthen the weak links, and boost supply-side structural reform. To this end, the new administration regards a leaner government as the key to supply-side structural reform. It has streamlined administration, delegated power, strengthened regulation and improved services in a broader scope and at a deeper level. The reform of the administrative system has continued to transfer function and improve efficiency. Administrative review and approval items were slashed. Steps have been taken to reform the commercial system, strengthen the management of the responsibility and power list of local governments, advance price reform and supervision and conduct enterprise credit information management.

III. Achievements and deficiencies in streamlining administration and delegating power

The greatest achievement of streamlining administration and delegating power is the reduction of institutional transaction costs in economic development. Institutional transaction costs refer to the economic, time and opportunity costs caused by institutional and mechanism hiccups, especially the costs that enterprises have to bear for complying with various systems, rules and policies formulated by the government.

At the beginning of the seventh round of administrative streamlining in 2013, there were over 1700 items for review and approval by the authorities under the State Council with processes that were complicated, costly, time-consuming and inefficient. This administration is committed to building a learner government. As of May 2016, 618 items of administrative review and approval were canceled or delegated, and non-administrative license approval was eliminated, which has greatly stimulated the vitality of the market. Since 2015, market players have increased by 40,000 every day, including 12,000 new businesses. A report released by the World Bank shows that the Chinese mainland has moved up six places in the global ranking of ease of doing business every year since 2015. It is estimated that since the start of the reform to streamline administration and delegate power by this administration, the burden on enterprises has been reduced by more than RMB150 billion each year.

While remarkable achievements have been made in the reform, there are still some problems in the practice of streamlining administration and delegating power in China, which are reflected in the following three aspects.

First, there is insufficient delegation of power. Although some items requiring government review and approval have been abolished or adjusted in the reform, there are still many such items, especially at the local government level, and it still takes a long time for enterprises to invest in a project and the cost remains high. In addition, as the reform started at easier issues, now the remaining items to be removed or adjusted are generally hard nuts to crack. Some of them concern the immediate departmental interests and have naturally met with resistance. Some involve multiple departments with conflicting policies. In other cases, the power of one department has been canceled or adjusted, but the supporting policies of other departments remain unchanged, and the cost of policy coordination between government departments is high.

The second is poor service delivery. According to a survey conducted by the People's Daily in May 2016, some measures to streamline administration and delegate power are often stuck in the "last mile" in implementation. As a result, some good policies have become "empty promises". The main reason is the weak capability of the government to provide follow-up services. For example, after power is delegated, primary-level government offices are not able to properly exercise power or deliver prompt and efficient services due to their limited capacity and manpower. Another example is the power of professional evaluation of various industries transferred to social organizations. As the market for professional industry evaluation in China is not mature, such services, which are often characterized by high fees, long processes, low efficiency and poor service quality, have drastically increased the financial burden on enterprises.

Third, weak regulation. Over the years, the Chinese government has been used to the practice of review and approval and has limited experience and sense of follow-up regulation. The problem of "being strict in prior review but weak in regulation" is widespread in the government. In the past, the government had large discretionary power and tended to select the best projects. However, when its responsibility shifts to regulation, the government finds it difficult to gain full information concerning the project and perform its regulatory functions. In addition, as an effective regulatory mechanism and a standardized regulatory system have not yet been established, problems such as unfair law enforcement, arbitrary inspection, lack of oversight and weak supervision are still prominent.

The Content of Streamlining Administration, Delegating Power, Improving Services and Strengthening Regulation

To streamline administration and delegate power, departments of the State Council, local governments and free trade zones have made active explorations and collected much valuable experience. To ensure the success of the reform, we need to work in the following three areas.

I. Improve regulation of power delegation with three lists

To streamline administration and delegate power, it is important to take a principled approach as to what kind of powers should be transferred and what should be kept in the government's hand. To this end, it is necessary to adopt three lists, namely, the negative list for market access, the list of the government's powers and the list of the responsibilities of the government and its departments.

The first is the negative list of market access, which defines the red line and the off-limit areas for market players. It also means that market players can try anything that is not written in the negative list in the principle of "anything can be done unless prohibited by law". The negative list can effectively strengthen business confidence because previously, in the principle of "he who files the claim shall present the evidence", market players had to prove by themselves which legal provisions backed their practice. Now with the negative list in place, the only thing they have to do is to prove that they have not breached the list.

The second is the government's power list, which specifies what the government can do, but at the same time, it also means that the government cannot intervene in things not mentioned in the power list, or in other words, "it cannot do anything without legal mandate". The power lists of various departments of the central and local governments need to be clarified to prevent policy conflicts among them. The list of government powers defines the boundary of the government's roles and the way of exercising them. It is an important form of law-based administration, as it enables market players to further enhance confidence and prevents rent-seeking behaviors.

The third is the list of responsibilities of the government and its departments, which specifies the services provided by the government and its departments for market and social entities and the procedures for performing their duties, in the principle that "the government must fulfill their statutory duties". The list of responsibilities of various departments of the central and local governments also need to be drawn to prevent overlapping responsibilities. It establishes the standards and contents for the government's work for the market and the public to exercise scrutiny.

II. Optimizing services and stimulating market vitality

To streamline administration and delegate power, we need to improve government services, which means that the government should provide quality and efficient public services to make the process of entrepreneurship and innovation of market players smoother and the business environment more convenient, efficient, fair and equitable for greater market vitality.

First, the government should provide comprehensive, one-stop services for mass entrepreneurship and innovation through streamlined services, policy support and information consultancy. Government service centers and online government services should be improved. All-around services should be delivered through "single window application, one-stop review and approval, and whole-process service". We will further cut administrative review and approval items related to private investment and fees charged from enterprises, regulate the processing steps and the conduct of intermediary organizations, and simplify administrative procedures to ease the burden on enterprises by lowering the costs. The government should support innovation and entrepreneurship through a combination of fiscal support and policy-based, development, commercial and cooperative financial support as well as a wide range of sustainable investment and financing cooperation mechanisms. It should also strengthen policy, legal and information consultancy services and do a good job in intellectual property protection, employment and entrepreneurship guidance and vocational skills training.

Second, capacity building of governments at all levels needs to be strengthened, especially those at the primary level, in an effort to build a service-oriented government. "Absence and inadequacy" of government services must be addressed to leave no areas unattended to. When market entities encounter difficulties, the government should provide prompt services to help them overcome the challenges through consultation and proper guidance. At the same time, the government should encourage social organizations and public institutions to provide public goods and services, help businesses make plans, set standards, promote competition and strengthen regulation.

Third, the government should improve social security to remove concerns of market entities. The government should invest more human, financial and material resources into public services that bear people's vital interests, such as implementing policies to assist those encountering setbacks in their businesses and encourage them to try again. Full coverage of the social security system is needed, such as providing universal medical insurance, alleviating poverty, helping people in need, and carrying out livelihood projects of rebuilding rundown urban areas and renovating dilapidated rural houses.

III. Combining power delegation with better regulation and improving systems and laws

A leaner government must combine delegating power with strengthening regulation. In the context of building a country under the rule of law, the government needs to further improve institutions and laws and strengthen law-based regulation while streamlining administration and delegating power.

The ultimate purpose of regulation is not to put shackles on businesses but to create a level playing field, stimulate the initiative of market entities, and protect their rights through better regulation. Regulatory means generally include not only administrative licensing but also information monitoring, standard setting, incentives offering and so on. Canceling or delegating the power of administrative licensing does not mean that the government will no longer perform its regulatory functions. Instead, the government should adjust its approach of regulation to boost market vitality and move from prior review to *interim and ex post* supervision.

Effective regulation needs support from a sound system that encompasses regulatory means, the structures, roles and responsibilities of regulatory bodies, capacity building of their staff and logistic services. It also calls for combining government regulation with industrial self-discipline and regulatory coordination among government departments, regulatory decision-making procedure settings, rectifying law-breaking regulatory activities and holding relevant officials accountable. In this context, it is important to improve relevant systems and laws as soon as possible and promote law-based and effective regulation.

The Practice of Streamlining Administration and Delegating Power in Suqian City, Jiangsu Province

Suqian is located in northern Jiangsu Province and northern Yangtze River Delta. Established in July 1996 with the approval of the State Council, it covers the counties of Shuyang, Siyang and Sihong, districts of Suyu and Sucheng, as well as the Suqian Economic Development Zone, Hubin New Area, Suzhou-Suqian Industrial Park and Yanghe New Area. With an area of 8555 km^2 and a population of 5.8 million, Suqian is the youngest prefecture-level city in Jiangsu Province.

Suqian Municipality was established on the basis of four provincial-level poverty-stricken counties previously under the jurisdiction of Huaiyin City, with a GDP of only RMB12.49 billion. Due to its late start and weak foundation, Suqian came behind other cities in Jiangsu in economic and social development and faced many difficulties in its own growth. In view of the growth challenges and its special development stage, the municipal government demonstrated an unyielding spirit in pushing for transformation. Decisions were made to stay united and make pioneering and dedicated efforts to achieve self-reliance and self-improvement as well as protect the ecology and encourage entrepreneurship in the urbanization process. The government encourages the people to embrace innovation and entrepreneurship and develop broader visions. The city has been known for its ambition, pioneering spirit, sense of responsibility and commitment and the ability to take on challenges.

Reform has always been a hallmark of Suqian. Over the past 20 years, under the strong leadership of the provincial Party committee and government, thanks to the joint efforts of successive municipal party and government leadership and the local communities, Suqian started by addressing fundamental issues such as industrial clustering and development-based poverty alleviation. Reform intensified in key areas of the economic system, agriculture, rural development and social undertakings as well as minimized government involvement in reviews and approvals and the issuance of qualifications and certifications. Thus, a development path that carries distinctive local features and fits into local conditions has been created. The economy has soared with a fast pace where four poor counties were located and a new city was born with the most drastic transformation, the best ecological environment and the highest growth rate compared with other cities in Jiangsu. It now has a GDP of RMB212.619 billion, up 10% from a year earlier, or 16 times the amount in its early days of development, and per capita GDP of RMB43853 or USD7041.

The third Plenary Session of the 18th CPC Central Committee adopted the blueprint of an all-round deepening of the reform. Following the general requirement of comprehensively deepening the reform, the municipal leadership has been committed to building a leaner government to boost market vitality and modernize the capacity and system of governance. In the principle of cutting power, removing interest and highlighting market roles, it has vigorously advanced the reform of the administrative management system and minimized the government's intervention in business affairs. The market sets to play a decisive role in the allocation of resources, while the government improves the efficiency of its own functions through orderly delegation of power, improvement of services and strengthened regulation. Efforts have been made to nurture market and business vitality. Suqian launched the reform of granting licenses before permits one year ahead of the national tryout, integrated four permits into one a year before other regions, and piloted three-in-one licenses 6 months in advance. Suqian was the first city in China to roll back government's power in review and approval as well as qualification and certification issuance, and it was also the first city to launch the "one number for one certificate" reform. It is now among the regions in China with the smallest number of administrative approval items and the highest service efficiency.

I. Regulate power delegation to unleash market vitality

Suqian has carried out reforms on the commercial registration system, the administrative review and approval system, removal of government involvement in granting certifications and licenses and cleaning up of non-administrative licensing items. The reform aims to minimize explicit and implicit approval items, return power to the market and society and forestall side-stepping or overstepping the government mandate. Less government power brings more market incentives.

In September 2013, Suqian launched a new round of reform in the administrative review and approval system focusing on commercial registration. In recent years, in the principle of "less power, no self-interest, transparency and check and balance", a road map for reform was adopted to start from easier issues before addressing more difficult ones and go for a city-wide rollout after successful trials. In 2015, after the success in introducing the "four-in-one certificate" and "three-in-one permit", a system of license issuance, information collection and coordinated supervision based on single social credit coding was set up to break departmental barriers, minimize administrative costs, fully release reform benefits, and boost market vitality at a deeper level and in a wider scope. Since 2014, Suqian has cut expenses by RMB35.608 million for 48 industrial users of water, electricity and heat that have participated in the reform.

In June 2015, Suqian took the lead among prefecture-level cities in the province in sorting out the list of government responsibilities to regulate power delegation and unleash market vitality. In the past, businesses and individuals complained about "cold shoulder treatment" or "buck-passing" when they sought help from the government. A departmental responsibility list was made to avoid such scenarios. When you log onto the Suqian municipal government organizational structure website, you can find the section "Responsibility List of Municipal Government Departments" on the home page, which specifies 480 specific responsibilities for 41 departments. The "responsibility list" divides responsibilities and names the lead departments of 295 cross responsibilities that involve 34 departments and distinguishes the relationship between leading and supporting agencies. A comprehensive review of the 455 public services items provided by 36 municipal government departments was performed. It clarified 4368 items of administrative power corresponding to the functions of 41 departments of the municipal government, released 731 flowcharts for the exercise of administrative power and established 181 *interim and ex post* supervision items. By setting a clear boundary of responsibilities among various government departments, the list has effectively addressed the issue of government side-stepping or overstepping its mandate and significantly boosted the confidence and vitality of market entities.

As of June 2016, the number of prior review items for industrial and commercial registration in the city was reduced from 199 to 7, with a reduction rate of 96.5%. The approval efficiency in key areas has more than doubled, making Suqian one of the cities in China with the fewest administrative approval items and the best approval efficiency. In 2015, there were 11,920 newly developed corporate enterprises in the city with a registered capital of RMB46.663 billion, up 207.06% and 179.15%, respectively, compared with 2012 before the reform. From January to May 2016, there were 6,816 newly registered private enterprises in the city, with a registered capital of RMB28.515 billion, up 10.63% and 82.10% year on year, respectively. Among them were 6002 newly registered corporate enterprises with a registered capital of RMB25.245 billion, up 33.28% and 60.17%, respectively.

II. Improve public services

In recent years, Suqian has comprehensively improved the quality of public services through "Internet Plus". With the opening of the "Internet Plus" municipal government service cloud platform on December 30, 2014, government services were upgraded, benefiting service applicants, government staff and citizens all at the same time. First, the work process is integrated. Applicants now find it easier to go through the process with less time and effort, and their level of satisfaction has increased. Second, resources are shared among multiple databases. This saves the government staff a lot of time in reviewing the applications and raises their work efficiency. Third, full coverage of online supervision is realized. This makes public oversight easier and guarantees the right to know, participate and supervise for the general public.

To improve social governance, efforts have been made to help communities build self-governance capacity and promote the model of social governance, which is "led by the Party and the government and participated by local communities under the rule of law". Reforms have been made to nurture such social organizations as intermediaries and industry associations, build a social credit system, optimize the structure of social governance, encourage orderly participation by all stakeholders in social governance, and improve the self-governance ability of social organizations. By June 2016, 5774 social organizations had been registered in the city, an increase of 3306 over the period before the reform, with 10 social organizations per 10,000 people. In early 2016, 19 local social organizations were ranked among the first provincial "model social organizations", surpassing other cities in northern Jiangsu.

III. Promote reform with power delegation and better regulation

1. Formulate regulatory guidelines to ensure parallel progress in delegating power and strengthening regulation. The government released the *Guidelines for Strengthening the Regulatory System in the Reform of Administrative Review and Approval.* Detailed processes were designed for every step covering program design, implementation and expansion. Meanwhile, capacity building activities for regulatory personnel were enhanced to ensure fairness of the reform.
2. Strengthen interdepartmental interactions to form synergies in regulation. Suqian has pooled resources for intensive use to ensure basic need and advanced coordinated regulation among government departments to avoid any regulatory vacuums. A joint regulatory platform on licenses and certificates was established to carry out "parallel approval" and "joint regulation". The government departments concerned must strengthen regulation upon receiving tips from the platform and promptly upload information such as administrative penalties, routine regulation and judicial judgment. The platform monitors and collects information on platform use and data upload, records and processing from agencies of joint regulation, makes assessments and notifications and ensures accountability. The efforts are meant to ensure that the joint regulation on certificates and licenses is institutionalized, standardized and runs on a routine basis.
3. Improve the credit system and give play to the role of market supervision. Suqian took the lead in Jiangsu Province to establish a credit system with a clear division of responsibilities and functions, driven by both the government and the market, each with its own roles. The city was among the first to use third-party credit reports and select through open bidding third-party credit evaluation agencies that are responsible for collecting and evaluating credit information such as enterprise qualification, key executives, contract performance and bad records and issuing third-party credit reports. All corporate credit information shall be publicized on the Internet for public scrutiny. In 2016, Suqian was among the first group of model cities in China to build a national social credit system and became one of the best cities in Jiangsu in terms of credit system building. In the *Chinese*

Cities Credit Monitoring Monthly Report released by the National Development and Reform Commission in June 2016, Suqian ranked first among 259 prefecture-level cities, with a credit score of 86.74 points.

Bibliography

Bai, T. et al. These costs should be lowered before others. *People's Daily*, 2016-5-19.

Ge, M., et al. Suqian deepens administrative reform: Controlling the 'intruding hand' of the government [OL]. [2015-11-25]. Suqian Website.

http://www.suqian.gov.cn

Huang, J., & Liao, W. (2015). Four historical leaps in repositioning the party's role in the market since reform and opening-up. *Journal of Zhuhai School of Administration of Zhuhai Party School*, (1).

Li, K. Speech at the national video and teleconference on promoting the reform of streamlining administration, delegating power, strengthening regulation and improving services. *People's Daily*, 2016-5-23.

Li, K. Speech at the national video and teleconference on the work of streamlining administration, delegating power, strengthening regulation and transforming functions [OL] [2015-5-17]. Xinhuanet.

Li, Y. (2013). *Dual transition of the Chinese economy*. China Renmin University Press.

Li, Y. Our understanding of streamlining administration and delegating power has deepened. *Beijing Daily*, 2015-10-19.

Li, H., et al. (2016). *The great change: Progress of streamlining administration and delegating power*. China Yan Shi Press.

Wei, G. (2016, June). *The reform of Suqian in 2015*. Reform Office of Suqian Municipal CPC Committee.

Xi, J. The new type of government-business relationship is characterized by "caring" and "clean". *Beijing Youth Daily*, 2016-3-5.

Xi, J. A letter to Fujian entrepreneurs. *Fujian Daily*, 2014-7-21.

Yao, X. Power list and government transformation [J/OL] *People's Daily Online*, 2014-4-1.

Correction to: The Chinese Path Toward a Leaner Government

Yining Li and Zhiqiang Cheng

Correction to:
Y. Li and Z. Cheng (eds.), *The Chinese Path Toward a Leaner Government*, https://doi.org/10.1007/978-981-19-6718-4

In the original version of the book, the following belated correction has been incorporated: the funder information "This book is published with financial support from the Chinese Fund for Humanities and Social Sciences." has been included on the Copyright page. The book has been updated with the change.

The updated version of the book can be found at
https://doi.org/10.1007/978-981-19-6718-4

Y. Li and Z. Cheng (eds.), *The Chinese Path Toward a Leaner Government*,
https://doi.org/10.1007/978-981-19-6718-4_28

The manufacturer's authorised representative in the EU is Springer Nature Customer Service Centre GmbH, Europaplatz 3, 69115 Heidelberg, Germany. If you have any concerns regarding our products, please contact ProductSafety@springernature.com

Printed and bound by CPI Group (UK) Ltd, Croydon, CR0 4YY
30/09/2026
02225237-0014